USING

Understanding by Design

IN THE

Culturally and Linguistically Diverse

CLASSROOM

USING
Understanding
by Design
IN THE
Culturally and
Linguistically
Diverse
CLASSROOM

AMY J. HEINEKE & JAY McTIGHE

 Alexandria, Virginia USA

1703 N. Beauregard St. • Alexandria, VA 22311-1714 USA
Phone: 800-933-2723 or 703-578-9600 • Fax: 703-575-5400
Website: www.ascd.org • E-mail: member@ascd.org
Author guidelines: www.ascd.org/write

Deborah S. Delisle, *Executive Director;* Stefani Roth, *Publisher;* Genny Ostertag, *Director, Content Acquisitions;* Julie Houtz, *Director, Book Editing & Production;* Darcie Russell, *Senior Associate Editor;* Donald Ely, *Senior Graphic Designer;* Mike Kalyan, *Director, Production Services;* Valerie Younkin, *Production Designer;* Kelly Marshall, *Senior Production Specialist*

All web links in this book are correct as of the publication date below but may have become inactive or otherwise modified since that time. If you notice a deactivated or changed link, please e-mail books@ascd.org with the words "Link Update" in the subject line. In your message, please specify the web link, the book title, and the page number on which the link appears.

PAPERBACK ISBN: 978-1-4166-2612-1   ASCD product #118084   n7/18

PDF E-BOOK ISBN: 978-1-4166-2614-5; see Books in Print for other formats.

Quantity discounts are available: e-mail programteam@ascd.org or call 800-933-2723, ext. 5773, or 703-575-5773. For desk copies, go to www.ascd.org/deskcopy.

Library of Congress Cataloging-in-Publication Data is available for this title.

Names: Heineke, Amy J., author. | McTighe, Jay, author.
Title: Using understanding by design in the culturally and linguistically
    diverse classroom / Amy J. Heineke and Jay McTighe.
Description: Alexandria, Virginia : ASCD, [2018] | Includes bibliographical
    references and index.
Identifiers: LCCN 2018006499 (print) | LCCN 2018036234 (ebook) | ISBN
    9781416626145 (ebook) | ISBN 9781416626121 (pbk.)
Subjects: LCSH: Curriculum planning--United States. | Curriculum-based
    assessment--United States. | Multicultural education--United States. |
    Minorities--Education--United States. | Linguistic
    minorities--Education--United States.
Classification: LCC LB2806.15 (ebook) | LCC LB2806.15 .H445 2018 (print) |
    DDC 375/.001--dc23
LC record available at https://lccn.loc.gov/2018006499

29 28 27 26 25 24 23 22 21   3 4 5 6 7 8 9 10 11 12

To the memory of
Dr. Grant Wiggins (1950–2015).
Grant's ideas live on
within these pages.

USING
Understanding by Design IN THE Culturally and Linguistically Diverse CLASSROOM

Acknowledgments

Many friends and colleagues directly and indirectly shaped the content of this text. At Loyola University Chicago, Kristin Davin, Aimee Papola-Ellis, Sarah Cohen, Amanda Roudebush, Brigid Schultz, Michelle Lia, and Beth Wright supported the groundwork and pilot of the preliminary framework for backward design with a lens on language development. With the support of the Chicago Community Trust, Peggy Mueller and Aida Walqui facilitated our ongoing collaboration and deliberation as we grappled with the nuances of culturally and linguistically responsive practice, specifically embedded in the diverse classrooms of Chicago. Others shaped this project indirectly through their partnership and mentorship in previous endeavors, including Grant Wiggins, Christian Faltis, Carmen Martínez-Roldán, and Jodi Swanson.

We are grateful for our partnership with the Chicago Public Schools, including the many teachers and administrators who have worked with us over the years. Of that larger group of committed educators, we would like to thank the teachers showcased in this text: Luke Carman, Jillian Hartmann, Bridget Heneghan, Lindsay Niekra, and Karen Tellez. Other teachers supported the collaborative work of instructional design, including Devansi Patel, Karoline Sharp Towner, Brandy Velazquez, and Teresa Garcia. In addition to these teachers who generously offered their time and expertise, their school leaders supported this work, including Scott Ahlman, Kyla Bailenson, Georgia Davos, Tami Forsline, Marie Garza-Hammerlund, Hiliana Leon, Edwin Loch, and Pilar Vazquez-Vialva. The Network One team was integral to ongoing work in schools, including Anna Alvarado, Becky Bancroft, Demetra Bolos-Hartman, Jason Major, Emily Mariano, Kate Ramos, Wendee Schavocky, Kerrin Staskawicz, and Camille Unger. A special thanks to Camille Unger, who served as a thought partner in early phases of this work and facilitated the connection between authors that ultimately brought this book to fruition.

We would like to thank our colleagues who provided integral feedback throughout the writing process. Many thanks go to Cynthia Bushar Nelson, who reviewed multiple versions of the full manuscript to ensure its clarity, practicality, and applicability for classroom teachers. Other doctoral students in Loyola University Chicago's Curriculum and Instruction program contributed their expert pedagogical and linguistic lenses, including Jenna Carlson, Wenjin Guo, and Ali Kushki. We are appreciative of the educators from Humble Independent School District—Chandra Torres, Deborah Perez, Martha Garcia, and Luma Blanco-Lajara—who used their dual expertise in UbD and English language learners to review and provide preliminary feedback.

We send our thanks to the editorial and production team at ASCD, specifically our editor, Darcie Russell, for getting this project across the finish line, in addition to Carol Collins, Julie Houtz, Genny Ostertag, Stefani Roth, Kathleen Florio, Megan Doyle, and Donald Ely.

Finally, we are thankful to our families who provided a constant source of support throughout this journey. To Amy's husband, Josh, many thanks for the patience and encouragement through the long stretches of writing, especially while preparing for Shea's arrival. To Amy's parents and sisters, thanks for being whatever was needed when the phone rang—cheerleader, sounding board, or distractor. Jay appreciates the ongoing understanding of his wife and veteran educator, Daisy, regarding the demands of writing, even as granddaughter, Sage, provides a delightful distraction.

Introduction

The Understanding by Design® framework (UbD® framework) has become widely used for curricular and instructional design in educational settings across the globe. Flexible by nature to promote purposeful thinking about curricular planning, the UbD framework focuses instruction on the development and deepening of understandings to promote the transfer of learning to both educational and real-world settings and performances. Rather than relying on textbooks and disjointed activities to transmit information to students, teachers plan instruction using a three-stage backward design process that begins with establishing long-term goals, followed by the crafting of authentic assessments and learning trajectories for students to successfully achieve those goals. In the last two decades, practitioners have used the UbD framework to transform teaching and learning—setting aside scripted curricula to instead design their own units of study to facilitate student learning in meaningful and authentic ways.

At the same time that educators have undertaken these pedagogical shifts promoting deeper learning and understanding, demographic shifts have changed the faces of students in classrooms and schools. Fueled by globalization and immigration, previously homogenous communities around the world now serve as homes to increasingly diverse populations. Typically with scant preparation, practitioners have found themselves teaching large and growing numbers of students who are *culturally and linguistically diverse* (CLD), an umbrella term used to capture a heterogeneous population of learners who use a language or language variety other than Standard English at home. These changes have led to the all-important question: How can educators best serve and support CLD students in schools and classrooms?

Stakeholders have struggled to respond to this question and changing reality, and the result has often been inequitable educational practices and outcomes for CLD students. We consistently see schools characterized by silos, where students are placed or pulled into separate classrooms apart from their so-called mainstream peers to focus on skill-based language curricula. Even in schools where teachers collectively embrace their roles in fostering all students' learning and language development, instructional considerations for CLD students are often characterized by one-size-fits-all strategies, after-the-fact lesson modifications, watered-down curriculum, and lowered expectations for learning. This is due not to the teachers, but to the larger educational system that has systemically limited CLD students' access to rigorous, grade-level teaching and learning.

Recent shifts in policy have resulted in stakeholders rethinking these previous approaches, leading to developments such as the New Standards formulated by the National Governors Association (NGA) and the Council of Chief State School Officers (CCSSO). With increasingly rigorous expectations for disciplinary learning and language use spanning kindergarten through 12th grade (K–12), as outlined in the Common Core State Standards for English Language Arts and Mathematics, the Next Generation Science Standards, and the C3 Social Studies State Standards, educators have negotiated how to carry out instruction that meets the needs of all learners. Fortunately, there is a growing consensus that CLD students must engage in grade-level academic learning and develop language throughout a school day to stay on pace with long-term expectations. Nonetheless, this is easier said than done, particularly within the institutionalized structures that have long limited CLD students' equitable access to rigorous instruction.

This book provides a means to respond to these challenges faced by practitioners and educational stakeholders. By focusing on UbD for CLD students, we merge the widely used UbD framework for rigorous and authentic instruction with principles and effective practices to promote students' learning and language development in culturally and linguistically diverse classrooms. Our goals are twofold: (1) to provide CLD students with equitable access to rigorous curriculum and high-quality instruction and (2) to support simultaneous language development and disciplinary learning. We achieve these goals by purposefully integrating and maintaining an explicit lens on language throughout the instructional design process, rather than inserting one-size-fits-all strategies or after-the-fact modifications. This inclusive and holistic approach to instructional design applies in every educational setting, in recognition of the pertinence of language in all learning and the need to focus on its development throughout the school day and beyond.

How This Book Is Organized

Part I of this book provides readers with the foundations for understanding backward design and the role of language in learning and instruction. Chapter 1 provides an overview of the UbD framework, including its overarching principles of learning and understanding and its three stages of curricular design that prompt practitioners to set goals, gather evidence, and plan instruction. Chapter 2 lays the groundwork for readers to grapple with the complexity of language and to understand how it develops as a part of disciplinary learning and instruction. Chapter 3 begins the application of the language lens to the UbD framework by considering how culturally and linguistically responsive practice can inform instructional planning. Teachers probe the nuanced backgrounds and abilities of students within the various labels ascribed in schools as a way to begin instructional design that taps into students' strengths and needs.

Part II adds the lens on language development to the three stages of UbD instructional design at the unit level. Chapter 4 explores Stage 1, in which teachers determine end goals by considering the discipline-specific language functions and features needed to engage in unit learning. Chapter 5 delves into Stage 2, which prompts curriculum designers to design culturally and linguistically responsive assessments to measure students' progress toward goals. Chapter 6 fleshes out Stage 3, in which practitioners plan learning trajectories to support students in reaching goals for disciplinary learning and language development. Student vignettes frame each chapter to illustrate how classroom diversity requires responsive and rigorous instruction. After reviewing the key aspects of UbD for each stage, we explore and demonstrate how to add the language lens throughout instructional design. We then summarize key steps for classroom application and provide snapshots of teachers' backward design and implementation of rigorous and meaningful instruction to support students' learning and language development.

Part III extends beyond unit planning to consider how UbD can be used to support students in daily practice in diverse classrooms and schools. Chapter 7 hones in on daily work in classrooms to probe how backward design can bolster language development at the lesson level. We explore how to create classroom environments that purposefully build community among learners, authentically promote communication and collaboration, and consistently scaffold for language development. Practitioners also learn how to plan daily lessons using backward design to set rigorous goals for content and language learning, design engaging and interactive instruction, and check for understanding and progress toward goals. Chapter 8 pans out to the school level to consider how the UbD framework with a language lens can be used to influence students' long-term achievement across classrooms, disciplines, and grade levels. We pull together key ideas from throughout the book to provide actionable steps that stakeholders can take to implement UbD in effective ways across schools.

PART I

Backward Design
and the Role of
Language
Development

1

Fostering Deeper Learning: The Understanding by Design Framework

CHAPTER GOALS

- **Transfer:** Educators will be able to independently use their learning to...

  – Apply the Understanding by Design framework (or UbD framework) to design curriculum units that support students' learning and understanding.

- **Understandings:** Educators will understand that...

  – Effective curriculum design involves an iterative, three-stage process, planned *backward* from clear goals.

  – Understanding by Design is a way of thinking and planning, not a prescriptive formula for planning or teaching.

  – Understanding must be developed by students; thus, the teacher's job is to facilitate meaning-making by the learner.

  – Understanding is revealed when students can apply their learning effectively in new situations (i.e., transfer).

- **Essential questions:** Educators will keep considering...

  – What is effective curriculum design? Why plan *backward?*
  – How do we teach for understanding and transfer?
  – How will we know that students *really* understand?

- **Knowledge:** Educators will know...

  – The tenets of the UbD framework.
  – The three stages of backward design.

In this chapter we introduce the Understanding by Design (UbD) framework and its three-stage process of curricular design. The framework is intended to guide educators toward the goal of enabling all students to transfer learning across contexts and to develop broad understandings, knowledge, and skills.

What Is Understanding by Design?

Understanding by Design is a curriculum planning framework that reflects research from cognitive psychology and neuroscience. As its title suggests, UbD reflects the convergence of two independent ideas: (1) research on learning and cognition that highlights the centrality of teaching and assessing for understanding and transfer, and (2) a time-honored process for designing curriculum.

The Understanding by Design framework is based on seven key tenets:

1. Learning is enhanced when teachers think purposefully about curricular planning. The UbD framework supports thoughtful curriculum design without offering a rigid process or prescriptive program.

2. The UbD framework helps focus curriculum and teaching on the development and deepening of student understanding and the transfer of learning—that is, the ability to effectively use content knowledge and skill.

3. Understanding is revealed when students can make sense of, and transfer, their learning through authentic performance. Six facets of understanding—the capacity to explain, interpret, apply, shift perspective, empathize, and self-assess—can serve as indicators of understanding.

4. Effective curriculum is planned *backward* from long-term outcomes through a three-stage design process. This process helps avoid three common educational problems: (a) treating the textbook as the curriculum rather than a resource, (b) activity-oriented teaching in which no clear priorities and purposes are apparent, and (c) test prep in which students practice the format of standardized tests (usually selected-response items) while concentrating only on tested content.

5. Teachers are coaches of understanding, not mere purveyors of content knowledge, skill, or activity. They focus on ensuring that transfer of learning happens; they do not assume that what was taught was learned.

6. Regular reviews of curriculum against UbD design standards enhance curricular quality, leading to deeper learning, whereas concomitant reviews of student work in professional learning communities (PLCs) inform needed adjustments in curriculum and instruction to maximize student learning.

7. Teachers, schools, and districts can *work smarter* and more effectively by sharing their curriculum and assessment designs with others in various ways, including through web-based tools such as the Eduplanet21 Unit Planner and shared database (https://www.eduplanet21.com/).

Understanding as an Educational Aim

The heading for this section may strike readers as unnecessary. Don't all teachers want students to understand what they teach? Perhaps. But an examination of numerous classrooms reveals that instruction is often focused on superficial *coverage* of lots of content specified by national, state, or provincial standards, or contained in textbooks. Moreover, teaching for understanding may be undercut by the pressures associated with standardized accountability tests. Too often, teachers are expected to engage in test prep as a means of raising achievement scores. At its worst, this practice encourages multiple-choice teaching that results in superficial learning at the expense of exploring ideas in greater depth and allowing authentic applications.

Understanding by Design proposes a sound alternative to these prevailing methods. UbD is predicated on the idea that gains in long-term achievement are more likely when teachers teach for understanding of transferable concepts and processes while giving learners multiple opportunities to apply their learning in meaningful and authentic contexts. Students learn the requisite knowledge and skills by actively constructing meaning—that is, coming to an understanding—and transferring learning to new situations.

Support for an understanding-based approach to instruction and classroom assessment comes from research in cognitive psychology. Here are brief summaries of several findings (Bransford, Brown, & Cocking, 2000) that provide a theoretical base for the instructional and assessment practices of Understanding by Design:

- To be widely applicable, learning must be guided by generalized principles. Knowledge learned at the level of rote memory rarely transfers; transfer most likely occurs when the learner knows and understands underlying concepts and principles that can be applied to problems in new contexts. Learning with understanding is more likely to promote transfer than simply memorizing information from a text or a lecture.
- Experts first seek to develop an understanding of a problem, which often involves thinking in terms of core concepts or big ideas. Novices' knowledge is much less likely to be organized around big ideas; novices are more likely to approach a problem by searching for correct formulas and pat answers that fit their already-held conceptions.
- Research on expertise suggests that superficial coverage of many topics in the domain is a poor way to help students develop the competencies that will prepare them for future learning and work. Curricula that emphasize breadth of knowledge may prevent effective organization of knowledge because they do not allow enough time to learn anything in depth. Curricula that are a mile wide and an inch deep run the risk of developing disconnected rather than connected knowledge.
- Many assessments measure only propositional (factual) knowledge and never ask for conditional knowledge—whether students know *when, where,* and *why* to use what they have learned. Given this real-world goal,

assessments and feedback must focus on understanding and not simply on memory of procedures or facts.

Additional validation of the principles and practices of Understanding by Design comes from the emerging research on the neuroscience of learning (Willis, 2006). Consider the following salient points on how the brain learns:

- Patterning is the process whereby the brain perceives and generates patterns by relating new material to previously learned material or chunking material into patterns it has not used before. Whenever new material is presented in a way that enables students to see relationships, greater brain cell activity is generated (forming new neural connections), and students can more successfully store learning in long-term memory and retrieve it.
- Experiential learning that stimulates multiple senses in students, such as hands-on science, is not only the most engaging form of learning but also the most likely to be stored as long-term memories.
- The best-remembered information is learned through multiple and varied exposures followed by authentic uses of the knowledge.
- The neural networks that control the brain's *executive functions* develop and mature during the school years through the mid-20s. These networks control the abilities of highest cognition, including focusing one's attention, critical analysis, reasoning and judgment, risk assessment, flexible and creative innovation, and metacognitive self-management. Instruction that engages the use of these functions strengthens them.

These research findings provide a conceptual underpinning for Understanding by Design and guide the design of curriculum and assessment, along with instructional practice.

What Is Understanding?

The term *understanding* can be tricky. Its ambiguity reflects the fact that it can be used with different connotations and intentions. In fact, you may be aware that Benjamin Bloom and his colleagues avoided using the term in their taxonomy of the cognitive domain (Bloom, 1956) because they found it imprecise.

One way to explore its meaning is to consider how understanding is shown. Try the following mental exercise: Think about something that you understand deeply, such as a subject that you teach or ideas related to a hobby. Now, think about the ways in which your understanding is shown: How would others know you have that understanding? Given your understanding, what can you do that a person without that understanding cannot? When we use this exercise in workshops, we receive predictable responses from participants, such as those shown in the chart in Figure 1.1.

Figure 1.1 | **Deep Versus Surface Understandings**

Indicators of a Little Knowledge but Not Deep Understanding

You can...

• Give back what you were told (recall).

• Apply a skill only in the way it was learned (i.e., you cannot transfer your learning to a new situation).

(But you are less able to do the things listed under Indicators of Deep Understanding.)

Indicators of Deep Understanding

You can...

• Explain things clearly and completely.

• Teach others effectively.

• Apply your understanding flexibly in new situations (transfer).

• Analyze and evaluate.

• Justify and support your ideas/positions.

• Interpret meaning (e.g., of text, data, experiences).

• Generate new questions.

• Recognize different points of view on an issue.

• Empathize with others.

• Diagnose errors and correct them.

• Self-assess and monitor your progress.

• Adjust in midcourse.

• Reflect on your own learning.

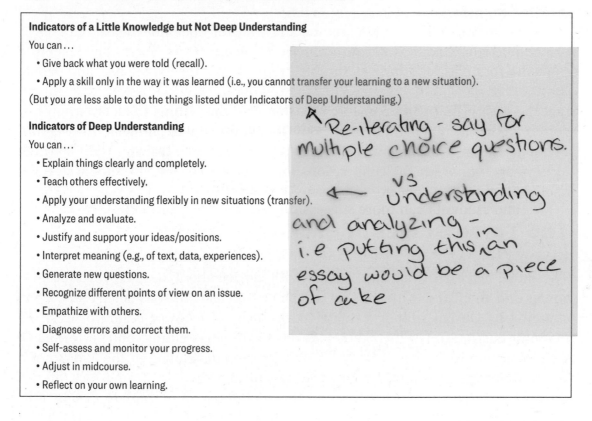

Re-iterating - say for multiple choice questions.

vs understanding and analyzing - i.e putting this in an essay would be a piece of cake

The indicators of deep understanding help us to understand understanding. They not only highlight the various ways in which the term is used but also offer specific ideas for assessment. In other words, when we want to see if students understand a concept or a process, we can ask them to do one or more of the things listed. The students' response will show the extent to which they understand. Notice that the abilities listed as indicators of a little knowledge are associated with the brain's executive functions. Indeed, this recognition lies at the heart of this book—that teaching and assessing for deep understanding builds the neural networks in the prefrontal cortex of the brain. At the same time, as these networks mature and expand, students' capacity to understand and transfer their learning is enriched.

In its essence, the UbD framework is intended to help educators identify the big ideas that we want students to come to understand at a deep level so that they can transfer their learning to new situations. Such ideas are inherently abstract. They take the form of concepts (e.g., adaptation), principles (e.g., *F=MA*), and processes (e.g., Writers draft and revise their writing to achieve clarity of expression). The ability to effectively transfer knowledge and skill involves the capacity to take what we know and use it creatively, flexibly, and fluently, in different settings or with different problems. Rote learning will not equip a student for transfer. Transfer requires understanding.

A focus on student understanding and transfer does not mean that educators should ignore basic skills or refrain from teaching facts. Basic knowledge and skills are foundational. Indeed, thinking requires a knowledge base, and people cannot apply learning effectively if they lack basic skills. However, we contend that the basics should be considered the floor, not the ceiling! In an era when students can Google much of the world's knowledge on a smartphone, it makes sense to put a greater premium on preparing them to be able to transfer their learning to new, even unpredictable, situations. In other words, schools should develop *know-how* as well as *knowing*.

The Three Stages of Backward Design

Teaching is a means to an end, and curriculum planning precedes instruction. The most successful teaching begins with clarity about desired learning outcomes *and* about the evidence that will show that learning has occurred. Understanding by Design supports this view through a *backward design* process for planning curriculum units that include desired understandings and performance tasks that require transfer. Daily lessons are then developed in the context of a more comprehensive unit design. More specifically, the UbD framework offers a three-stage curriculum design process that includes a unit template, design tools that support the process, and a set of design standards for quality control. A key component of a curriculum based on the UbD framework is alignment, with all three stages clearly aligned not only to standards but also to one another.

The concept of planning curriculum *backward* from desired results is not new. In 1948, Ralph Tyler advocated this approach as an effective process for focusing instruction; William Spady (1994) popularized the idea of *designing down* from exit outcomes; and in his best-selling book *7 Habits of Highly Effective People*, Stephen Covey (1989) notes that effective people always plan "with the end in mind." Although it is not a novel idea, we have found that the intentional use of backward design results in more clearly defined goals, more appropriate assessments, and more purposeful teaching. In the following sections, we summarize the three stages of backward design used in UbD curriculum planning.

Stage 1: Identify Desired Results

In this first stage, curricular planners grapple with what they want learners to understand, know, and do at the end of the instructional unit of study. They consider the following questions: *What do we want students to be able to do with their learning (long-term transfer)? What should students come to understand in order for them to transfer their learning? What essential questions will students explore? What knowledge and skill will students need to acquire?*

This first stage in the design process calls for clarity about instructional priorities and long-term versus short-term goals. In Stage 1 we consider the *big ideas* that we want students to come to understand and the long-term transfer goals that those ideas enable. We examine established content standards and related curriculum outcomes, such as 21st century skills, in order to identify the big ideas and the related transfer performances. We frame companion *Essential Questions* around these targeted *Understandings* and *Transfer Goals*. Finally, we identify more specific objectives related to *Knowledge* and *Skill*.

Stage 2: Determine Acceptable Evidence

In this second stage, curricular planners determine the evidence needed for learners to demonstrate transfer and understanding as tied to unit goals. They consider these questions: *What performances and products will reveal evidence of student understanding and ability to transfer? What additional assessment evidence will be used to assess other learning outcomes?*

Backward design encourages us to think like assessors *before* planning lesson activities in Stage 3 (Wiggins & McTighe, 2005, p. 78). In other words, we think about the assessment that will show the extent to which our students have attained the learning outcomes set forth in Stage 1. It is one thing to say that students should understand X and be able to do Y; it is another to ask: What *evidence will show* that they understand X and can effectively apply Y? We have found that considering the needed assessment evidence helps to focus and sharpen the learning plan in Stage 3.

Evidence of understanding is obtained through performance tasks that ask students to explain the meaning(s) they have made and to apply—to transfer—their learning to new situations. We recommend that the performance assessments be set in a meaningful and authentic context whenever possible. Supplementary assessments, such as a quiz on facts or a skills check, provide additional evidence of students' knowledge acquisition and skill proficiency.

Stage 2 of UbD embodies a fundamental *if-then* proposition: *If* you acknowledge that a primary goal of a modern education is to equip students to be able to transfer their learning to new situations, *then* you should design curriculum backward from authentic performances of transfer, not from long lists of discrete topics or skills.

Stage 3: Plan Learning Experiences and Instruction

In this third stage, curricular designers design experiences for learners to reach and demonstrate attainment of goals. They consider the following questions: *What activities, experiences, and lessons will lead to achievement of the desired results and success at the assessments? How will the learning plan help students to acquire the desired knowledge and skills, make meaning, and transfer?*

How will the unit be sequenced and differentiated to optimize achievement for all learners?

With clearly identified learning results and appropriate assessment evidence in mind, we now plan the most appropriate instructional activities for helping learners acquire targeted knowledge and skills, come to understand important ideas, and apply their learning in meaningful ways. The various types of learning goals identified in Stage 1—acquisition of knowledge and skills, understanding of big ideas, and transfer—inform the selection of instructional strategies and pedagogical roles, such as direct instructor, facilitator, and coach. In other words, instructional practices need to be aligned to the desired results (Stage 1) and their assessments (Stage 2).

We have found that when teachers follow this three-stage planning process, they are more likely to avoid the familiar "twin sins" of planning and teaching (Wiggins & McTighe, 2005). The first sin, which occurs more widely at the elementary and middle school levels, may be labeled *activity-oriented teaching*. Teachers plan and conduct various activities, which may be engaging, hands-on, and kid-friendly. These are fine qualities as long as the activities are purposefully focused on clear and important goals *and* if they yield appropriate evidence of learning. However, too often the collection of activities does not add up to coherent and focused learning. Haven't we all seen examples of classroom activities that fail these tests? Such activities are like cotton candy—pleasant enough in the moment but lacking long-term substance.

The second sin, more prevalent at the secondary and collegiate levels, goes by the name of *coverage*. In this case, teaching consists of marching chronologically through the content, often in the form of long lists of grade-level standards or material in textbooks. With all due respect to the content-related challenges of secondary teaching, a teacher's job is not to simply cover what is in a book; a teacher's job is to *uncover* the content in ways that develop and deepen student understanding of important ideas and equip them to transfer their learning in meaningful ways. The textbook should serve as a resource, *not* the syllabus. We have found that backward design is key to helping teachers better understand their priorities and the role of the textbook and other resources.

The UbD Unit Template

We have created a unit-planning template for teachers to use when planning a UbD unit. The template provides a graphic organizer that embodies the various elements of UbD and reflects the logic of backward design. Figure 1.2 presents the template with questions that teachers consider when planning a UbD unit.

When teachers first encounter UbD, especially without a thorough introduction, they may think that this approach to curriculum planning is simply a matter of filling in boxes on a template. This view confuses a *tool* (the unit template) with the *process* of backward design. We contend that backward design has an important logic; it reflects a way of thinking and planning to ensure clarity of outcomes, appropriate assessments, and focused teaching by always keeping the *ends* of understanding and transfer in mind.

Although completing the unit template is not the goal of UbD, the template has proven to be a valuable tool for curriculum planning. Like any effective graphic organizer, the UbD template serves as a guide for users, resulting in a *mental template* that helps teachers internalize a robust curriculum planning process. The UbD template has another virtue: its common layout enables teachers to share units in a recognizable format with other teachers throughout a school, across a district or state, and anywhere in the world!

A Driving Example

To illustrate the backward design process in action, let's consider how UbD could be used in driver training (Wiggins & McTighe, 2011). In Stage 1, we reference the *National Driver Development Standards* from the American Driver and Traffic Safety Education Association:

- Demonstrate a working knowledge of rules, regulations, and procedures of operating an automobile.
- Use visual search skills to obtain correct information and make reduced-risk decisions for effective speed and position adjustments.
- Interact with other users within the Highway Transportation System by adjusting speed, space, and communications to avoid conflicts and reduce risk.
- Demonstrate balanced vehicle movement through steering, braking, and accelerating in a precise and timely manner throughout a variety of adverse conditions.

We then specify the information that a beginning driver will need to know, such as (1) basic car parts and their functions, (2) the driving rules and regulations for the driver's jurisdiction, (3) the meaning of traffic signs and signals, and (4) procedures to follow in case of an accident.

We also identify the various skills that a beginning driver will need to practice, including (1) adjusting the driver's seat and car mirrors, (2) coordinating the gas and brake pedals, (3) signaling intentions to other drivers, (4) merging into traffic on a highway, and (5) parallel parking.

In addition to targeting knowledge and skills, teachers planning with UbD will also identify the *big ideas* that they want their students to understand. Here are several understandings for driving:

- A motor vehicle can become a lethal weapon, and driving one demands constant attention to avoid damage, injuries, or death.

Figure 1.2 | **The UbD Template with Planning Questions**

Stage 1—Desired Results		
Established Goals What content standards and program- or mission-related goal(s) will this unit address?	**Transfer** *Students will be able to independently use their learning to . . .* What kinds of long-term, independent accomplishments are desired?	
	Meaning	
	Understandings *Students will understand that . . .* What specifically do you want students to understand?	**Essential Questions** *Students will keep considering . . .* What thought-provoking questions will foster inquiry, meaning making, and transfer?
	Acquisition	
	Students will know . . . What facts and basic concepts should students know and be able to remember?	*Students will be skilled at . . .* What discrete skills and processes should students be able to use?

Stage 2—Evidence

Evaluative Criteria	Assessment Evidence
• What criteria will be used in each assessment to evaluate attainment of the desired results? • What are the most important qualities for student performance?	**Performance Task(s)** How will students demonstrate their understanding (meaning making and transfer) through transfer performance(s)? *Consider the six facets when developing assessments of understanding. Optional: Use the GRASPS elements to frame an authentic context for the task(s).* **Supplementary Evidence** What other evidence will you collect to determine whether Stage 1 goals were achieved?

Stage 3—Learning Plan

What pre-assessments will be used to check students' prior knowledge, skill levels, and potential misconceptions?   *Pre-assessment*

Learning Events

• What teaching and learning experiences will be used to help students . . .
  – Acquire targeted knowledge and skills?
  – Make meaning of big ideas?
  – Be able to transfer their learning?
• How will you help learners know the learning goals, recognize the value of this learning, and understand how their learning will be assessed?
• How will you hook and engage learners' interest?
• How will you tailor (i.e., differentiate) the learning plan to address the varied interests and achievement levels of all students?
• How will you help learners self-assess their performance, reflect on their learning, and set future goals?

Formative Assessments

• What ongoing assessments will be used to monitor students' progress toward acquisition, meaning making, and transfer throughout the unit?

• How and when will students get the feedback they need and have opportunities to make use of it?

Source: From *The Understanding by Design Guide to Creating High-Quality Units* (pp. 16–17), by G. Wiggins and J. McTighe, 2011, Alexandria, VA: ASCD. Copyright 2011 by Grant Wiggins and Jay McTighe. Adapted with permission.
*See p. 122 for information on GRASPS.

- Defensive driving assumes that other drivers are inattentive and might make unexpected or dangerous moves.
- Effective drivers constantly adapt their driving to various traffic, road, and weather conditions.

Notice that these are not facts, but rather conceptual understandings that guide experienced drivers in safely operating a motor vehicle.

Finally, ask yourself: What are the ultimate goals of a driver training program? Certainly, effective driving demands more than simply having novice drivers memorize the rules of the road and master discrete driving skills. Long-term transfer goals for driving should be goals such as these: "Effective drivers drive courteously and defensively without accidents or needless risk. They adapt their knowledge of safe driving to various traffic, road, and weather conditions." Keeping these long-term *ends* in mind focuses teaching and learning. Indeed, a successful driver training program should be designed backward from such goals.

You may have noticed that the Stage 1 template includes one category that we have not yet referenced in this example—*Essential Questions*. Such questions are open-ended; that is, they do not seek a single correct answer. Rather, they are meant to be considered over time as a means of helping students construct meaning and deepen their understanding. Given the targeted understandings and transfer goals for driver education, here are two essential questions that could be used to frame the entire course:

- *What must I anticipate and do to minimize risk and accidents when I drive?*
- *What makes a courteous and defensive driver?*

Essential questions like these provide a conceptual umbrella for a unit or a course. They remind both teachers and students that simply acquiring information or basic skills is insufficient; the ultimate goal is transfer, and transfer requires understanding. Figure 1.3 presents the driver education example within Stage 1 of the UbD unit template.

Let's continue examining the backward design process by moving into Stage 2 for the driver education example. In Stage 2, we ask teachers to think like an assessor or to consider the evidence needed to determine the extent to which students have achieved the identified knowledge, skills, understandings, and transfer goals established in Stage 1 (Wiggins & McTighe, 2005, p. 78). The logic of backward design asks teachers to carefully consider what these different goals imply for the assessments (in Stage 2) and then for instruction (in Stage 3).

You saw in Figure 1.2 that Stage 2 of backward design contains three main categories: *Performance Tasks*, *Supplementary Evidence*, and *Evaluative Criteria*. We believe that performance tasks are generally best suited to assess whether students understand important ideas and can transfer their learning to new

Figure 1.3 | **Stage 1 of the UbD Unit Template with Driver Education Example**

Stage 1—Desired Results	
Established Goals	**Transfer**
National Driver Development Standards	*Students will be able to independently use their learning to…*
• Demonstrate a working knowledge of rules, regulations, and procedures of operating an automobile.	• Drive courteously and defensively without accidents or needless risk. • Adapt their knowledge of safe driving to various traffic, road, and weather conditions.
	Meaning
• Use visual search skills to obtain correct information and make reduced-risk decisions for effective speed and position adjustments.	**Understandings** *Students will understand that…* • A motor vehicle can become a lethal weapon, and driving one demands constant attention.	**Essential Questions** *Students will keep considering…* • What must I anticipate and do to minimize risk and accidents when I drive?
• Interact with other users within the Highway Transportation System by adjusting speed, space, and communications to avoid conflicts and reduce risk.	• Defensive driving assumes that other drivers are inattentive and might make unexpected or dangerous moves. • Effective drivers constantly adapt their driving to various traffic, road, and weather conditions.	• What makes a courteous and defensive driver?
	Acquisition
• Demonstrate balanced vehicle movement through steering, braking, and accelerating in a precise and timely manner throughout a variety of adverse conditions.	*Students will know…* • Basic car parts and functions. • Driving laws and rules of the road for their jurisdiction. • Meaning of traffic signs and signals. • What to do in case of an accident.	*Students will be skilled at…* • Adjusting driver's seat and car mirrors. • Coordinating the gas and brake pedals. • Signaling intentions. • Merging into traffic on a highway. • Parallel parking.
Source: Goals from American Driver and Traffic Safety Education Association		

situations. Indeed, an effective performance task sets up an authentic situation that calls for transfer.

The *Supplementary Evidence* section of the template offers a place to list other (often more traditional) assessments of knowledge, skill, and standards that are not otherwise assessed by the performance task. For example, if we want to see whether students *know* state capitals or math facts, we might use a multiple-choice, matching, true-false, or fill-in-the-blank assessment format to provide the needed evidence in an efficient manner. Similarly, we can assess for proficiency of individual *skills* by using a skill check or simple demonstration. In the driving example, teachers can use traditional tests to check students' knowledge of driving regulations and the meaning of traffic signs and signals.

Evaluative criteria are needed for performance tasks and any other open-ended assessments that do not have a single correct answer. These criteria, shown on the left side of the template, serve as the basis for assessing student performance. (Note: Identified criteria can be used to develop more detailed scoring rubrics as needed.)

Figure 1.4 displays a completed Stage 2 template for the driver education example. The example shows six performance tasks with associated criteria. Six is an appropriate number because this is an entire course and driving is a performance-based activity. (Note: In most shorter curriculum units designed for academic subject matter, we would typically see one or two performance tasks.) The supplementary assessments include tests of knowledge and observations of particular skills because these are also listed goals in Stage 1 and should be assessed.

Stage 3 is where teachers develop the learning plan for a unit or course. Again, the logic of backward design reminds us that our learning plan needs to be tightly aligned with our goals (as identified in Stage 1) to help learners *acquire* targeted knowledge and skills, *make meaning* of important ideas, and be equipped to *transfer* their learning in meaningful ways. The learning plan should also prepare students for the corresponding assessments outlined in Stage 2.

Because a fundamental process of the brain involves linking new information to memory networks related to prior knowledge, teachers must find out what students already know (or think they know) before introducing a new topic. Accordingly, you'll note a section at the top of the Stage 3 template (see Figure 1.2) for identifying the *pre-assessments* that will be used to check students' prior knowledge, skill levels, and potential misconceptions related to the unit topic.

The Stage 3 template includes a separate column on the right side for planning the *formative assessments* that will be used to gauge learning along the way and to provide the feedback needed for adjustments. As the video game model (and an extensive research base) reminds us, frequent, timely, and understandable feedback is one of highest-yielding classroom strategies. Accordingly, we should include formative assessments in our learning plans—by design!

Figure 1.4 | **Stage 2 of the UbD Unit Template with Driver Education Example**

	Stage 2—Evidence
Evaluative Criteria	**Assessment Evidence**
• Skillful • Controlled • Defensive • Attentive • Courteous • Responsive • Accurate • Clear and complete explanation • Passed	**Performance Task(S)** *Task 1*: Drive to and from a designated location (e.g., from home to school and back) during daylight hours in light traffic to demonstrate skillful, responsive, courteous, and defensive driving under real-world conditions. *Task 2*: Same as Task #1 but in rainy conditions. *Task 3*: Same as Task #1 but in rush-hour traffic. *Task 4*: Same as Task #1 but after dark. *Task 5*: Study Guide: Develop a study guide of advice for beginning drivers to introduce and explain key understandings about safe and effective driving. *Task 6*: Road test required for obtaining a driver's license.
• Knowledgeable • Controlled • Skilled • Passed	**Supplementary Evidence** • Quiz on rules of the road and knowledge of signs and symbols. • Observation of student driver in a driving simulator or while practicing in car (off road). • Skill tests—backing up, parallel parking, merging into traffic. • Written test required for obtaining a driver's license.

Source: Based on *The Understanding by Design Guide to Creating High-Quality Units* (pp. 18–20), by Grant Wiggins and Jay McTighe, 2011, Alexandria, VA: ASCD. Copyright 2011 by Grant Wiggins and Jay McTighe. Adapted with permission.

When drafting a unit, designers need not develop Stage 3 into full-blown lesson plans with all details mapped out. The key in unit design is to see the bigger picture; that is, to determine what learning experiences and instruction are needed, what resources will be used, and what sequence will optimize learning and student engagement. Once designers have developed a general outline, they can flesh out lesson plans with more detail as needed. Figure 1.5 presents a brief outline of the learning plan for the driver training course.

UbD Design Standards

Accompanying the UbD template is a set of design standards corresponding to each stage of backward design (see Figure 1.6). The standards offer criteria, framed as questions, for use during unit development and for quality control of completed unit designs. Framed as questions, the UbD design standards serve curriculum designers in the same way that a scoring rubric serves students, so that teachers can periodically check to see, for example, if the identified understandings are truly big ideas or if the assessment evidence is properly aligned to the goals.

Teachers can also use these standards to guide peer reviews when they work collegially to examine their draft units and identify needed refinements *before* enacting them in the classroom. Our profession rarely subjects teacher-designed units and assessments to this level of critical review. Nonetheless, we have found structured peer reviews, guided by UbD design standards, to be enormously beneficial, and participants in peer review sessions regularly comment on the value of sharing and discussing curriculum and assessment designs with colleagues.

Chapter Summary

In this chapter, we introduced the UbD framework as a means to foster students' learning and understanding through rigorous and meaningful curriculum across disciplines and academic settings. By using the three stages of backward design to craft classroom instruction, practitioners begin with the end in mind to promote the transfer of learning across contexts, as well as provide opportunities for students to develop holistic understandings and nuanced knowledge and skills.

With this book, we hone in on the role of language in learning to consider how to design high-quality curriculum and instruction for culturally and linguistically diverse classrooms. In particular, we explore how to use the UbD framework to design instruction that promotes deeper learning and understanding among all students while simultaneously supporting language development. In the next chapter, we build on these foundational understandings of the UbD framework to consider the central role of language in learning and instruction.

Figure 1.5 | Stage 3 of the UbD Unit Template with Driver Education Example

Stage 3—Learning Plan	Pre-assessment
Pre-assessment of driving knowledge and skills using a pre-test (nongraded) and driving simulators.	*Formative Assessments* Formative assessment and feedback by the instructor as students apply skills on the simulator and on the road. Instructor looks for common misconceptions and skill deficits, such as the following: • Failure to check mirrors and use peripheral vision. • Not adapting to changing road, weather, or traffic conditions. • Failure to give complete attention when driving. • Inaccurately judging the speed of oncoming cars during merges and turns. • Following other cars too closely.

Learning Events

Note: The following provides a brief overview of a learning plan.

• Driving skills are developed and formatively assessed based on a four-level rubric distinguishing degrees of skill proficiency and autonomy:

 - The skill is introduced and modeled via video and the driving instructor.

 - The skill is practiced under instructor's direction in a controlled situation with instructor feedback.

 - The skill is practiced independently in a controlled situation with instructor feedback.

 - The skill is autonomously and effectively applied in varied situations (e.g., daylight, wet roads, nighttime, highway, city, country, rush hour).

Car Check	Reversing
Safety Checks	Parking
Controls and Instruments	Emergency Stopping
Starting, Moving, and Stopping	Anticipation and Planning Ahead
Safe Positioning	Use of Speed
Mirrors	Other Traffic
Signals	Intersections
Circles	Darkness
Pedestrian Crossings	Weather Conditions
Highways	Rules and Laws
Turns	

• Student and instructor discuss the essential questions after each virtual and actual driving experience.

• Students self-assess after each virtual and actual driving experience.

Source: Based on *The Understanding by Design Guide to Creating High-Quality Units* (pp. 18–20), by Grant Wiggins and Jay McTighe, 2011, Alexandria, VA: ASCD. Copyright 2011 by Grant Wiggins and Jay McTighe. Adapted with permission.

Figure 1.6 | **UbD Design Standards**

3 = Meets the standard; 2 = Partially meets the standard; 1 = Does not meet the standard.

To what extent does the unit plan...			
Stage 1	**3**	**2**	**1**
1. Identify important, transferable ideas worth exploring and understanding?			
2. Identify understandings stated as full-sentence generalizations: *Students will understand that...*?			
3. Specify the desired long-term transfer goals that involve genuine accomplishment?			
4. Frame open-ended, thought-provoking and focusing essential questions?			
5. Identify relevant standards, mission, or program goals to be addressed in all three stages?			
6. Identify knowledge and skills needed to achieve understanding and address the established goals?			
7. Align all the elements so that Stage 1 is focused and coherent?			
Stage 2			
8. Specify valid assessment evidence of all desired results; i.e., Stage 2 aligns with Stage 1?			
9. Include authentic performance tasks based on one or more facets of understanding?			
10. Provide sufficient opportunities for students to reveal their achievement?			
11. Include evaluative criteria to align each task to desired results and to provide suitable feedback on performance?			
Stage 3			
12. Include learning events and instruction needed to help learners—			
a. Acquire targeted knowledge and skills?			
b. Make meaning of important ideas?			
c. Transfer their learning to new situations?			
13. Effectively incorporate the WHERETO elements so that the unit is likely to be engaging and effective for all learners?*			
Overall			
14. Align all three stages as a coherent whole?			

*See Chapter 6 for information on WHERETO.

Source: *The Understanding by Design Guide to Creating High-Quality Units* (p. 27), by G. Wiggins and J. McTighe, 2011, Alexandria, VA: ASCD. Copyright 2011 by Grant Wiggins and Jay McTighe. Adapted with permission.

2

Promoting Language Development: Language, Learning, and Instruction

---

CHAPTER GOALS

- **Transfer**: Educators will be able to independently use their learning to…

    – Apply the UbD design process to support students' disciplinary learning and language development.

- **Understandings**: Educators will understand that…

    – Language mediates learning and communication inside and outside schools.
    – Language and language development are complex and dynamic; nuances of language are used in disciplinary classrooms.

- **Essential question**: Educators will keep considering…

    – How do students learn and develop language?

- **Knowledge**: Educators will know…

    – Facets of academic language.
    – Four domains of language.
    – Stages of second language acquisition.

To understand how language development can be incorporated with disciplinary learning in the UbD approach to instructional design, we first need to understand more about language itself. This understanding includes being knowledgeable about the role of language in learning and instruction, including its functions, features, complexities, and how it is acquired.

The Role of Language in Learning

To develop, deepen, and communicate understandings, we rely upon language (Vygotsky, 1978; Walqui & van Lier, 2010). Think about your use of language for learning in this very instance: You are reading this text and making interpretations based on your classroom practice and experiences. You might stop and process what you read in your head, asking and answering questions like these: *What are they saying here? Do I do this? How would this look in my classroom?* Perhaps you are taking notes and writing down the key ideas that stand out. In upcoming days, you may discuss the text and your related understandings and classroom applications with your colleagues or professors. Your understandings and learning rely upon language: it is the medium that we use to process information, make meaning of content, organize thoughts and questions, and communicate and share ideas with one another.

Language has always played an integral role in learning, but recent educational policies and standards have prioritized academic language in instructional design. *Academic language* is the medium by which individuals understand, learn, and communicate about disciplinary topics, concepts, and ideas (Uccelli et al., 2015; Walqui & van Lier, 2010). As learners make meaning and communicate via higher-order thinking processes—such as interpreting, evaluating, and critiquing—they use particular sets of words, grammatical patterns, sentence structures, organizational strategies, and text features (Zwiers, 2014). Academic language is multifaceted, ranging from words to texts. In addition, academic language has various linguistic *registers* based on the focal discipline. For example, the language of mathematics is different than the languages of social studies or fine arts. Even within disciplines, we use language in nuanced ways to actively engage in understanding and learning, as is evident in social studies in the variances among the languages of history, civics, economics, and psychology.

Despite its centrality to understanding, academic language is often misunderstood and misused when educators design instruction (see Figure 2.1). Teachers may falsely assume the need to preteach language as a prerequisite to content learning or focus only on a list of subject-area vocabulary terms. Many teachers understand academic language to be the generic language of school—an assumption that fails to capture the nuances of discipline-specific language needed to engage in learning inside and outside school (Heineke & Neugebauer, in press). The term *disciplinary language* better captures the connection between language and disciplinary learning, while also avoiding the common misunderstandings of academic language. (We use *disciplinary language* throughout this text.) But regardless of terminology, this important concept guides policy and practice in today's classrooms. Nonetheless, it requires deeper exploration to conceptualize the complex and dynamic nature of language in learning.

The Complexities of Academic Language

Think about how you and your students use language in the classroom. What purposes and functions does language serve throughout the school day? Where do you see patterns or trends in words, phrases, sentences, texts, or classroom discourse? How is language used in various ways to process and communicate ideas? Who uses diverse linguistic mediums, such as Spanish or African American Vernacular English (AAVE), to learn and understand? When do learners need targeted support to actively use and develop disciplinary language? Most likely you are not able to provide quick and easy responses to these questions, mainly because of the complex and dynamic ways we use language to actively engage in learning, understanding, and communication. However, it is important to consider these complexities when grappling with how language influences our daily work in classrooms with students.

Figure 2.1 | **Academic Language: Understandings and Misunderstandings**

Academic language is…	Academic language is not…
• Discipline-specific language with unique word, sentence, and discourse features. • Intertwined with understanding, learning, development, and communication. • Used by all individuals, including students, teachers, and professionals. • Oral and written, spanning languages.	• The generic language of schools. • Solely vocabulary (e.g., words, terms). • The opposite of social language. • A prerequisite to academic learning. • Language used only by teachers. • Solely written texts and artifacts. • Limited to the English language.

As learners actively use language to develop, deepen, and communicate understandings, they employ a variety of *language functions*. Consider the various ways that you and your students use language across the school day: greeting one another, summarizing previous learning, interpreting text, predicting hypotheses, evaluating equations, analyzing political debates, negotiating ideas, and explaining homework. Language can be more communicative in nature, as when we exchange greetings, share feelings, and request information. The functions of academic language connect to higher-order thinking and cognitive skills, such as analyzing, comparing, critiquing, and inferring (Assessment and Accountability Comprehensive Center at WestEd [AACCW], 2010; O'Malley & Pierce, 1996). Despite the distinction in terminology, these language functions are not used separately or discretely at different times throughout the school day. Whether doing an experiment in chemistry class or engaging with friends at lunchtime, students intermix and use both communicative and academic language functions across their daily interactions.

While explaining, arguing, or synthesizing ideas, individuals dynamically merge their knowledge and skills related to various *language features*. In addition to applying knowledge of micro-level linguistic components like sounds, letters, and word parts, learners must use words, phrases, sentences, and discourses that correspond with the register of the focal discipline (Brown & Abeywickrama,

2010; WIDA, 2012). Consider the language of language arts, specifically when students interpret, evaluate, and create poetry. Students must use *words and phrases* particular to the disciplinary learning (e.g., figurative language, words with multiple meanings). They also must use discipline-specific *sentence* structures including grammar, conventions, and mechanics (e.g., predicate nouns, pronouns, less common punctuation). Learners must also maneuver unique forms of *discourse*, or the overarching organization and structure of texts and language (e.g., diverse poetic forms and structures by word, phrase, or clause; various language varieties based on time period).

We authentically merge both language functions and features to interpret and communicate ideas through four *language domains*: listening, speaking, reading, and writing (Nagy & Townsend, 2012). Consider how students use language to engage in learning in your classroom: They *listen* while you present information and provide directions for learning experiences. They *speak* with one another to grapple with essential questions and share developing understandings. They *read* texts, articles, websites, and other sources to interpret and make meaning of diverse perspectives and ideas. They *write* to synthesize and convey ideas, as well as to apply learning by producing reports, scripts, plans, projects, and presentations. In this way, disciplinary language involves both oral language (listening and speaking) and literacy (reading and writing), with learners dynamically developing and deepening understandings through these four interconnected domains (see Figure 2.2).

Figure 2.2 | **Language Domains in Classrooms**

	Receptive Language	**Productive Language**
Oral Language	Listening	Speaking
Literacy	Reading	Writing

Despite these varied language functions, features, and domains, students do not learn language through a formal progression of discrete linguistic knowledge and skills. Instead, learners develop language and cognition concurrently and authentically, as they actively engage in learning within and across classrooms, through disciplinary topics, texts, and tasks (Heritage, Walqui, & Linquanti, 2015; Walqui & Heritage, 2012; Walqui & van Lier, 2010; Zwiers, 2014). When designing instruction to develop and deepen understandings through authentic disciplinary experiences, effective practitioners recognize and attend to these linguistic complexities and nuances to support students' simultaneous advancement in language development and content learning in language arts, math, science, social studies, fine arts, and other disciplines. In this way, instructional design bolsters all learners' academic registers and repertoires, while also enhancing access to and mastery of important and rigorous disciplinary understandings, knowledge, and skills.

Language Development and Acquisition

Because of these complex nuances of language both within and across disciplines and learning settings, scholars and practitioners alike recognize that all students are academic language learners (Gottlieb, 2006). As students become apprenticed into the disciplines, deepening their understandings over time through authentic learning experiences, they use increasingly complex language to engage with content, make meaning of concepts, and communicate ideas. In this way, *all* students benefit from instruction with an explicit lens on language, strategically designed and implemented to promote language development concurrent with disciplinary learning.

Nonetheless, within that sizeable population of all students who are developing academic language, it is imperative to consider and prioritize the needs of individual learners. If all learners must develop language in disciplinary classrooms, including monolingual English speakers who have spent their lives in English-medium educational settings, then consider those students whose primary language is something other than English. For students who speak Spanish, Arabic, Urdu, Polish, Navajo, or another language at home, how do they acquire and develop proficiency in a second language? The answer has two key components: students develop a second language (1) by transferring knowledge and abilities from their diverse cultural and linguistic backgrounds and (2) through social interaction during disciplinary learning experiences with teachers' strategic integration of scaffolds and supports.

All students bring rich resources for learning to the classroom, even those who may not seemingly align with the dominant culture and language in a given learning setting. Imagine you have been transported to a Cambodian literature classroom. Although the instruction is in Khmer, you still possess valuable knowledge, skills, and abilities that can be used as resources for learning. As teachers and students around you use Khmer to learn and communicate, you can tap into your cultural background knowledge to access the content (e.g., reading stories at home, visiting cultural institutions in the community, knowing about particular genres from previous schooling) and your linguistic abilities to make meaning of the language (e.g., organization of sounds and words, print directionality in texts and resources). Regardless of the medium of instruction, you are still highly capable of learning and understanding.

This premise remains true for students who enter our classrooms from diverse cultural and linguistic backgrounds: the most valuable resources for learning are those brought from unique and diverse homes, communities, and schools (Herrera, 2016). Students' background knowledge, often shaped by cultural experiences outside school, provides the schema with which they make meaning in classrooms. Regardless of how different these experiences may be from those of the teacher or other students, these resources must be used to foster learning. Equally important is the linguistic background knowledge brought to classrooms, as learners use their dominant language to (1) make meaning of disciplinary concepts and ideas and (2) transfer linguistic knowledge and skills from one language to another (August & Shanahan, 2008). Teachers should embrace the role of multiple languages in classroom learning, because we never turn off our home language. Whether prompting students to think and discuss in their preferred language or demonstrating how languages are similar and different, first and second language development promotes learning and understanding.

As described earlier, all students develop academic language while engaged in meaningful and collaborative disciplinary learning with their peers (Nagy & Townsend, 2012; Zwiers, 2014). This reality is no different for learners from diverse cultural and linguistic backgrounds, including those who are still developing proficiency in English. In other words, students acquire language at the same time that they develop socially, cognitively, and academically (Collier & Thomas, 2007). Nonetheless, students cannot be thrown into English-medium classrooms and learning experiences with the expectation that they will simply jump in as active participants. For students who are still developing proficiency in the medium of instruction—English, for example—both disciplinary learning and language development occur when teachers strategically scaffold instruction (Walqui & van Lier, 2010). By designing instruction in specific ways—such as attending to disciplinary language demands, tapping into background knowledge, providing visuals and graphic organizers, or grouping students by linguistic background—teachers provide students with equitable access to learning while simultaneously supporting and promoting language development.

While interacting socially with peers in classroom communities, students develop language by progressing through stages of second language acquisition (Krashen, 1981, 1982). Whereas students may begin by silently taking in the world or producing words or short phrases, they develop language over time by using and expanding their word choice, grammar and sentence structures, and complex texts and oral discourse. Teachers can strategically scaffold learning and language development by attending to students' individual needs based on where they are on the path to language proficiency, as well as their backgrounds and abilities in languages other than English. Students pass through these stages at variable rates, depending on factors such as previous schooling experiences and native-language literacy skills (Collier, 1989). Figure 2.3 shows some of the various labels used in the United States to indicate students' progress with regard to stages of second language acquisition, including those adopted by individual states (Arizona, California, New York, and Texas) and two multistate consortiums (WIDA and English Language Proficiency Assessment [ELPA] 21). Whereas different contexts employ distinct numbers of proficiency level descriptors (e.g., six for WIDA, three for California), all are grounded in second language acquisition theory and ultimately result in the same advanced level of language proficiency (Krashen, 1981, 1982).

Figure 2.3 | **Consortium and State Labels for Stages of Second-Language Acquisition**

WIDA	Entering	Beginning	Developing	Expanding	Bridging	Reaching

ELPA21	Emerging	Progressing	Proficient

Arizona	Pre-Emergent	Emergent	Basic	Intermediate

California	Emerging	Expanding	Bridging

New York	Entering	Emerging	Transitioning	Expanding	Commanding

Texas	Beginning	Intermediate	Advanced	Advanced High

As students develop language, they concurrently engage in disciplinary learning with their grade-level peers. Even students at the earliest stages of language proficiency can participate in rigorous and authentic classroom experiences with the appropriate scaffolds and supports provided by teachers. It is important to note that students will make mistakes in their language use; such mistakes are expected when learning a second language and should be embraced and encouraged by teachers. Imagine if you as an English-dominant teacher ended up in a professional development session facilitated in another language, such as Spanish or Polish. By tapping into your rich background knowledge as an educator and using scaffolds provided by the facilitator (e.g., visuals, graphic organizers, grouping with other English-dominant peers), you engage in learning alongside your bilingual colleagues. You may well make errors because you are developing proficiency in the other language, but you can still interact with peers and make meaning of the content. In short, learners develop and deepen understandings while developing and practicing language.

Learning a second language—particularly English, with its many irregularities and idiosyncrasies—is a lengthy and complex process. Research has indicated that it takes 4 to 10 years for students to achieve proficiency in a second language and 7 to 9 years to catch up to native English-speaking peers on measures of academic achievement (Collier, 1989; Cummins, 2009; Hakuta, Butler, & Witt, 2000). These facts require an explicit focus on language in instruction, with all teachers—across school years and school days—embracing their pertinent roles in supporting students' language development. By tapping into students' strengths and maintaining a lens on language within and across classrooms, educators can develop and deepen students' understandings while simultaneously promoting disciplinary language development.

The Role of Language in Instruction

To begin exploring the role of language in classroom instruction, let's return to the driver education example introduced in Chapter 1. As someone who has likely driven within a particular jurisdiction for a few or more years, you might find the goals of the instructional unit of study to be relatively straightforward. We obviously want to prepare drivers who are safe, responsible, courteous, and responsive to common risks like traffic, weather, road conditions, and inattentive drivers. You can think back to your own experiences in learning how to drive and consider the specific knowledge and skills involved in becoming an effective driver, such as knowing how to position your hands on the steering wheel or being able to parallel park between cars on city streets.

These goals become less straightforward when we shift the focus away from you as a seasoned driver in your community to consider a driver education classroom with students from diverse backgrounds. Driving rules and procedures vary by context, so certain students may bring unique sets of background knowledge that influence their understandings and learning experiences, such as driving on the left side of the road or using the metric system for calculating speed and distance. Driving norms also differ across social settings, so a student who has observed drivers' linguistic interactions in Argentina or New York City may be at odds with those assumed or presented in the current context. Others may have little to no direct experience with driving, whether coming from a remote rural area in another country or an urban center dominated by mass transit.

Regardless of the varying experiences that students bring to the classroom, we want all students to reach the end goal of safe and effective driving. Using our knowledge of students' divergent experiences with driving, we critically consider the disciplinary language needed to interact, understand, and learn in the driver education unit. Some students may need to build linguistic knowledge and skills—such as terminology for automobile parts (e.g., steering wheel) and interacting with drivers and law enforcement in culturally appropriate ways—at the same time they are learning how to drive. Other students may need to transfer linguistic knowledge and skills from other settings to develop disciplinary language, such as translating road signage or calculating speed and distance in miles rather than kilometers.

Thus, the driver education unit will look distinct based on the unique and diverse group of learners. As the course instructor, you surely want to maintain the larger unit goals to ensure the preparation of effective drivers; however, you realize that additional considerations are needed to ensure that all students have equitable access to fully achieve these goals. Recognizing the background knowledge and experiences that students bring to the classroom, you strive to design instruction that will meet both the disciplinary learning and the language development needs of this diverse group of students. You can accomplish this by adding an explicit lens on language to the UbD framework.

Language and the Understanding by Design Framework

Chapter 1 began by presenting the seven tenets that underlie UbD, the instructional design framework implemented widely across the world because of its effectiveness in developing and deepening students' understanding and learning across disciplines. These tenets center on the need to intentionally plan curriculum and instruction that promote students' understanding using the three-step backward design process. Spanning schools and disciplines, expert teachers embrace roles as coaches and facilitators of in-depth student learning through authentic experiences with disciplinary topics, concepts, and ideas.

In this book we focus on using the UbD framework as a means to mediate all students' learning *and* language development, specifically focused on providing equitable access for CLD students with diverse backgrounds, experiences, and abilities. With this in mind, we add three tenets to frame this important work in contemporary classrooms:

1. All teachers have the responsibility to support students' learning and language development. Language develops in the context of disciplinary learning in subject areas, such as mathematics, social studies, sciences, and fine arts. Thus, language cannot be separated and maintained as the sole obligation of particular classrooms, such as English as a Second Language (ESL), or courses, such as English language arts.

2. All students are capable of achieving rigorous, grade-level goals for learning and understanding, regardless of particular variables or ascribed labels—for example, students who speak languages or language varieties other than Standard English, recent immigrants, and refugees from other countries—that have often unintentionally prompted lower expectations in classrooms and schools.

3. All students bring rich resources for learning to the classroom, including those with knowledge, experiences, and language repertoires that differ from those of white, middle-class, English-dominant students. Teachers should embrace and integrate students' backgrounds and multifaceted language abilities into instructional design to support learning and language development.

These tenets provide the foundation for the ideas presented in this book, which center on using the UbD framework to promote the learning and language development of all students, including CLD students.

Language and the Three Stages of Backward Design

As described earlier, UbD consists of three interconnected and aligned stages of unit-level instructional design, which prompt practitioners to identify the desired results for learning (Stage 1), determine acceptable evidence of reaching unit goals (Stage 2), and plan corresponding learning experiences and instruction (Stage 3). When adding a lens on language to curricular design, these three stages remain the same, but we enhance instructional planning by specifically considering students' language development along with their disciplinary learning. Our goal is to provide all students equitable access to the rigorous and authentic instruction designed and implemented using the UbD framework.

Stage 1 of UbD asks teachers to define what they expect learners to understand, know, and do at the end of instructional units of study. As illustrated with the driver education example, the goal is to maintain the desired outcomes for both transfer and meaning (as expressed in the UbD framework's *Transfer Goals, Understandings,* and *Essential Questions*), recognizing that all learners can and should have access to rigorous disciplinary instruction. Nonetheless, students need to develop and use language in particular ways to actively engage in disciplinary learning and successfully achieve the unit goals, which requires teachers to pinpoint essential linguistic *knowledge* (language features at the word, sentence, and discourse levels) and *skills* (language functions and domains) to guide subsequent assessment and instruction.

Stage 2 of UbD prompts the design and selection of suitable evidence for learners to demonstrate transfer and understanding as tied to the Stage 1 unit goals, including *Performance Tasks, Supplementary Evidence,* and the corresponding *Evaluative Criteria.* When adding a language lens, we consider how to design fair and bias-free assessments that tap into students' background knowledge and abilities, while accounting for varying levels of language proficiency. The aim is to provide all learners with authentic opportunities across instructional units of study to demonstrate what they understand, know, and can do in relation to disciplinary unit goals, without being hampered by or evaluated on English language proficiency or presumed cultural background knowledge.

Stage 3 of UbD involves the design of aligned and appropriate learning experiences for students to reach and demonstrate attainment of goals, as indicated in Stages 1 and 2. *Pre-assessments* prompt teachers to discern students' background knowledge of the disciplinary content, including unique and diverse experiences from students' homes, communities, and prior schooling. *Learning Events* in Stage 3 encompass the bulk of the teacher's instructional time in any given unit of study, and the language lens ensures the consistent integration of students' background knowledge across daily instruction, as well as the needed scaffolds and supports to provide equitable access to disciplinary learning and language development. *Formative Assessments* embedded in instruction prompt the ongoing collection of data to inform future teaching and drive students' understanding, learning, and language development

By adding and maintaining a lens on language throughout the three stages of backward design, teachers design instruction that promotes both disciplinary learning and language development for all students. Further, the language lens ensures that the backgrounds, abilities, and needs of diverse students are prioritized in classroom instruction. The ultimate goal is equity: that all students—specifically those from culturally and linguistically diverse backgrounds who are often marginalized in schools—have equitable access to rigorous and authentic disciplinary instruction that effectively develops and deepens their understandings, learning, and language development.

Chapter Summary

In these introductory chapters, we have introduced the central tenets and components of the widely used and effective UbD framework (Wiggins & McTighe, 2005, 2011). We also added a lens on language to critically consider the complexity of language and its impact on teaching and learning. Indeed, students in today's schools engage simultaneously in academic learning and language development across various programs, curricula, and instruction. Despite the reliance on the English language in many schools, students speaking other languages or language varieties at home and in communities have rich resources for learning and development. The goal of this book is to provide teachers with an effective way to plan rigorous and meaningful instruction that values and responds to students' linguistic and cultural resources and needs.

Grounded in these foundational understandings of UbD and language development, we now shift to the in-depth exploration of curriculum and instructional design with an explicit lens on language. In the next chapter, we consider the pertinent steps involved in preplanning for language development, including the collection and analyses of varied sources of data on students' backgrounds, strengths, and needs. By merging the UbD framework with principles of culturally and linguistically responsive practice (Gay, 2010; Lucas, Villegas, & Freedson-Gonzalez, 2008), we lay the groundwork for Part II of the book, which tackles instructional design for language development at each stage of unit planning, including Stage 1 in Chapter 4, Stage 2 in Chapter 5, and Stage 3 in Chapter 6.

3

Starting with Students: Preplanning for Language Development

CHAPTER GOALS

- **Transfer**: Educators will be able to independently use their learning to...
    - Embrace, validate, and incorporate the rich diversity of students to enhance their academic and language learning.

- **Understandings**: Educators will understand that...
    - Each individual student brings unique backgrounds, strengths, and needs into the classroom across dimensions of learning and development.
    - Instruction must build upon the linguistic and cultural resources and assets that students bring to classrooms.

- **Essential questions**: Educators will keep considering...
    - How do labels shape our perceptions of students?
    - How do students' languages influence learning?
    - What resources do students bring to classrooms?

- **Knowledge**: Educators will know...
    - The sociocultural, linguistic, cognitive, and academic dimensions of student learning and development.
    - The stages and domains of language development.

- **Skills**: Educators will be skilled at...
    - Analyzing multiple sources of data as an entry point to culturally and linguistically responsive instructional design.

Understanding and gathering information about the many facets of students' cultural and linguistic diversity is the prerequisite for planning instruction that responds to students' unique backgrounds, strengths, and needs.

Student Diversity in Classrooms and Schools

In 2014, white students ceased to be the majority in U.S. schools, dropping below 50 percent of total student enrollment for the first time in the history of contemporary American schooling (National Center for Education Statistics [NCES], 2015a). The population of K–12 schools has indeed shifted in recent decades (see Figure 3.1), driven by expanding globalization and increased immigration from Latin America and around the world (Suárez-Orozco & Suárez-Orozco, 2006). With more and more people from every corner of the globe migrating to the United States, as well as to other countries such as Canada, France, Germany, and the United Kingdom, cultural and linguistic diversity has grown rapidly. In the United States, one in five people speak a *language other than English* (LOTE) at home, with more than 350 different languages represented in households across the country (American Community Survey, 2015). This heterogeneity emerges most noticeably in classrooms and schools, where urban, suburban, and rural educators seek to support the learning, development, and achievement of students with varied and unique backgrounds, strengths, and needs (Herrera, 2016; Wrigley, 2000).

Figure 3.1 | Enrollment in K–12 Schools by Race

Census Category	1995	2015
White	64.8%	49.3%
Black	16.8%	15.6%
Hispanic	13.5%	25.9%
Asian/Pacific Islander	3.7%	5.3%
American Indian/Alaska Native	1.1%	1.0%
Two or more races	n/a	2.9%

Sources: U.S. Department of Education, National Center for Education Statistics, Common Core of Data, "State Nonfiscal Survey of Public Elementary and Secondary Education," 1995-96 through 2011-12; and National Elementary and Secondary Enrollment Projection Model, 1972 through 2023.

Here we introduce two students, Zaia and Lorenzo. They, along with other children and adolescents who will be featured throughout this book, represent the large and growing population of CLD students.

Zaia, 3rd Grader

Born and raised in a culturally and linguistically diverse urban neighborhood, Zaia grew up speaking Assyrian and Arabic, as well as reading and writing in Arabic. Her parents came to the United States as adolescents, escaping the conflict in their homeland of Iraq. After meeting, settling, and marrying, they opened a small business in the main commercial region of the community. Zaia spent a lot of time at the store, where primarily Middle Eastern families came to rent movies and video games, send and receive wire transfers, use the fee-based Internet services, and socialize with one another. When she was as young as 3 years old, she interacted and supported business transactions in both Assyrian and Arabic, able to switch back and forth flawlessly between languages depending on customers' linguistic preferences. Due to the family's strong Christian faith, weekends included religious services in the Assyrian community. When Zaia turned 5, her parents enrolled her at the neighborhood primary school, with predominantly Spanish-speaking students, as well as children speaking different African languages. In a self-contained kindergarten classroom of diverse students with families from around the globe, she began learning English as her third language. After two years of schooling, her 2nd grade teacher recognized her advanced intellect and referred her for gifted services. Now in 3rd grade and labeled both as gifted and as an English learner (EL), Zaia loves learning through inquiry projects that use her rich resources from home, community, and school.

Lorenzo, 12th Grader

Born and raised in a midsize industrial town in the United States, Lorenzo has been enrolled in general education classes at school since kindergarten. Now a senior in high school, he looks forward to enrolling at the local community college while he continues to work at his father's small business. A roofer by trade, his father established his own contracting company when Lorenzo was 10 years old, encouraging the boy to help with both construction and administrative tasks that became more demanding as he got older. When he isn't in school or working, Lorenzo enjoys making his own music and playing baseball. His music is a unique mix of his biracial identity and community surroundings, where he aims to tell stories through hip-hop that include both the African American Vernacular English spoken by his father, coworkers, and friends, as well as the Chicano English spoken by his mother's extended family, whom he visits on weekends. Growing up in a predominantly African American neighborhood and spending the majority of the time with his father, Lorenzo had self-identified as African American for most of his childhood. After making the high school baseball team, his social circle extended to include a number of his Mexican American teammates, and he began to explore more of his Latino identity. Following high school graduation, Lorenzo plans to travel with his mother to Guerrero, Mexico, as well as enroll in Spanish classes at the community college.

Responsive Pedagogy and Practice

With the increasing diversity in schools, many practitioners have embraced *culturally responsive pedagogy* to improve the educational experiences and outcomes of students from diverse backgrounds. Rather than provide students with one-size-fits-all curricula, this approach to teaching recognizes the need to facilitate learning and development that align with and tap into students' cultural backgrounds, knowledge, and experiences. Geneva Gay (2010) defines culturally responsive pedagogy as instruction that validates and incorporates "cultural knowledge, prior experiences, frames of reference, and performance styles of ethnically diverse students to make learning encounters more relevant to and effective for them" (p. 31). Because of the vast array of cultural diversity, culturally responsive pedagogy is a dynamic framework rather than a prescriptive curriculum or instructional approach, taking different shapes and forms depending on the students in the classroom. In other words, teachers use personalized knowledge of individual students' cultural backgrounds and lived experiences to shape and craft meaningful classroom instruction. When learning goals and activities are situated within students' unique and diverse experiences and perspectives, students demonstrate increased motivation, engagement, and learning (Gay, 2010; Herrera, 2016).

Narrowing the broader lens on culture and cultural diversity, *linguistically responsive teaching* emphasizes practices that specifically recognize and respond to language and linguistic diversity (Lucas & Villegas, 2010; Lucas et al., 2008). In this approach to pedagogy and practice, teachers plan instruction with an explicit lens on language development, which results in rigorous disciplinary teaching and learning that vary depending on students' language backgrounds, experiences, and proficiencies. To be linguistically responsive, educators first work to understand principles of language learning and development and recognize students' unique and diverse language backgrounds and abilities as resources for learning. Linguistically responsive instruction then explicitly attends to language demands in academic tasks and scaffolds tasks to support language development and disciplinary learning (Heritage et al., 2015; Lucas et al., 2008; Walqui & Heritage, 2012). Linguistically responsive practice spans contexts and disciplines: whether teaching literacy, mathematics, science, social studies, special areas, or electives in early childhood, elementary, secondary, or special education settings, with bilingual or monolingual mediums of instruction, *all* teachers support students' language development. See Figure 3.2 for key points of both culturally and linguistically responsive practice.

As noted earlier, this book adds an explicit lens on language to the design of instruction for disciplinary learning as outlined in the UbD framework. The overarching goal of this framework is to provide equitable access to meaningful, authentic, and rigorous learning goals and experiences by tapping into students' rich and diverse backgrounds and supporting their language development (see Figure 3.3). To accomplish this, we embed the UbD framework within the principles of culturally responsive pedagogy (Gay, 2010) and linguistically responsive teaching (Lucas et al., 2008). Thus we place CLD students at the center of curricular design and embrace an asset-based approach by conceptualizing students' backgrounds as resources for learning. Our framework differs from traditional approaches, in which students receive separate instruction apart from peers, such as ESL pull-out sessions; deficit-based accommodations, such as simplified texts and materials; or one-size-fits-all strategies within larger instructional plans, such as a differentiation box at the end of a lesson plan. To plan instruction that is culturally and linguistically responsive, teachers begin by recognizing, prioritizing, and integrating students' linguistic backgrounds, strengths, and needs.

Figure 3.2 | **Key Points of Culturally and Linguistically Responsive Practice**

Culturally Responsive Pedagogy	Linguistically Responsive Teaching
• Teaching is dynamic and flexible to reflect students' backgrounds.	• Teaching is grounded in theoretical principles of language learning and development.
• Facilitation of learning taps into background knowledge and experiences.	• Facilitation of learning taps into language backgrounds and proficiencies.
• Teachers shape and craft instruction to align with students' backgrounds.	• Teachers attend to language demands and scaffold instruction by language proficiency.
• Goal is to make learning more relevant, engaging, and effective for students.	• Goal is to promote disciplinary learning and language development for students.

Sources: Based on *Culturally Responsive Teaching: Theory, Research, and Practice* (2nd ed.), by Geneva Gay, 2010, New York: Teachers College Press; and "Linguistically Responsive Teacher Education: Preparing Classroom Teachers to Teach English Language Learners," by T. Lucas, A. M. Villegas, and M. Freedson-Gonzalez, 2008, *Journal of Teacher Education, 59*(4), 361–373.

The upcoming sections of this chapter, organized to explore the myriad nuances of language development and cultural backgrounds, lay the groundwork for pertinent preplanning steps that precede the drafting of UbD units of instruction. We begin by looking within the labels commonly used by educators in classrooms, schools, and districts.

Looking Within Labels: Language Development and Today's Students

In our discussion throughout this book of instructional design for *CLD students*, we use that terminology strategically because of its wide reach across multiple facets of diversity. Whereas many labels specify ethnicity (e.g., Latino), country of origin (e.g., Romanian), circumstances of immigration (e.g., newcomer), cultural background (e.g., Mexican American), native language (e.g., Spanish-speaking), or second language (e.g., English learner), the term *CLD* encompasses learners more broadly to capture those who do not fall into what has been referred to as *mainstream*: U.S.-born, white, and English-speaking. Other formal educational terms and labels used frequently in instructional design fall under this umbrella, specifically those focused on various facets of language, linguistic diversity, and language learning.

Figure 3.3 | **Critical Components of Instructional Planning**

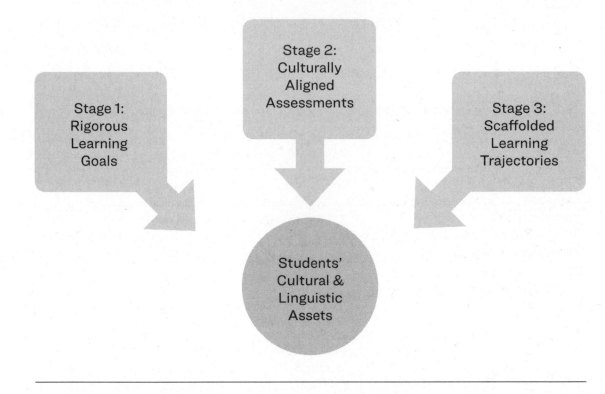

Bilingual Students

Approximately 10 million students in the United States speak a language other than English (LOTE), making up 20 percent of school-aged children nationwide (American Community Survey, 2015). Approximately half of these students enter schools as proficient (or fluent) in both English and another language, meaning they are *bilingual,* with backgrounds and abilities in two languages. Although schools typically do not have formal labels to capture the bilingualism of students, scholarly literature provides important terminology to better conceptualize students with abilities in a LOTE. For example, children raised learning two languages concurrently are referred to as *simultaneous bilinguals,* whereas *sequential bilinguals* first develop their home language and then learn a second language, typically in school. Although the demographics of bilingual learners typically center on students from nonnative English backgrounds, seemingly dominant English users can also be considered bilingual, including those raised in simultaneous bilingual homes or others participating in long-term, dual-language education programs. We must also expand our terminology to include *multilingual students*, like 3rd grader Zaia, introduced earlier, who are proficient in multiple languages (de Jong, 2011).

English Learners

Of the larger population of students who speak a LOTE, approximately half are labeled as *English learners* (ELs), comprising around 4.6 million learners, or 9.1 percent of the U.S. student population (NCES, 2017). Similar to the label for bilingual students, the EL label includes many different linguistic backgrounds (see Figure 3.4), including Spanish, Arabic, Chinese, English varieties, and Vietnamese (NCES, 2015). Synonymous with *English language learner* (ELL), this terminology specifies those students who have not yet demonstrated English proficiency as measured by standardized tests of listening, speaking, reading, and writing (Linquanti & Cook, 2013). Although *EL* has become the preferred term in most settings, teachers may be familiar with the *limited English proficient* (LEP) label, which emerged through No Child Left Behind despite criticism because of the deficit-based emphasis on a student's limitations in acquiring the nonnative language (English). Students who had not yet passed standardized language tests received the LEP label, whereas students who had recently passed were reclassified as *fluent English proficient* (FEP). In contrast to the deficit lens of LEP, *emergent bilingual* is a relatively new label that is becoming popular among scholars and educators because of its asset-based discourse (Garcia, 2009b): *emergent* implies that the student is still learning English, but in so doing is becoming *bilingual* because of already existing abilities in his or her native language.

Newcomers and Long-Term English Learners

While ample heterogeneity exists within the formal EL label, which we explore in upcoming sections, additional labels attempt to differentiate the unique needs of learners based on time spent in U.S. schools. On the early end of the temporal spectrum, *newcomers* are those students who have just enrolled and begun formal, school-based language learning in EL or bilingual programming. Identified with the label commonly ascribed to recent immigrants and refugees, newcomers typically do not speak English and are developing familiarity with cultural norms and school expectations (Cohen & Daniel, 2013). Whereas the *newcomer* label calls attention to recent entrants, the formal classification of *long-term English learner* (LTEL) refers to a student who has been enrolled in English-medium schools and labeled as an EL for an extended period of time, normally six or seven years (Menken & Kleyn, 2009; Olsen, 2014). Typically enrolled in middle and high schools, LTELs are often orally bilingual and sound proficient in English, but they struggle with native language and academic literacy skills (Menken & Kleyn, 2009). Although both newcomers and LTELs fall within the same overarching *EL* label, they have widely divergent learning needs that must be accounted for when designing and implementing instruction.

Figure 3.4 | **Top 10 Home Languages of English Learners in U.S. Schools in 2015**

Home Language	Number of ELs	Percentage of Total ELs
Spanish/Castilian	3,770,816	76.5%
Arabic	109,170	2.2%
Chinese	107,825	2.2%
English	91,669	1.9%
Vietnamese	89,705	1.8%
Hmong	39,860	0.8%
Haitian/Haitian Creole	37,371	0.8%
Somali	34,472	0.7%
Russian	33,821	0.7%
Korean	32,445	0.7%

Sources: U.S. Department of Education, National Center for Education Statistics, EDFacts file 141, Data Group 678; Common Core of Data, "State Nonfiscal Survey of Public Elementary and Secondary Education." See *Digest of Education Statistics 2015*, table 204.27.

Students with Limited or Interrupted Formal Education

Another subgroup of ELs is organized based on formal educational experiences. A *student with limited or interrupted formal education* (SLIFE) has lacked consistent exposure to school settings for a variety of reasons depending on previous circumstances, such as living in isolated geographic locales, needing to enter the workforce, dealing with repercussions of civil strife or natural disasters, or aligning with societal expectations for school attendance (Wisconsin Center for Educational Research, 2014). SLIFE students are often newcomers, arriving as immigrants or refugees from difficult situations in varying contexts around the world. A similar label, *student with interrupted formal education* (SIFE), can also encompass students from established immigrant families, including LTELs who struggle in part due to extended breaks in school attendance to return to countries of origin. Students with limitations or interruptions in their educational trajectories may lack literacy abilities and academic skills in native languages, as well as familiarity with the dynamics of formal schooling. Additionally, SLIFE students often have significant social and emotional needs due to traumatic events and experiences such as war, violence, and family separation.

Standard English Learners

Whereas the labels just discussed focus on users of a LOTE, the overarching population of CLD students can also include children and adolescents who speak varieties of the English language. As described in the previous chapter, language is complex and dynamic, with no single standard used across all members of a society. Language varieties and dialects exist within the same defined language (e.g., English, Spanish), with varying rules, forms, and structures spanning the linguistic components of phonology, morphology, syntax, lexicon, or semantics (LeMoine, 1999). Although English is formally considered as the home language, students' language use is influenced by ancestral linguistic structures, resulting in language varieties such as African American Vernacular English (AAVE) and Chicano English (Delpit, 2006). Nonetheless, Standard English is the consistently expected language for demonstrating mastery and achievement in schools, often without recognition of the fact that language varieties influence learning and language development (Lippi-Green, 1997). Just as EL and bilingual students' home languages play an integral role in school-based learning, nonstandard varieties of English must be recognized and tapped into as resources for instruction.

Labels such as those listed in Figure 3.5 exist in education for good reason. Within the complexity of classrooms, labels highlight students' particular learning needs. By being familiar with common labels used to describe CLD students, practitioners can ensure explicit attention to those students' abilities and needs when planning and implementing instruction. Nonetheless, the seemingly homogenous terms can mask ample heterogeneity, such as home language, language proficiencies, language varieties, and cultural backgrounds. To engage in culturally and linguistically responsive practice via UbD instructional design, teachers should first explore the diversity within labels to recognize the individual strengths and needs of students. We consider nuances of students' languages in the next section.

The Linguistic Dimension of Learning and Development

The labels in Figure 3.5 emphasize one key dimension of student learning and development: language, or what we refer to as the *linguistic dimension* (Collier & Thomas, 2007; Herrera, 2016). Looking beyond these homogenous labels commonly used in schools, we consider students' first, home, native, or dominant language (L1) and their second language (L2) to know and use linguistic backgrounds, strengths, and needs, as well as the pertinent interconnection between students' languages and linguistic repertoires.

Figure 3.5 | **Common Labels and Corresponding Acronyms and Abbreviations**

Acronym/Abbreviation	Label
CLD	Culturally and Linguistically Diverse
EB	Emergent Bilingual
ELL	English Language Learner
EL	English Learner
FEP	Fluent English Proficient
LEP	Limited English Proficient
LOTE	Language Other Than English
LTEL	Long-Term English Learner
SEL	Standard English Learner
SIFE	Student with Interrupted Formal Education
SLIFE	Student with Limited or Interrupted Formal Education

Native Language Abilities

Research demonstrates that students' L1 is integral to their literacy and content learning (Lindholm-Leary & Borsato, 2006). Thus it is important to know students' linguistic abilities so that teachers can tap into and develop their L1 in instruction. For the heterogeneous population of CLD students, L1 includes a vast array of formally defined languages (e.g., Spanish, English) and language varieties (e.g., Castellano, AAVE). Whereas some languages share commonalities with English, such as Indo-European languages that use similar alphabets and phonological systems (e.g., German, Spanish), others are quite distinct—such as nonalphabetic systems that use characters instead of letters (e.g., Chinese, Japanese). Regardless of similarities or differences between L1 and L2, linguistic abilities transfer across languages. Put simply, you only have to learn to listen, speak, read, or write in one language; those skills then transfer to other languages (August & Shanahan, 2008). Facilitating this transfer requires understanding of students' abilities in the L1, as well as knowledge about the language itself. In Figure 3.6 we provide examples of the sign systems for the four primary languages spoken by students in U.S. schools—Spanish, Arabic, Chinese, and English.

Figure 3.6 | **Sign Systems of Spanish, Arabic, Chinese, and English**

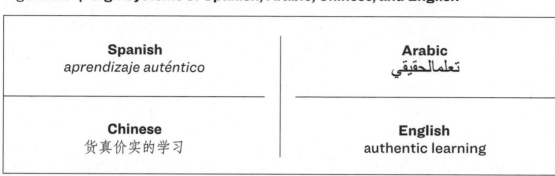

Spanish *aprendizaje auténtico*	**Arabic** تعلمالحقيقي
Chinese 货真价实的学习	**English** authentic learning

Spanish

The most commonly used language after English in the United States, Spanish is spoken in the homes of over three-quarters of ELs (Lipski, 2008; NCES, 2015b). Because both are Indo-European languages, Spanish and English share various features, including similar alphabets (Spanish has three additional letters: *ch, ll, ñ*), print directionality (reading and writing is done from left to right and top to bottom), and lexicon (e.g., *cognates,* or words that look, sound, and mean the same across languages). Examples of key differences between Spanish and English are phonological (Spanish is highly phonetic, whereas English has multiple ways to spell various phonemes) and syntactical (e.g., different rules for word order, such as noun-adjective in Spanish and adjective-noun in English). Despite millions of students sharing a common, mutually intelligible language, there are many varieties within the Spanish language in the United States. Depending on the dialect (e.g., Mexican American, Puerto Rican, Cuban, Dominican, Central American), Spanish speakers may pronounce words distinctly or have entirely different words to describe the same object or action (Lipski, 2008). This complexity is further exacerbated by regional linguistic variations in both the country of origin and the United States (Zentella, 2005). Consider, for example, the differences that might be apparent in the Spanish spoken in urban Mexico City versus rural Jalisco, or the differences in English spoken in New York City versus Southern California.

Arabic

A language dating back over 2,000 years, Arabic is the L1 used throughout the Middle East and in parts of Africa. Whereas Classic Arabic is used for religious purposes and Modern Standard Arabic is the official language of 22 countries, colloquial Arabic has various dialects depending on region (e.g., the Arabian Peninsula, Iraq) and contextual factors such as education and urbanization (Versteegh, 2014). In their use of the language of the Muslim faith, people around the world have varying oral language and literacy abilities in Arabic as L1 and L2 as they engage in religious traditions (Razfar & Rumenapp, 2014). Rapid immigration from Muslim nations in recent years has further increased the use of Arabic; in U.S. schools, Arabic is the fastest-growing L1 of English learners, increasing by 68 percent in the past five years (NCES, 2017). Notably different from English is the language's sign system (see Figure 3.6), which uses the Arabic script (as do other Middle Eastern languages such as Urdu and Farsi) and is read from right to left, rather than left to right. Phonologically, vowels operate much differently than in English; whereas English is marked by complex vowel usage (e.g., short vowels, long vowels, vowel patterns, diphthongs, *r*-controlled vowels), Arabic's vowel system is so straightforward in oral language that vowels are not represented in writing (Razfar & Rumenapp, 2014). Thus Arabic users learning English may emphasize consonants when reading and omit vowels when writing.

Chinese

The Chinese language is complex, even prompting disagreement among linguists. For some, Chinese is conceptualized as one language with multiple dialects used in particular regions, including Mandarin (prevalent in Beijing) and Cantonese (prevalent in Hong Kong), which are the dialects most widely spoken in the United States (Kurpaska, 2010; NCES, 2017). For others, Chinese is a family of languages, thus situating Mandarin and Cantonese (among others) as distinct languages that share a written sign system but are otherwise mutually unintelligible (Razfar & Rumenapp, 2014). Chinese is tonal, meaning that intonations distinguish between seemingly identical words; however, the various languages (or dialects) use different tones, often resulting in incomprehensibility across speakers (Sin-wai, 2016). Although Mandarin, Cantonese, and other regional varieties differ to the point that some speakers cannot orally comprehend one another, their common sign system allows for written communication. Chinese is one of the few remaining *logographic* languages: unlike alphabetic systems in which letters correspond phonetically with sounds, logographic systems use symbols (see Figure 3.6) to represent words or ideas; a helpful comparison is the use of emojis or emoticons, in which a symbol captures meaning (Razfar & Rumenapp, 2014). Due to this sign-word correspondence (rather than letter-sound correspondence), Chinese users learn tens of thousands of characters, differing significantly from phonics-based learning in U.S. schools.

English

Readers may be surprised to see English as an L1 of ELs. Possible rationales for this statistic include students living in simultaneous bilingual households (therefore English and another language are *both* considered home languages) or children born abroad and adopted into English-dominant households (McFarland, 2016). Whatever the reason, the data provide an opportunity to consider the diversity among English users, as Standard English cannot be considered the norm in every household. A prime example is AAVE, also known as *Black English* or *Ebonics,* a common dialect spoken in African American homes and communities (Perry & Delpit, 1998). Lippi-Green (1997) defines AAVE as a "functional spoken language which depends on structured variation to layer social meaning into discourse" (p. 176). AAVE is not simply a derivative of Standard English, but rather a hybrid language variety with linguistic influences from Africa, the Americas, and the Caribbean and historical origins dating back to slavery (Delpit, 2006). Thus, phonological, grammatical, and cultural variances in the language are not random but follow rules grounded in the storied African ancestry of its speakers (Lippi-Green, 1997). Similar to the languages just described, AAVE varies based on social and regional influences, such as differing vocabulary between the urban Midwest and the rural South (Lippi-Green, 1997). In sum, nonstandard varieties of English *are* home languages and should be used as resources for learning during instruction.

Focused on only four languages of the 350 spoken in homes by students and families, these nuances just scratch the surface of the heterogeneity and complexity of the linguistic landscape in the United States. Whether coming to school with oral language or literacy abilities in Bengali, Cherokee, Norwegian, Pashto, Puget Sound Salish, or Tarascan, students' L1 is an incredible asset and should be embraced and tapped into as a resource for instruction. Per federal law, U.S. schools must administer the *Home Language Survey* to collect data on all students' L1 upon enrollment. Educators can use this information as a starting point to learn more about the nuances of particular languages, as well as to support opportunities, resources, and personnel for formally and informally assessing students' L1 oral language, reading, and writing. For languages that are more common, schools should have access to assessments, texts, and individuals to discern and evaluate students' L1 abilities. For less common languages, educators can seek out web-based resources, as well as enlist the support of parents, families, and community organizations. Although assessments of students' L1 abilities are not required or commonplace in schools, the data are invaluable, allowing teachers to tap into students' linguistic strengths to support learning.

Second Language Abilities

CLD students enter schools with abilities in their L1, which can then be used as resources to develop their L2. In the case of the United States, as well as other countries such as the United Kingdom, Canada, and Australia, L2 typically refers to English. In Chapter 2, we described theory and research related to the nuances of language in academic settings, as well as how students develop languages with discipline-specific learning. In this subsection, we put theory into practice by considering how language is used in schools, or the particular skills needed to actively engage in learning (see Figure 3.7). We also consider what learners can do across language domains (listening, speaking, reading, writing) based on levels of English proficiency. Whereas authentic learning tasks integrate all language domains, it is important to understand, recognize, and develop individuals' abilities, strengths, and needs within *receptive* language, which encompasses listening and reading, and *productive* language, which encompasses speaking and writing (O'Malley & Pierce, 1996).

Receptive language

Of the two receptive language domains—listening and reading—the latter gets the lion's share of explicit emphasis in classroom instruction. Starting in preschool and continuing through college and career, reading is central to learning. Whether reading picture books, poetry, recipes, manuals, reports, charts, maps, textbooks, letters, diaries, novels, essays, or policy documents, learners must access and comprehend written text to actively participate in instruction and develop disciplinary understandings, knowledge, and skills. Students apply knowledge of language and print—such as letters, sounds, word parts, words, sentence structures, text structures, and print directionality—to comprehend meaning, make inferences, and evaluate ideas. To accomplish this, students tap into their background knowledge and interact with the text to construct new knowledge related to the text's concepts, arguments, and ideas. Additionally, students use a variety of strategies to aid in comprehension (e.g., visualization, predictions, self-monitoring), which vary depending on the myriad genres and texts spanning grades and disciplines.

Receptive oral language, or *listening*, receives less attention or overt support in classroom instruction. We often (falsely) assume listening to be a straightforward prerequisite to other language domains; however, effective listening requires ample knowledge and skills, particularly in the classroom context. Whereas reading involves comprehension of written texts, listening requires learners to make meaning of speech, which is characterized by various rates of delivery, run-on sentences, redundancies, elaborations, corrections, pauses, and colloquial language (Brown & Abeywickrama, 2010). Authentic listening involves interaction with others, thus requiring the use of nonlinguistic cues such as facial expressions, body language, and personal proximity to aid in comprehension and performance. Similar to reading, listening requires comprehension—processing information, making meaning using background knowledge, and pulling out important ideas and concepts. In classrooms, students need to listen to extended discourse by teachers and classmates, being strategic in how they capture the ideas and information.

Figure 3.7 | **Domain-Specific Language Use in Schools**

Domain: Listening
Sample Language Skills:
- Discriminate among the distinctive sounds and stress patterns in speech.
- Process speech at different rates of delivery with varying pauses and errors.
- Infer situations, participants, and goals of speech using real-world knowledge.
- Use facial, kinesthetic, and nonverbal cues to decipher meaning.
- Use listening strategies, such as detecting key words and self-monitoring.

Domain: Speaking
Sample Language Skills:
- Monitor speech and use strategic devices (e.g., pauses, fillers, self-corrections).
- Produce speech in appropriate phrases with related pause and breath patterns.
- Use appropriate styles, registers, conventions, and conversation rules.
- Make links and connections between events, ideas, feelings, and information.
- Use speaking strategies, such as rephrasing and providing context for meaning.

Domain: Reading
Sample Language Skills:
- Distinguish among letters, letter combinations, and orthographic patterns.
- Recognize words and interpret word-order patterns and their significance.
- Recognize rhetorical conventions and communicative functions of written texts.
- Infer context that is not explicit by activating and using background knowledge.
- Use reading strategies, such as skimming and discerning meaning from context.

Domain: Writing
Sample Language Skills:
- Express meaning using different words, phrases, and grammatical forms.
- Communicate for various purposes (e.g., persuade, inform) with related form.
- Convey connections between events, such as main idea and supporting details.
- Distinguish between literal and implied meanings while writing.
- Use writing strategies, such as prewriting and using feedback for revising.

Source: Based on "Principles of Language Assessment," by H. D. Brown & P. Abeywickrama, 2010, *Language Assessment: Principles and Classroom Practices* (2nd ed., pp. 25–51), Boston: Pearson.

Although disciplinary listening and reading in classrooms can be difficult for all learners, consider the additional challenges for those who are doing so in their second language. Tune in to a Spanish-speaking radio station or browse a Japanese biology textbook, and it won't take long to empathize with CLD students who are attempting to decipher and comprehend oral and written texts in

English. Because we all use linguistic background knowledge to facilitate effective listening and speaking, it is beneficial to consider what students can do with language, including dealing with the linguistic complexity of speech and text, various language forms and conventions, and overall vocabulary usage (WIDA, 2012). Students in the early stages of acquiring English can process information via patterned sentence structures and recognizable content-related terminology. As students progress through levels of English proficiency, as illustrated in Figure 3.8, they understand more complex language at the discourse, sentence, and word/phrase levels. Being familiar with students' domain-specific abilities in listening and reading is integral to instructional planning with a language lens.

Productive language

The productive counterpart to listening, *speaking* is rarely used in isolation from other domains, which is why we usually refer to *oral language* to encompass both listening and speaking. Often used unknowingly by educators and noneducators alike, speaking abilities serve as the litmus test to gauge an individual's overall language proficiency. Consider a first encounter with a student, a coworker, or an acquaintance, which led you to make broader linguistic assumptions based on that person's speech. Because speaking is productive and is frequently used in daily interactions, we can hear the manifestations of a person's linguistic knowledge, including phonology (e.g., production of sounds), syntax (e.g., verb tense and agreement, pluralization, word order), and lexicon (e.g., reduced forms of words, expressions, idioms). Similar to listening, speaking requires understanding of sociolinguistic cues, rules, and expectations for oral conversation to assess comprehension and know when to interrupt, rephrase, or provide context (Brown & Abeywickrama, 2010). Speakers must produce language for a variety of social and academic purposes, with varying background knowledge depending on the topic.

Productive literacy, or *writing*, occurs in various genres and for varied purposes in instruction. We ask students to write essays, reports, stories, poems, journals, and letters, as well as less formal documents including lists, schedules, notes, forms, reminders, e-mails, and exit tickets. Writing may conjure up memories of your own schooling: learning print and cursive with appropriate penmanship, taking spelling tests, and diagramming sentences based on grammar rules. Most contemporary classrooms have embraced a more authentic approach to writing, in which students apply linguistic knowledge (e.g., of grammatical forms) and writing skills (e.g., communicating ideas) in ways that align with real-world practice, depending on the discipline. To effectively produce academic writing across the curriculum, students use their knowledge of the focal topic (such as global warming or geometry) and writing conventions (such as spelling and punctuation), and their skills related to organizing ideas (as displayed in the formatting and sequencing or grouping of ideas) and applying related strategies (such as prewriting and revising) (O'Malley & Pierce, 1996). Learners also consider purpose, voice, and audience, and then use particular words, sentences, and discourse structures to meet their intended goals.

Figure 3.8 | **Receptive Language by Proficiency Level**

WIDA Performance Definitions—Listening and Reading, Grades K–12		
Within sociocultural contexts for processing language…		
Discourse Dimension	Sentence Dimension	Word/Phrase Dimension
Linguistic Complexity	Language Forms and Conventions	Vocabulary Usage
Level 6—Reaching Language that meets all criteria through Level 5, Bridging		
At each grade, toward the end of a given level of English language proficiency, and with instructional support, English language learners will process…		
Level 5 Bridging • Rich descriptive discourse with complex sentences • Cohesive and organized related ideas	• Compound, complex grammatical constructions (e.g., multiple phrases and clauses) • A broad range of sentence patterns characteristic of particular content areas	• Technical and abstract content-area language • Words and expressions with shades of meaning across content areas
Level 4 Expanding • Connected discourse with a variety of sentences • Expanded related ideas	• A variety of complex grammatical constructions • Sentence patterns characteristic of particular content areas	• Specific and some technical content-area language • Words or expressions with multiple meanings across content areas
Level 3 Developing • Discourse with a series of extended sentences • Related ideas	• Compound and some complex (e.g., noun phrase, verb phrase, prepositional phrase) grammatical constructions • Sentence patterns across content areas	• Specific content language, including expressions • Words and expressions with common collocations and idioms across content areas
Level 2 Emerging • Multiple related simple sentences • An idea with details	• Compound grammatical constructions • Repetitive phrasal and sentence patterns across content areas	• General content words and expressions, including cognates • Social and instructional words and expressions across content areas
Level 1 Entering • Single statements or questions • An idea within words, phrases, or chunks of language	• Simple grammatical constructions (e.g., commands, Wh- questions, declaratives) • Common social and instructional forms and patterns	• General content-related words • Everyday social and instructional words and expressions

Source: Based on WIDA ELP Standards © 2007, 2012 Board of Regents of the University of Wisconsin System. WIDA is a trademark of the Board of Regents of the University of Wisconsin System. For more information on using the WIDA ELD Standards, please visit the WIDA website at *www.wida.us*. Used with permission.

Instructional design should integrate ample opportunities for authentic language production, with specific attention to ELs. As illustrated in Figure 3.9, students develop speaking and writing over time, beginning with common words and patterned phrases and expanding to complex sentences with a range of grammatical structures, sentence patterns, and technical and abstract language (WIDA, 2012). It is imperative to note that ELs can produce discipline-specific language while still developing proficiency in their L2. Students should be encouraged to express ideas in L2 speaking and writing despite errors in fluency, mechanics, and conventions. In other words, correct spelling, appropriate punctuation, and flawless grammar are not prerequisites to engaging in academic tasks. ELs will make errors in productive language as they maneuver and develop their L2, often due to transfer from their L1, and their effort should be encouraged and supported. These miscues provide helpful data, opening windows into students' thought and language for educators to understand how learners are processing and producing L2 and using L1 to do so (Goodman, 1973). By considering students' domain-specific abilities, teachers can plan instruction that taps into strengths (such as speaking to support writing) and scaffolds by needs (e.g., using particular sentence patterns by discipline).

Distinct from L1, ample formal data exist in a student's L2. Per federal requirements, any student using a LOTE at home must be screened for identification, classification, and placement. For students labeled as ELs, standardized language proficiency tests are then given each academic year to monitor growth and provide snapshots of students' language abilities, strengths, and needs. For example, WIDA consortium members give the ACCESS test to students annually, which yields composite and domain-specific scores in listening, speaking, reading, and writing; these numeric scores correspond to "Can Do Descriptors," detailing what students *can do* with language depending on proficiency levels (WIDA, 2016). These data provide a starting point to understand the L2 abilities of ELs; however, practitioners need additional information to accompany the formal data collected only once per year, as well as to glean L2 data on non-ELs. Formative assessments of language across domains, as well as anecdotal data captured during authentic learning, can support the understanding of the linguistic dimension.

Bilingual and Multilingual Abilities

When home and second languages are considered as separate entities, we get only a limited sense of students' linguistic abilities. Daily discursive practices are complex and dynamic, not bound by what are considered formal languages, such as Standard English. In other words, bilingual individuals do not operate as two separate monolinguals, thinking and talking in one language at a time—for example, English at school and Spanish at home. Instead, when learning and

Figure 3.9 | **Productive Language by Proficiency Level**

WIDA Performance Definitions—Speaking and Writing, Grades K–12		
Within sociocultural contexts for language use...		
Discourse Dimension	Sentence Dimension	Word/Phrase Dimension
Linguistic Complexity	Language Forms and Conventions	Vocabulary Usage
Level 6—Reaching Language that meets all criteria through Level 5, Bridging		
At each grade, toward the end of a given level of English language proficiency, and with instructional support, English language learners will produce...		
Level 5 Bridging	• Multiple, complex sentences • Organized, cohesive, and coherent expression of ideas	• A variety of grammatical structures matched to purpose • A broad range of sentence patterns characteristic of particular content areas	• Technical and abstract content-area language, including content-specific collocations • Words and expressions with precise meaning across content areas
Level 4 Expanding	• Short, expanded, and some complex sentences • Organized expression of ideas with emerging cohesion	• A variety of grammatical structures • Sentence patterns characteristic of particular content areas	• Specific and some technical content-area language • Words and expressions with expressive meaning through use of collocations and idioms across content areas
Level 3 Developing	• Short and some expanded sentences with emerging complexity • Expended expression of one idea or emerging expression of multiple related ideas	• Repetitive grammatical structures with occasional variation • Sentence patterns across content areas	• Specific content language, including cognates and expressions • Words or expressions with multiple meanings used across content areas
Level 2 Emerging	• Phrases or short sentences • Emerging expression of ideas	• Formulaic grammatical structures • Repetitive phrasal and sentence patterns across content areas	• General content words and expressions • Social and instructional words and expressions across content areas
Level 1 Entering	• Words, phrases, or chunks of language • Single words used to represent ideas	• Phrase-level grammatical structures • Phrasal patterns associated with common social and instructional situations	• General content-related words • Everyday social, instructional and some content-related words

Source: Based on WIDA ELP Standards © 2007, 2012 Board of Regents of the University of Wisconsin System. WIDA is a trademark of the Board of Regents of the University of Wisconsin System. For more information on using the WIDA ELD Standards, please visit the WIDA website at *www.wida.us.* Used with permission.

communicating inside and outside school, they draw simultaneously from their vast array of linguistic resources (Grosjean, 1989). They cannot (and should not) turn off one language to prioritize the other. Nonetheless, traditional approaches to educating CLD students have exacerbated dual-monolingualism by separating languages in classroom environments, assessments, and instruction. Consider general education classrooms that allow students to use only English, or bilingual classrooms that rigidly separate language by teacher or content area. Formal assessments maintain the division of linguistic mediums, as seen in standardized language proficiency tests (e.g., ACCESS) that evaluate abilities in English only.

Collecting anecdotal data allows educators to capture students' authentic language use as they draw from all linguistic resources to engage in learning. Through observation and conversation with learners, teachers can glean ample information to better and more fully understand the linguistic dimension. Note that we want to consider students' *language preferences*. With multiple linguistic resources to draw from, students might prefer to use particular languages depending on the task or topic—for example, the elementary student who feels confident using English in the balanced literacy block but prefers Korean to process and solve mathematical problems. Depending on students' previous experiences with literacy and disciplinary learning, their language preferences will vary by both domain (e.g., speaking or reading) and content area (e.g., mathematics or physical education). Other students may prefer to simultaneously draw from multiple languages, tapping into unique abilities possessed by bilinguals, known as *translanguaging* (Garcia, 2009a). Because the UbD approach to curricular design builds upon students' backgrounds and strengths, it is important to recognize these preferences and abilities before planning instruction.

Facilitating the connection between languages is integral in instruction. A learner's L1 is a rich resource for literacy and disciplinary learning, as L1 abilities transfer to L2 development and academic learning. When they are familiar with students' primary languages, teachers can be aware of how languages compare and contrast. They can use this awareness first to understand linguistic transfer, or how learners use L1 to make sense of L2. For example, a Spanish-speaking EL may interchange the noun and adjective in English because of the syntactical structure in Spanish (e.g., *la casa roja* translates to "the house red"). We want to encourage students' linguistic transfer to develop *metalinguistic awareness* (Bialystok, 1993; Nagy & Townsend, 1995). When students recognize how linguistic knowledge transfers across languages, they tap into the multiple resources that they bring to school. For example, Zaia's literacy in Arabic supports her literacy skills in English, including similarities (such as comprehension strategies) and differences (such as print directionality). Lorenzo might engage in contrastive analyses between AAVE and Standard English to understand linguistic components like morphology, syntax, and pragmatics (Siegel, 2006). Using anecdotal data to understand how students connect and transfer language skills, teachers can facilitate metalinguistic awareness in instruction.

Throughout this book, we explore how to design efficacious instruction for culturally and linguistically diverse classrooms, specifically attending to language development within the UbD framework. This approach is purposefully broad to support practitioners as they plan for diverse educational settings and programs, including bilingual, ESL, sheltered, and general education classrooms. Although not the explicit focus of this book, principles of bilingualism and biliteracy underlie our framework of UbD with a lens on language development. Thus, regardless of context, home languages and language varieties should be the primary resources that are tapped into, authentically incorporated, and purposefully maintained in schools. Nonetheless, language is not the sole variable among CLD students, nor is it the only resource that learners bring to classrooms. In the next section, we consider the value of students' cultural backgrounds as they shape and influence language development and disciplinary learning.

Cultural Diversity and Today's Students

Homogenous labels, such as *ELs*, tend to make us think of homogenous groups of students with similar needs in the classroom, with an emphasis on English-language abilities. In addition to heterogeneity in the linguistic dimensions, *culture* influences classroom diversity and corresponding instruction. Despite common misconceptions, culture is much more than an ethnic ascription or demographic category, such as Mexican, African American, or Latino. Gay (2010) defines culture as "a dynamic system of social values, cognitive codes, behavioral standards, worldviews, and beliefs used to give order and meaning to our own lives as well as the lives of others" (p. 9). In short, culture shapes every aspect of learning and development (Rogoff, 2003). To plan UbD instruction that is culturally and linguistically responsive, we first consider how language *and* culture influence school-based learning and development.

As we've said before, this book focuses on the simultaneous support of students' language development and their authentic literacy and disciplinary learning as planned through the UbD framework. To accomplish plans for language-integrated curricular design, it is imperative to understand that language development does not exist in a vacuum. To consider how language and culture intersect to influence learning and development, we use the prism model, which illustrates the multiple dimensions of language acquisition at schools (Collier & Thomas, 2007; Thomas & Collier, 1997). As you can see in Figure 3.10, this model emphasizes the interconnected nature of language development, cognitive development, and academic development, all centered on social and cultural processes from inside and outside school. Across dimensions, students' L1 and L2 play integral roles in holistic learning and development. We explored the nuances of students' language development in the previous section. Now we consider the cognitive, academic, and sociocultural dimensions as a means to explore the cultural diversity of students in today's classrooms.

Figure 3.10 | **The Prism Model: Language Acquisition for School**

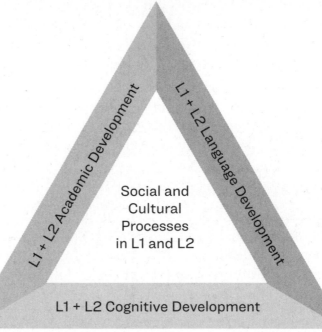

The Cognitive Dimension: Cultural Ways of Knowing and Learning

As learners develop language in schools, they also develop cognition, which refers to how a student's brain subconsciously processes and learns (Collier & Thomas, 2007). Often overlooked in instructional planning, the *cognitive dimension* considers how culture uniquely drives individual students' thoughts, knowledge, learning, and development (Herrera, 2016; Rogoff, 2003). Gay (2010) explains: "Even without our being consciously aware of it, culture determines how we think, believe, and behave, and these, in turn, affect how we teach and learn" (p. 9). Learners process information using culturally specific lenses and schema to tell stories, solve problems, and make decisions. These cultural ways of making meaning are mediated by students' multiple linguistic repertoires; for example, depending on the linguistic dimension (such as L1/L2 strengths and preferences) and academic dimension (such as prior disciplinary learning in L1/L2), students will process information in a particular language or mix of languages. Despite traditional approaches to EL education that reduced schooling to low-level activities lacking cognitive rigor, theory and research support the premise that language and cognition develop simultaneously in schools (see, for example, Bowerman & Levinson, 2001; Clark, 2004; Collier & Thomas, 2007; Dromi, 1993; van Lier & Walqui, 2012; Vygotsky, 1962). As learning experiences increase in cognitive demand, students use and develop more advanced language (Walqui & van Lier, 2010). Thus, instructional design must embrace students' multiple perspectives, ways of knowing, cognitive and metacognitive strategies, and overall approaches to learning.

The Academic Dimension:
Language Development for Learning

When exploring language development in schools, we also connect to student learning in the *academic dimension*. Academic development "includes all school work in language arts, mathematics, the sciences, social studies, and the fine arts for each grade level, K–12 and beyond" (Collier & Thomas, 2007, p. 335). In this era of accountability as measured by standardized tests, this dimension maintains primary importance in schools when considering educational goals for academic achievement more broadly; however, this dimension has often been removed in traditional approaches to teaching CLD students, based on false assumptions that language development precedes academic learning. With the demonstrated connection between language and cognition, as students learn and develop through their use of cultural and linguistic schema, the extension to learning and development in school-based academics becomes obvious. To engage in disciplinary learning in mathematics, for example, students use cultural lenses to conceptualize ideas and solve problems and linguistic abilities to process and communicate results. As illustrated in Figure 3.10, the academic dimension also includes attention to L1 and L2, as academic content knowledge and skills in a student's L1 transfer to L2 (Collier & Thomas, 2007). To support academic achievement in English-medium or other classrooms, effective teachers plan instruction that addresses linguistic, cognitive, and academic development equally, in both L1 and L2, while also tapping into the sociocultural dimension.

The Sociocultural Dimension:
Background Knowledge for Learning

All facets of learning and development—language, cognitive, and academic—occur through social and cultural processes (Thomas & Collier, 1997; Vygotsky, 1978). The final facet to explore, the *sociocultural dimension,* represents what students bring to the classroom from the assets and resources that they have learned from since birth, also referred to as *background knowledge* (Herrera, 2016). The heart of a learner's identity, these social and cultural processes are essential to learning across dimensions (Herrera, 2016). Because the sociocultural dimension is so essential to student achievement, we want to glean information on learners' background knowledge from home, community, and school. As shown in Figure 3.11, these three sources of background knowledge can be referred to as *funds of knowledge, prior knowledge,* and *academic knowledge,* respectively (Herrera, 2016). The sources are interconnected and should be considered holistically to capture the multiple dimensions of learners, but categories allow us to initially conceptualize these resources and explore related data sources. As will become evident throughout this book, the sociocultural dimension should underlie instructional planning, with teachers using students' backgrounds as a starting place for learning.

Figure 3.11 | **Sources of Student Background Knowledge**

Funds of Knowledge *from Home*	Prior Knowledge *from Community*	Academic Knowledge *from School*
Traditions	Community environment	Previous content knowledge
Values	Linguistic landscapes	School literacy practices
Native languages	Family employment	Academic language abilities
Home literacy practices	Community support systems	School-based cooperation and collaboration skills
Home numeracy practices	Bilingual speech communities	Formal school dynamics
Family dynamics	Language brokering	

Source: From *Biography-Driven Culturally Responsive Teaching,* 2nd ed. (p. 82), by Socorro G. Herrera, New York: Teachers College Press. Copyright 2016 by Teachers College, Columbia University. Reprinted by permission of the Publisher. All rights reserved.

Funds of knowledge from home

Central to an asset-based approach to teaching and learning, funds of knowledge emphasize the resources and experiences of students and families where they spend ample time—at home. *Funds of knowledge* refers to the "historically accumulated and culturally developed bodies of knowledge and skills essential for household or individual functioning and well-being" (Moll, Amanti, Neff, & González, 1992, p. 133). As active members in households, children learn varied knowledge and skills related to agriculture, business, construction, repair, and medicine. Additionally, cultural and religious affiliations shape family values and traditions, such as moral knowledge, ethics, baptisms, and holidays (Moll et al., 1992). Family dynamics include the roles that students play in their homes; for example, in many Mexican families, children are central contributors to daily household management in areas such as cooking, cleaning, and childcare (Orellana, 2001). Amid these activities, family members use unique repertoires of language, literacy, and numeracy while playing, singing, dancing, praying, debating, telling stories, reading newspapers, making lists, or tutoring siblings (Heath, 1983; Zentella, 2005).

Getting to know students' funds of knowledge takes effort beyond looking at formal data provided by schools. Whereas teachers can glean basic information—such as home language, country of origin—from enrollment forms, rich information on students' experiences at home emerges from the collection of anecdotal data via meaningful and authentic interaction with students, parents, and families. To collect data on funds of knowledge, we recommend going straight to the source—the home. Home visits allow for firsthand observation, participation, and conversation to gain a holistic sense of students' daily lives (Moll & González, 1997). Following home visits, teachers can maintain open lines of communication between home and school. Rather than conceptualize parent-teacher conferences and school-based family events as opportunities for school personnel to pass information to parents, these should be embraced as two-way conversations to learn about students' homes, families, and funds of knowledge (García-Sánchez, Orellana, & Hopkins, 2011). When analyzing data, educators should deconstruct their own assumptions and biases as to what at-home practices are valuable for school-based learning; although they may have grown up with ample books and bedtime stories, other experiences are also valuable to classroom learning (Heath, 1983; Zentella, 2005).

Prior knowledge from the community

When students are not at home or school, they are interacting with friends, family, and others in various locales in the community—a restaurant, store, church, workplace, community organization, library, museum, sporting event, or social gathering. Connected to funds of knowledge accumulated at home, *prior knowledge* refers to students' experiences and understandings accrued from living in and being a part of a larger community (Herrera, 2016). Based on family employment, students might engage with language, literacy, and numeracy in workplaces, as illustrated by Zaia's many roles at the family store and Lorenzo's hands-on tasks for his father's small business. Using affiliations from work, cultural background, and religion, families regularly develop social networks, building mutually beneficial support systems to meet childcare, financial, educational, and other needs (Moll et al., 1992). Whether in an informal social network or a formal community organization, members participate in bilingual speech communities that merge linguistic repertoires via authentic engagement with religion, sports, and activities (Herrera, 2016; Zentella, 2005). Children and adolescents play integral roles in these diverse linguistic landscapes, often serving as language brokers between L1 and L2 for other members of the community (Morales & Hanson, 2005).

Beyond the general inferences that can be made from formal data such as address and family or parent employment, anecdotal data elucidate the varied sources of prior knowledge. Just as home visits yield context-specific data on funds of knowledge, community walks provide genuine opportunities to observe and document trends in social interaction, linguistic repertoires, and cultural practices within the community (Moll et al., 1992; Zentella, 2005). Partnerships with community entities and stakeholders—such as collaboration between classroom teachers and community members who work with the same students in churches, language classes, or sports leagues—can support recognition and understanding of prior knowledge (Kenner & Ruby, 2013). In classrooms, conversations with students provide invaluable opportunities to collect data on any facet of background knowledge, including prior knowledge from community-based experiences. Whether orally or in writing, students and teachers can dialogue about out-of-school experiences, activities, and interests. Teachers can also glean helpful anecdotal data about how prior knowledge manifests in classrooms by observing students as they engage with authentic learning tasks, including think-alouds that provide windows into students' cultural ways of making meaning (Herrera, 2016; Rogoff, 2003).

Academic knowledge from schools

Whereas prior knowledge from homes and communities is often disregarded in instructional planning—particularly for CLD students, who likely have different experiences than the predominantly white, English-proficient teaching corps—academic knowledge is the form of background knowledge that is most widely used in classrooms. Herrera (2016) describes academic knowledge as that which students have acquired in formal educational settings, both in students' countries of origin and in the current school context. Academic knowledge includes students' understandings of and abilities with literacy and content, as well as experiences with formal school dynamics and patterns of collaboration. For students with previous schooling experiences in other countries, teachers can tap into their L1 abilities, content knowledge and skills, and familiarity with schooling practices; however, in many countries, schools maintain different expectations for student behavior and learning. By being aware of divergent school dynamics and norms, such as teacher-directed instruction with limited student interaction or expectations to find the right answer without showing work, teachers can recognize where students may need additional support to actively engage in learning.

Academic knowledge is the one type of background knowledge for which formal data are often readily available for educators to begin to understand students' holistic backgrounds, abilities, and needs. For students with prior schooling in the United States, educators can access and explore academic records, such as grades and standardized test scores. Additionally, they can use knowledge of state standards and local curricula to gain a general sense of students' previous scope and sequence of learning. For students entering schools from other countries, often without formal documentation or school records, school personnel can research the broad educational trends and characteristics, such as what languages are used in instruction, the trajectory of various disciplinary curricula, and formal school norms and dynamics in the country of origin (Flaitz, 2006). Practitioners can then use this information as a backdrop to make meaning of anecdotal data collected in classrooms, such as teachers' observations and students' self-assessments of overall school engagement, content and literacy abilities, and preferences regarding language and learning.

In summary, with vast diversity among students in every classroom—ranging in age, ethnicity, cultural background, religion, native language, learning preferences, socioeconomic status, gender identity, and beyond—we embrace the need to be responsive in the design and implementation of UbD instruction. With a specific lens on CLD students, practitioners move beyond the educational labels ascribed by schools and embrace the complexity and multiple dimensions of student learning, including sociocultural, linguistic, cognitive, and academic (Collier & Thomas, 2007; Thomas & Collier, 1997). Doing so requires that teachers first deconstruct what is typically perceived to be valuable background knowledge in mainstream American schools, and then collect and analyze various sources of data (as shown in Figure 3.12) to understand students as holistic learners (Herrera, 2016). After preplanning for UbD instruction, teachers can then set goals and design classroom experiences that integrate students' unique backgrounds, strengths, and needs as learners.

Classroom Application: Supporting Students' Backgrounds, Strengths, and Needs

Drawing from the multiple dimensions of students' learning and development, we now outline the specific steps to follow in instructional planning using the UbD framework. In this section, we describe how to collect, analyze, and apply appropriate data to effectively preplan instruction for diverse students.

Amass Formal Data

Given the plethora of educational policies, related forms, and required assessments, educators should have access to ample data to begin to get to know students. When enrolling students in school, parents and guardians submit various forms that include general developmental information (such as age, grade) and specific cultural and linguistic details (such as ethnic background, home language). Given annually, standardized tests, such as ACCESS, produce data related to students' language development; others, such as PARCC, produce data on academic achievement. Other assessment data may also be available for individual students, including data from screening tests for gifted services and individualized education plans (IEPs). Whether your school or district uses cumulative folders with data housed in the main office, computer software with data organized on online platforms, or a combination of both, you can purposefully seek and assemble helpful information related to students' learning and development.

Figure 3.12 | **Collecting Data on Students' Backgrounds**

Data Source	Directions
Classroom observations	Watch and listen to how students communicate and interact with other students and texts. Note how they use language to engage in tasks both inside and outside classrooms.
Community walk	Walk around the community of your school where your students live. Observe authentic language and literacy in action. Note community support systems and resources for learning.
Dialogue journals	Have students write about home, community, and school experiences in journals. Respond to their entries, creating a form of written dialogue. Provide prompts and questions to probe pertinent facts.
Home visits	Schedule time to visit a student's home. Draft open-ended questions to engage in a dialogue with the caregivers. Encourage caregivers to informally share information about the learner.
Parent-Teacher conferences	Use parent-teacher conferences as a two-way dialogue to collect information about students' background knowledge and experiences that can be tapped into as resources in classrooms.
Student records	Seek out extant data in cumulative folders or electronic databases, including age, grade, ethnicity, home language, country of origin, prior schooling, and standardized test scores of language and content.
Student self-assessments	Allow students to share strengths, needs, and preferences through self-assessments on language use and classroom learning. Have students set goals for learning and self-assess progress toward goals.
Student-Teacher conversations	Structure informal and formal opportunities to individually interact with students. Draft open-ended questions to engage in dialogue about interests, experiences, and preferences and evaluate oral language.
Think-alouds	Encourage students to think aloud. Observe and note how they process information to glean information on linguistic skills and culturally and linguistically specific cognitive and metacognitive processes.

Collect Anecdotal Data

Formal measures provide a starting place to get to know students on paper, but these data yield static and often limited snapshots of students' abilities. Moving beyond traditional tests and tools that are normed with mainstream students, you can produce richer portraits of learners by gleaning additional information related to background knowledge, cultural ways of making meaning, and language preferences in social and academic settings. In this way, you can collect anecdotal data on students' learning and development by seeking information directly from students and families—often while engaged in learning in classrooms and communities. Prioritizing qualitative methods such as observations and interviews, you can collect anecdotal data through formative assessment—using vehicles such as dialogue journals and student self-assessments, daily classroom interaction in situations such as reading conferences and small-group work, and family engagement during home visits and parent-teacher conferences.

Analyze Students Holistically

After amassing formal data and collecting anecdotal data to get to know students holistically as learners, you then analyze the data to discern individual students' backgrounds, strengths, and needs. To plan instruction that responds to students, consider the multiple dimensions of learners, including the *sociocultural* (background knowledge from home, community, and school), *linguistic* (listening, speaking, reading, and writing in L1 and L2), *cognitive* (culturally specific approaches to learning and problem solving), and *academic* (abilities spanning literacy and content areas). The Holistic Student Profile in Figure 3.13 is a tool to help organize and analyze multiple sources of formal and anecdotal data to identify an individual's resources, abilities, strengths, and needs. As we emphasize throughout the book, this holistic analysis focuses on students' assets to bolster learning and development.

Set Long-Term Learning Goals

After tapping into both formal and anecdotal sources to holistically profile students, use these data to set individual and whole-class goals. This process will vary by teacher and classroom context; for example, elementary teachers may target each student in a self-contained classroom, whereas high school teachers might generalize across a particular class section. Long-term learning goals for CLD students should align with the rigorous course-level goals for all learners, specifically when considering desired achievement in cognitive and academic dimensions. Add goals related to the sociocultural dimension—for example, acculturating to U.S. school practices and developing cultural identity; and the linguistic dimension—for example, maintaining L1 and improving L2 writing. Plan instruction for the academic year using these goals for student learning across sociocultural, linguistic, cognitive, and academic dimensions.

Figure 3.13 | **Holistic Student Profile**

Dimension	Formal Data	Anecdotal Data	Analyses and Goals
Sociocultural	Age: Grade: Country of origin: Prior schooling: Time in US:	Funds of knowledge (Home): Prior knowledge (Community) Academic knowledge (School):	Strengths: Need(s): Goal(s):
Cognitive	Gifted: IEP: 504: RtI tier: Other:	Student processing: Learning preference(s): Preferred grouping:	Strengths: Need(s): Goal(s):
Linguistic	Native Language (L1): L1 Overall: L1 Listening: L1 Speaking: L1 Reading: L1 Writing: Second Language (L2): L2 Overall: L2 Listening: L2 Speaking: L2 Reading: L2 Writing:	Language preference(s): Literacy preference(s): Language variety: Metalinguistic awareness: Translanguaging abilities:	Strengths: Need(s): Goal(s):
Academic	Standardized content test scores: Reading: Math: Science: Other:	ELA abilities/self-efficacy: Math abilities/self-efficacy: Science abilities/self-efficacy: Other:	Strengths: Need(s): Goal(s):

Sources: Based on "Predicting Second Language Academic Success in English Using the Prism Model," by V. P. Collier and W. P. Thomas, in J. Cummins & C. Davison (Eds.), *International Handbook of English Language Teaching, Part 1,* 2007, New York: Springer; and *Biography-Driven Culturally Responsive Teaching* (2nd ed.), by S. G. Herrera, 2016, New York: Teachers College Press.

Design Supportive Environments

Although this book focuses on instructional planning, specifically through the culturally and linguistically responsive UbD framework, contextual features of culturally and linguistically diverse classrooms and schools are equally important in supporting language development and disciplinary learning. Contextual features are broader elements, not limited to actual instruction, that aim to create, foster, and maintain positive learning environments that support students' multiple dimensions of development, including sociocultural, cognitive, and linguistic dimensions. These contextual features should respond to students' backgrounds and needs; examples include classroom communities that support students' risk taking with language and literacy-rich environments that provide multilingual celebrations and scaffolds for learning.

Plan Meaningful Instruction

As you seek to support students' achievement of long-term learning goals, plan meaningful and authentic instruction using the UbD framework. The chapters that follow will explore how to plan instruction to foster students' learning and development across dimensions, drawing from the holistic data analyses and long-term goals described earlier. In Stage 1 (Chapter 4), teachers analyze the unit of study for language demands and set unit learning goals via knowledge and skill indicators. In Stage 2 (Chapter 5), teachers analyze and revise for possible cultural and linguistic bias in performance tasks, summative tests, and other assessments. In Stage 3 (Chapters 6 and 7), teachers tap into background knowledge and provide appropriate scaffolds and supports before, during, and after instruction.

Classroom Snapshot: Starting with Students

Mrs. Karen Tellez is the 8th grade language arts teacher at Newton Bateman Elementary School in the vibrant and diverse Albany Park community on the northwest side of Chicago. Taught by 60 teachers spanning preschool through middle school, approximately one thousand students attend Bateman. Eighty percent, or 800, of those students speak a LOTE at home. At a school that is 85 percent Latino, the large majority of those students use Spanish at home, with a wide array of language varieties spoken by families from Mexico, Guatemala, El Salvador, Ecuador, Colombia, Puerto Rico, and Spain. In addition to Spanish, students come to school with linguistic backgrounds in Arabic, Tagalog, Farsi, Urdu, Malayalam, Russian, Swahili, Thai, Burmese, and French. Within the broader population of CLD learners, approximately one-third of Bateman students are labeled as EL based on scores from the ACCESS language proficiency test. Thus, one in three students across the school community is still developing proficiency in listening to, speaking, reading, and writing English.

In the departmentalized middle school setting, Mrs. Tellez serves approximately 95 students across multiple sections of 8th grade language arts. In spite of teaching many students, she recognizes the importance of getting to know students' backgrounds and abilities before undertaking instructional design. Using data compiled by Bateman's EL specialist, Mrs. Tellez begins each school year by analyzing students' language abilities, including L1 backgrounds and L2 proficiencies. First, using the student list with L1 as indicated on the Home Language Survey, she familiarizes herself with any new languages not previously represented in her classroom, such as one newcomer and SLIFE student whose L1 is Swahili. Then, for each class section, she plots students' standardized language proficiency test scores, which gives her a snapshot of students' language abilities and needs by domain (listening, speaking, reading, writing) to inform instructional planning and supports.

In addition to using these formal data, Mrs. Tellez also purposefully integrates meaningful and interactive opportunities to get to know students and collect anecdotal information on their sociocultural, cognitive, linguistic, and academic backgrounds. She consistently fosters a collaborative classroom environment where learners feel safe, comfortable, and encouraged to share their own stories and develop their individual identities. Early in the school year, she designs community-building efforts for learners to tell stories and share ideas, simultaneously building rapport and capturing pertinent data about students' backgrounds, experiences, interests, and preferences. Throughout the school year, Mrs. Tellez documents observations from literacy conferences and constructivist learning contexts, such as literature circles and journals. Doing so helps her to build her awareness of the diversity in students' backgrounds in terms of family structure, religion, language preferences, previous schooling, and other factors, and to note specific sets of background knowledge that learners bring from home, community, and school. She also strategically uses parent-teacher conferences as a two-way dialogue to glean additional information about learners' holistic backgrounds, abilities, strengths, and needs.

These formal and anecdotal data provide her with pertinent information to design instruction that responds to and incorporates students' cultural and linguistic backgrounds. Consider her 8th grade language arts unit focused on journeys and identity development (see Figure 3.14). Being familiar with her students' backgrounds, Mrs. Tellez specifically selects the book *Red Glass* (Resau, 2009) as the mediating text. In this book, the protagonist, Sophie, travels through Mexico to Central America to find the family of her 5-year-old adopted brother, Pablo, the only survivor of a group crossing the border in Arizona. Facing many hardships and challenges on this dangerous journey, Sophie finds inner strength and develops a sense of identity and self-awareness when faced with trauma, challenges, and death.

From her collection of preplanning data, Mrs. Tellez knows that the majority of her students are immigrants or the children of immigrants with both personal and familial stories of border crossing, family separation, and other related hardships. Whereas many students have direct knowledge of the setting in Mexico and Central America, other students have experienced similar journeys from Iraq, Myanmar, and the Congo. By selecting a culturally relevant text based on her students' experiences, she allows students to use their background knowledge to build understandings, grapple with essential questions, and develop the knowledge and skills indicated in Stage 1 of the UbD framework. By integrating her students' journeys and identities throughout the unit, including the performance assessment in Stage 2 and the learning plan in Stage 3, she maintains a language lens for CLD students throughout her instructional design.

Mrs. Tellez also plans the unit in response to other elements of learners' profiles. Using preplanning data on students' linguistic dimensions, she prioritizes the development of discipline-specific language. Bateman's heterogeneous class sections include students who are labeled as ELs and English-proficient. Other than the recent arrival from the Congo, most of her labeled ELs are in the latter stages of L2 development. She uses this information to target disciplinary language to develop students' linguistic knowledge in areas such as vocabulary, literary devices, and expository text structures as well as their skills in particular language functions and domains, such as paraphrasing and debate. As a part of her linguistic analysis in Stage 1, Mrs. Tellez recognizes she can use cognates for her Spanish bilingual students (e.g., desert/desierto, immigration/inmigración), while other learners will need additional support to develop disciplinary language. Regardless of her students' language background, including Arabic, Tagalog, Thai, and Burmese, Mrs. Tellez wants to embrace and build upon their L1 in the classroom setting. To accomplish this, she designs the Stage 2 performance task and the Stage 3 learning plan to incorporate frequent opportunities for bilingualism, biliteracy, and translanguaging. Because most of the learning plan is student-centered through literature circles, Mrs. Tellez also recognizes the need to support her Congolese student and others newer to the classroom community who may not be familiar with these collaborative dynamics of schooling.

Chapter Summary

Focused on preplanning for language development, this chapter has emphasized the need to acknowledge, discern, and plan instruction that responds to students' unique backgrounds, strengths, and needs across dimensions of learning and development (Herrera, 2016). Throughout the chapter, we have explored the heterogeneity of students' cultural and linguistic backgrounds and abilities within the homogenous labels commonly used in schools, as well as specific ways to collect and use multiple sources of data to capture individual students as unique and

Figure 3.14 | Mrs. Tellez's 8th Grade Language Arts Unit

Stage 1—Desired Results

Transfer

Students will be able to independently use their learning to…

- Read critically, analyzing how themes are developed in a text as connected to real-world experiences.

Meaning

Understandings	Essential Questions
Students will understand that…	*Students will keep considering…*
• People take many journeys, including physical, emotional, spiritual, and cultural.	• What journeys can a person take?
• Our journeys shape our identities.	• How do our journeys change us?
• Our values develop through the choices that we make.	• What is most important in life?
• Powerful story writing helps us make connections to our lives and the lives of others through the development of themes.	• How do fictional texts help us make personal connections?
	• How do the themes of a text help us better understand others?

Acquisition

Established Goals	Students will know…	Students will be skilled at…
CCSS-ELA-RL-8.4: Determine the meaning of words and phrases as they are used in a text; analyze the impact of specific word choices on meaning and tone.	• Unit- and text-specific vocabulary (e.g., journey, destination, desert, immigration, undocumented, shard, insecurity, protagonist, antagonist).	• Determining a speaker's argument and claims and evaluating relevance of the presented evidence.
CCSS-ELA-RL-8.6: Analyze how differences in points of view of characters or reader create such effects as suspense or humor.	• Literary devices (e.g., simile, metaphor, hyperbole, assonance, personification, alliteration).	• Paraphrasing the argument and claims of a peer regarding Sophie's change.
CCSS-ELA-W-8.1: Write arguments to support claims with clear reasons and relevant evidence.	• Expository texts with particular sentence structures and signal words.	• Debating the events that most influence Sophie to change.
CCSS-ELA-SL-8.5: Integrate multimedia and visual displays into presentations to clarify information, strengthen claims and evidence, and add interest.		• Identifying the events that most influence Sophie's change.
		• Producing an argument and supporting claims regarding the events that most influence Sophie to change.

Stage 2—Evidence

Assessment Evidence

Evaluative Criteria	Assessment Evidence
• Authentic • Evidence-based • Convincing • Engaging • Rich language	**Performance Tasks(s)** **Sophie's Immigrant Journey** Your task is to tell the journey of an individual. You are a local reporter charged with informing the public about personal stories of immigration. The upcoming segment centers around Sophie's journey, including your argument and supporting claims about the events that defined her journey. You will create a video segment with your peers, which includes interviews, role-playing, and supplemental video and pictures to craft the story of Sophie's journey. You should use your cultural and linguistic resources to accomplish this task, including your own journeys and native languages. Your performance needs to tell her story while convincing the audience with your crafted storyline.
• Collaborative • Interpretive • Engaged	**Supplementary Evidence** • Participation in interactive learning events (i.e., Socratic seminar, literature circles) • Teacher-student conferences based on focal text (i.e., *Red Glass*) and related texts

Stage 3—Learning Plan

Pre-assessment

• Glean background knowledge about journeys: Use a form of graffiti where students walk around the room and respond to the unit essential questions with words or pictures. Groups share out key ideas from posters.

• Interactive anticipation guide (in English and Spanish): Students respond to sentence prompts and use their ideas to interact with one another around the big themes of *Red Glass*.

Learning Events

• Modeling and application of nonfiction article about immigrant border crossing: Text annotation using Think Marks and summarization using the 5W+1H graphic organizer (bilingual).

• Ongoing reader responses: To begin each class, students use reader response strategies based on the target theme and focus for the class. (e.g., sketch to stretch, webbing, character comparison).

• Ongoing reading minilessons: Prior to each literature circle, give a minilesson on reading strategy to make meaning (e.g., self-monitoring, making inferences, visualizing, analyzing events) using related graphic organizers (e.g., characterization chart, bridge graphic organizer, say/mean T-chart, pictures).

• Ongoing literature circles: After reading set portions of the novel *Red Glass*, students get together to discuss and make meaning of the overarching themes as related to essential questions using roles.

• Modeling and application: Connections between focal novel and other genres, including poetry ("I carry your heart in my heart" by e e cummings) and graphic novel (*Safe Area Gorazde*, by Joe Sacco).

• Socratic seminar: What prompted the change from Sophie La Delicada to Sophie La Fuerte? Provide students with sentence frames based on levels of language proficiency (L1 for emerging students).

• Extension of language development through culturally relevant picture books: *Harvesting Hope: The Story of Cesar Chavez* (Krull, 2003), *Ziba Came on a Boat* (Lofthouse, 2007), *Pancho Rabbit and the Coyote* (Tonatiuh, 2013), *The Arrival* (Tan, 2007), *Migrant* (Trottier, 2011), *Grandfather's Journey* (Say, 2008), *My Diary from Here to There* (Perez, 2009), *Landed* (Lee, 2006), and *Bread Song* (Lipp, 2004).

• In-class time to plan, rehearse, and share performance tasks (reporting segments; see above).

Formative Assessment

• Artifacts from reader responses and interactive literature discussions (e.g., posters, reflections)

• Artifacts from daily instruction (e.g, bridge graphic organizer for citing text evidence, characterization chart, say/mean T-chart, context clue chart, one-minute summaries)

• Personal glossaries of related vocabulary

• Checklist on daily checks for understanding

Source: Used with permission from Karen Tellez, Newton Bateman Elementary School, Chicago.

holistic learners. We have described how to plan instruction that builds upon the resources and assets that students bring to classrooms, including home languages and cultural backgrounds. Unlike traditional approaches to teaching CLD students, in which one-size-fits-all strategies pervade instruction, our approach has emphasized the need to first recognize and then respond to the diverse students in classrooms, resulting in what has been called, in the educational literature, culturally and linguistically responsive pedagogy (Gay, 2010; Lucas et al., 2008).

Throughout upcoming chapters, we integrate foci on language and culture into the UbD framework for curricular design and instructional planning. As we explore the three stages of instructional design, you will see the pertinence of the data amassed in the preplanning stage. In Stage 1, data on students' linguistic dimension support the determination of relevant language and corresponding goals for language development. In Stage 2, various data inform the design of performance tasks that appropriately tap into background knowledge and differentiate opportunities to demonstrate learning based on language proficiency. In Stage 3, all data merge to devise learning trajectories that incorporate students' unique strengths and interests while scaffolding and supporting equitable access to authentic learning tasks and complex texts. In the next chapter, we begin our exploration of using the UbD framework in culturally and linguistically diverse classrooms by focusing on Stage 1 of instructional design.

PART II

The Three Stages
of Backward
Design for
Language
Development

4

Setting Goals for Learning:
Stage 1 for Language Development

CHAPTER GOALS

- **Transfer**: Educators will be able to independently use their learning to...
  - Recognize language demands within and across academic disciplines.
  - Target and define desired results for students' language development.

- **Understandings**: Educators will understand that...
  - Language usage varies within and across academic disciplines.
  - Language demands vary by learner, task, and classroom context.
  - By recognizing and attending to language demands in units of study, teachers provide CLD students equitable access to learning.

- **Essential questions**: Educators will keep considering...
  - What is language?
  - How does language vary by discipline, context, and unit of study?

- **Knowledge**: Educators will know...
  - Language functions tied to six facets of understanding.
  - Academic registers of mathematics, science, social studies, English language arts, and other disciplines.
  - Language features at word, sentence, and discourse levels.
  - The four domains of language (listening, speaking, reading, writing).

- **Skills**: Educators will be skilled at...
  - Analyzing the language demands inherent within and across academic disciplines and units of study.
  - Distinguishing how discrete skills and processes can target and develop students' language development in units of study.

When we add a lens on language development to UbD, our overarching goal is equity. This focus on equity for CLD students begins in Stage 1 of instructional planning when we define the desired results for learning. First, we want all students to be able to engage in authentic learning to achieve learning goals and enduring understandings. Second, we recognize the need to explicitly focus on disciplinary language to develop all students' language and to provide equitable access to the desired results for CLD students. With those goals in mind, we focus this chapter on recognizing the linguistic demands of academic tasks, including language functions and features. We consider these demands across disciplines and units of study and then use them to fine-tune the Stage 1 desired results, including transfer goals, meaning goals, and acquisition goals.

Language Development in Classrooms and Schools

Recognition of the many facets of language development—including how it varies depending on discipline, classroom, student, task, and text—informs the work of Stage 1. Here we introduce Fatima and Vinh, two students whose situations illustrate some of the nuances that come into play when undertaking Stage 1 of the UbD framework.

Fatima, 7th Grader

A native Spanish speaker, Fatima began learning English in 3rd grade, when her family immigrated to the United States from Guaymas, Mexico, and enrolled her in the neighborhood elementary school. Now at a culturally and linguistically diverse middle school, Fatima moves from classroom to classroom to learn different content areas with her peers, many of them Spanish speakers from Mexico, Central America, and South America. In language arts class, Fatima's teacher engages students in reading, writing, and orally reciting different forms and structures of poetry, including limericks and haiku. Fatima learns about statistics in math class: reading random samples of census data, making inferences on population, and writing justifications for claims. In science, she and her classmates apply learning from textbook readings and learning experiences by designing and explaining the structure and function of cells through models. Fatima enjoys the current focus on immigration in social studies, where the class is reading *Dreamers* (Truax, 2015), an expository, journalistic-type narrative profiling undocumented students across the United States, and conducting oral history interviews to capture stories of immigration. Just as she did in elementary school, Fatima loves learning and embraces her teachers' high expectations; however, she sometimes struggles to access the content because of the complex language used distinctly in each class period. Whether making inferences based on figurative language in poems, justifying claims from census-based data tables, applying concepts from the science textbook, or navigating the specific people, legal proceedings, and acronyms of the U.S. immigration debate, Fatima must develop disciplinary language to fully participate and engage in learning.

Vinh, 10th Grader

Vinh, a sequential bilingual, grew up speaking Vietnamese at home with his parents, a nurse and a local restaurant owner, as well as his grandparents and siblings. Vinh began learning English when his parents enrolled him in kindergarten. Now a 10th grader in a suburban public high school, Vinh is considered a long-term EL. Strong in listening and speaking, he struggles with reading and writing, particularly in discipline-specific academic settings. Last year in 9th grade, Vinh failed history class. Despite being interested in social studies in elementary and middle school, he struggled to comprehend the teacher's lectures and access the textbook, which consistently used passive voice, complex sentences, technical vocabulary, and words with multiple meanings. After Vinh lost interest in the content due to its inaccessibility, his teacher provided him with simplified texts and rote worksheets different from the texts and tasks of his English-proficient peers. This year Vinh was placed in a history class with a different teacher, one with specific preparation for ELs, including an understanding of disciplinary language and language development. This teacher plans instruction with simultaneous lenses on history content and language. She plans and implements instruction to engage students in deep, authentic, and interactive learning around understandings and essential questions, while scaffolding access to the language demands and functions inherent in the history-focused units of study. Because of the teacher's language lens, Vinh can now access classroom-based disciplinary learning, build deeper understandings, and grapple with essential questions, leading to his enhanced self-efficacy, engagement, and motivation.

Stage 1 for Understanding and Language Development

As described in Chapter 1, the overarching goal of UbD is to develop and deepen student understanding. We want educators to plan instruction so that students make meaning and apply understandings, knowledge, and skills in new situations (Wiggins & McTighe, 2011). Stage 1 of backward design is where we define the desired results of instruction, including goals for transfer, meaning, and acquisition. *Transfer* refers to long-term goals of instruction—specifically, preparing students to transfer and use their learning beyond the scope and sequence of an instructional unit of study. To facilitate transfer, we teach for *meaning*, with students actively inquiring and grappling with *essential questions* to build deep *understandings*. The building blocks for meaning-making and transfer, *acquisition goals* aim to build related *knowledge* and *skills* (Wiggins & McTighe, 2011). Taken together, these interconnected goals set rigorous expectations for authentic learning that guide subsequent instructional planning. In the next sections, we examine these various elements through the lens of language development.

Transfer and Meaning Goals with a Lens on Language

We begin UbD instructional planning with a lens on language by considering the language students need to achieve *transfer goals* and *meaning goals*. Teachers use these goals first to determine the language needed for all students to engage in learning and then to scaffold and support students' language development throughout the stages of instructional design and implementation.

As demonstrated in the following sections, language development occurs within a sociocultural context (Walqui & van Lier, 2010). This context includes a register (e.g., the language of mathematics), a unit topic (e.g., algebraic slope), tasks (e.g., using neighborhood maps), texts (e.g., word problems), and students, including their linguistic background (WIDA, 2012). We begin with the *sociolinguistic lens* on *language functions* across disciplines and units, as students use language for social interaction and cognitive processing. We then consider the *linguistic lens*, focused on the *language demands* at the discourse, sentence, and word/phrase levels within disciplines and units of study.

Language Functions Across Disciplines: A Sociolinguistic Lens

Language mediates communication inside and outside school, both orally and in writing. However, to accomplish specific goals and tasks, we use language in different ways, referred to as *language functions* (Fairclough, 2003; Halliday, 1975). Throughout the school day, teachers and students use various language functions to engage in daily learning experiences. Using *communicative language functions*, students greet one another, ask for a hall pass or to go to the bathroom, give information or assistance to their peers, and express their feelings and emotions (O'Malley & Pierce, 1996). Students incorporate *academic language functions* while participating in classroom learning experiences, such as identifying and labeling geographic features on a map, sequencing and explaining the steps in a mathematical equation, hypothesizing the outcome of a science experiment, or critiquing the author of a literary work (AACCW, 2010; O'Malley & Pierce, 1996). Language functions span disciplines and prompt students to use language in distinct ways, including merging and enacting words, phrases, sentences, and discourses to take part in social interaction, cognitive processing, and authentic learning.

In this section, we use the *six facets of understanding* (Wiggins & McTighe, 2005) to consider language functions, or the ways in which students use language as tied to cognition. These facets of understanding are explanation, interpretation, application, perspective, empathy, and self-knowledge. They can be used to design and assess the deep and authentic learning that is the ultimate goal of

UbD—the design of instruction that enables students to go beyond simple recall of facts related to a specified standard and instead to make meaning of important concepts and to transfer learning to other contexts. By adding a lens on language, our overarching goal is to ensure that all students have equitable access to the transfer and meaning goals in units of study, ensuring equity for CLD students in particular. Because transfer and meaning goals require higher cognitive functions by design, we consider the language functions needed to achieve those desired results. This linguistic analysis aims to reduce the *expert blind spot*, the phenomena in which educators—the disciplinary and pedagogical experts in classrooms—have difficulty empathizing with students who are novices in the field and may have radically different experiences than their own (Wiggins & McTighe, 2005). This blind spot is exacerbated by language, particularly for educators who are English dominant. Thus we aim to build awareness of discipline-specific language demands, allowing educators to support students' language development throughout the three stages of instructional design.

Explanation

The first facet of understanding, *explanation,* centers on students' use of productive language via speaking or writing to demonstrate their understanding of big ideas. Wiggins and McTighe (2005) assert, "When we truly understand, we can explain via generalizations or principles, providing justified and systemic accounts of phenomena, facts, and data [to] make insightful connections and provide illuminating examples or illustrations" (p. 84). Distinct from the regurgitation of rote knowledge of facts and terms, this facet of understanding recognizes the need for students to explain what they know by making inferences, generalizing principles, synthesizing ideas, and substantiating claims with evidence. With understanding demonstrated by explanation of concepts, ideas, theories, and events, students use language in authentic ways that are embedded in content learning. The assumption is that students with in-depth understanding can express these nuanced connections and provide particular examples using both oral and written language.

When adding a lens on language, teachers consider the language that students need to use to articulate understandings and respond to essential questions. *Explanation* as a language function requires that students use "phrases and sentences to express the rationale, reasons, causes, or relationship related to one or more actions, events, ideas, or processes," as well as related *discourse markers,* including "so, for, therefore, as a result, for that reason" (AACCW, 2010, p. 3). But expanding to consider explanation as a broader facet of understanding, additional language functions become pertinent, such as sequencing, describing, comparing, generalizing, inferring, predicting, and synthesizing, with corresponding linguistic features that vary in complexity (AACCW, 2010; Wiggins &

McTighe, 2005, 2011). With our primary purpose being that all students engage cognitively with disciplinary concepts and achieve transfer and meaning goals, we must consider the varied language functions and features needed to demonstrate understanding. See Figure 4.1 for an overview of language functions and related language features.

Figure 4.1 | **Language Functions and Features**

Language Function	Related Language Features
Identify	A word or phrase to name an object, action, event, idea, fact, problem, or process
Label	A word or phrase to name an object, action, event, or idea
Enumerate	Words or phrases to name distinct objects, actions, events, or ideas in a series
Classify	Words, phrases, or sentences to associate an object, action, event, or idea with the category to which it belongs
Sequence	Words, phrases, or sentences to express the order of information with adverbials such as *first, next, then, finally*
Organize	Words, phrases, or sentences to express relationships among events and ideas with coordinating conjunctions (*and, but, yet, or*) and adverbials (*first, next, then, finally*)
Compare	Words, phrases, or sentences to express similarities or differences with coordinating conjunctions (*and, but, yet, or*) and adverbials (*similarly, likewise, in contrast*)
Inquire	Words, phrases, or sentences to solicit information (e.g., yes-no questions, WH-questions, statements used as questions)
Describe	Words, phrases, or sentences to express or observe attributes or properties of an object, action, event, idea, or solution
Define	Words, phrases, or sentences to express the meaning of a given word or phrase
Explain	Phrases or sentences to express rationales for actions, events, ideas, or processes with coordinating conjunctions (*so, for*) and adverbials (*therefore, as a result*)
Retell	Phrases or sentences to relate or repeat information with coordinating conjunctions (*and, but*) and adverbials (*first, next, then, finally*)
Summarize	Phrases or sentences to express important ideas and relevant details about one or more objects, actions, events, ideas, or processes
Interpret	Phrases, sentences, or symbols to express understanding of the intended or alternate meaning of information
Analyze	Phrases or sentences to indicate parts of a whole or relationship among parts with relationship verbs (*contain, entail*), partitives (*a part of*), and quantifiers (*hardly any*)
Generalize	Phrases or sentences to express an opinion or conclusion based on facts, statistics, and other information to extend that opinion to other contexts

Language Function	Related Language Features
Infer	Words, phrases, or sentences to express understanding based on available information using inferential logical connectors (*although, while, thus, therefore*)
Predict	Words, phrases, or sentences to express an idea about a future action or event based on available information using adverbials (*maybe, perhaps, evidently*)
Hypothesize	Phrases or sentences to express an expectation or possible outcome based on available information using adverbials (*generally, typically, obviously*)
Argue	Phrases or sentences to present a point of view and communicate a particular position with expressions (*it seems to me*) and adverbials (*although, however*)
Persuade	Phrases or sentences to present ideas with the intent to create agreement around a position with expressions (*in my opinion*) and adverbials (*since, because*)
Negotiate	Phrases or sentences to engage in a discussion with the purpose of creating mutual agreement from two or more different points of view
Synthesize	Phrases or sentences to express relationships among ideas with relationship verbs (*contain, entail*), partitives (*a segment of*), and quantifiers (*almost all, hardly any*)
Critique	Phrases or sentences to express a focused review or analysis of an object, action, event, idea, or text
Evaluate	Phrases or sentences to express a judgment about the meaning, importance, or significance of an action, event , idea, or text
Symbolize	Symbols, numerals, and letters to represent meaning within a conventional context

Source: From "Language for Achievement" handout from the Assessment and Accountability Comprehensive Center at WestEd, 2010. Reprinted with permission.

After deconstructing the particular ways that language is required to demonstrate understanding in this facet, teachers then consider how CLD students might use language differently to demonstrate understandings based on their unique and diverse linguistic backgrounds and abilities. For example, students at earlier stages of language proficiency might explain understandings by *sequencing* ideas and events, using simple sentences and adverbial cues such as *first, next, then*, and *finally*; whereas those in later stages might *synthesize* those same ideas and events in more complex sentences using relationship verbs such as *entail* and *consist of,* and quantifiers such as *almost all* and *a good number of* (AACCW, 2010). Starting with what students can do with language, as described in Chapter 3, effective practitioners analyze language to ensure that all students have equitable opportunities to explain their understandings regardless of their language proficiency, as well as consider how students might use their native languages and cultural background knowledge to support their explanations.

Interpretation

The second facet of understanding, *interpretation*, emphasizes students' use of receptive language via listening and reading of "narratives, translations, metaphors, images, and artistry that provide meaning" (McTighe & Wiggins, 2004, p. 155). In addition to receptive language, students articulate these interpretations through speaking and writing, thus merging language domains in a way that emulates real-world practices with texts and tasks. Wiggins and McTighe (2005) explain that true understanding means that "we can interpret [to] tell meaningful stories, offer apt translations, provide a revealing historical or personal dimension to ideas and events, [and] make the object of understanding personal or accessible through images, anecdotes, analogies, and models" (p. 84). Divergent from comprehension questions requiring rote recall of story elements and events after listening to or reading a text passage, interpretation as a facet of understanding focuses on making meaning, gaining insight, and drawing conclusions based on ideas and events, specifically connecting to past and current experiences and perspectives.

When considering this facet of understanding with a lens on language, we recognize the language needed to demonstrate learning through interpretation across the domains of listening, speaking, reading, and writing. *Interpretation* as a language function requires that students use "phrases, sentences, or symbols to express understanding of the intended or alternate meaning of information" (AACCW, 2010, p. 3). However, students also tap into additional language functions—such as identifying, retelling, summarizing, critiquing, and evaluating (see Figure 4.1)—to accomplish the larger purpose of interpretation as a facet of understanding (AACCW, 2010; Wiggins & McTighe, 2005, 2011). By critically considering the complexity of language functions and related features needed to interpret stories, ideas, and events, teachers can provide equitable access to transfer and meaning goals. Whereas some students might develop and express interpretations through symbols and illustrations paired with high-frequency words and phrases, others might incorporate technical words and figurative language (AACCW, 2010).

In addition to linguistic considerations related to language domains, functions, and features, we must pay particular attention to culture when approaching this facet of understanding. As Wiggins and McTighe (2005) remind us, meaning is in the eye of the beholder; in other words, we all approach, transact, and make meaning of tasks and texts in our own ways (Rogoff, 2003; Rosenblatt, 2004). As described in Chapter 3, culture shapes students' sociocultural and cognitive dimensions with interpretations influenced by the rich diversity in background knowledge and habits of mind derived from homes, communities, and schools. In addition to cultural background knowledge and schema, consider how culture shapes students' language use in interpretation. For example, when asked to interpret and tell meaningful stories, students may tap into unique cultural approaches to storytelling that differ from the linear approach of mainstream American traditions (Heath, 1983). By analyzing the language involved in interpretation, teachers build awareness of how learners' multiple dimensions influence understanding (Herrera, 2016).

Application

The third facet of understanding, *application*, involves students' authentic and integrated use of knowledge and skills in real-world situations spanning diverse settings. Wiggins and McTighe (2005) describe it this way: "When we truly understand, we can apply [and] effectively use and adapt what we know in diverse and real contexts—we can 'do' the subject" (p. 84). Rather than superficially demonstrating understanding on a worksheet or a paper-and-pencil test, students engage in language-rich tasks in which they apply knowledge and skills in meaningful and diverse contexts. When given the opportunities to tackle practical problems and realistic tasks situated outside classrooms and schools, students engage in decision making, problem solving, and performances that merge listening, speaking, reading, and writing (O'Malley & Pierce, 1996). Whether applied in mathematics, science, social studies, language arts, or another content area, this facet of understanding has the potential to tap into students' interests and background knowledge while simultaneously mediating learning and language development with hands-on tools and materials.

Application as a facet of understanding is context dependent (Wiggins & McTighe, 2005), resulting in varied language usage depending on the situation. With the emphasis on real-world tasks and problems, students use language connected to cognitive processes and academic content when they integrate and apply knowledge and skills to adapt, build, create, design, and perform (Wiggins & McTighe, 2011). For example, if students' understanding of a social studies unit manifests in the creation of a museum exhibit chronicling the hardships of pioneer life, students might use language to identify, label, sequence, organize, summarize, and synthesize; however, when students apply scientific learning by building switches for model railroads, language functions might include enumerating, inquiring, predicting, hypothesizing, and evaluating (McTighe & Wiggins, 2004). When adding a linguistic lens to this facet of understanding, we can better conceptualize the complexity and dynamism of how students use language in disciplinary learning. As discussed in Chapter 2, language cannot be easily dichotomized or separated into categories, such as *social* versus *academic* language. Consider how students might use language as they collaboratively create museum exhibits or build railroad switches, using multiple language functions to brainstorm ideas, discuss and seek out classroom materials, and negotiate procedures and project organization. Students mix various communicative and academic language functions as they engage in learning.

In addition to language functions, other linguistic features may emerge as demanding when considering the nature of this facet of understanding, particularly in relation to the push for students to apply learning to new problems and diverse situations (Wiggins & McTighe, 2005). With transfer and meaning goals centering on application for understanding, teachers might expect students to employ knowledge and skills in novel contexts, but some may lack the cultural and linguistic background knowledge needed to engage with those contexts and achieve instructional goals. For example, consider a mathematics unit with goals focused on applying knowledge and skills to real-world problems, such as a contractor estimating the cost of drywall to draft a work proposal for a new homeowner (McTighe & Wiggins, 2004). In addition to the mathematical understandings, knowledge, and skills from the unit of study, students require particular background knowledge and related words, such as *contractor* and *drywall*, and discourse structures, such as *written proposal*. For students to be able to engage with this facet of understanding, teachers respond to individual students to support disciplinary learning and language development as embedded in the specific context and unit of study.

Perspective

The fourth facet of understanding, *perspective*, centers on students' use of receptive and productive language to develop and share "critical and insightful points of view" (McTighe & Wiggins, 2004, p. 155). The crux of this facet is that students recognize the complex and multifaceted nature of issues: questions and problems can be approached from multiple standpoints, and ideas and events can be perceived distinctly, depending on viewpoints. Wiggins and McTighe (2005) assert, "When we truly understand, we have perspective [to] see and hear points of view through critical eyes and ears [and] see the big picture" (p. 84). Moving beyond first-person language use in which they develop and share their own perspectives (e.g., I think, I believe), students demonstrate understanding by shifting to third-person points of view to critically consider, evaluate, and share the perspectives of others. Perspective as a facet of understanding has great potential in CLD settings, where multiple perspectives shaped by the rich array of cultures and languages are inherent in the classroom context.

Students use language in unique ways when taking perspectives to demonstrate understanding, with a variety and range of related language functions. When instruction includes opportunities to confront various viewpoints related to the big ideas of a unit of study, learners engage in comparing, contrasting, analyzing, inferring, arguing, persuading, and critiquing (AACCW, 2010; Wiggins & McTighe, 2011). In addition to the language of the particular content area and unit topic (which we explore in more depth later in this chapter), students use language functions and related features to consider and share multiple perspectives.

For example, *comparing* and *contrasting* require words, phrases, and sentences to distinguish among viewpoints on an issue and communicate the specific similarities and differences using coordinating conjunctions, such as *and, but, or,* and adverbials, such as *similarly, in contrast* (AACCW, 2010). Often requiring more complex language, *persuading* requires students to use discourse to present and support a particular position or idea, including expressions such as *in my opinion, it seems to me,* and adverbials such as *although* and *however* (AACCW, 2010). By adding a lens on language to this facet of understanding, teachers can ensure appropriate linguistic supports for all students to engage with the big ideas of the unit.

Building on these linguistic considerations, cultural implications tie to the various language functions of perspective taking. In short, some students may not be accustomed to the critical lens attached to this facet of understanding, depending on their cultural backgrounds, values, and traditions. If children and adolescents have been raised with the cultural expectation that they do not argue or critique established principles, ideas, or authorities, then they may lack cognitive and linguistic repertoires to appropriately use these language functions (Bunch, Kibler, & Pimentel, 2012). In addition to supporting language in this facet of understanding, consider deep-seated cultural schema that may influence students' ability to take perspective on a topic or issue. For example, consider an instructional unit focused on World War II in a diverse classroom context with both U.S.-born and immigrant students from nations including Russia, Korea, and Japan. Particularly for those with previous schooling in their countries of origin and exposed to ideologies and opinions of family and community members, students bring distinct viewpoints on the war's origins, events, and outcomes. To support all students in critically considering multiple perspectives, effective practitioners attend to these unique, diverse, and intersecting sociocultural, cognitive, and linguistic dimensions (Herrera, 2016).

Empathy

The fifth facet of understanding, *empathy*, pushes students to "get 'inside' another person's feelings and world view" (McTighe & Wiggins, 2004, p. 155). Distinct from perspective, in which students consider distanced, detached, and critical viewpoints on issues and events, empathy centers on our human capacity for warmth, compassion, and kindness to foster open-mindedness and intercultural consciousness. Wiggins and McTighe (2005) state, "When we truly understand, we can empathize [to] find value in what others might find odd, alien, or implausible [and] perceive sensitively on the basis of prior direct experience" (p. 84). The emphasis here is on bridging differences, helping students "to understand people whose values, views, and behavior are different from our own" (Calloway-Thomas, 2010, p. 18)—a facet integral to building classroom community in CLD settings, as well as designing instruction that prepares students for our diversifying and globalizing world.

Because empathy is complex, it requires multifaceted language functions to achieve transfer and meaning goals (Calloway-Thomas, 2010). Spanning receptive and productive language domains, empathetic learning goals engage students in *listening* and *reading* to make meaning of the experiences of others, as well as producing *speech* and *writing* to describe and explain their emotions, opinions, and identities. In initial stages of empathy, learners use language to *compare* themselves to others, specifically to recognize similarities as a starting place for understanding (e.g., "We are around the same age"). Next, they *inquire* into the experiences of others to be able to figuratively enter into someone's world (e.g., "Who is this person? What is he feeling? How might I feel if this were me?"). Students then attempt to express another's experiences, often needing to first *infer* current emotions and *predict* future behaviors based on available information, and then *describe* and *explain* these sentiments and actions as situated in another's values and worldviews. Due to the complexity of human emotions, including ample nuances and shades of meaning—as illustrated in the terms *sad, depressed, devastated, heartbroken*—students across levels of language proficiency use various words, phrases, and sentences to demonstrate their understanding.

Self-Knowledge

The sixth facet of understanding, *self-knowledge* requires students to consider their individual understandings and misunderstandings by deconstructing their own identities, lenses, and biases. Understanding in this facet centers on *metacognition*, or students' thinking about their own thinking and reflection on their learning. Wiggins and McTighe (2005) assert, "When we truly understand, we...have self-knowledge [to] show metacognitive awareness; perceive the personal style, prejudices, projections, and habits of mind that both shape and impede our own understanding; are aware of what we do not understand; [and] reflect on the meaning of learning and experience" (p. 84).

The focus on self-knowledge in UbD instruction provides inordinate value and opportunity with CLD students, as this particular facet emphasizes students' individual identities as shaped by their native languages, cultural backgrounds, and corresponding values, traditions, and experiences. By reflecting upon understandings, knowledge, skills, and habits of mind, students can recognize their unique and diverse identities as individuals, influenced by myriad factors inside and outside school. In addition to embracing students' cultural and linguistic identities, self-knowledge as a facet of understanding can support learners' motivation, engagement, and autonomy.

When adding a lens on language development, this facet of understanding appears to provide more opportunities than challenges for CLD students. Due to the nature of self-knowledge, students demonstrate understanding by sharing their own thoughts and reflections, which automatically taps into students' background knowledge and incorporates a first-person singular perspective (e.g., I think, I believe). From an affective standpoint, students often feel more comfortable taking risks with language when speaking and writing about themselves (Herrera, 2016; O'Malley & Pierce, 1996). In addition to these opportunities to reduce students' affective filter by tapping into personal and cultural background knowledge, teachers can differentiate the linguistic complexity of how students demonstrate understanding. For example, emergent ELs can reach desired results and self-assess using simple sentences and familiar words and phrases, whereas more advanced students can incorporate more complex sentences, verb tenses, and vocabulary terms.

In addition to having learners demonstrate understanding of self-knowledge in English, effective practitioners consider and tap into students' L1 and language varieties. Returning to the abundant theories and research regarding the value of students' L1 shared in Chapter 3, teachers adding a language lens on Stage 1 goals should also consider the role of native language. Students' native languages should be perceived as resources for all facets of understanding, but self-knowledge, in particular, requires giving priority to languages and language varieties other than English. Because many CLD students think in their L1, in the act of thinking about thinking, we must embrace their preferred linguistic medium of cognition. Additionally, the metacognitive focus of this facet presents valuable opportunities for teachers to explicitly build *metalinguistic awareness*, which involves students reflecting upon their own language use and learning to recognize and use the transfer of linguistic knowledge and skills across languages (Bialystok, 1993; Nagy & Anderson, 1995).

Teachers are not expected to use all six facets of understanding in every lesson. Instead, we encourage looking for natural opportunities to employ one or more of the facets in support of disciplinary and linguistic outcomes.

Language Demands Within Disciplines: A Linguistic Lens

Whereas language *functions* are similar across school-based learning experiences, language *features* vary significantly within particular disciplines. In this section, we consider discipline-specific language at the discourse, sentence, and word/phrase levels (see Figure 4.2). *Discourse-level* language features center on overall linguistic complexity, or the quantity, density, variety, and organization of oral and written texts (WIDA, 2012). Complex texts and classroom discourse tend to be longer, with varied sentence types, multiple ideas per sentence, inclusion of nonessential ideas, and higher-level text structures (AACCW, 2010).

Sentence-level features include types, structures, conventions, and mechanics of sentences (WIDA, 2012). More intricate syntax includes long sentences with modifying words, phrases, and clauses, as well as use of progressive and perfect verb tenses (AACCW, 2010). *Word-level* demands focus on the specificity of words and phrases, such as vocabulary terms, multiple-meaning words, and figurative language (WIDA, 2012). Complex lexicons include nuances and shades of meaning, as in closely related verbs or adjectives, and collocations, or common sequences of words.

Figure 4.2 | Features of Academic Language

The features of academic language operate within sociocultural contexts for language use.

	Performance Criteria	Features
Discourse Level	**Linguistic Complexity** *(Quantity and variety of oral and written text)*	Amount of speech/written text Structure of speech/written text Density of speech/written text Organization and cohesion of ideas Variety of sentence types
Sentence Level	**Language Forms and Conventions** *(Types, array, and use of language structures)*	Types and variety of grammatical structures Conventions, mechanics, and fluency Match of language forms to purpose/perspective
Word/Phrase Level	**Vocabulary Usage** *(Specificity of word or phrase choice)*	General, specific, and technical language Multiple meanings of words and phrases Formulaic and idiomatic expressions Nuances and shades of meaning Collocations

The sociocultural contexts for language use involve the interaction between the student and the language environment, encompassing the…
- Register
- Genre/Text type
- Topic
- Task/Situation
- Participants' identities and social roles

Source: Based on WIDA ELP Standards © 2007, 2012 Board of Regents of the University of Wisconsin System. WIDA is a trademark of the Board of Regents of the University of Wisconsin System. For more information on using the WIDA ELD Standards, please visit the WIDA website at *www.wida.us*. Used with permission.

In unique and diverse educational contexts, students use language in distinct ways when they are engaged in learning around discipline-specific topics via particular texts and classroom tasks (Zwiers, 2014). To support teachers in analyzing

Stage 1 goals with a lens on language, we now explore the linguistic features of mathematics, sciences, social studies, language arts, and other disciplines and units of study.

Mathematics

As a school-based discipline, mathematics refers to the study of "numbers, quantities, and shapes and the relations between them" (https://www.merriam-webster.com/dictionary/mathematics). Ranging from numerical and spatial sense in kindergarten to advanced algebra, trigonometry, and calculus in high school, the breadth and depth of mathematics teaching and learning center around building enthusiasm and value for core mathematical practices, skills, and concepts to yield real-world problem solvers (CCSSO & NGA, n.d.). Despite its direct association with numbers, equations, and variables, mathematics as a discipline centers on language—both inside and outside schools. As teacher Kay Toliver (1993), a nationally known middle school mathematics teacher in Spanish Harlem in New York City, consistently asserted, mathematics is a communication art. Thus mathematical teaching and learning require listening, speaking, reading, writing, touching, and creating, grounded in students' cultures and experiences. Scholars have also described the unique language needed to engage in mathematical practices, referred to as the mathematics register, or the "subset of language composed of meaning appropriate to the communication of mathematical ideas" (Kersaint, Thompson, & Petkova, 2013, p. 36). Thus, students predict, explain, justify, hypothesize, and evaluate mathematical practices and concepts using language specific to the academic discipline of mathematics (Cloud, Genessee, & Hamayan, 2009). See Figure 4.3 for a sampling of language demands in mathematics.

Typically spiraled across K–12 curricula, various fields of study exist within the larger discipline of mathematics, such as algebra, geometry, and statistics. Within the different mathematical fields and units of study, students use language in distinct ways to engage in authentic content learning. The study of algebra relies heavily on equations that intermix numbers, symbols, and variables (e.g., $y = 2x + 6$), in addition to narrative text in the form of word problems and directions (e.g., "Write an equation in slope-intercept form..."). In geometry, students write geometric proofs to explain and argue theorems, which incorporate specific text structures (e.g., two-column proof) with varied features (e.g., figures, statements, reasons), as well as punctuation and complex sentences (e.g., "When a segment is bisected, the two resulting segments are congruent"). Statistics instruction uses texts with features such as dot plots, box plots, scatter plots, histograms, and frequency tables, and requires students to use language to summarize, interpret, infer, and justify with language features such as conditional structures (e.g., if a, then b) and logical connectors (e.g., such that, thus, therefore). Instruction also engages students in mathematical practices and communication around concepts including numbers, operations, ratios, proportions, measurement, and models, each requiring specific language functions with related text structures, classroom discourse patterns, sentence constructions, and unique phrases and words (Moschkovich, 2013).

Figure 4.3 | **Examples of Language Demands in Mathematics**

Component	Feature	Examples
Discourse	Amount of speech/text	Short texts with up-down and left-right reading
	Structure of speech/text	Intermixing of words, numbers, variables, symbols
	Density of speech/text	Conceptually packed, high density of unique words
	Organization of ideas	Varying text features (graphs, charts, diagrams)
Sentence	Sentence types	Passive voice: *A ball is dropped from 100 feet.*
	Sentence structures	Cause-effect, reason-result, chronological
	Logical connectors	*if and only if, such that, consequently*
	Lexical bundles	*as much as, greater than or equal to, such that*
	Use of prepositions	*divided by, divided into; percent off, percent of*
Word	Discipline-specific words	*hypotenuse, parabola, isosceles, coefficient*
	Discipline-specific phrases	*greatest common factor, least common multiple*
	Words used in new ways	*mean, carry, odd, table, column, set, prime, foot*
	Synonyms	*subtract, minus, less; add, plus, combine, sum*
	Idioms	*ballpark figure, split fifty-fifty, on the hour*

To support students' language development and equitable access to the depth and breadth of mathematical understandings, concepts, and processes, effective practitioners deconstruct the unique linguistic demands within each unit of study. Consider the high school geometry unit in Figure 4.4, which is focused on real-world mathematical problem solving with the use of two- and three-dimensional geometric objects and related formulas for volume. Using the transfer and meaning goals for the unit, we can add a lens on language to ensure that all students have equitable access to reach these desired results. For example, to synthesize attributes and relationships of geometric objects, students use

Figure 4.4 | **Transfer and Meaning Goals for a High School Geometry Unit**

Stage 1—Desired Results		
Established Goals	**Transfer**	
CCSS Math (GMD.B.3, GMD.B.4, MG.A.3)	*Students will be able to independently use their learning to...*	
• Use volume formulas for cylinders, pyramids, cones, and spheres to solve problems.	• Synthesize the attributes and relationships of geometric objects.	
	• Adapt mathematical methods and models to investigate dynamic geometric phenomena.	
• Identify the shapes of 2D cross-sections of 3D objects, and identify 3D objects generated by rotations of 2D objects.	• Solve real-world problems using mathematical reasoning.	
	Meaning	
• Apply geometric methods to solve design problems.	**Understandings**	**Essential Questions**
	Students will understand that...	*Students will keep considering...*
	• The adaptation of mathematical models and ideas to human problems requires careful judgment and sensitivity to impact.	• How well can pure mathematics model messy, real-world situations?
	• Mapping three dimensions onto two (or two onto three) may introduce distortions.	• When is the best mathematical answer not the best solution to a problem?
	• Sometimes the best mathematical answers are not the best solutions to real-world problems.	

Source: From Understanding by Design Professional Development Workbook (p. 11), by J. McTighe and G. Wiggins, 2004, Alexandria, VA: ASCD. Copyright 2004 by ASCD. Adapted with permission.

discourse to describe attributes and explain relationships between objects. Such discourse includes relationship verbs (e.g., entail, consist of); partitive grammatical constructions—that is, phrases indicating partialness (e.g., a segment of, a portion of); quantifiers (e.g., some, almost all); technical academic terminology (e.g., tetrahedron, vertex, oblique); and multiple-meaning words (e.g., volume, face, cone) (AACCW, 2010). In addition to tasks, the unit goals reference texts to mediate learning—specifically, word problems that ask students to solve real-world problems by applying their understandings of geometric principles and concepts. Word problems typically feature discourse that is packed with concepts, and diagrams that require multiple readings. They often use sentence constructions with the passive voice and combine various types of language—including social, academic, and technical words and phrases—into a brief narrative. To achieve the transfer and meaning goals of the unit, students must be able to access and develop the related language functions and features.

Science

Science is defined as the "systematic gathering of information through various forms of direct and indirect observations and the testing of this information by methods including, but not limited to, experimentations" (National Science Teachers Association, 2000, p. 1). Whereas science is typically approached as a broad content area in self-contained elementary classrooms, secondary settings hone in on particular areas, such as biology, chemistry, physics, and earth sciences. Crosscutting scientific concepts and practices span the sciences, which require students to use academic registers of scientific disciplines. As students grapple with scientific ideas and questions across fields, they use particular language functions as they identify questions, define problems, organize investigations, hypothesize findings, analyze and interpret data, synthesize findings, argue from evidence, and evaluate information (AACCW, 2010; National Research Council, 2013). Central to teaching and learning in science classrooms is the notion of scientific inquiry that mirrors the authentic practices of scientists as they study and develop ideas about nature and the universe, including the use of language to inquire, discover, and communicate via oral language, reading, and writing (Nutta, Bautista, & Butler, 2011). See Figure 4.5 for a sampling of language demands in science.

Schools typically organize the study of sciences into subjects in the fields of life, physical, and earth and space sciences (Nutta, Bautista, & Butler, 2011). Across fields, students use similar language functions aligned to scientific practices and processes (e.g., analyze, interpret, argue, evaluate), as well as common text structures and organization (e.g., diagrams, tables, graphs, pictures, figures) and complex sentence structures with frequent use of the passive voice. In the life sciences, which focus on characteristics, processes, and interactions of living organisms, students use species names (e.g., soapberry bug, or jadera haematoloma), multiple-meaning words (e.g., cell, base, bonds, branch), abbreviations (e.g., ES cells, iPS cells), and morphological constructions (e.g., solution, solute, solvent, soluble; hydrogen, hydroxide, hydronium). In the physical sciences, which focus on the physical and chemical properties of objects and materials, students solve real-world problems (e.g., speed of moving cars, chemistry of airbags) by integrating scientific principles and concepts (e.g., Newton's laws, Dalton's laws) with corresponding mathematical equations (e.g., using variables, symbols, numbers). Within earth and space science, instruction promotes inquiry spanning various areas of study, including astronomy, meteorology, geology, oceanography, and environmental sciences, each with its own academic register. In disciplines across science, technology, engineering, and mathematics (STEM), language demands also emerge as students maneuver measurement systems to investigate and solve problems, including length (e.g., millimeter, centimeter), mass (e.g., gram, metric ton), temperature (e.g., kelvin), and substance (e.g., mole).

Figure 4.5 | **Examples of Language Demands in Science**

Component	Feature	Examples
Discourse	Amount of speech/text	Extended lectures, long texts, and passages
	Structure of speech/text	Varied structures (lab report, summary, glossary)
	Density of speech/text	Dense textbooks often written above grade level
	Organization of ideas	Varied text features (illustrations, diagrams, photos)
Sentence	Sentence types	Complex sentences with multiple embedded clauses
	Sentence structures	Cause-effect, problem-solution, compare-contrast
	Verb tenses	Conditional tense (what *could* or *might* happen)
	Logical connectors	*because, therefore, unless, consequently*
	Lexical bundles	*in the form of, as a result of, the nature of*
Word	Discipline-specific words	*organism, symbiosis, tsunami, conductivity*
	Discipline-specific phrases	*gravitational potential energy, root mean square velocity*
	Words used in new ways	*matter, gas, space, order, solution, wave, crust*
	Nominalizations	*observe/observation; analyze/analysis*

To engage all students in authentic learning and corresponding language development around scientific understandings, concepts, and processes, teachers first consider the language of particular units of study. Consider the middle school science unit shown in Figure 4.6, which integrates scientific fields for learners to grapple with big ideas and essential questions related to weather, climate, energy, and geography. To achieve the desired results—explaining weather patterns by drawing from multiple disciplines—students engage in various tasks and texts that require specific language. Classroom discourse includes expressions of cause and effect and other relationships between weather events, using language elements such as adverbials (e.g., as a result), and adverbs (e.g., frequently, evenly). Various demands emerge at the word level, including technical phrases and abbreviations (e.g., intertropical convergence zone, ITCZ), multiple-meaning words (e.g., front, cycle), morphological constructions (e.g., troposphere, stratosphere, mesosphere, thermosphere, exosphere; thermometer, barometer, anemometer, hygrometer), proper nouns (e.g., Doppler effect, Coriolis effect), and collocations (e.g., trade winds, jet stream). To mediate learning related to unit goals, students use a science textbook that integrates scientific narrative with complex sentences, weather maps with multiple symbols, tables showing characteristics of air mass, diagrams of the water cycle, and figures indicating global flows of air and water. To allow all students equitable access to the desired results of the unit, teachers should recognize and target these language demands.

Social Studies

Social studies education is "concerned with how people, past and present, live together" (Cruz & Thornton, 2013, p. 47). As we can tell from that definition, social studies as a discipline is expansive, including the fields of anthropology, archeology, economics, geography, history, law, philosophy, political science, psychology, religion, and sociology (National Council for the Social Studies [NCSS], 2016). Within the breadth of this content area, K–12 teachers seek to build students' conceptual understandings, content knowledge, inquiry skills, and civic values that are "necessary for fulfilling the duties of citizenship in a participatory democracy" (NCSS, 2016, p. 1). Not surprising, given the disciplinary focus on the *social* components of society, language plays an integral role within social studies instruction, whether approached broadly in elementary settings or via specific courses within secondary settings, such as geography, world history, or Western civilization. Students use language to pose questions, investigate issues, solve problems, evaluate situations, communicate conclusions, and take informed action (NCSS, 2017). Using a variety of primary sources such as historical documents and photographs, and secondary sources such as textbooks and guidebooks, students use various linguistic registers related to the discipline of social studies as they seek to understand and grapple with social, historical, cultural, and economic ideas, concepts, and questions. See Figure 4.7 for a sampling of language demands in social studies.

Figure 4.6 | Transfer and Meaning Goals for a Middle School Science Unit

Stage 1—Desired Results		
Established Goals	**Transfer**	
NGSS MS ESS2, S2-5 & S2-6	*Students will be able to independently use their learning to…*	
• Collect data to provide evidence for how the motions and complex interactions of air masses result in changes in weather conditions.	• Explain weather patterns by drawing from multiple disciplines, including earth, space, and physical science, as well as geography.	
	• Produce and use models to make meaning of scientific phenomena.	
	Meaning	
• Develop and use a model to describe how unequal heating and rotation of the Earth cause patterns of atmospheric and oceanic circulation that determine regional climates.	**Understandings**	**Essential Questions**
	Students will understand that…	*Students will keep considering…*
	• The unequal heating between the equator and poles, Earth's rotation, and the distribution of land and ocean generate the global wind patterns that determine climate.	• What causes weather and wind patterns?
		• What factors affect climate?
	• Most of what goes on in the universe involves some form of energy being transformed into another.	• How do events in one geographical area affect another?
		• How does climate affect agriculture?
	• Transformations of energy usually produce some energy in the form of heat, which spreads around by radiation and conduction into cooler places.	• How can I apply these factors to locations on Earth to determine the climate?

Source: From Understanding by Design Professional Development Workbook. (p. 42), by J. McTighe and G. Wiggins, 2004, Alexandria, VA: ASCD. Copyright 2004 by ASCD. Adapted with permission.

Figure 4.7 | **Examples of Language Demands in Social Studies**

Component	Feature	Examples
Discourse	Amount of speech/text	Extended lectures, long texts, and passages
	Structure of speech/text	Mixing of various sentences types and structures
	Density of speech/text	Mixing of proper, common, and temporal nouns
	Organization of ideas	Varied text features (maps, photos, time lines)
Sentence	Sentence types	Passive construction, indirect/reported speech
	Sentence structures	Chronological, compare-contrast, cause-effect
	Logical connectors	*from that time forward, by the 20th century*
	Lexical bundles	*at the same time, as a result of, the fact that*
Word	Discipline-specific terms	*medieval, revolutionary, patriotism, superdelegate*
	Discipline-specific phrases	*substantive due process, wholly owned subsidiary*
	Words used in new ways	*period, party, assembly, market, depression, cycle*
	Nominalizations	*explore/exploration; occur/occurrence*
	Collocations	*rich culture, strong opponent, heavy rain*
	Use of abbreviations and acronyms	*WWI, NAFTA, WPA, SEC, NRA, OMB*

Various fields of study exist within the larger discipline, including geography, U.S. history, world history, government and civics, economics, anthropology, sociology, and psychology (Cruz & Thornton, 2013). Within the study of these disciplines, students use language in varied ways to actively participate in learning. In history, students engage in learning via primary and secondary sources about historic events possibly unrelated to their own life experiences, with ample details including names, dates, places, concepts, and systems (e.g., Industrial Revolution, John D. Rockefeller, capitalism, manufacturing). In geography, students use maps, visuals, and texts to learn specific geographical features (e.g., Mississippi River), to generalize classes of phenomena (e.g., rivers versus streams, creeks, and brooks), and to make inferences based on learning (e.g., why people live near rivers). Civics education engages students in political processes and concepts that might be distinct from those in students' countries of origin (e.g., democracy, Electoral College, straw poll), while incorporating everyday words in political discourse (e.g., left, right, party, lobby, house). Whether interwoven with other fields of social studies in elementary and middle school or explicitly targeted in high school, the study of economics includes words and abbreviations tied to economic concepts (e.g., gross domestic product, or GDP), sentence structures and connectors indicating relationships (e.g., based on, were seen as), and text narrative connected to features such as economic models (e.g., supply and demand curves). Other focal areas in social studies, such as anthropology, sociology, and psychology, have their own nuanced language functions and features, as well as pertinent and culturally specific background knowledge needed to engage with content.

Across the fields and units of study within the broader discipline of social studies, there are complex and diverse features across discourse, sentence, and word/phrase levels to purposefully develop students' language and allow equitable access to learning. Consider the integrated social studies unit of study in Figure 4.8, written for intermediate grades in the elementary setting and focused on the American pioneer spirit across history. When analyzing transfer and meaning goals with a lens on language, specifically those related to comparisons between pioneers from earlier times and the present day, ample demands become apparent, beginning with the dual definitions of *pioneer* upon which the unit is based. To achieve the unit goals and express similarities and differences between historical accounts and current events, students must tap into discourse patterns that include coordinating conjunctions (e.g., and, but, yet, or) and adverbials (e.g., similarly, likewise, instead) (AACCW, 2010). The comparisons of past and present also require discipline-specific classroom discourse including an intermixing of verb tenses, as well as culturally specific background knowledge of U.S. history, society, geography, and cultures. To grapple with the essential questions of the unit, students interact with various texts spanning multiple genres and media, including historical documents, oral histories, letters, photographs, time lines, and maps. Each text has distinct features and varying types of sentences, grammatical constructions, phrases, and words needed to access the stories and ideas related to the pioneer spirit.

Language Arts

The overarching discipline of language arts focuses broadly on the teaching and learning of English through listening, speaking, reading, writing, viewing, and visually representing (Roe & Ross, 2005). Various terminology identifies this content area, including *literacy*, *language arts*, and *English*. The prototypical term in primary grades is *literacy*, which engages students in balanced instruction across language domains with varied grouping strategies for reading and writing (e.g., read aloud, guided reading, independent reading). *Language arts* is the common terminology in intermediate grades, where students engage in integrated learning spanning language, literacy, literature, and visual arts. Secondary education settings often organize instruction around separate components, such as English classes focused on reading or literature, writing or composition. Despite the explicit focus on language inherent in this discipline, students encounter

Figure 4.8 | **Transfer and Meaning Goals for an Elementary Social Studies Unit**

Stage 1— Desired Results		
Established Goals	**Transfer**	
• Students pose relevant questions about events they encounter in historical documents, eyewitness accounts, oral histories, letters, diaries, artifacts, photographs, maps, artworks, and architecture.	*Students will be able to independently use their learning to . . .* • Seek out, compare, and critique different historical accounts. • Compare the lives of pioneers on the prairie and pioneers of today. • View interactions of civilizations, cultures, and peoples with greater perspective and empathy.	
• Students trace why their community was established, how individuals and families contributed to its founding and development, and how the community has changed over time, drawing on maps, photographs, oral histories, letters, newspapers, and other primary sources.	**Meaning**	
	Understandings *Students will understand that . . .* • Many pioneers had naïve ideas about the opportunities and difficulties of moving west. • People move for a variety of reasons—for new economic opportunities, greater freedoms, or escape from something. • Successful pioneers rely on courage, ingenuity, and collaboration to overcome hardships and challenges. • The settlement of the West threatened the lifestyle and culture of Native American tribes living on the plains. • History involves making sense of different stories.	**Essential Questions** *Students will keep considering . . .* • Why do people move? Why did the pioneers leave their homes to head west? • How do geography and topography affect travel and settlement? • What is a pioneer? What is *pioneer spirit?* • Why did some pioneers survive and prosper while others did not? • Whose story is it? • What happens when cultures interact?

Source: From The Understanding by Design Guide to Creating High-Quality Units (p. 29), by G. Wiggins and J. McTighe, 2011, Alexandria, VA: ASCD. Copyright 2011 by Grant Wiggins and Jay McTighe. Adapted with permission.

ample and diverse linguistic demands as they maneuver copious amounts of language and literacy across multiple genres and mediums. Instruction should be organized around authentic learning experiences that engage learners in literacy practices, such as informing, analyzing, critiquing, and arguing via complex texts, varied perspectives, and meaningful interaction. Within these language-rich classrooms, it is important to maintain precise attention to language demands, particularly for CLD students (Bunch et al., 2012). See Figure 4.9 for a sampling of language demands in language arts.

Figure 4.9 | **Examples of Language Demands in Language Arts**

Component	Feature	Examples
Discourse	Amount of speech/text	Amounts vary by genre (poetry, autobiography)
	Structure of speech/text	Variety of sentence types and verb tenses
	Density of speech/text	Linguistic abstraction with figurative language
	Organization of ideas	Features vary by genre (graphic novel, nonfiction)
Sentence	Sentence types	Compound, complex, compound-complex
	Sentence structures	Temporal, comparison, cause and effect
	Verb tenses	Present, past, and future progressive and perfect
	Conventions and mechanics	Punctuation marks, capitalization rules
Word	Discipline-specific words	*fable, rhyme, interjection, onomatopoeia, homonym*
	Discipline-specific phrases	*exclamation point, thesis statement, logical fallacy*
	Multiple-meaning words	*period, blend, mood, pitch, stress, style, shift*
	Synonyms	*happy, blissful, jovial, elated, cheerful, delighted*
	Nominalizations	*write/writing, illustrate/illustration*
	Shades of meaning	*acquaintance, ally, friend, confidant*
	Figurative language	simile, metaphor, onomatopoeia, personification
	Idiomatic expressions	*burn bridges, spill the beans, feeling blue, on thin ice*

Because of the broad focus of language arts as a discipline, language demands vary depending on the genre, subgenre, and form used to mediate oral language, reading, and writing. *Nonfiction* increasingly serves as the vehicle for teaching and learning, as students make arguments and cite evidence with informational texts, persuasive essays, autobiographies, and biographies. Distinct from other nonfiction, *biographies* often use sequential historical discourse, third-person point of view, complex sentences with multiple clauses, and both present and past tense (Ranney, Dillard-Paltrineri, Maguire, & Schornack, 2014). Using a variety of *fiction*, including realistic, historical, and science fiction, students interpret, relate, and recount elements and events of various texts. In addition to the varying use of language across fictional subgenres, form influences linguistic demands, such as the unique text features used in graphic novels (e.g., captions, speech balloons, internal versus external dialogue, special-effects lettering) (Ankiel, 2016). In instruction focused on poetry, students recite, represent, interpret, explain, and produce various forms of poems (e.g., haiku, free verse, sonnet); whereas poetic use of figurative language remains a relatively consistent language demand across the genre, other linguistic features vary based on the poem (e.g., structure, organization of ideas, grammatical clauses/stanzas, verb tenses, punctuation). *Folklore* as a genre, including myths, legends, tall tales, fairy tales, and fables, also demonstrates variation across texts and resulting tasks, which present particular challenges for ELs—for example, when they rely on literal interpretations of tall tales or need additional background knowledge to make meaning of culturally situated legends. Regardless of the text or task, additional demands stem from the needed and often assumed background knowledge that enables students to access big ideas, develop understandings, and grapple with essential questions.

To ensure equitable access to the language arts curriculum while simultaneously supporting students' language development, consider how language is used within each unit in terms of the literary genre and related tasks. In Figure 4.10, the unit centers on *The Catcher in the Rye* (Salinger, 1951), which has been deemed to be "one of the handful of essential American books" (Bloom, 2007, p. 25). Living in mid–20th century Manhattan, adolescent protagonist Holden Caulfield narrates the four-day series of tangible and psychological events following his departure from an elite New York City prep school. Realistic fiction written in the form of a novel, the text structure is episodic, with a series of flashbacks throughout the 200-plus pages. Based on the publication date and the protagonist narration, the text has been characterized as a unique linguistic window into 1950s teenage vernacular, specifically the "informal speech of an intelligent, educated, Northeastern American adolescent" (Costello, 2000, p. 12). This discourse pattern leads to a variety of language demands, including words used in different ways (e.g., crap, crazy, killed), adjectivization (e.g., Christmasy, perverty, hoodlum-looking), profanity (e.g., bastard, sonuvabitch, goddam), and figurative language (e.g., sharp as a tack, feel like a horse's ass) (Costello, 2000). Connecting the linguistic analysis directly to the goals of the unit—specifically, the essential question about who is genuine versus phony—students must recognize narrator Holden's use of

Figure 4.10 | **Transfer and Meaning Goals for a High School English Unit**

Stage 1—Desired Results		
Established Goals	**Transfer**	
CCSS ELA-Literacy (RL.11-12.2 RL.11-12.5, W.11-12.1) • Determine two or more themes or central ideas of a text and analyze their development over the course of the text. • Analyze how an author's choices concerning how to structure specific parts of a text contribute to its overall structure, meaning, and aesthetic impact. • Write arguments to support claims in an analysis of substantive topics or texts, using valid reasoning and relevant and sufficient evidence.	*Students will be able to independently use their learning to . . .* • Read, comprehend, and critically analyze fictional texts. • Consider and evaluate how fictional texts contribute to our broader understanding of real-life experiences. • Craft arguments to persuade others to take a particular position or perspective.	
	Meaning	
	Understandings *Students will understand that . . .* • Novelists often provide insights about human experience and life through fictional means. • Writers use a variety of stylistic techniques to engage and persuade their readers. • Holden Caulfield reflects common adolescent experiences but masks deep-seated personal problems about growing up and relating to others.	**Essential Questions** *Students will keep considering . . .* • What is the relationship between fiction and truth? What truths can best be rendered fictionally? • Does Holden represent adolescence? Is he abnormal, or are all adolescents abnormal? Who is genuine and who is phony? Why do people act phony? • How do authors hook and hold readers? How does J. D. Salinger engage you? • How do writers persuade readers?

Source: From *Understanding by Design Professional Development Workbook,* (p. 64), by J. McTighe and G. Wiggins, 2004, Alexandria, VA: ASCD. Copyright 2004 by ASCD. Adapted with permission.

particular nouns (e.g., prince, angels), adjectives (e.g., grand, snobby, bourgeois), and phrases (e.g., traveling incognito, licorice stick, little girls' room) to describe characters and events (Costello, 2000, p. 18). To comprehend, consider, and craft arguments related to *The Catcher in the Rye*, students must be able to access the language of the mediating text and then use it to actively participate in unit tasks.

Other Disciplines

Whereas WIDA and other language proficiency standards typically focus on the core content areas just described, language spans all school disciplines, including world languages, electives, and special areas. Language functions, as well as the related word-, sentence-, and discourse-level features, should be considered for each discipline. Here we explore and provide examples for special-area courses.

Art education

Art education focuses instruction on visual and tangible arts (Latta & Chan, 2010). In addition to creating art, students use various discourse and syntax structures to critique, compare, analyze, and reflect on artistic works and processes. Text features include descriptive narratives and historical accounts of artwork, paired with visual images and numeric dates. A complex sentence construction for ELs involves passive voice, which artistic registers often use to describe the artwork itself, rather than active voice focused on the artist—for example, "The sketch was drawn in charcoal" rather than "Delacroix drew the sketch in charcoal." Equally difficult for ELs who interpret texts literally, discourse includes figurative language with metaphors, imagery, and symbolism describing works of art. Shades of meaning emerge in artistic language, including colors (e.g., white, ivory, pearl, cream, bone, eggshell) and other descriptive adjectives (e.g., big, huge, immense, vast, towering). Other word-level demands include discipline-specific vocabulary (e.g., acrylics, hue, monochromatic, expressionism), words used in new ways (e.g., contrast, media, rhythm, cool, warm), and nominalizations (e.g., abstract, abstraction). By embracing the visual and kinesthetic nature of the arts, a teacher can purposefully design instruction to foster students' language development while they are engaging in authentic learning.

Music education

Music education centers on learning about, listening to, and making music (Latta & Chan, 2010). In addition to singing and engaging directly with music, students also use language to describe and evaluate musical performances and to explain and justify various musical techniques. Written texts include textual narratives, as well as symbolic representations of musical elements, including lines, clefs, notes, rests, repetition, and codas, along with lyrics in the form of stanzas that may not form complete sentences. The language of music education includes discipline-specific vocabulary within musical units of study (e.g., chord, instrument, orchestra, percussion, xylophone), as well as the consistent incorporation of words used in new ways (e.g., measure, signature, flat, bar, note). An interesting and unique facet of the language of music is the prevalence of words borrowed from other languages, such as Italian and French. For example, a unit focused on the elements of music might emphasize discipline-specific language derived from standard Italian (e.g., allegro, crescendo, forte, lento, moderato, tempo), whereas a unit merging music and dance would require disciplinary language from French (e.g., arabesque, chassé, jeté, pirouette, plié, sissonne). By tapping into the multimodal and interactive classroom setting, music teachers can embrace their central roles in fostering students' language development.

Physical education

Physical education prioritizes instruction in sports, exercise, and well-being (Constantinou & Wuest, 2015). Relying on oral language, students use varied skills in the domains of listening and speaking to actively participate in learning. Classroom discourse is often characterized by intermixing a variety of verb tenses (e.g., ran, run, will run, are running, have run), with students receiving and producing varied sentence structures to follow and give sequential directions and to compare and contrast sports and activities. To partake in activities, students maneuver prepositions of place (e.g., above, behind, between, on the left, inside, outside) and verbs with varying shades of meaning (e.g., walk, jog, run, sprint). Additionally, words are frequently converted and used as verbs and nouns (e.g., to throw the ball, make a good throw). Adjectives play an important role for students engaging in particular sports, such as recognizing the distinction between a penalty kick, a free kick, a corner kick, and a goal kick in soccer. Compound words (e.g., handball, baseball), discipline-specific vocabulary (e.g., dribble, calisthenics), and words used in new ways (e.g., pepper, flag) are also common in the language of physical education. By explicitly planning instruction with a lens on language, physical education teachers can maximize the low-anxiety and interactive learning setting to promote students' language development.

Acquisition Goals with a Lens on Language

In the previous sections, we considered the language needed to engage in learning and understanding within and across disciplines. By analyzing transfer and meaning goals with a lens on language development, we aim to maintain rigorous results for all learners, building awareness and uncovering blind spots (particularly among English-dominant educators) on how language might serve as a gatekeeper to student learning. The purpose of our earlier linguistic analyses is not to shelter students from these linguistic demands and complexities, but instead to purposefully define acquisition goals in order to (1) provide equitable access to transfer and meaning goals and (2) scaffold instruction to build the linguistic knowledge and skills needed to achieve the desired results in the unit of study. After analyzing Stage 1 goals for disciplinary language functions and features, teachers now use those analyses to respond to the following question: *What must students know and do with language to achieve the desired results, engage in active learning, and grapple with essential questions?* We explore acquisition goals with a lens on language in this section.

As described early in the chapter, *acquisition goals* focus on what students need to know and do to reach the larger transfer and meaning goals of the unit. Whereas transfer and meaning goals capture the wider applicability and deeper understandings that we desire for learners, knowledge and skill indicators are those pertinent substeps needed to achieve the larger outcomes. When we add a lens on language development, we explicitly define the language students must acquire to achieve the desired results of the unit, as connected to pertinent content-based knowledge and skills. Stemming from linguistic analyses of transfer and meaning goals, acquisition goals should focus on the linguistic knowledge and discrete skills needed to foster students' language development to engage in content learning (see Figure 4.11).

Figure 4.11 | **Acquisition Goals for Language Development**

Knowledge Indicators	Skill Indicators
• *Language features* needed to achieve transfer and meaning goals of the unit (e.g., text structures, classroom discourse patterns, sentence types, academic words and phrases)	• *Language functions* tied to cognitive processes (e.g., explaining, intepreting, arguing, critiquing, evaluating) • *Language domains* (listening, speaking, reading, writing) aligned to students' areas of need

Knowledge indicators in UbD are the *declarative knowledge* students must acquire by the end of the unit, including factual information, vocabulary, and basic concepts needed to reach the overarching transfer and meaning goals (Wiggins & McTighe, 2011). When adding a lens on language, we expand beyond vocabulary to consider the linguistic knowledge needed to engage in learning throughout the unit of study. To define acquisition goals, specifically the declarative knowledge related to language development, teachers analyze the linguistic features embedded in the unit, including those at the discourse, sentence, and word/phrase levels (WIDA, 2012). Rather than analyzing every task and text included in the unit, we use the transfer and meaning goals to consider the language required for achieving the established goals, understanding the big ideas, and grappling with the essential questions. We then use this declarative knowledge of language to draft knowledge indicators that strategically target students' language development while simultaneously providing students equitable access to big ideas and understandings in the unit. By drafting knowledge indicators with a language lens, we aim to develop students' language and support their equitable access to content learning.

Skill indicators in UbD are the *procedural knowledge* students must acquire by the end of the unit, including basic know-how and discrete skills needed to reach transfer and meaning goals (Wiggins & McTighe, 2011). When adding a lens on language, we specifically consider the linguistic skills that students need to actively participate in learning and meaning making throughout the unit of study. To define acquisition goals, specifically the procedural knowledge related to language development, teachers first consider the language functions that students use while engaging in tasks and related cognitive processes, as tied to the six facets of understandings. Next, teachers consider the linguistic strengths and needs of students to prioritize students' language development across the four domains—listening, speaking, reading, and writing (see Figure 4.12). Teachers then draft skill indicators that pinpoint the pertinent language functions and domains to strategically develop students' language as authentically embedded in content learning. Skill indicators should align with knowledge indicators, to the extent that language functions require particular words and phrases, as well as sentence, grammatical, and discursive structures. By drafting skill indicators with a language lens, we aim to develop students' language skills and content skills simultaneously.

Figure 4.12 | **Sample Verbs by Language Domain for Skill Indicators**

Listening	Speaking	Reading	Writing
Identify	Produce	Identify	Communicate
Categorize	Express	Interpret	List
Sequence	Recite	Explore	Record
Follow directions	Describe	Classify	Produce
Recognize	Convey	Match	Create
Detect	Present	Infer	Compose
Distinguish	Discuss	Summarize	Explain
Evaluate	Explain	Critique	Justify

Consider the previously introduced high school mathematics unit focused on the attributes and relationships of geometric objects (see Figure 4.4). After defining and maintaining the desired results for disciplinary learning, the math teacher, Mrs. Peña, analyzes the transfer and meaning goals in order to uncover her linguistic blind spot as an expert mathematician. In so doing, she recognizes that students need to develop disciplinary language to achieve the transfer and meaning goals, including particular discourse (i.e., word problems), sentence constructions (i.e., relationship verbs, partitive grammatical constructions, quantifiers), and words (i.e., technical terminology, multiple-meaning words). To draft acquisition goals, she specifically considers the linguistic abilities of her sophomores who are primarily reclassified and long-term ELs, including Vinh. When pinpointing knowledge indicators, she focuses on disciplinary language such as math-specific, multiple-meaning words, rather than vocabulary like *cylinder* and *sphere* that students already know from previous units and courses. When drafting skill indicators, she prioritizes related language functions (e.g., compare, contrast) and domains most in need of development (e.g., read, compose). In this way, Mrs. Peña embeds language development in disciplinary learning, specifically targeting the learning and development of her CLD students. Figure 4.13 shows the geometry unit resulting from Mrs. Peña's efforts.

In summary, Stage 1 with a lens on language begins by analyzing the language needed to access the transfer and meaning goals, which remain the same for all learners. The preliminary linguistic analysis then leads to the drafting of acquisition goals with a specific lens on the language that is tied to disciplinary learning. Knowledge indicators pinpoint the pertinent language features of texts and tasks, and skill indicators highlight the language functions that are connected to cognitive processing and skills. Additionally, skill indicators should target goals for listening, speaking, reading, and writing embedded in authentic learning and meaningful interaction around understandings and essential questions. Moving forward in future stages of the curricular planning process, the language-focused knowledge and skills indicated in Stage 1 of instructional design will guide the design of performance assessments in Stage 2 and of learning experiences in Stage 3.

Classroom Application: Language Development in Stage 1

Drawing from the lenses on language development in Stage 1 as described in this chapter, we now shift to consider the specifics of classroom application. In this section, we detail the steps to integrate language into Stage 1 of the UbD planning template to provide equitable access for all learners.

Figure 4.13 | **Stage 1 of a High School Mathematics Unit, Geometry**

Stage 1—Desired Results		
Established Goals	**Transfer**	
CCSS Math (GMD.B.3, GMD.B.4, MG.A.3) • Use volume formulas for cylinders, pyramids, cones, and spheres to solve problems. • Identify the shapes of 2D cross-sections of 3D objects, and identify 3D objects generated by rotations of 2D objects. • Apply geometric methods to solve design problems.	*Students will be able to independently use their learning to...* • Synthesize the attributes and relationships of geometric objects. • Adapt mathematical methods and models to investigate dynamic geometric phenomena. • Solve real-world problems using mathematical reasoning.	
	Meaning	
	Understandings *Students will understand that...* • The adaptation of mathematical models and ideas to human problems requires careful judgment and sensitivity to impact. • Mapping three dimensions onto two (or two onto three) may introduce distortions. • Sometimes the best mathematical answers are not the best solutions to real-world problems.	**Essential Questions** *Students will keep considering...* • How well can pure mathematics model messy, real-world situations? • When is the best mathematical answer not the best solution to a problem?
	Acquisition	
	Students will know... • Mathematical formulas for calculating surface area and volume. • Cavalieri's Principle. • Related geometric terminology (e.g., face, edge, vertex, oblique). • Related sentence constructions (e.g., relationship verbs). • Discourse structures of word problems and solutions.	*Students will be skilled at...* • Calculating surface area and volume for various three-dimensional figures. • Comparing and contrasting volumes of figures using Cavalieri's Principle. • Reading and solving word problems by applying geometric formulas. • Composing mathematical explanations to real-world problems.

Source: From *Understanding by Design Professional Development Workbook* (p. 11), by J. McTighe and G. Wiggins, 2004, Alexandria, VA: ASCD. Copyright © 2004 by ASCD. Adapted with permission.

Analyze Transfer and Meaning Goals for Language

Begin with *transfer goals*—long-term, authentic goals of independent learning; *meaning goals*—enduring understandings and essential questions; and *established goals*—content standards. Analyze the language that students need to achieve these goals, considering the topic, texts, and tasks, including language functions and related features at the discourse, sentence, and word/phrase levels. Consider the language demands in the unique context of your classroom, including how students' cultural and linguistic backgrounds and abilities influence language use and what they might or might not find linguistically challenging in the unit of study.

Prioritize Language That Is Pertinent to Engaging in Learning

Our earlier linguistic analysis of broader disciplines and specific units of study undoubtedly uncovered a number of language demands. In addition to general awareness of the language needed to engage in classroom instruction, prioritize language that is (1) *important* for students as they work to access the big ideas and grapple with essential questions across the unit of study, (2) *aligned* with needed cognitive processes and content learning and understandings, (3) *prevalent*, in that multiple students will find the language demanding in their attempt to engage with academic content learning, and (4) *versatile*, in that students can transfer and use knowledge and skills across units of study, disciplines, and settings.

Draft Knowledge Indicators to Target Language Demands

Write acquisition goals for the declarative knowledge—including factual information and basic concepts—that is related to the unit's transfer and meaning goals. Add the language lens to draft additional acquisition goals for declarative knowledge of language, drawing from analyses at the word, sentence, and discourse levels. Although these language-focused knowledge indicators may be added separately from content-specific knowledge indicators, they should be inherently connected in that the end goal is to build students' language to allow access to content learning.

Draft Skill Indicators to Identify Language Functions

Write acquisition goals for the procedural knowledge—including discrete skills and cognitive processes—related to the unit's transfer and meaning goals. Add the language lens to revise the skill indicators so that they prioritize language development through appropriate language functions and domains. Remember that the goal of writing skill indicators with a language lens is to develop students' language and content-specific skills simultaneously. Thus, each skill indicator should include a *language function* and related *content stem*. Once all skill indicators are drafted, prioritize the specific language domains—listening, speaking, reading, writing—invoked by the verbs in the skill indicators.

Review Transfer and Meaning Goals to Ensure Equitable Access

Transfer and meaning goals should remain rigorous for all learners, with instructional plans that incorporate acquisition goals to ensure equitable access to those high expectations regardless of language proficiency. Nonetheless, all students should be able to access the goals themselves, particularly to grapple with the essential questions across the unit of study. In reviewing essential questions with a lens on language, analyze for word- and sentence-level language demands and reword to avoid possible language demands that would limit access, as illustrated in Figure 4.14. You might also provide essential questions in students' native languages.

Figure 4.14 | **Sample Essential Questions with Demanding Language**

Language Demands	Sample Essential Questions Needing Revision
Words	What do effective problem solvers do when they get *stuck*? Why did the pioneers leave their homes to *head* west? What is the role of *serendipity* in scientific advances?
Idioms	How do you read between the lines? If practice makes perfect, what makes perfect practice? To what extent is the pen mightier than the sword?
Sentence/Grammar Structures	How does art reflect, as well as shape, culture? How are stories from other places and times about me? What couldn't we do if we didn't have or couldn't use numbers?
Passive Sentence Construction	Whose story is it? Why is that there? Is there a pattern?

Source: From *Understanding by Design Professional Development Workbook* (pp. 8–9, 90–91, 93–101), by J. McTighe and G. Wiggins, 2004, Alexandria, VA: ASCD. Copyright 2004 by ASCD. Adapted with permission.

Revise Acquisition Goals to Foster Language Development

Consider the formal and anecdotal data on students' backgrounds, strengths, and needs, particularly the language proficiencies and abilities of your ELs, as described in Chapter 3. Using overall language proficiency as a guide, revise *knowledge indicators* to ensure appropriate goals for language development based on proficiency levels. Using domain-specific assessment data, revise *skill indicators* to target language functions and domains based on what students *can do* with language, as well as where they need additional support on the path to language proficiency. (In addition to unit-level acquisition goals focused on the prioritized language demands, teachers target language at the lesson level through learning objectives. We explore lesson-level objectives further in Chapter 7.)

Classroom Snapshot: Setting Goals for Student Learning

Ms. Jillian Hartmann is a secondary science teacher at Theodore Roosevelt High School, a neighborhood public high school serving 1,500 9th through 12th graders on the northwest side of Chicago. Nestled in the culturally and linguistically diverse Albany Park community, the school welcomes students who speak 35 different languages, as well as multiple language varieties including AAVE and Chicano English. Seventy-five percent of the student body is Latino, making Spanish the primary LOTE spoken in homes, followed by Arabic, Tagalog, Burmese, Karen, Gujarati, Swahili, and Oromo, among others. Eighty percent of Roosevelt students use a LOTE at home, with approximately 25 percent labeled as ELs as measured by the ACCESS scores of English language proficiency. Students labeled as ELs range from newcomers recently arrived in the United States to long-term ELs who have been enrolled in Albany Park community schools since kindergarten. Organized by disciplinary departments, 80 teachers support the learning of the CLD student body, spanning mathematics, science, social studies, English, world languages, career and technical education, and the fine arts. Labeled ELs are typically placed in separate sheltered sections of content-area classes.

Ms. Hartmann teaches an array of classes within the science department, including one section of 9th grade sheltered biology, one section of 10th grade sheltered chemistry, one section of 10th grade chemistry, and two sections of mixed-grade earth and space science. In addition to the various branches of science and grade levels, her students vary significantly across periods. She works with 43 labeled ELs—20 in sheltered biology, 21 in sheltered chemistry, and 2 in earth and space science. Across her five class sections, students in her classroom come from households where 15 different languages are spoken. Thirteen of those learners are newcomers who have recently arrived in the United States and Chicago from a variety of countries around the world, including a number who have recently experienced trauma and loss. Before designing her instructional units of study, Ms. Hartmann considers these cultural and linguistic data, as well as the many other social, emotional, and academic factors influencing her adolescent students' learning and development. She pairs these considerations about learners with her keen awareness that students need to develop particular disciplinary language to learn biology, chemistry, and earth and space science.

After teaching biology and chemistry in previous school years, Ms. Hartmann was recently assigned two sections of earth and space science, an area that was new to her professional repertoire as a high school science teacher. With her graduate degree focused on EL teaching and learning, she prepared for her new discipline with lenses on both content and language. As she dove into the curricular design for the school year and individual units of study, Ms. Hartmann maintained a language lens to recognize the disciplinary language needed to access scientific understandings, rigorous learning, and inquiry-based exploration. For example, in the unit focused on weather and climate (see Figure 4.15), she recognized that the transfer and meaning goals required disciplinary language, as exemplified when interpreting multiple sources of scientific evidence (e.g., maps, graphs, charts), describing weather using words that may be familiar from other contexts (e.g., humidity, temperature), and comparing climates between local and global settings using distinct measurement systems (i.e., Fahrenheit, Celsius). After analyzing the language that her unique CLD student population would need to achieve transfer goals, deepen understandings, and grapple with essential questions, Ms. Hartmann used her findings to target linguistic knowledge indicators (e.g., weather maps and graphs, particular vocabulary terms, comparative sentence structures) and skill indicators (e.g., analyzing weather-related data, interpreting weather patterns, comparing and contrasting climates).

By adding an explicit lens on language to Stage 1 goals, Ms. Hartmann then automatically prioritized disciplinary language development in Stages 2 and 3. In Stage 2, she designed a performance task aligned to Stage 1 goals, with learners taking on roles as potential weather reporters who use multiple sources of evidence to describe how weather affects human life around the globe. Simulating an authentic, language-rich performance, students use disciplinary language to compare and contrast how weather and climate have influenced one facet of human life—for example, sports or child rearing—in various contexts of the world. In addition to the performance task, she collected other evidence of learning and language development aligned to Stage 1 goals, including personal glossaries of academic vocabulary, journals of scientific responses and explorations, and artifacts from various in-class uses of graphs, maps, and weather-related data. In Stage 3, Ms. Hartmann designed a learning plan that sets students up to achieve the Stage 1 goals, tapping into their cultural and linguistic background knowledge and attending to disciplinary language development through modeling and application with strategic scaffolds such as sentence frames and graphic organizers. In other words, with all stages of curricular design aligned, she ensured a consistent and deliberate lens on language throughout the unit of study by beginning with analysis and prioritizing disciplinary language in Stage 1.

Figure 4.15 | **Ms. Hartmann's High School Earth Science Unit**

Stage 1—Desired Results		
Established Goals	**Transfer**	
NGSS HS-ESS3-5 Analyze geoscience data and the results from global climate models to make an evidence-based forecast of the current rate of global or regional climate change and associated future impacts to Earth systems. **CCSS RST.11-12.7** Integrate and evaluate multiple sources of information presented in diverse forms and media to address a question or solve a problem.	*Students will be able to independently use their learning to…* • Present and argue appropriate solutions to problems, including drawing from multiple sources of scientific evidence and information.	
	Meaning	
	Understandings *Students will understand that…* • Various components of the Earth system interact in complex ways to regulate climate. • Weather influences humans, and humans influence weather. • Science involves particular ways of knowing, requiring empirical evidence, logistical arguments, skepticism, and peer review. • We revise scientific ideas over time as new evidence becomes available.	**Essential Questions** *Students will keep considering…* • How does weather vary across the world? • What effect does weather have on human life? • How do humans affect weather on a local scale? • How do humans affect weather on a global scale? • How can we use scientific data to argue for solutions?
	Acquisition	
	Students will know… • Weather/climate distinctions. • Weather maps and graphs. • Fahrenheit/Celsius conversions. • Weather concepts with related vocabulary (e.g., altitude, air pressure, precipitation, humidity, atmosphere, temperature). • Sentence structures/clauses (i.e., cause/effect, compare/contrast). • Problem/solution discourse.	*Students will be skilled at…* • Analyzing weather-related data in weather maps and graphs. • Interpreting weather patterns and events using data analyses. • Comparing and contrasting climates and weather patterns in various regions around the world. • Developing and arguing solutions to weather-related problems.

Stage 2—Evidence

Evaluative Criteria	Assessment Evidence
• Thorough investigation • Evidence-based findings • Multiple sources • Effective presentation • Convincing argument	**Performance Task(s)** **The Weather Channel** Your goal is to demonstrate the effects of weather on human life. You and your team are being interviewed for a job at the Weather Channel. The search committee is particularly interested in finding a team that can investigate how weather affects various aspects of human life around the world (e.g., climate change, severe weather). Your challenge is to select one aspect of human life (e.g., sports, child rearing, travel) and draw from multiple sources of evidence to make your argument about the effects of weather. You will produce a 10-minute video segment to share with the committee. To further demonstrate your qualifications for global weather reporting, use other languages in addition to English.
• Thorough analyses • Accurate findings • Diverse media • Scientific language	**Supplementary Evidence** • Article analyses: Reading and responding to scientific articles • Graph analyses: Layers of atmosphere temperature and pressure • Map analyses: Weather maps around the world lab • Data analyses: Temperature change over 25 years in global cities

Stage 3—Learning Plan

Pre-assessment

• Carousel brainstorming using translanguaging to glean students' background knowledge from home, community, and school (e.g., watching weather segment of the news, checking weather app before getting dressed in the morning, previous learning about water cycle and precipitation)

• Multilingual word wall and personal glossaries: Using students' background knowledge, start display of related weather terms in multiple languages (e.g., rain with related translation into all students' L1). Students begin personal glossaries with disciplinary language that they already know.

Learning Events

• Chicago-specific hook (journal with sentence frames and discussion): How does weather affect your life in the Windy City? How does it compare with other places that you have lived in or visited?

• Model disciplinary language to make scientific claims/arguments and justify the claims with evidence, including overall organization of argument with specific sentence frames and key words.

• Analysis partners, Round 1: Teacher-selected pairs analyze graphs on relationship between altitude, temperature, and pressure, including conversions between Fahrenheit and Celsius.

• Analysis partners, Round 2: Each pair selects a severe weather event to read, analyze, and discuss related research using a graphic organizer. Pairs will exchange their written analyses with another group to then analyze and critique the other group's interpretations.

• Global inquiry teams: L1-based groups analyze weather maps of one continent of their choice (i.e., North America, South America, Africa, Europe, Asia, Australia) using a graphic organizer.

• Expert groups: Graphing the average temperature in a city over the past 25 years (i.e., Chicago, USA; Santo Domingo, Dominican Republic; Gulu, Ghana; Sarajevo, Bosnia; Yangon, Myanmar; Santiago, Chile); jigsaw by city, then mixed groups (one student per city) share and compare results.

• Performance task preparation and completion: Students work in small groups to design, research, rehearse, and perform the 10-minute video segment regarding weather events and human impacts. Graphic organizers, bilingual dictionaries, and other instructional supports available.

Formative Assessments

• Journal with specific prompts across unit (e.g., "What are the signs of global climate change?")

• Personal glossaries with academic vocabulary, including translation into L1 and visuals

• Observations during instruction using student checklist and anecdotal notes

• Daily checks for understanding on progress toward learning objectives

Source: Used with permission from Jillian Hartmann, Theodore Roosevelt High School, Chicago.

Chapter Summary

Focused on Stage 1 of UbD, the goals of this chapter have centered on educators recognizing language demands to target desired results for students' language development in classroom instruction. Throughout the chapter, we have explored the nuances of disciplinary language, building awareness of how language varies and develops across disciplines, classrooms, students, tasks, and texts. Two overarching goals guide the principles in practice for Stage 1 with a lens on language: educators define desired results for rigorous and authentic learning that (1) develops *all* learners' language and (2) provides CLD students equitable access. After drafting Stage 1 UbD plans, teachers analyze for language demands and revise goals to build linguistic knowledge and skills for students to engage in discipline-specific units of study. These linguistically responsive goals for learning then guide the meaningful assessment and scaffolded instruction in Stages 2 and 3, respectively. We explore Stage 2—the collection of assessment evidence—with a language lens in the next chapter.

5

Assessing Student Learning: Stage 2 for Language Development

CHAPTER GOALS

- **Transfer**: Educators will be able to independently use their learning to...

  – Design performance tasks and other assessments that tap into students' background knowledge and support language development.

- **Understandings**: Educators will understand that...

  – Well-designed performance assessments involve authentic tasks that integrate language functions and domains as applied to disciplinary topics.
  – Performance tasks must be differentiated to enable students to tap into cultural background knowledge and allow for linguistic accessibility.
  – By collecting multiple sources of evidence across units of study, teachers can dynamically capture students' holistic learning and development.

- **Essential questions**: Educators will keep considering...

  – How do students use language to engage in authentic tasks?
  – How can culture and language influence students' performance?
  – What role does assessment play in my understanding of students?

- **Knowledge**: Educators will know...

  – Examples of oral, written, and displayed performance tasks.
  – The GRASPS task elements for designing performance tasks.
  – Sensory, graphic, and interactive supports for performance tasks.
  – Criteria for culturally and linguistically responsive assessments.

- **Skills**: Educators will be skilled at...

  – Identifying the language needed to authentically engage in performance tasks aligned with transfer, meaning, and acquisition goals.
  – Analyzing and modifying assessment tasks and tools to reduce cultural and linguistic bias and enhance validity of assessment results.
  – Collecting and documenting various sources of evidence of learning, including language development embedded in disciplinary learning.

Stage 2 of UbD focuses on designing assessments that will provide evidence of students' progress toward the learning goals defined in Stage 1. Whereas other approaches to planning consider assessment as an afterthought, backward design prioritizes the integral role of assessment in instruction. By considering the needed assessment evidence (Stage 2), teachers gain goal clarity (Stage 1) while sharpening their instructional foci (Stage 3).

Assessing Learning in Classroom Instruction

Before we begin our in-depth exploration of Stage 2, we introduce two students, 2nd grader Absame and 6th grader Emma. Their backgrounds and experiences set the context for our discussion of assessment with a lens on language.

Absame, 2nd Grader

Absame recently arrived in the United States with his mother and two siblings, having escaped the civil war in Somalia. After losing her husband amid the ongoing violence, Absame's mother moved her children to a refugee camp in Kenya, where they lived for two years before gaining refugee status in the United States. The family moved to the urban Midwest, where they had an established network of extended family members and other Somalis to support their transition into U.S. society and schooling, as well as maintain their Sunni Muslim traditions and Somali language. Absame struggled at first to settle into a context that was different from the schools at the refugee camp, where international volunteers set up tents to teach basic skills with limited materials. But he began to thrive with the collaborative support of his classroom teacher and his ESL resource teacher, who used coteaching methods to actively include him in 2nd grade instruction while supporting his unique learning needs.

During the balanced literacy block, the class has been engaged in a descriptive writing unit, and Absame has excelled with the teachers' high expectations, interactive workshop format, and scaffolded instructional supports to communicate his ideas in writing. The unit culminates in a performance task in which students write songs for a music recital with the hope of capturing the attention of a record producer and a famous artist who are in the audience. But Absame does not fully demonstrate his learning and development because of his unfamiliarity with concepts such as *music recital*, *record producer*, and *famous artist*. Growing up without access to these cultural constructs, Absame's prior experiences do not align with the background knowledge needed to engage with this task.

Emma, 6th Grader

Emma, born and raised in the suburbs, has white, English-dominant parents with conversational Spanish abilities and an extended family including two Spanish-dominant uncles and four bilingual cousins. Recognizing the importance of bilingualism, her parents placed Emma in a two-way immersion program starting in kindergarten so that she could learn in both Spanish and English.

After six years in the program at her public elementary school, Emma moved to the local middle school, with students from various schools and programs. Other than the foreign language Spanish class during 5th period, her other courses are facilitated solely in English. In Spanish class, her teacher gives traditional tests to measure isolated knowledge and skills related to grammar and vocabulary. In most content classes, including language arts, science, and social studies, teachers maintain expectations of English use for students engaging in performance tasks and other learning experiences.

Only in mathematics, where her bilingual teacher consistently integrates Spanish-English cognates and other facets of students' bilingualism, is Emma encouraged to use both languages. As a native English speaker, she has no formal label ascribed to indicate a particular language proficiency; however, as a sequential bilingual with all formal schooling previously mediated in two languages, she has unique abilities and needs that go unrecognized and unused with the current assessment practices implemented across the middle school classrooms.

Stage 2 for Understanding and Language Development

In Stage 2 of UbD, we aim to integrate various assessment tasks and tools to collect ample data on student learning and development corresponding to unit goals for transfer, meaning, and acquisition. Taking center stage in UbD instructional design, *performance tasks* actively engage learners in authentic situations that require the transfer of unit understandings, knowledge, and skills to real-world problems and practices (Wiggins & McTighe, 2005). In addition to performance tasks, educators integrate frequent opportunities to collect *supplementary evidence* to assess student learning (see Figure 5.1). By using varied assessments embedded in instruction, including academic prompts, tests, quizzes, observations, dialogues, and checks for understanding, teachers have multiple data points to discern students' progress toward all transfer, meaning, and acquisition goals.

Figure 5.1 | **Continuum of Assessments**

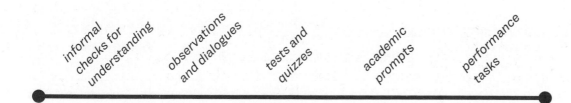

Source: From *Understanding by Design Professional Development Workbook* (p. 142), by J. McTighe and G. Wiggins, 2004, Alexandria, VA: ASCD. Copyright 2004 by ASCD. Adapted with permission.

By focusing a language lens on Stage 2 of UbD, we continue the pledge to promote equity for CLD students in classrooms. When designing units of study, we aim to design authentic assessment tasks and tools that provide equitable opportunities for students to demonstrate progress toward Stage 1 goals. With this intent in mind, we integrate language-rich, culturally responsive, and linguistically accessible assessments that provide multiple sources of data to track students' learning and development across sociocultural, cognitive, linguistic, and academic dimensions (Herrera, 2016; Thomas & Collier, 1997). Our goal is to craft assessments that use the rich resources and linguistic abilities that students bring to classrooms while maintaining academic rigor and learning expectations. Grounded in culturally and linguistically responsive practice, this alignment bolsters the validity of the assessment data by measuring students' disciplinary learning rather than background knowledge or language-proficiency levels. By adding a language lens to Stage 2, we validate the cultural and linguistic backgrounds of students like Absame and Emma while providing equitable opportunities for them to demonstrate disciplinary learning.

Designing Performance Tasks

Taking the form of tangible performances and products, performance tasks engage students in "complex challenges that mirror issues and problems faced by adults" (Wiggins & McTighe, 2005, p. 153). A critical component of the UbD framework, performance tasks directly align to Stage 1 learning goals. Because of their authentic nature, performance tasks relate to transfer goals and meaning goals, whereas acquisition goals are measured by collecting supplementary evidence via means such as quizzes and checks for understanding. Thus we begin with Stage 1 goals and then brainstorm the evidence needed for students to demonstrate understandings in the form of *understanding performances*. We then flesh out broad understanding performances into specific performance tasks (see Figure 5.2; McTighe & Wiggins, 2004).

Figure 5.2 | **Aligning Stages 1 and 2**

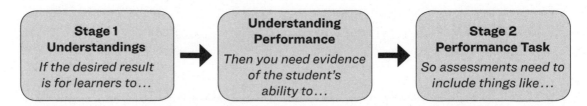

Source: From *Understanding by Design Professional Development Workbook* (p. 138), by J. McTighe and G. Wiggins, 2004, Alexandria, VA: ASCD. Copyright 2004 by ASCD. Adapted with permission.

In this section, we add a language lens on performance tasks to yield language-rich assessments that align with disciplinary language goals from Stage 1.

Language-Rich Authentic Tasks

Performance tasks should involve ample use of language, as tasks are meant to engage students in real-world practices that involve using language to communicate with others. When directly aligned to Stage 1 learning goals, authentic performance tasks have the potential to prioritize and further develop discipline-specific language.

In Chapter 4, we explored the nuances of disciplinary language, such as the functions and features related to a given discipline—for example, mathematics, earth science, history—and then targeted and integrated language development into Stage 1 goals. By beginning with these goals, already drafted with a language lens, we can design performance tasks and pinpoint evaluative criteria that align to both disciplinary learning and language development. Now moving into Stage 2 of instructional design, we want to maintain the explicit lens on language. To accomplish this, we first consider how to use the six facets of understandings and related language functions to generate possible performances. We then work to flesh out performance tasks that prioritize language use across domains via oral, written, and displayed products and performances.

Tasks by language functions

As emphasized throughout this book, *understanding* is the integral goal of UbD curricular design. Rather than rote instruction that prompts the passive recall of facts related to a specified standard, students actively make meaning of important concepts in order to transfer learning to other contexts. Working from Stage 1 goals, we now design aligned and appropriate performance tasks for students to demonstrate disciplinary learning and language development. To maintain rigorous expectations for all students' learning in Stage 1 and assess all students' progress toward unit goals via performance tasks in Stage 2, we connect the two stages, as noted earlier, by brainstorming possible performances aligned to transfer and meaning goals, referred to as *understanding performances* (McTighe & Wiggins, 2004).

Grounded in Stage 1 transfer and meaning goals, understanding performances emerge, as illustrated in Figure 5.3, by combining performance verbs and disciplinary generalizations (McTighe & Wiggins, 2004). Remember the central tenet of the UbD framework: if students truly understand, then they should be able to explain, interpret, apply, take perspective, empathize, and self-reflect. Thus, we consider possible performances by using performance verbs spanning one or more of the six facets of understanding (see Figure 5.4).

Figure 5.3 | **Aligning Goals with Performances**

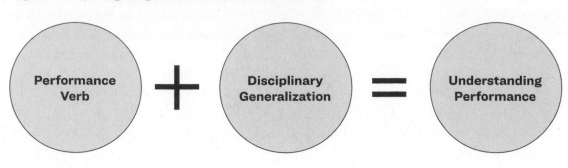

z

Source: From *Understanding by Design Professional Development Workbook* (p. 159), by J. McTighe and G. Wiggins, 2004, Alexandria, VA: ASCD. Copyright © 2004 by ASCD. Adapted with permission.

Notice that performance verbs align to language functions, such as explaining, critiquing, arguing, and inferring (AACCW, 2010; O'Malley & Pierce, 1996). Language functions span disciplines; for example, we compare and contrast characters in language arts, geometric figures in mathematics, weather patterns in science, and historic events in social studies. Although the language functions are used across classrooms to demonstrate understanding, languages features will vary by discipline, as varying words, phrases, sentence structures, and discourse are used in language arts, math, science, and social studies. Because we aim to develop language embedded in particular disciplines, we brainstorm understanding performances by specifying a disciplinary generalization attached to the performance verb. By merging performance verbs (language function) and disciplinary generalizations (discipline-specific language features), we brainstorm possible performances that will allow students to demonstrate disciplinary learning and language development aligned to Stage 1 goals.

Figure 5.4 | **Examples of Performance Verbs by Facet of Understanding**

Explain	Interpret	Apply	Perspective	Empathy	Self-Knowledge
Describe	Critique	Adapt	Analyze	Believe	Be aware of
Express	Document	Create	Argue	Consider	Realize
Justify	Evaluate	Decide	Compare	Imagine	Recognize
Predict	Represent	Invent	Contrast	Relate	Reflect
Synthesize	Translate	Produce	Infer	Role-play	Self-assess

Source: From *Understanding by Design Professional Development Workbook* (p. 161), by J. McTighe and G. Wiggins, 2004, Alexandria, VA: ASCD. Copyright 2004 by ASCD. Adapted with permission.

Recall the elementary social studies unit focused on the pioneer spirit introduced in the previous chapter. In this unit, desired results aim for students to transfer learning by comparing historical and current accounts of pioneers and today's migrants, as well as taking perspective and empathizing with interactions between civilizations, cultures, and people. Thus, learners must understand the complexity of the pioneer experience, including why people moved, what challenges they faced, and how they negotiated life on the prairie—specifically, interactions with Native Americans. With these transfer and meaning goals in mind, the social studies teacher uses the six facets of understanding to consider possible performances, specifically by merging *performance verbs* with *disciplinary generalizations* from unit goals. To measure learners' progress toward these big goals regarding pioneer life, the teacher needs evidence of students' ability to *explain* the challenges of the pioneer experience, *interpret* real-life stories of pioneers, *produce* a story detailing the hardships of pioneer life, *compare* perspectives of pioneers and Native Americans, *imagine* their own emotions as a Native American or a pioneer, and *reflect* on a personal pioneer-like experience. Grounded in Stage 1 goals, these understanding performances then provide the stepping-stone for the teacher to further plan performance tasks.

Tasks across language domains

Because of their direct alignment to the language functions needed to engage in disciplinary learning, understanding performances should engage students with authentic language use that integrates the four domains: listening, speaking, reading, and writing. When working to flesh out more detailed performance tasks, practitioners can consider an array of products and performances that fall into three categories: oral, written, and displayed (McTighe & Wiggins, 2004). Although authentic tasks typically integrate all four domains of language in meaningful ways, performances and products prioritize specific domains, particularly the productive domains of speaking, in the form of *oral performance tasks*, and writing, in the form of *written performance tasks*. Further, *displayed performance tasks* can strategically integrate supports for language development via hands-on products, graphic displays, and kinesthetic movements. Thus, teachers can design tasks to prioritize domains in response to students' linguistic strengths and needs, as discussed in Chapter 3, and aligned to Stage 1 learning goals, as described in Chapter 4.

Oral performance tasks prioritize listening and speaking to simulate real-world situations and problem solving. With the flexibility to span disciplines, oral performance tasks engage learners in debating issues, presenting proposals, sharing reports, giving speeches, telling stories, and conducting interviews. Various products and performances result from discipline-specific tasks that spotlight oral language (see Figure 5.5). Oral *products*, such as recitations and speeches, focus on fixed artifacts of oral language in which students practice and rehearse over time. Oral *performances* are more dynamic in nature, relying on on-the-spot interaction with classmates through debates, discussions, and improvisations. Although they prioritize oral language, these authentic tasks typically require reading and writing, such as reading about the sides of an argument to prepare for a debate, or writing questions and notes to facilitate an interview. Being responsive to students' strengths and needs is integral to designing performance tasks. The goal is to build off students' strengths—so they can equitably demonstrate disciplinary learning—while simultaneously supporting their areas of need. For example, for students with strong speaking skills, a podcast would highlight oral language while integrating disciplinary reading and writing as learners prepare and rehearse in the less threatening setting of small groups. In this way, performance tasks are rigorous, authentic, and responsive to students.

Figure 5.5 | **Examples of Performances and Products**

Oral	Written	Displayed
Debate	Blog	Advertisement
Discussion	Critique	Artistic performance
Improvisation	Essay/analysis	Artistic visual media
Interview	Law/policy	Blueprint
Oral report	Letter	Constructed model
Podcast	Magazine article	Demonstration
Proposal	Narrative	Diorama
Recitation	Poem	Electronic media exhibit
Role-play	Proposal/plan	Graph/table/chart
Simulation	Report	Storyboard
Speech	Script	Website
Storytelling	Song lyrics	

Source: From *Understanding by Design Professional Development Workbook* (p. 174), by J. McTighe and G. Wiggins, 2004, Alexandria, VA: ASCD. Copyright 2004 by ASCD. Adapted with permission.

Written performance tasks prioritize reading and writing to engage students in authentic practices of portraying ideas through written texts. Regardless of the discipline, adults use writing in the real world, whether drafting legislation, authoring articles, creating proposals, summarizing research findings, drawing up game plans, composing music, or scripting plays. Because of the focus on productive language, written performance tasks primarily result in products, such as essays, letters, blog posts, and reports (see Figure 5.5). Nonetheless, performances can be added as a component of written performance tasks to authentically integrate other domains, as when students read poems aloud at poetry slams, enact scripts via dramatic performances, or perform musical compositions and lyrics.

When adding a language lens, we design performance tasks aligned to Stage 1 goals while also highlighting strengths and supporting needs of students. For example, consider a unit with goals centered on writing in a discipline where students bring academic knowledge in L1. To tap into students' L1 and develop their L2 writing, the task might ask students to draft bilingual proposals to present to multinational North American corporations. The task simulates real-world practice in our globalizing world, allows students to demonstrate learning through linguistic strengths, and integrates scaffolds to target and develop language aligned to unit goals.

Displayed performance tasks merge language domains, including authentic and interactive uses of listening, speaking, reading, and writing. In addition to simulating real-world experiences particular to various disciplines, such as advertising products, constructing models, developing websites, and producing exhibits, displayed products and performances build in graphic and sensory supports for language development (see Figure 5.5). Displayed *products* are typically artifacts created using hands-on materials or technology, such as models, blueprints, dioramas, and visual media. Displayed *performances*, such as dramatic interpretations, musical recitals, and disciplinary demonstrations, tend to integrate auditory, kinesthetic, and visual scaffolds. Whether products or performances, displayed tasks allow the time and space for students to create and rehearse in low-anxiety settings, which supports language development tied to disciplinary learning.

Like tasks in oral and written mediums, displayed performance tasks can be designed to align to Stage 1 goals, as well as respond to students' strengths and needs in classrooms. Consider a student like Absame, an emergent bilingual student who is just beginning to learn English in elementary school. By designing a performance task in which students use storyboards to recount something important to them, Absame can demonstrate what he learned in the writing unit through visuals, background knowledge, and culturally specific ways of storytelling. To differentiate the task for others, the teacher can add expectations regarding written captions for storyboards. (Differentiation of tasks by language proficiency will be discussed further in the next section.)

Consider the unit on pioneer life mentioned earlier and featured here as planned and executed by a 6th grade social studies teacher, Ms. Piccioni (see Figure 5.6). In her class is Emma, along with many other students who have recently exited a two-way immersion program that spanned kindergarten through 5th grade. To select a performance or product for this class, Ms. Piccioni considers the bilingualism and biliteracy these students gained from six years in a

Figure 5.6 | **Elementary Social Studies Unit on Pioneer Life**

Stage 1—Desired Results

Established Goals

- Students pose relevant questions about events they encounter in historical documents, eyewitness accounts, oral histories, letters, diaries, artifacts, photographs, maps, artworks, and architecture.
- Students trace why their community was established, how individuals and families contributed to its founding and development, and how the community has changed over time, drawing on maps, photographs, oral histories, letters, newspapers, and other primary sources.

Transfer

Students will be able to independently use their learning to...
- Seek out, compare, and critique different historical accounts.
- Compare the lives of pioneers on the prairie and pioneers of today.
- View interactions of civilizations, cultures, and peoples with greater perspective and empathy.

Meaning

Understandings

Students will understand that...
- Many pioneers had naïve ideas about the opportunities and difficulties of moving west.
- People move for various reasons, such as seeking economic opportunities or fleeing situations.
- Successful pioneers rely on courage, ingenuity, and collaboration to overcome challenges.
- The settlement of the West threatened Native American cultures and communities living on the plains.
- History involves making sense of different stories.

Essential Questions

Students will keep considering...
- Why do people move? Why did the pioneers leave their homes to move west?
- How do geography and topography influence travel and settlement?
- What is a pioneer? What is the *pioneer spirit*?
- Why did some pioneers survive and prosper while others did not?
- Who owns a story?
- What happens when cultures and communities come together?

Acquisition

Knowledge

Students will know...
- Facts about the westward movement and pioneer life on the prairie.
- Facts about Native American tribes and interactions with settlers.
- Dual definitions of *pioneer*.
- Related geographical terms (e.g., travel routes, settlements).
- Comparative grammatical structures (e.g., conjunctions, adverbials).
- Linguistic features of novels written from two perspectives.

Skills

Students will be skilled at...
- Interpreting various texts across genres and mediums (e.g., historical documents, oral histories, maps, photographs, timelines, letters).
- Comparing and contrasting the experiences of pioneers from historical accounts and current events.
- Critically analyzing perspectives of pioneers and Native Americans.
- Conducting and producing web-based research on pioneer life.

Stage 2—Evidence

Evaluative Criteria	Assessment Evidence
• Historically accurate • Detailed • Well-crafted • Revealing & informative • Effective exhibit • Clear oral presentation	**Performance Task(s)** **Bilingual Museum Exhibits** Your task is to tell the story of one real-life pioneer family. You and your team members work at the local history museum. Your target audience is primary students who are bilingual in Spanish and English. The challenge involves capturing the stories and struggles of pioneers and portraying those stories in two languages. You will create a museum exhibit using photos, artifacts, and narrative. You will find and use primary sources and Internet resources to research the pioneer family. You will give an oral presentation to compare historical and modern pioneers.
• Historically accurate • Unique perspectives • Social studies language	**Supplementary Evidence** • Ongoing quizzes assessing facts about the westward movement, pioneer life, Native American tribes, and interactions with settlers. • Dialogue journals with academic prompts for students to take the perspectives of both pioneers and Native Americans.

Stage 3—Learning Plan

Pre-assessment

• Provide journal prompts to encourage connections with personal experiences of human movement (e.g., immigration), and cultural/community displacement (e.g., gentrification).

• Use KWL to glean students' previous academic knowledge about Native Americans, the westward movement, and pioneer life on the prairie.

• Have students reflect and set individual learning and language development goals for the unit.

Learning Events

• Personal glossaries: Students begin the individual notebooks to capture pertinent language throughout the unit, including Spanish translations.

• Critically read and collaboratively compare fictional texts that represent different perspectives: *Little House on the Prairie*, by Laura Ingalls Wilder, and *The Birchbark House*, by Louise Erdrich.

• Critically read nonfiction texts (e.g., *Life on the Oregon Trail, Diaries of Pioneer Women*, and *Dakota Dugout*) along with related primary source documents from the Library of Congress website.

• Reading discussions and responses: Graphic organizers and prompts to reflect upon readings on the nature of a pioneer and the effects of cultural and linguistic interactions between pioneers and native peoples.

• Reading storyboard: Students develop an interactive timeline and map of a pioneer family's journey west using pertinent geographical terms.

• Simulation: Use Oregon Train card game to simulate pioneer experience.

• Simulation: Council of elders of a Native American tribe living on the plains where students consider perspectives and develop empathy for displaced Native Americans. Discuss: What should we do when threatened with relocation: fight, flee, or agree to move? How would each decision impact our lives?

• Inquiry groups: Have teams research different modern-day pioneers in different fields (preselected by the teacher). Compare and contrast to develop ideas about how we are all pioneers in some ways.

• Linguistic exploration of personal glossaries to support bridging and comparative analysis between English and Spanish (e.g., cognates, word parts).

Formative Assessment

• Observations of students' reader responses and discussions while interpreting texts

• Personal glossaries of geographical terms and other pertinent vocabulary, including drawings and bilingual translations

Source: From *The Understanding by Design Guide to Creating High-Quality Units* (pp. 29–30), by G. Wiggins and J. McTighe, 2011, Alexandria, VA: ASCD. Copyright 2011 by G. Wiggins and J. McTighe. Adapted with permission.

dual-language program with equal emphasis on Spanish and English. After brainstorming possible performances that would provide evidence of Stage 1 goals, Ms. Piccioni then fleshes out what the assessment should include—what would allow students to demonstrate their disciplinary learning while tapping into their backgrounds, strengths, and abilities. She decides to have students work in small groups to create museum exhibits in which photos, artifacts, and bilingual narratives tell one nuanced authentic story of pioneer life. Like displays at many of the cultural institutions in the area, the museum exhibits will need to be bilingual to provide access to a larger population of students. By incorporating visual elements (photos) and sensory scaffolds (artifacts), both English- and Spanish-dominant students have supports to produce bilingual museum displays. Additionally, strategic grouping of students by language background allows for experts in both languages to contribute to the performance task. In this way, Ms. Piccioni designs a performance task for students to demonstrate learning related to unit goals but does so in a way that embraces, aligns with, and responds to students' backgrounds and abilities.

Authentic, language-rich performance tasks support the language development of all students in UbD instructional design. Specific attention to language functions and domains allows teachers to align tasks to Stage 1 goals while shifting attention to students' linguistic abilities, strengths, and needs. Using the broad understanding performances aligned to Stage 1 transfer and meaning goals, which are rigorous by design and maintained for all learners, particular performance tasks are designed in response to students in classrooms. In this way, whereas unit goals may remain the same from class to class, performance tasks may change depending on students' abilities, strengths, and needs. In the next section, we flesh out performance tasks in more depth using the GRASPS framework (McTighe & Wiggins, 2004; Wiggins & McTighe, 2005) to explore specific task considerations for CLD students. Within a general sense of the performance that will provide appropriate evidence of student learning, the GRASPS elements prompt additional details that guide completion of the task. The goal is to provide equitable access for all students to engage with and demonstrate learning via Stage 2 assessments, so we specifically design performance tasks with lenses on students' unique and diverse cultural and linguistic backgrounds.

Specific Task Considerations for CLD Students

The UbD framework includes the GRASPS design tool (see Figure 5.7) to assist in the creation of authentic performance tasks, with each letter corresponding to a task element—Goal; Role; Audience; Situation; Product, performance, and purpose; and Success criteria (Wiggins & McTighe, 2005). The *goal* frames the assessment by establishing the goals, problems, challenges, or obstacles that students will address within the task. The *role* explicitly defines the persona or job that students assume to complete the task. The *audience* identifies the individuals to whom the student will deliver the performance or product. The *situation* elaborates the scenario by describing the context and explaining the situation. The *product, performance, and purpose* includes a statement of what students will produce and why. Finally, *success criteria* specify how the performance or product will be evaluated and serve as the basis for developing detailed rubric(s). In this section, we explore how to differentiate GRASPS tasks to allow CLD students equitable access to demonstrate learning, first by using the cultural lens to align with background knowledge and then the linguistic lens to support language proficiency.

Figure 5.7 | **Prompts for Writing GRASPS Tasks**

Element		Prompts	Language Lens
G	Goal	Your task is to… Your goal is to… The problem or challenge is… The obstacle to overcome is…	Does students' background knowledge align with the stated goal of the task?
R	Role	You are… You have been asked to… Your job is to…	Are students familiar with the target role based on their prior knowledge (e.g., jobs, careers, positions)?
A	Audience	Your clients are… The target audience is… You need to convince…	Do students know the cultural values and practices that shape how they would interact with target audience?
S	Situation	The context you find yourself in is… The challenge involves dealing with…	How can students use language in authentic ways to engage in the situation?
P	Product, Performance, and Purpose	You will create a… You need to develop…	How can students use language in varied ways to demonstrate learning? What linguistic supports do students need to demonstrate learning?
S	Success Criteria	Your performance needs to… Your work will be judged by… Your product must meet these standards… A successful result will…	What are the expectations for students' language use? How does language develop as embedded in disciplinary learning?

Source: From *Understanding by Design Professional Development Workbook* (p. 172), by J. McTighe and G. Wiggins, 2004, Alexandria, VA: ASCD. Copyright 2004 by ASCD. Adapted with permission.

Cultural lens on performance tasks

When focusing a cultural lens on performance tasks, the primary goal is to design assessments that tap into students' background knowledge while still prompting them to transfer their learning to a novel context, situation, or problem. This is a delicate but pertinent line to walk when designing UbD instruction: we cannot place CLD students at a disadvantage in demonstrating understandings based on any background knowledge assumed or required to complete the performance or product. Therefore, we must ask: Are students familiar with the activities, objects, people, and places required to understand and engage with the performance task? Is the task linked to students' background knowledge to provide equitable access to a demonstration of learning and understanding? All three areas of background knowledge should be considered when designing performance tasks—*funds of knowledge* from home, *prior knowledge* from community, and *academic knowledge* from school (Herrera, 2016)—as well as students' linguistic backgrounds, including L1, L2, and interconnections between L1 and L2. Here we consider these kinds of background knowledge by analyzing the goal, role, audience, and situation elements of GRASPS tasks.

Goal. As is the norm in backward design, GRASPS tasks begin with the end in mind—by clearly and explicitly establishing the goals to be reached upon completion. In real-world practice, we enter situations with a clear goal. As educators, we engage in daily problem solving shaped by well-defined goals: to draft an individualized education plan (IEP) for a particular student, to organize professional learning communities across our school, to increase parental involvement in classroom curriculum, to negotiate a fair contract with the school board, or to design a UbD unit to foster language development. To mimic authentic experiences and prepare students for independent practice, it is imperative to set clear goals to frame performance tasks; however, we must consider students' background knowledge, which may align or misalign with the stated goal. Academic knowledge from formal schooling experiences often influences students' equitable access to the goal of the GRASPS task. For example, a performance task goal might prompt students to plan a fundraiser or design an experiment. These goals require culturally specific background knowledge that students without extensive exposure to American schools may not possess, such as the notion of fundraising or the process of scientific inquiry. The intention is to prompt transfer to novel contexts while not putting particular students at a disadvantage in demonstrating their learning.

Throughout this chapter we have focused on the pioneer unit to consider the design of Stage 2 assessments aligned to Stage 1 learning goals. After brainstorming possible performances using the six facets of understanding, Ms. Piccioni, the social studies teacher, decides to use a displayed performance task—specifically, museum exhibits. Now seeking to flesh out the performance task using the

Do students know what they're working on?

Its important to have an end-goal in mind to see the task through like backwards design

Reminder: Not all students have the same background knowledge ie kids not from America might not know about fundraising

GRASPS elements, Ms. Piccioni first defines the goal. Thinking about the Stage 1 learning goals, as well as the students in her classroom, she strategically frames the performance task with the goal that learners will *tell the story of one real-life pioneer family*. Following six years in self-contained, dual-language classrooms, her students are in their first year in a departmentalized setting with a separate class focused solely on social studies. Because of this, she remains relatively unclear about students' knowledge of discourse that is specific to social studies. Thus, instead of asking students to chronologically document the history of pioneers, she sets the goal for learners to tell a story—specifically tapping into their familiarity with and affinity for telling stories. Additionally, rather than insist upon the often linear trajectory of stories in mainstream American culture, Ms. Piccioni sees the broad construct of storytelling as a way to tap into students' home and community experiences and allow for various approaches to completing the task.

Role. Following the statement of the goal, the GRASPS task then provides learners with roles or jobs that they must assume to complete the task. Sometimes, it is appropriate for students to be themselves, such as when writing a short autobiography or developing a personal position on an issue. In other cases, a task may ask students to assume a real-world role and take on the persona and perspective of another individual, therefore prompting transfer to a novel and authentic context. The role that we ask students to assume becomes central to the performance or product, requiring background knowledge of the role itself to be able to complete the task. We want to contemplate how roles defined in GRASPS tasks align to students' prior knowledge in the community—specifically, familiarity with various jobs, careers, and positions (see Figure 5.8). Consider Absame, who recently lived in a refugee camp, being asked to take the role of a caterer or a choreographer. Or think of Zaia, who has never traveled outside her urban community, needing to know the nuanced perspectives of a forest ranger or a farmer. Nevertheless, both Absame and Zaia have ample prior knowledge to take on other roles to complete tasks and demonstrate learning.

When designing the social studies unit on the pioneer experience, the teacher has already selected the language-rich performance task of creating museum exhibits, with the goal that students tell the stories of pioneer families. Using the GRASPS task elements, she then determines that the appropriate role for learners to take is that of *workers at a local history museum*. With all students enrolled in the district for multiple years—most since kindergarten due to the required long-term commitment to participate in the dual-language program—Ms. Piccioni is confident that learners possess the needed background knowledge about museums and museum workers. Students have been to museums throughout elementary school, including the local history museum during a previous social studies unit. Despite this similarity in prior experiences, she acknowledges that students may vary in knowledge of specific museum roles; for this reason, she chose not to use the terminology of museum *curator* or *docent*, which may be unfamiliar to some students in the classroom.

Figure 5.8 | Possible Student Roles and Audiences

Actor	Family member	Newscaster	School official
Biographer	Farmer	Novelist	Ship's captain
Businessperson	Geologist	Observer	Social worker
Candidate	Historian	Parent	Statistician
Celebrity	Judge	Park ranger	Student
Choreographer	Lawyer	Photographer	Teacher
Elected official	Literary critic	Playwright	Traveler
Embassy staff	Lobbyist	Police officer	Travel agent
Engineer	Meteorologist	Pollster	Website designer
Eyewitness	Neighbor	Researcher	Zookeeper

Source: From Understanding by Design Professional Development Workbook *(p. 173), by J. McTighe and G. Wiggins, 2004, Alexandria, VA: ASCD. Copyright 2004 by ASCD. Adapted with permission.*

Audience. Directly connected to the roles of GRASPS tasks, the audience defines the individuals to whom the students will deliver the performance or product. When considering the design of performance tasks for CLD students, the statement of audience, like that of roles, prompts considerations regarding students' background knowledge: Do learners know enough about the target individual or group to be able to culturally and linguistically shape their performance or product? To engage in authentic interaction between the task-defined roles and audiences, students tap into their funds of knowledge from home—those cultural values and practices that shape how they interact and use language with particular individuals and groups. Consider a performance task from the role of a teacher; the audience will influence the language used in the performance or product, as teachers might use distinct registers when interacting with students, parents, board members, firefighters, or celebrities. Performance may vary further based on students' previous experiences, just as teachers' interaction with students or parents looks distinct in countries such as Mexico, India, and Saudi Arabia. This situation is further exacerbated if students are altogether unfamiliar with the audience, such as a recent immigrant from Cuba being asked to speak to a jury or an elected official. Audience—particularly the expected interaction between defined roles and targeted audiences—influences students' access to the task.

Let's return to the museum exhibit performance task in the pioneer unit. Assuming roles as museum workers, learners design exhibits for *bilingual students* who come to the museum to learn about pioneers. Ms. Piccioni recognizes that all learners have firsthand familiarity with the target audience, as they have been students themselves for a number of years. Thus they know the *register of schooling*—how educators and students use language and interact with one another in formal settings like classrooms and museums. Additionally, younger learners provide an opportune audience for CLD students, as they can create linguistically appropriate products to demonstrate their understanding and proficiency. Because this social studies class consists primarily of students who recently exited the district's dual-language program, the addition of *bilingual* students further aligns with their previous experiences. By selecting the audience of bilingual primary students, rather than targeting museum board members or donors (which would require distinct background knowledge and linguistic registers), the task requires transfer to a novel context while aligning with background knowledge.

choose an audience they know

Situation. After briefly defining the goal, role, and audience, a GRASPS task elaborates on the scenario by describing the context and explaining the situation. These additional details build on the previous elements to provide students with the needed real-world backdrop to successfully transfer their learning and complete the performance task. When adding a lens on language to designing performance tasks, the particular situation described in a GRASPS task provides the opportunity to tap into students' linguistic background knowledge. Think about how people use language in today's world: the interaction between individuals in linguistically diverse communities, across generations of families living in different countries, or among businesspeople working in the globalized economy. We use multiple languages, code-switch between languages, and rely upon the linguistic expertise of others to connect with family, friends, community members, colleagues, partners, and strangers. Because performance tasks aim to simulate real-world practice and CLD students bring rich linguistic backgrounds to classroom learning, we can shape the situation of a performance task to integrate learners' unique abilities with language, such as multilingualism and translanguaging.

Understanding how they should speak. Tone, syntax and vocab.

Consider the draft performance task for the pioneer unit. For museum workers laboring to design and prepare exhibits for bilingual students, the situation involves *capturing the stories and struggles of pioneers using primary sources and portraying those stories in two languages.* By having students portray the stories of pioneer life in two languages, the situation both deepens the authenticity of the task and taps into students' linguistic strengths. The large and growing Spanish-speaking population in the United States has prompted many museums and other cultural institutions to use both Spanish and English to expand access to exhibits

conscious accessibility

and displays. By explicitly integrating a situation requiring students to use both languages, the performance task authentically simulates real-world practice in museums in the local community. The inclusion of both languages also validates students' bilingualism and biliteracy, allowing them opportunities to continue to develop disciplinary Spanish beyond the dual-language program. Remember that this departmentalized social studies classroom is an English-medium disciplinary setting—reinforcing the notion that non-English languages and language varieties can be used as resources for learning in any educational context, regardless of the teacher's language background and proficiency.

Linguistic lens on performance tasks

With the cultural lenses just described, we analyzed performance tasks based on students' background knowledge. In this section, we continue to use the GRASPS task elements to consider how students' language proficiency factors into *products, performances, and purposes*, as well as *success criteria* (McTighe & Wiggins, 2004; Wiggins & McTighe, 2005). Regardless of language proficiency level, all students should have equitable access to participate in the real-world simulation and demonstration of disciplinary learning via designated performances and products. Because of varying linguistic abilities in both L1 and L2, students' participation and contributions to the resulting performance or product will vary based on what we know they *can do* with language (WIDA, 2012). Additionally, because of their authenticity and rich use of language, performance tasks provide ideal locales to collect data on students' language development as aligned to Stage 1 goals. By designing rubrics with criteria by language proficiency level, we scaffold access to the task while gleaning meaningful data on students' language development.

Product, performance, and purpose. With this GRASPS element, practitioners provide details to expand upon the predetermined performance tasks that have emerged from Stage 1 goals—that is, the understanding performances attached to oral, written, or displayed tasks. Teachers describe how students will use language while doing the task, with attention across language domains—oral language, reading, writing—connected to pertinent language functions, such as *explain* and *argue*. As described earlier, all performance tasks are language-rich thanks to their authenticity in simulating real-world practices of disciplinary learning and communication. By designing tasks that authentically integrate language functions and domains for all learners, we open opportunities to differentiate performances and products by language proficiency—both through *linguistic expectations* and *linguistic supports*.

Linguistic expectations focus on how students use language in varied ways to demonstrate disciplinary learning. This is where a state's English language proficiency (ELP) or English language development (ELD) standards and tools are helpful. Consider the WIDA Can Do Descriptors, discussed in previous chapters, which use students' ELP test scores to provide snapshots of what students can do with language. Organized by grade and proficiency levels, Can Do Descriptors provide age-appropriate, developmental trajectories of language organized by domain with sample language functions (WIDA, 2016). Thus we can use the Can Do Descriptors to differentiate linguistic expectations on performance tasks. For example, we know that all learners can *argue* disciplinary ideas in a given performance task; however, as shown in Figure 5.9, students will process and produce language differently based on proficiency (WIDA, 2016). When considering the domain of speaking, we see how students can use language in different ways to participate in the performance task while progressing through proficiency levels: stating claims, sharing reasons for claims, asking and answering questions, defending claims and posing solutions, providing evidence to defend ideas, and summarizing opinions from two sides. These differentiated linguistic expectations will support the subsequent design of task rubrics.

We can also differentiate performance tasks by providing *linguistic supports*, organized into three categories—sensory, graphic, and interactive—as shown in Figure 5.10 (WIDA, 2007). *Sensory supports* use students' sight, sound, and touch as impetuses for language comprehension and production; examples include videos, manipulatives, and gestures. *Graphic supports* aim to visually and conceptually organize information and related language; they include graphic organizers, tables, time lines, and concept maps. *Interactive supports* tap into the collaborative nature of learning with peers and experts, paired with strategic scaffolding via technology and L1. In the design of performance tasks, these linguistic supports have the potential to foster students' language use while enhancing the authenticity of the product or performance. Consider how we use various supports when we engage in real-world tasks, such as designing instruction using exemplar units (sensory) and UbD planning templates (graphic) with grade-level or departmental teams (interactive). Along with authentic supports for all students' disciplinary language use, teachers can incorporate further supports to target students' needs by language proficiency. As a general rule, supports should decrease in number and intensity as students progress with language (WIDA, 2007). Linguistic supports will be covered in more depth in the next chapter in the discussion on scaffolding Stage 3 instruction for CLD students.

Let's return to the sample social studies unit with the performance task prompting students to assume roles as museum workers to tell the stories of pioneer families for bilingual student visitors. Aligning to Stage 1 goals and responding to overall student abilities, Ms. Piccioni has already opted to use the language-rich, displayed performance task of a museum exhibit. In this performance/product portion of the GRASPS task, she more thoroughly details the performance task with attention to language. For writing, students will create a museum exhibit using photos, artifacts, and writing. For reading, learners will use primary sources and Internet resources to research the pioneer family. Focused on oral language, which includes both listening and speaking, students will give an oral presentation to compare historical and modern pioneers. Still simulating authentic, real-world practice, the teacher calls attention to the four domains with language functions that directly connect to the task at hand.

Figure 5.9 | **Sample WIDA Can Do Descriptors**

By the end of each of the given levels of English language proficiency, English language learners can...

	ELP Level 1 Entering	**ELP Level 2 Emerging**	**ELP Level 3 Developing**	**ELP Level 4 Expanding**	**ELP Level 5 Bridging**	**ELP Level 6 Reaching**
LISTENING	**Process arguments by** • Indicating personal points of view in response to oral phrases or short sentences *(e.g., by thumbs up/ thumbs down; agree/disagree cards)* • Identifying preferences from short oral statements	**Process arguments by** • Distinguishing opinions from facts in peer's oral presentations • Categorizing content-based pictures or objects from oral descriptions *(e.g., "animals that form groups to help members survive")*	**Process arguments by** • Identifying similarities and differences from oral content-related materials or equipment • Identifying different points of view in short oral dialogue	**Process arguments by** • Interpreting oral information from different sides • Identifying opposing sides of arguments in dialogues	**Process arguments by** • Comparing oral arguments with representations and models • Identifying claims in oral presentations	**Process arguments by** • Identifying evidence to support claim/ opinion from multimedia • Following agreed-upon rules for discussions around differing opinions
SPEAKING	**Argues by** • Stating a claim or position from models or examples • Sharing facts as evidence using sentence starters or sentence frames	**Argues by** • Telling what comes next and showing why • Sharing reasons for opinions or claims *(e.g., science experiments)*	**Argues by** • Describing own organizing categories for content-related information *(e.g., fish/birds, forests/deserts)* • Asking and answering questions in collaborative groups	**Argues by** • Defending claims or opinions to content-related topics • Posing different solutions to content-related issues or problems	**Argues by** • Expressing and supporting different ideas with examples • Providing evidence to defend own ideas	**Argues by** • Connecting personal comments to the remarks of others to build a case for ideas or opinions • Summarizing ideas or opinions from two sides

Source: Based on WIDA ELP Standards © 2007, 2012 Board of Regents of the University of Wisconsin System. WIDA is a trademark of the Board of Regents of the University of Wisconsin System. For more information on using the WIDA ELD Standards, please visit the WIDA website at *www.wida.us.* Used with permission.

Figure 5.10 | **Linguistic Supports for Performance Tasks**

Sensory Supports	Graphic Supports	Interactive Supports
Realia and manipulatives	Charts	Pairs or partners
Pictures and photographs	Graphic organizers	Triads or small groups
Illustrations and diagrams	Tables	Cooperative group structures
Magazines and newspapers	Graphs	Use of related technology
Gestures and movement	Time lines	Use of native language
Videos, films, and broadcasts	Number lines	Mentors
Models and figures	Concept maps	

Source: Based on WIDA ELP Standards © 2007, 2012 Board of Regents of the University of Wisconsin System. WIDA is a trademark of the Board of Regents of the University of Wisconsin System. For more information on using the WIDA ELD Standards, please visit the WIDA website at *www.wida.us.* Used with permission.

Within each language domain, the task allows for variability in how students contribute to their small group's creation of exhibits, use of primary sources and Internet resources, and oral presentation. The use of two languages automatically allows for variance in how students use linguistic abilities to collaboratively complete the task; however, let's consider how these performance task details allow for differentiation in one language. Students at early stages of language proficiency might sequence photos and artifacts, label key words and phrases associated with images, and orally state facts from the exhibit, whereas students at later stages might paraphrase stories using primary sources, write detailed interpretations of images, and orally elaborate upon big ideas from the exhibit. Either way, students use language at their proficiency levels to demonstrate disciplinary learning, as well as constructively contribute to the small-group process and product.

The assessment design also incorporates various supports for students to access and develop language while engaging with the task. In a classroom where most students previously had dual-language programming, Ms. Piccioni recognizes the need to foster students' language development and to scaffold access to L2 (whether English or Spanish) through sensory, graphic, and interactive supports. In this way, the museum exhibit task authentically integrates sensory supports (hands-on artifacts and photographs), graphic supports (primary source documents), and interactive supports (cooperative groups based on students' L1). Although it is not explicitly stated in the task itself, students can use supports that are consistently integrated into classroom instruction, such as Spanish-English bilingual dictionaries and personal glossaries compiled throughout the unit. The teacher strategically suggests additional supports based on individual students' abilities and needs.

[handwritten margin note: Early learners may use pics to associate stories]

[handwritten margin note: Others will use primary sources to story-tell]

Success criteria. To round out performance task design, this final element prompts instructional designers to connect back to Stage 1 goals by defining the criteria that will be used to evaluate performances and products. Performance tasks aim to measure students' progress toward Stage 1 goals, including transfer goals and meaning goals requiring authentic, real-world application of learning, and related acquisition goals. In this way, criteria on performance tasks should emerge from the Stage 1 goals for disciplinary learning and language development. Using the overall themes of the unit goals, evaluative criteria should respond to the most salient features of the authentic task. Wiggins and McTighe (2012) organize criteria into categories: content (Was the work accurate?), process (Was the approach sound?), impact (Was the work effective?), and quality (Was the performance/product of high quality?). Whereas content-focused criteria prioritize disciplinary learning, process-focused criteria prioritize language development—highlighting how students use language to engage with and complete the task.

After defining criteria aligned to Stage 1 goals, the next step is to develop detailed rubrics for scoring performance tasks and capturing valuable data on students' disciplinary learning and language development. Educators opt between two types: (1) *holistic rubrics*, which provide an overall rating of students' performance to yield one score, or (2) *analytic rubrics*, which divide performances and products into distinct dimensions to evaluate and glean more detailed feedback. Designed to capture multiple aspects of performance tasks, analytic rubrics allow teachers to evaluate students' language development as embedded in disciplinary tasks. For content criteria focused on disciplinary learning, rubrics aim to evaluate students' understanding, ranging from novice to expert (Wiggins & McTighe, 2012). For process criteria prioritizing language development, rubrics should correspond to students' language proficiency levels, ranging from emergent to proficient. Using preplanning data on students' language abilities, paired with readings and resources detailing how language develops as embedded in disciplinary learning (e.g., Gottlieb, 2006; O'Malley & Pierce, 1996; WIDA, 2012, 2016; Wiggins & McTighe, 2012), teachers draft rubrics that respond to students' abilities and maintain the rigor of disciplinary learning.

Stage 1 goals provide the starting place to define criteria for the pioneer unit task. Drawing from the unit goals, the teacher defines six evaluative criteria: *A successful exhibit will be historically accurate, detailed, well-crafted, revealing and informative, and effective, with a clear oral presentation* (Wiggins & McTighe, 2011). Content criteria focus on the *historical accuracy* and nuances, or *details* of pioneer stories, which align to meaning goals (e.g., "People move for various reasons...") and acquisition goals (e.g., facts, related terms) and prompt students to demonstrate unit learning using disciplinary language. Process criteria hone in on language domains and functions as embedded in disciplinary learning:

[handwritten margin note: Ask yourself the right questions to grade]

[handwritten margin note: Stage 1 goals should kind of outline what you're looking for.]

well-crafted relates to reading and interpreting primary sources, *revealing and informative* relates to writing and crafting the story, and *clear oral presentation* relates to comparing historical and current experiences of pioneers. Impact and quality merge in the criterion of *overall effectiveness* of the exhibit, including the prioritized goal requiring bilingual communication of information.

Using these evaluative criteria that link Stage 1 goals with Stage 2 tasks, Ms. Piccioni fleshes out an analytic rubric to represent what students can do at each performance level—considering both disciplinary learning and language development. She drafts the rubric based on the particular students in her 6th grade classroom, which includes bilingual students with language that is *expanding* (WIDA Level 4), *bridging* (WIDA Level 5), and *reaching* (WIDA Level 6). She uses WIDA's *performance definitions* (WIDA, 2012) and Can Do Descriptors for 6th grade (WIDA, 2016) to first understand what her students can do with language at each proficiency level and then provide corresponding expectations at each performance level. The final rubric, shown in Figure 5.11, maintains the overall authenticity and flexibility of the performance task but hones in on particular elements in order to evaluate students' dynamic disciplinary learning and language development.

Overall considerations and revisions

As just described, performance tasks with a language lens emerge when we design tasks that (1) provide evidence of students' learning and language development as aligned to Stage 1 goals, (2) simulate real-world situations that authentically integrate language, (3) require transfer of learning while connecting to students' background knowledge, (4) integrate linguistic scaffolds allowing learners to demonstrate progress, and (5) provide evidence of discipline-specific language development. The GRASPS elements support task design to simulate real-world application by prompting students to work toward authentic goals, assume unique roles, target specific audiences, consider nuanced situations, plan products or performances, and meet success criteria. After drafting tasks with cultural and linguistic lenses, we revise narratives so that students can equitably access and engage with tasks (see Figure 5.12). We want to ensure the narrative does not disadvantage students by using language that is unnecessary or misaligned to unit learning. For example, the narrative for the pioneer unit task conveys the needed information by using student-friendly words and phrases and simple sentences with one idea or direction per sentence. The teacher also plans to provide bilingual narrative aligned to task expectations.

We would be remiss if we closed this section without discussing how performance tasks connect to grading within units of study, particularly for ELs who are developing L2 at the same time they are learning math, science, social studies, language arts, and other disciplines. In short, students' performance should

Figure 5.11 | **Pioneer Spirit Performance Task and Rubric**

Criteria	NOVICE	PROFICIENT	EXPERT
Historically Accurate	Designs a museum exhibit about pioneer life that is inaccurate; numerous errors detract from the exhibit.	Produces a museum exhibit about pioneer life that is generally accurate; minor inaccuracies do not affect the overall exhibit.	Creates a museum exhibit about pioneer life that is completely accurate; all facts and concepts are correct.
Good Detail	Includes scant details of the pioneer family's story and uses general terminology and language.	Integrates some details of the pioneer family's story and uses related content terminology and language.	Captures ample details of the pioneer family's story and uses appropriate content terminology and language.
Well-Crafted (*Reading*)	Identifies and orders narrative, visuals, and artifacts using primary sources and web research. (*Level 4—Expanding*)	Sequences main ideas, events, and conclusions and matches to content-related concepts of pioneer life. (*Level 5—Bridging*)	Evaluates primary sources and resources in detail to introduce, illustrate, and elaborate on pioneer story. (*Level 6—Reaching*)
Revealing and Informative (*Writing*)	Tells story of one pioneer family by reproducing the sequence of events using transitional words. (*Level 4—Expanding*)	Summarizes the sequence of the pioneer family's story by recounting events using multiple sources. (*Level 5—Bridging*)	Conveys the story sequence by signaling shifts from one time frame to another and showing relationships among detailed events. (*Level 6—Reaching*)
Clear Oral Presentation (*Speaking*)	Paraphrases and summarizes content-related ideas to compare historic and current pioneers. (*Level 4—Expanding*)	Evaluates the significance and evolution of the pioneer spirit throughout history to the present day. (*Level 5—Bridging*)	Extends comparisons of historic and current pioneers by building on others' ideas and questions. (*Level 6—Reaching*)
Effective Exhibit	Designs an exhibit in one language that is somewhat effective in telling the story of one pioneer family.	Produces an exhibit that is partially bilingual and generally effective in telling the story of one pioneer family.	Creates an exhibit that is completely bilingual and highly effective in telling the story of one pioneer family.

be graded based on individualized expectations that directly correspond to their levels of language proficiency. They should *not* be evaluated by the same linguistic standards as English-proficient students or graded down for performing or producing language that is developmentally appropriate. Remember that L2 learning is a complex developmental process that takes 4 to 10 years. During that time, we want to encourage—not penalize—language development. Critically consider your use of the rubrics described previously to target and measure students' language as embedded in discipline-specific performance tasks. For discipline-specific rubric criteria, the strategic design of culturally and linguistically responsive performance tasks should glean data that can be tied to and graded based on progress toward Stage 1 goals. Language-specific rubric criteria, detailing expectations for student performance based distinctly on levels of language proficiency, either should not be factored in to students' grades or should be weighed more lightly than discipline-specific criteria. Instead, the language-specific data should be used to dynamically track students' progress and inform future instruction—a topic that will be discussed in more depth later in this chapter.

Figure 5.12 | **Linguistic Considerations, Questions, and Prompts for Performance Tasks**

Linguistic Consideration	Questions and Prompts for Task Revisions

Vocabulary Usage
 Word-level demands
	• Does the task narrative contain any words or phrases that may be unknown or unclear with regard to the task?
	   - Avoid unnecessary use of words with multiple meanings.
	   - Replace terms and phrases that do not align with the unit of study.

Language Conventions
 Sentence-level demands
	• Does the task narrative contain unnecessary or complex linguistic structures that might encumber students' comprehension?
	   - Restate and revise complex and compound sentences containing grammatical structures such as *if-then* clauses and conditionals.
	   - Use the active voice, rather than the passive voice.

Linguistic Complexity
 Discourse-level demands
	• Does the task narrative contain the information needed to successfully engage with the performance task?
	   - Reduce any redundant and superfluous information that may unnecessarily weigh down students while reading.
	   - Use bullets, fonts, and other formatting techniques to organize the task and highlight specific information.

Linguistic Medium
 Bilingual considerations
	• Does the task narrative align with language(s) used for learning during instruction?
	   - Use students, teachers, or parents to support translation of task narrative to support multiple students' access.
	   - Revise translations based on students' L1 varieties (e.g., a folder is *un cuaderno* in Mexico and *una carpeta* in Argentina).

Accumulating Supplementary Evidence of Learning

Whereas performance tasks prioritize transfer and meaning goals, other evidence should be collected to determine mastery of all unit goals. Supplementary evidence includes both *formative assessments* of learning goals throughout a unit to inform instruction, such as quizzes and journals; and *summative assessments* of learning goals at the close of a unit, such as traditional end-of-unit tests. Collecting multiple sources of data ensures that students have varied opportunities and mediums to demonstrate learning, and provides ample information to inform instruction—assembling a photo album rather than a single snapshot of student performance (Wiggins & McTighe, 2005). Using a procedure similar to that used for performance tasks, we design, select, and revise summative and formative assessment tools to enhance validity by reducing cultural and linguistic bias. In this way, assessments (1) measure content knowledge and skills, rather than language proficiency, (2) tap into students' backgrounds, rather than require ancillary knowledge, (3) authentically integrate content and language, and (4) maintain cognitive complexity while reducing language demands.

Summative Assessment and Language

Non-performance-based summative assessments typically take the form of traditional paper-and-pencil tests. Particularly in later grades in middle and high school settings, teachers may opt to use summative tests in addition to performance-based measures to collect data corresponding to all learning goals, as well as to prepare students for procedures related to state-mandated standardized tests. Traditional tests are often straightforward, easy-to-score tools that inform teachers about students' mastery of acquisition goals, such as declarative knowledge of facts and terminology and discipline-specific discrete skills. Nonetheless, assessments can be fraught with bias, requiring analyses with lenses on language and culture to ensure that the tools yield valid and reliable data on disciplinary learning. Remember that the overarching goal for summative tests should be to evaluate students' content-related knowledge and skills rather than to assess language proficiency or background knowledge.

Before using summative tests with CLD students, teachers should analyze the assessment tool for *linguistic bias* to ensure that they assess Stage 1 disciplinary learning without unnecessary language demands and requirements. By their very nature, tests require students to use language to demonstrate learning, particularly reading and writing. Nevertheless, the goal is to measure discipline-specific knowledge and skills without placing certain students at a disadvantage due to language background or proficiency level. The full text of testing tools—including both test directions and all test items—should be drafted, analyzed, and revised with a lens on linguistic bias, specifically reducing unnecessary language demands at the word/phrase, sentence, and discourse levels that may place particular students at a disadvantage.

Selected-response test items rely heavily upon reading. Students read questions or prompts and respond by selecting between options. Examples of item types include multiple choice, binary choice, matching items, and interpretive exercises (see Figure 5.13). In addition to being contrived and inauthentic (rarely

Figure 5.13 | **Considerations for Summative Test Items**

	Item Type	Definition	Linguistic Considerations
Selected Response	Multiple choice	Question or statement stem with alternatives to select	• Use clear, direct, simple stems. • Avoid negatively stated stems. • Maintain syntactical consistency between stem and alternatives. • Keep alternatives short. • Place alternatives in logical order (e.g., alphabetical).
	Binary choice	Statements with two options to select (e.g., yes/no, true/false)	• Focus item on a single concept. • Avoid negative statements. • Never use double negatives.
	Matching	List of premises to match with correct responses	• Use fairly brief lists on one page. • Include similar items in each list (e.g., nouns, verb infinitive). • List responses in logical order.
	Interpretive	Information or data (e.g., map) with several questions	• Use items from everyday life. • Align with classroom instruction. • Be clear in introductory material.
Constructed Response	Completion	Incomplete statement requiring word or phrase response	• Paraphrase classroom texts. • Craft to reduce correct options. • Insert blank at end of sentence. • Only use one blank per item. • Avoid required verb agreement.
	Short answer	Brief student-generated written response to an item	• Draft items as direct questions. • Seek brief, unique responses. • Supply sufficient answer space. • Make all answer spaces equal.
	Essay	Extended student-generated written response to a prompt	• Explicitly outline the task. • Specify response length. • Use more questions requiring shorter answers. • Provide a reasonable number of options for student selection.

Source: Based on *Classroom Assessment: Principles and Practice for Effective Standards-based Instruction* (6th ed.), by James McMillan, 2013, New York: Pearson.

do we engage in similar exercises in the real world), selected-response items are often laden with linguistic demands and inconsistencies that make them difficult for students to decipher and maneuver. Multiple-choice items, common in summative tests, often use long-winded stems and alternatives that require multiple readings. Although certain alternatives may be grounded in disciplinary learning, distractors might require certain knowledge of unknown words and phrases. The use of negative stems and statements in multiple- and binary-choice items can interrupt students' interpretation with only one word. Multiple-choice and matching items with long lists of options in no particular order add another layer of linguistic demands for students. Although selected-response items can be worthwhile to glean information on students' declarative knowledge, such as content-related facts and concepts, valid and reliable tools must reduce any linguistic bias.

Constructed-response items typically require both reading and writing, as students read questions or prompts and respond by constructing answers in the form of words, sentences, or extended narrative corresponding to completion, short-answer, and essay items (see Figure 5.13). Although these are slightly more authentic than selected-response items, more potential linguistic biases emerge because students must use both receptive and productive language. Similar to the situation with selected-response items, the stems or prompts requiring reading should be brief and clear, with direct questions and explicit expectations. When drafting essay items with multiple options, teachers should weigh the time required for students to read, comprehend, and select one option. When considering students' written production, teachers must be particularly cognizant of rubrics and procedures for scoring. If the constructed-response items align to specific goals for disciplinary learning, such as completing sentences about the westward expansion or explaining the interactions between pioneers and Native Americans, then students should not be scored down for errors in spelling and grammar. Students can demonstrate disciplinary learning while still developing English proficiency, and effective practitioners look to pull out related ideas without pulling out the red pen to highlight errors. Therefore, we can reduce linguistic bias by crafting clear prompts and questions and remaining focused on disciplinary learning goals when evaluating student responses.

In addition to linguistic bias in the form of unnecessary language demands, *cultural bias* emerges in summative tests when students need certain background knowledge to correctly select or construct responses. We have emphasized the lens on culturally specific background knowledge throughout this book, underscoring its importance when seeking to provide equitable opportunities for CLD students to demonstrate learning. In short, cultural bias refers to assessments that require ancillary background knowledge unrelated to disciplinary learning. A good example comes from the time one of the authors spent teaching in

Arizona, where she came across a 3rd grade reading test measuring students' ability to interpret functional text. The interpretive task, entitled Ants on a Log, required use of a recipe to answer a series of multiple-choice items. Readers who grew up in a particular era and locale may know that *ants on a log* refers to celery sticks lined with peanut butter and raisins. For the large majority of Latino students in Phoenix, this would be an unfamiliar snack, placing them at a disadvantage to interpret the recipe and respond to test items. Students labeled as ELs had additional difficulty, as many read the words literally rather than figuratively, perceiving the text to be about insects on a tree. To reduce cultural bias and glean more valid and reliable data on students' ability to interpret functional texts, the test could have been revised to include a recipe for a food from students' everyday lives, such as tamales or pizza.

To reduce both cultural and linguistic bias to maximize the validity and reliability of results with CLD students, we need assessment tools that factor in students' diverse backgrounds and abilities, which vary by classroom and community. Thus we recommend teachers begin with Stage 1 learning goals and independently create summative assessment tools, rather than using form tests or test items from textbooks or prescribed curricula. On the whole, tests in U.S.-based curricula and settings are typically written for and normed with English-dominant students from mainstream backgrounds (such as those who have eaten the snack called ants on a log). As a result, these tests do not consistently glean valid and reliable data for CLD students. If form tests must be used, whether per practitioner preference or school or district policy, teachers should critically analyze and thoroughly revise test directions and items to provide fair and suitable evidence appropriate to students' heterogeneous cultural backgrounds and linguistic abilities.

Along with analyzing and revising the actual assessment tools, teachers should consider modifying the assessment procedure used when students take tests. *Accommodations* can enhance the validity of traditional testing results by specifically altering the timing, setting, presentation, or response expectations based on individual students' learning needs, particularly for students labeled as ELs (Rivera, Collum, Willner, & Sia, 2005). Teachers might provide extended time to complete assessments, factoring in the additional cognitive and linguistic processing time needed in two languages. They might present test directions and items in students' L1 and allow use of bilingual dictionaries or resource materials. To ensure the focus on disciplinary learning, students could be allowed to use word-processing software with spelling and grammar checking for constructed-response items. Accommodations should not be used randomly but selected specifically in response to individual students' needs and provided consistently in classroom assessments and instruction across contexts.

Formative Assessment and Language

In addition to summative assessments, teachers should amass supplementary evidence throughout units of study. Formative assessment happens during instruction and includes (1) formal data collection where students directly participate in the assessment activity (e.g., academic prompts, quizzes) and (2) informal (or anecdotal) data collection where teachers gather data without direct student involvement (e.g., observations, dialogues; see Figure 5.14). Whether using formal or informal measures, the overarching goal is to collect authentic data of student learning and language development tied to unit goals. Remember that we conceptualize (and therefore measure) language development as embedded in disciplinary learning. Thus we design formative assessments to simultaneously capture data on students' language and content abilities. We want to evaluate students' progress toward acquiring linguistic knowledge and skills, such as academic terminology or disciplinary writing, but we do so by embedding assessments in content-based learning—no separate spelling tests or grammar drills.

Figure 5.14 | **Types of Formative Assessments and Related Linguistic Considerations**

Assessment Type	Definition	Linguistic Considerations
Academic Prompts	Open-ended questions or problems for students to solve and respond	• Design to require rich language usage as embedded in disciplinary thinking. • Provide appropriate scaffolds for students' language development (e.g., graphic organizer, L1 partners).
Quizzes	Test-like items to assess acquisition (e.g., terminology, discrete skills)	• Organize quiz items consistently. • Use clear and direct language aligned to disciplinary learning in classroom. • Provide appropriate accommodations.
Observations	Examination of student learning through interaction and work samples	• Observe various learning events to capture language functions and domains. • Use procedures to document data aligned to unit goals (e.g., checklist).
Dialogues	Communication with students either orally or in writing	• Use oral dialogue assesses listening and speaking and written dialogue to assess reading and writing. • Use discipline-specific questions and prompts, differentiated by language background and proficiency.
Checks for Understanding	Students' self-evaluation of learning during instruction	• Design checks for understanding that prompt multiple language domains (not only speaking or writing). • Integrate self-assessment toward goals for disciplinary learning, as well as language development.

Formal formative measures are integrated into Stage 2 instructional design for implementation throughout units of study. When teachers formally collect evidence, students explicitly know that they are being assessed through tools including academic prompts and quizzes (McTighe & Wiggins, 2004). Typically corresponding with meaning goals, *academic prompts* are open-ended, critical-thinking questions or problems for students to collaboratively or independently respond to and solve. Students authentically use disciplinary language to engage in cognitive processing related to unit learning, often spanning language domains—for example, reading the prompt, listening and speaking with a small group, writing the response. *Quizzes* use test-like items to assess acquisition goals—such as terminology, facts, and discrete skills—during units of study that should be drafted with the same linguistic considerations as summative tests.

In the social studies unit focused on the pioneer experience, various formal assessments are integrated during instruction to capture multiple sources of data on students' progress toward learning goals. Using dialogue journals, the teacher has students respond to academic prompts, specifically taking the perspectives of both pioneers and Native Americans. Quizzes throughout the unit assess students' knowledge of facts about the westward movement, pioneer life, and Native American tribes and their interactions with settlers. These supplementary sources of evidence provide the teacher with valuable information to formally grade and track student learning, specifically corresponding to Stage 1 goals.

Conversely, informal formative measures do not directly involve students or contribute to their larger course grade. Aligned with Stage 3 learning events, these data sources emerge as students engage in disciplinary learning, such as peer interactions, teacher conversations, and various products and artifacts. Educators use procedures such as observational notes, checklists, and rubrics to anecdotally document students' progress toward unit goals during instruction. *Observations* and *dialogues* are the overarching categories for anecdotal data collection during instruction, including various ideas presented in Chapter 3: think-alouds, interviews, conferences, dialogue journals, observational checklists, and student work samples. Depending on the quality and quantity of anecdotal data collected, informal formative assessments can be used to capture students' progress toward both meaning goals and acquisition goals. For example, individual student conferences might yield data related to understandings (and misunderstandings), whereas observational checklists can provide quick snapshots of students' knowledge and skills. In the social studies unit, informal formative assessments target particular Stage 1 acquisition goals and include analyzing personal glossaries—lists of unit terms with drawings and bilingual translations—and observing reader responses and discussions as students interpret various texts, such as oral histories, time lines, and letters.

In addition to ongoing assessments in which teachers collect supplementary evidence formally, through such means as academic prompts and quizzes, and informally, through observations and dialogues, *checks for understanding* provide data points centered on students' self-evaluation of learning and progress toward goals. Typically integrated into every lesson within larger units of study, checks for understanding are strategically planned learning events that prompt students to cognitively reflect upon their learning and share their reflections using related disciplinary language. Common examples include reflective probes regarding learning and lingering questions (e.g., 3-2-1, circle-square-triangle) or rapid responses to essential questions or disciplinary prompts (e.g., one-minute essay, quick write, exit ticket, timed pair-share). Regardless of the strategy used to collect evidence, self-assessment data can inform future instruction—for example, by identifying concepts, ideas, or terminology requiring additional attention in subsequent lessons. Because these are embedded directly in instruction, we will discuss and provide additional examples of formative assessments and checks for understanding when considering Stage 3 in Chapters 6 and 7.

Ongoing Monitoring of Student Progress

By integrating multiple opportunities to collect evidence of student learning into instructional units of study, teachers will find themselves with ample data on students' learning and development to inform future instruction. In Chapter 3, we explored pertinent preplanning steps, which centered on collecting and analyzing data to better understand learners' sociocultural, cognitive, linguistic, and academic dimensions (Collier & Thomas, 2007; Herrera, 2016). In addition to diagnostic assessments at the beginning of the year, such as home visits and community walks, teachers should use performance tasks, as well as supplementary assessments embedded in units, to monitor student progress throughout the academic year. At the close of each unit, educators can update the Holistic Student Profile (HSP) with new information across sociocultural, cognitive, linguistic, and academic dimensions and evaluate progress toward long-term goals. In this way, teachers maintain the HSP to accurately capture the complexity and dynamism of students' learning and development, which helps them to design instruction that best supports and fosters progress toward course-level goals.

The *sociocultural dimension* focuses on how social and cultural processes influence learning, including the background knowledge and experiences that students bring into the classroom (Collier & Thomas, 2007). Diagnostic data have already informed sociocultural dimensions of the HSP, including basic information on students' background (e.g., age, grade, country of origin), as well as anecdotal notes regarding sources of background knowledge from home, community, and school (Herrera, 2016). When strategically designed and implemented in UbD units, formative assessments, such as oral or written dialogues and observations of students' social interactions, can provide insight into students' backgrounds. For summative tests, selected-response items rarely provide insight into students' backgrounds, but strategically crafted constructed-response items can allow students to draft short answers or essays using cultural and linguistic background knowledge. Similarly, well-designed performance tasks that tap into students' backgrounds can provide in-depth information to build on profiles of students' background knowledge and experiences.

The *cognitive dimension* centers on how a student's brain processes and learns, specifically considering how culture uniquely shapes students' thought, knowledge, learning, and development (Collier & Thomas, 2007; Herrera, 2016; Rogoff, 2003). Preplanning data can provide diagnostic information regarding students' cognitive dimension, including formal labels related to cognitive abilities (e.g., gifted, IEP, RTI tier), as well as observations of student processing, learning preferences, and preferred grouping. Ongoing assessments embedded in instructional units can be purposefully designed to glean data on students' cognitive dimension. For example, formative assessments might include think-alouds to capture student processing, self-evaluations to capture learning preferences, and observations to capture preferred grouping. Similarly, summative tests might integrate constructed-response items that prompt students to describe thought processes and problem-solving strategies. Central to gleaning data on transfer goals and meaning goals, performance tasks should first allow for multiple ways of making meaning and then incorporate teacher, peer, and self-evaluations of how various students solved problems or planned performances.

The *linguistic dimension* focuses explicitly on language, including students' L1, L2, and the interconnection between languages, language varieties, and linguistic repertoires (Collier & Thomas, 2007; Herrera, 2016). Standardized proficiency tests provide diagnostic data on the linguistic dimension, particularly for students currently or previously labeled as ELs. Additionally, the HSP should include preliminary notes on students' language preferences and bilingual abilities. After designing language-rich performance tasks with attention to background knowledge and language proficiency, teachers can gather data from students' rubric scores on language-specific criteria. Formative measures (word-, sentence-, and discourse-level knowledge indicators, and skill indicators by language function and domain) can also attend to language, whether embedded in disciplinary learning or specific to language-focused acquisition goals. In summative tests, selected-response items might specifically attend to knowledge (e.g., multiple-choice items on word or phrase definitions, interpretive tasks related to text structures and features), whereas constructed-response items can provide writing to analyze for language development (e.g., vocabulary usage, grammatical constructions, transfer errors).

The *academic dimension* refers to school-based learning across disciplines, including language arts, mathematics, science, social studies, and fine arts (Collier & Thomas, 2007; Herrera, 2016). Diagnostic data inform students' academic dimension, including students' content test scores, as well as anecdotal data on students' content-specific abilities and perceptions of self-efficacy. In addition to these formal and anecdotal data collected and analyzed to begin the school year, performance, summative, and formative assessments can provide dynamic data on students' academic abilities as they progress through disciplinary units of study. Consistent incorporation of formative tools for self-evaluation can also support teachers' ongoing understanding of students' self-efficacy within and across disciplines. Teachers should be wary of using data from non-teacher-designed summative tests, which may not produce valid and reliable results. As mentioned earlier, most traditional and standardized tests are normed with white, English-dominant students, so even established tools may not yield data that accurately add to the Holistic Student Profile.

Through the performance tasks at the center of UbD instruction, along with various formative assessments during units and summative assessments at the close of units, students have frequent and authentic opportunities to demonstrate disciplinary learning and language development. Teachers can use these assessments as rich sources of data that depict the complexity and dynamism of student learning and can inform future instruction, rather than relying on static and dated information often collected early in the school year. By using the HSP or another consistent procedure, teachers can document and organize these multiple sources of data to monitor students' progress toward learning and developmental goals spanning sociocultural, cognitive, linguistic, and academic dimensions. This is the heart of culturally and linguistically responsive practice—moving beyond homogenous labels to place students' dynamic abilities, strengths, and needs at the center of UbD instructional design and classroom practice. These data will then directly inform instructional design, particularly in Stage 3, which is the focus of the next chapter.

Classroom Application: Assessment and Evidence of Learning

Drawing from the lenses on language development in Stage 2 as described in this chapter, we now shift to consider the specifics of classroom application. In this section, we detail the steps for integrating language into Stage 2 of the UbD template, with the goal of providing all learners equitable access to opportunities to demonstrate learning on assessments.

Design Language-Rich Performance Tasks Aligned to Learning Goals

Using the learning goals defined in Stage 1, determine the evidence needed to demonstrate student learning. First, use the six facets of understanding to identify needed evidence via performance verbs and disciplinary generalizations, such as what students must explain, interpret, or apply related to unit learning. Then, flesh out possible performances into appropriate, authentic, language-rich tasks for students to demonstrate understanding. Consider students' abilities and needs when designing performance tasks—oral, written, or displayed—to gauge progress toward learning goals.

Analyze and Revise Assessment Tools for Cultural and Linguistic Bias

All students need equitable opportunities to demonstrate progress toward unit goals. After drafting the performance task, critically consider the background knowledge needed to make meaning and actively engage with it. Analyze the language needed to access the task and demonstrate disciplinary learning. You want students to transfer learning to new contexts without disadvantaging particular students based on cultural or linguistic backgrounds. To ensure equity and emphasize the value of bilingualism, deliberate how you might authentically integrate students' L1 in performance tasks.

Differentiate Assessments and Rubrics by Language Proficiency

After drafting and refining language-rich performances and products aligned to Stage 1 goals, differentiate tasks for the individual learners in your classroom, paying particular attention to how to allow your ELs to demonstrate disciplinary learning. Integrate appropriate sensory, graphic, and interactive supports to provide equitable access for students at varying language proficiency levels. Design rubric criteria and performance indicators to attend to and capture students' language development. Revise the overall task directions with attention to language demands, and provide directions in students' L1 as needed.

Collect Supplementary Evidence of Learning and Language Development

In addition to performance tasks, consider how to collect other evidence to measure students' progress toward all transfer, meaning, and acquisition goals. Strategically integrate opportunities to capture student learning, using vehicles such as tests, quizzes, prompts, journals, and work samples. Use assessment tools to glean data to inform all Stage 1 learning goals without disadvantaging students based on cultural background knowledge or language proficiency levels. Doing so allows you to holistically capture students' disciplinary learning and language development.

Design Procedures to Monitor Progress Toward Long-Term Goals

Nuanced understandings of unique and individual students' backgrounds, abilities, and needs drive instructional planning. As described in Chapter 3, diagnostic data should be collected and analyzed to understand students' holistic profiles. To capture the complexity and dynamism of a student's growth and progress throughout an academic year, design procedures to collect, analyze, and track data from classroom assessments embedded in instruction. At the close of each unit, update student profiles using the multiple sources of evidence collected and analyzed across the unit of study.

Classroom Snapshot: Assessing Student Learning

Mr. Luke Carman is a middle school mathematics teacher at Albany Park Multicultural Academy (APMA) in the Albany Park neighborhood of Chicago, which serves approximately 300 7th and 8th graders from 16 different language backgrounds. Approximately 10 percent of APMA students use English as their primary language at home, which means the remaining 270 students use diverse languages from around the world, including Spanish, Arabic, Khmer, Gujarati, Tagalog, Romanian, Somali, Urdu, and Vietnamese. Seventy-two percent of these middle schoolers are Spanish-dominant, with family origins spanning multiple countries in North America, Central America, South America, and the Caribbean. Despite the ample linguistic diversity in homes and communities, most students have developed English proficiency at school before arriving at the middle school setting. Thus 16 percent of students are labeled as EL, including long-term ELs who have been in Chicago schools since elementary school, and newcomers from various countries around the world. Organized by discipline (e.g., language arts, social studies, science), 20 teachers guide the learning of students at APMA, including Mr. Carman, who teaches mathematics to 60 7th graders and 60 8th graders. In his unit of study focused on systems of equations (see Figure 5.15), he maintains a lens on language in UbD instructional design to ensure his students have equitable access to mathematical understandings, processes, and practices.

Using Stage 1 goals and the six facets of understanding to brainstorm possible performances for students to demonstrate learning, Mr. Carman and his middle school departmental team[1] flesh out the *career counselor* performance task (see Figure 5.16). Together, they strategically craft the GRASPS task to tap into his students' background knowledge, particularly as it relates to the audience of self-employed individuals, including parents and community members

---

[1]APMA teachers collaboratively plan UbD units and corresponding assessments. For this unit, Luke Carman collaborated with math teachers Devansi Patel and Karoline Sharp Towner, as well as special education teacher Brandy Velazquez and ESL teacher Teresa Garcia.

Figure 5.15 | Mr. Carman's Middle School Mathematics Unit

Stage 1—Desired Results

Established Goals

CCSS-Math-8.EE.C.8: Analyze and solve pairs of simultaneous linear equations.

CCSS-Math-8.EE.C.8a: Understand that solutions to a system of two linear equations in two variables correspond to points of intersection of their graphs, because points of intersection satisfy both equations simultaneously.

CCSS-Math-8.EE.C.8b: Solve systems of two linear equations in two variables algebraically, and estimate solutions by graphing the equations. Solve simple cases by inspection.

CCSS-Math-8.EE.C.8c: Solve real-world and mathematical problems leading to two linear equations in two variables.

CCSS-Math-8.F.A.3: Interpret the equation $y=mx+b$ as defining a linear function, whose graph is a straight line; give examples of functions that are not linear.

Transfer

Students will be able to independently use their learning to…

- Make critical decisions about which strategies are most effective to solve a variety of real-world problems in math and beyond.

Meaning

Essential Questions

Students will keep considering…

- How can you manipulate information into a particular representation for a specific purpose?
- What's the value in having multiple ways to solve systems of equations?

Understandings

Students will understand that…

- There are many ways to represent linear equations.
- Being able to use multiple strategies to move between representations will build a deeper understanding of linear relationships in the world.
- There are many ways to solve systems of equation problems.
- Having a flexible understanding of linear equations allows you to select the most appropriate way to solve a systems problem.

Acquisition

Students will be skilled at…

- Translating $y=mx+b$ into standard form and vice versa.
- Testing real number values to see which make an equation true.
- Solving linear equation in two variables by graphing and algebraic methods.
- Testing values to see if they make all equations in a system true.
- Solving systems of linear equations with strategies (graphing and finding the point of intersection, writing all equations in $y=mx+b$, substituting and solving, using combinations to eliminate variable).
- Identifying systems with no and infinite solutions by graphing.
- Solving problems that involve systems of linear equations.
- Comparing and contrasting lines with varying equations.
- Explaining the appropriate method for finding the system of equations.

Students will know…

- $Ax+By=C$ as linear, standard form.
- Linear equation in $Ax+By=C$ form has infinitely many solutions (x, y).
- The forms $Ax+By=C$ and $y=mx+b$ are equivalent for linear equations.
- Options for solving systems of equations (i.e., no solution, one solution, infinite solutions).
- Solving a system of linear equations is the same as finding a value that makes all equations true.
- Strategies for solving problems.
- Related vocabulary (e.g., slope, intercept, coefficient).
- Everyday words used in new ways (e.g., intersection, solution, addition, substitution, cancellation, variable, combination).
- Lexical bundles (e.g., dependent variable, inverse operations).
- The use and reference of variables.
- Comparative sentence structures.
- Discourse for sequential directions.

(continued)

Figure 5.15 | **Mr. Carman's Middle School Mathematics Unit—**(*continued*)

	Stage 2—Evidence
Evaluative Criteria	**Assessment Evidence**
Real-world career overview Graphic representation Accurate algebraic solutions Math-based argument Mathematical language	**Performance Task(s)** **Career Counselor** Your goal is to find the point where a business will be profitable. You and your partner are career counselors for people who are self-employed, including Uber driver, hair stylist, personal trainer, neighborhood mechanic renting garage space, tutor, and food-truck operator renting kitchen space. A new client walks in and explains that she wants to make a career change. She is asking you what she needs to do to make money in her new career. You need to make an argument to your client about when and how to make a profit in her career. You need to inform the client exactly what she will need to do to be profitable, offering advice about whether you think this is a good career for her or not. Your presentation will need to include (1) an overview of what the expenses and revenues are for the career, (2) a graph representation of expenses and revenues, (3) an algebraic solution to the system of expenses and revenues, and (4) convincing advice about the career, which includes evidence from your graph or algebra solution.
Accurate algebraic solutions Thorough testing of values Graphic representations Narrative explanations	**Supplementary Evidence** • Check-up quiz—Investigation #1 • Check-up quiz—Investigation #2 • Partner quiz—Investigation #3 • Check-up quiz—Inequalities

Stage 3—Learning Plan

Pre-assessment

• Accessing prior knowledge and building background for unit learning: Word-based prompts to tap into previous school-based math learning (i.e., slope, intercept, coefficient, intersection, solution, addition, substitution, cancellation, variable, combination, dependent variable, inverse operations).

Learning Events

• Demonstration and application with Desmos (online graphical mathematics platform) to explore standard-form equations and solving systems graphically (for both Investigation #1 and Investigation #2).

• Modeling and discussion in L1 pairs: Matching activity to solve systems graphically. Students match equations to figure out where pairs of graphs intersect and orally suggest appropriate method to match equations to graphs. Students listen and interpret partner's suggestions to match equations to graphs.

• Demonstration and application: Substitutions for $y=mx+b$ equations (Investigation #3).

• Inquiry groups: L1 small groups solve systems of linear equations by writing all equations in $y=mx+b$, substituting, and solving. Students write equations using step-by-step directions (in L2, L1 as needed).

• Send-a-problem (video version): Students submit a sample problem via video using iPads, with other students critiquing the solutions the students have provided. Students pick a problem and partners videotape each other solving problems. Students trade with another partner and provide feedback.

• Home extension: Students conduct survey and interview with parents to collect information on *gig economy* jobs in which parents are their own bosses. Place specific evidence on the ways in which parents can share authentic information about expenses and revenue collected.

• Community extension: Students can also connect with strong neighborhood institutions (e.g., Albany Park Community Center, Albany Park Theater, Communities United) to interview others about doing business.

• Performance task: Students have in-class time to complete the Career Counselor performance task.

• Modeling and discussion in heterogeneous small groups based on language proficiency levels: Plotting inequalities on the number line using manipulatives and number lines.

• Demonstration and guided practice in homogenous small groups based on mathematical understandings: Using computer to graph inequalities in two dimensions with teacher support.

Formative Assessments

• Daily checks for understanding (e.g., exit slips, oral explanations)

• Post-investigation self-assessments

• Personal word wall of related math terms with translations, visuals, examples, and explanations

• Language-specific observations using WIDA speaking and listening rubric

• Writing-specific observations of student-produced artifacts using WIDA writing rubric

Source: Used with permission from Luke Carman, Teresa Garcia, Devansi Patel, Karoline Sharp Towner, and Brandy Velazquez, Albany Park Multicultural Academy, Chicago.

who commonly hold jobs such as hair stylist, personal trainer, mechanic, tutor, and food-truck operator. They know that students understand the construct of making money, including the related concepts and terminology of expenses and revenues. Thus they are confident that given the pertinent financial details (e.g., a hair stylist makes $65 per haircut profit with $5 per-haircut expense, $500 per month chair rental fee, $40 renters license, $150 insurance, and $50 for supplies), students can apply their understandings, knowledge, and skills around systems of equations to meaningful, real-world problems. APMA teachers then add the performance expectations that learners will make presentations to explain expenses and revenues, evaluate whether the career will be profitable, and argue whether it is a good or bad career choice. To prompt use of disciplinary language across domains, students will work with strategically selected partners to both draft scripts and perform the oral presentation.

After drafting the GRASPS task and critically considering lenses on students' background knowledge and language abilities, the team defines the specific evaluative criteria for success on the performance task. Aiming to capture both disciplinary learning and related language development, they use the Stage 1 goals to define four criteria for the performance itself—*real-world career overview, graphic representation, accurate algebraic solution, math-based argument*—and one for the narrative reflection using mathematical language that follows the task (see Figure 5.17). Two criteria capture the content, including graphic representations (i.e., understandings of graphs and word-level disciplinary language) and algebraic solutions (i.e., understandings of algebraic solutions, as well as sentence- and discourse-level disciplinary language). Two criteria—real-world career overview and mathematical language—focus on the process, honing in on students' development in the domain of writing. The criterion focused on the career argument captures students' oral language, as well as the impact and quality of the presentation. To draft the indicators for the language-specific criteria, the team uses the WIDA Can Do Descriptors for Grades 6–8 to capture the language development across stages of language proficiency as embedded in algebraic learning. Although the rubric supports the evaluation of learning and language development, the team also designs a student-friendly checklist to guide completion of the performance task (see Figure 5.17). With statements written in clear, concise, first-person language, the student checklist aligns to the rubric criteria (e.g., graphs/graphic representations). And, although Mr. Carman doesn't have any newcomers this year, he knows he can use Google Translate to provide translated versions of the checklist for emergent ELs with L1 literacy skills.

In addition to the authentic, language-rich performance task, Mr. Carman and his colleagues outline other evidence to ensure students' progress toward unit goals for disciplinary learning and language development. As listed in the *Supplementary Evidence* box of the unit plan (see Figure 5.15), they plan to use

Figure 5.16 | **Rubric for Mr. Carman's Performance Task in Middle School Mathematics**

Criteria	NOVICE	PROFICIENT	EXPERT
Career Overview	• Brief description of the career with list of expenses and revenue but without citations from reliable sources • Uses disciplinary language from word banks or sentence stems	• Clear description of the career that includes accurate overview of the connections between expenses and revenue • Uses disciplinary language in appropriate ways to describe the career	• Thorough evaluation of the career in the context of Chicago, with detailed and accurate description of expenses and revenue • Uses disciplinary language in appropriate and nuanced ways to describe the career
Graphic Representation	• Partially accurate solution that is difficult to follow, with unclear connections between lines to table of values and equations • Graph elements are unlabeled (i.e., axes, scale, line equations, independent/dependent variable)	• Generally accurate solution with (a) lines generally connected to table of values *or* equations and (b) point of intersection labeled • Graph elements are partially labeled (i.e., axes, scale, line equations, independent/dependent variable)	• Completely accurate solution with (a) lines clearly connected to table of values *and* equation and (b) point of intersection labeled • All graph elements are clearly labeled (i.e., axes, scale, line equations, independent/dependent variable)
Algebraic Solution	• Both equations have inaccuracies or the solution for the work is not shown • Method of solving is not clearly labeled • Missing one solution; have solution for x or y	• Both equations are somewhat accurate and make sense for the context • Method of solving (e.g., elimination, substation) is labeled and evident • Solution labeled for both x and y variables	• Both equations are completely accurate and make sense for the problem • Solved using more than one method *or* explained use of one particular method • Solutions explained for both x and y variable
Career Argument	• Explanation of the career without a clear argument • Argument shares some evidence to support claims, drawing from abilities in both English and the L1 • Audience is somewhat convinced of argument	• Effective argument that connects career advice with supporting details and evidence • Career advice somewhat supported by graphical and algebraic solutions • Audience is convinced of the argument	• Exceptional argument that clearly defends career advice with specific evidence and claims • Career advice highly supported by graphical and algebraic solutions • Audience is highly convinced of the argument
Mathematical Language	• Narrative reflection reproduces the sequence of events in problem solving, using transitional words • Reflection uses word banks and sentence stems to describe general experiences	• Narrative reflection summarizes conclusions reached from steps in problem solving • Reflection generalizes the good and challenging events in the problem solving process	• Narrative reflection connects and shows relationships between events in problem-solving process • Reflection evaluates what went well and what did not by providing specific examples

Source: Used with permission from Luke Carman, Teresa Garcia, Devansi Patel, Karoline Sharp Towner, and Brandy Velazquez, Albany Park Multicultural Academy, Chicago.

Figure 5.17 | **Student Checklist for Mr. Carman's Performance Task**

Overview	• I gave a detailed description of my career. • I explained why this career is important in Chicago. • I gave a detailed list of expenses and revenue. • I created a hypothesis. • I listed all my sources.
Graphs	• I created a table. • I created a graph consisting of both lines (i.e., expenses, revenue). • I labeled the point of intersection. • I labeled all elements of the graph (i.e., independent and dependent variables, scale, axis titles, line equations).
Equations	• Both equations are evident, with minor algebraic errors. • I used more than one method (e.g., substitution, elimination). • I accurately labeled my methods. • The solution is labeled for both x and y variables.
Argument	• I stated my hypothesis and acknowledged whether I was correct or incorrect. • I gave quality career advice using both my graph and equations. • I used the appropriate vocabulary and language to give career advice.
Reflection	• I described my specific process for solving the problem. • I explained what went well and challenges that I faced. • I reflected upon one thing that I could have done better. • I used specific examples from my project in my reflection.
Sentence Stems	• I created a project that (explain what you did on this project)… • The key concepts I learned in this project were… • Things that went well in my project were… because… • A challenge I had was… It was challenging because… • If I did this project again, I would change…

Source: Used with permission from Luke Carman, Teresa Garcia, Devansi Patel, Karoline Sharp Towner, and Brandy Velazquez, Albany Park Multicultural Academy, Chicago.

check-up quizzes for the three in-class investigations, followed by corresponding self-assessments (listed under *Formative Assessments*). Because of the diversity in his classroom, Mr. Carman analyzes and revises quizzes from the *Connected Math* curriculum to reduce bias and enhance relevance to his students. Drawing on materials from his graduate program on EL teaching and learning, he took an extant rubric originally used to analyze culturally relevant texts (Paulson & Freeman, 2003) and modified it to specifically apply to mathematical word problems for his middle schoolers (see Figure 5.18). By using this rubric himself and with his students, he is able to critically consider if students have the background knowledge to equitably engage with the word problems presented on paper-and-pencil quizzes. He probes relevance based on the problem itself, as well as both the context of the problem (e.g., location, time) and the characters involved (e.g., age, language, experiences). When the word problems receive a lower overall score on the relevance rubric—whether scored by him in advance of the assessment or afterward as a part of students' self-assessments of learning and performance on the corresponding quiz—Mr. Carman recognizes the need to revise and make changes to enhance the validity of results.

Figure 5.18 | **Mr. Carman's Analysis of Word Problems**

Prompt	4	3	2	1
Are the people in the problem like you, your family, and friends?	Just like people I know	No, but they seem similar	No, but I can imagine people like this in the real world	I have never met or can't imagine anyone really being like this
Have you ever lived or visited a place like the one in the problem?	Yes, definitely	No, but someone I know has	No, but I can imagine it	No, and I can't even imagine it
Could this problem take place this year?	Within 5 years	Within 10 years	Within a time I can imagine	Not a near time at all
Do the characters use tools and materials like ones you know about?	Yes, I've used tools or materials like this before	Yes, I've seen tools or materials like this in the real world	No, but I can imagine tools like these or have seen others use them	No, and I've never even been in a context to imagine these tools
How close are the characters in the problem to your age?	Very close (or slightly older, aspirational)	Somewhat close	Not very close	Definitely adults, not close at all
Do the characters in the problem talk like you, your family, or your friends?	That sounds a lot like me	That sounds like someone I know	That doesn't really sound like anyone I know, but I understand it	I don't understand the language being used
How often have you encountered a problem like this one before?	Frequently	I have seen a problem like this before	This problem looks similar but is not the same as others	This is a completely unique and new situation
Have you ever had an experience like the one described in the story?	Yes, more than once	Yes, once	No, but I know someone who has	No
Is this something related to your interests or experiences?	This is super-relevant	I'm kind of interested in this	I will work on this, but it has no intrinsic value	I am completely bored with this problem

Source: Used with permission from Luke Carman, Teresa Garcia, Devansi Patel, Karoline Sharp Towner, and Brandy Velazquez, Albany Park, Multicultural Academy, Chicago.

Whereas the quizzes provide formal measures of learning during the unit of study, Mr. Carman also plans to informally evaluate students' language development while they are engaged in collaborative and authentic disciplinary learning. To accomplish this, he collects artifacts and assignments produced as a part of the unit (e.g., personal word walls, exit slips) and conducts observations of learners engaged in classroom practice (e.g., small-group problem solving, independent application of learning). Using these artifacts and observations as data, Mr. Carman tracks students' language development using a modified WIDA rubric for grades 6–8 (see Figure 5.19). Connecting with the desired results, defined in Stage 1, of the unit on systems of equations, he and his ESL teaching colleague, Ms. Teresa Garcia, differentiate the discipline-specific linguistic expectations based

Figure 5.19 | **Mr. Carman's Disciplinary Language Development Rubric**

	Level 1: Entering	Level 2: Emerging	Level 3: Developing	Level 4: Expanding	Level 5: Bridging
Listening	Match instructional language with visual representations of linear equations.	Identify important systems information in tables and graphs based on oral directions.	Categorize types of two-variable linear equations based on oral directions.	Apply strategies presented orally to new systems of equations contexts.	Make inferences from systems of equations problems read aloud.
Speaking	Identify details of systems of equations with visual cues.	Define details of systems of equations using tables or graphs.	Restate some details about how to solve systems of equations.	Discuss with peers ways to represent many systems of equations.	Explain in detail the ways to represent all systems of equations.
Reading	Identify key language that provides information to solve real-life math problems using visual and graphic supports with a partner.	Identify key language that provides information to solve real-life math problems using labeled visual and graphic supports with a partner.	Identify key language that provides information to solve real-life math problems using graphic supports (e.g., charts, tables).	Identify key language patterns to solve real-life math problems using graphic supports.	Identify key language patterns to solve real-life math problems.
Writing	Show pictorial representations or label terms related to algebraic equations with two variables from models or visuals.	Give examples and express meaning of terms related to algebraic equations with two variables from models or visuals.	Describe math operations, procedures, patterns, or functions involving algebraic equations with two variables from models or visuals.	Produce everyday math problems with algebraic equations involving two variables and give problem-solving steps from models or visuals.	Summarize or predict information needed to solve problems involving algebraic equations with two variables.

Source: Used with permission from Luke Carman, Teresa Garcia, Devansi Patel, Karoline Sharp Towner, and Brandy Velazquez, Albany Park Multicultural Academy, Chicago.

on students' language proficiency levels. In other words, he maintains his high expectations that all students achieve disciplinary learning goals, while simultaneously understanding that his ELs, in particular, will demonstrate that learning by using language in developmentally appropriate ways. By collecting data throughout the unit, Mr. Carman is able to modify his instruction to support and foster students' language development, as well as monitor learners' progress over time to inform the instructional design of upcoming units of study.

Chapter Summary

Focused on Stage 2 of UbD, this chapter has centered on the design of performance tasks and other assessments that tap into students' background knowledge and support language development. To begin, we explored how performance tasks provide language-rich opportunities for students to demonstrate learning with appropriate scaffolds for cultural background knowledge and language development. We then considered how to collect and analyze supplementary evidence with a language lens, including potential biases in formal assessment tools and occasions to collect informal data merging content and language. In Stage 2, our overarching goal is for educators to design meaningful and authentic assessment tasks and tools that are (1) aligned to Stage 1 goals, (2) language-rich, (3) culturally responsive, and (4) equitable for CLD students. After drafting Stage 2 UbD plans, teachers critically consider and revise assessments with lenses on students' cultural background knowledge and language abilities. These linguistically responsive assessments of learning then guide the scaffolded instruction in Stage 3. We explore Stage 3 with a language lens in the next chapter.

6

Planning for Learning: Stage 3 for Language Development

CHAPTER GOALS

- **Transfer**: Educators will be able to independently use their learning to...

  – Design effective and engaging learning plans that support students' disciplinary learning and language development.

- **Understandings**: Educators will understand that...

  – Language-rich learning plans support all students' language development, including authentic and interactive opportunities for students to listen, speak, read, and write that are connected to disciplinary learning goals.
  – Effective curricular design consistently and strategically scaffolds for language development throughout the learning trajectory.
  – By incorporating tasks and texts that tap into cultural background knowledge and linguistic abilities, the learning plan enables students to engage and achieve at higher levels.

- **Essential questions**: Educators will keep considering...

  – How do disciplinary units of study connect to students' lives?
  – Why do we scaffold language embedded in disciplinary learning?
  – How do students participate in tasks while developing language?
  – What makes a text complex for heterogeneous CLD students?

- **Knowledge**: Educators will know...

  – The role of background knowledge in learning and language development.
  – Disciplinary instructional approaches that support language development.
  – Criteria for selecting appropriate texts to mediate student learning.
  – WHERETO elements for planning instruction with a language lens.

- **Skills**: Educators will be skilled at...

  – Sequencing learning plans to support students in achieving Stage 1 transfer, meaning, and acquisition goals.
  – Integrating authentic tasks and texts that purposefully scaffold language development in disciplinary learning.
  – Analyzing and selecting complex texts for cultural relevance and linguistic accessibility based on student backgrounds.

In Stage 3 of UbD curricular design, we plan instruction to yield the goals that we set for student learning in Stage 1, demonstrated by the assessment evidence outlined in Stage 2. As introduced in Chapter 1 and reiterated throughout this book, the UbD framework supports deep and authentic learning. Rather than *coverage* of required topics or texts, the emphasis is instead on encouraging *uncoverage* of "core ideas at the heart of understanding a subject," including any questions, issues, assumptions, and potential misunderstandings (Wiggins & McTighe, 2005, p. 46). Whereas coverage focuses on the actions and decisions of the teacher, uncoverage prioritizes learners and learning. Our aim is to design instruction that is both *engaging* and *effective*, provoking the thoughts and ideas of learners as they develop understandings, abilities, and competencies.

Language-Rich Learning in Classroom Instruction

We begin by introducing two more students whose background stories exemplify the diversity of today's classrooms and whose presence inspired their teachers to create language-rich environments for learning. In this case, we present Jin, a kindergartener born in China, and Itzel, an 8th grader from Guatemala.

Jin, Kindergartener

Jin was born and raised just outside Beijing, where he spoke Mandarin at home and regularly attended private English lessons focused on reading and writing. His parents, both experts in the field of biomedical engineering, recently received appointments as visiting professors at an American university. They enrolled Jin in kindergarten at the local elementary school serving a predominantly white student population in this rural-area college town. Upon enrolling, Jin was given the standardized assessment to determine English proficiency. Because of prior tutoring, Jin's reading and writing in English are strong for an EL of his age, but his oral language is still developing at early stages of proficiency. When first starting school, Jin tended to be reserved and quiet in whole- and small-group settings, preferring to draw, write, and read independently. Nonetheless, in the interactive setting of the kindergarten classroom, the teacher consistently engaged learners in authentic practices with literacy through readers' and writers' workshops, as well as inquiry-based math and science units. In a community without extensive linguistic diversity, the teacher initially struggled to engage Jin in instruction but experimented with various ways to foster his oral language use and development. She discovered that he thrived when she planned units of study that placed his abilities and needs at the forefront, maintaining the language-rich and collaborative learning practices while strategically sequencing learning experiences to model and demonstrate expectations and procedures and specifically tapping into his strengths in drawing and writing as impetuses for oral language production.

Itzel, 8th Grader

Itzel was born and raised in the central highlands of Guatemala, moving with her family at the age of 10 from the rural countryside to Guatemala City in hopes of improving their economic conditions. Instead Itzel and her family found rampant gang violence, which eventually resulted in her coming to the United States as an unaccompanied minor at age 12. After making the difficult journey through Mexico with her brother, Itzel lived in a holding facility at the border for months before legal proceedings allowed her to be reunited with an aunt and uncle. Upon starting middle school, she was labeled as an EL, based on developing English proficiency, and a SLIFE, due to interrupted educational experiences. At a school whose student body includes many unaccompanied minors from Honduras, Guatemala, and El Salvador, as well as other Spanish-speaking immigrants, formal structures support adolescents' social-emotional, linguistic, and academic needs. Nonetheless, most supports are provided in Spanish, and although Itzel knows Spanish from her experiences in Guatemalan schools, her native and dominant language is the Mayan language of Kaqchikel. After two years in U.S. schools, Itzel is improving in oral language, according to her scores on standardized proficiency tests, but is still developing in reading and writing. Although her 6th and 7th grade teachers tended to provide her with simplified texts and materials, her 8th grade language arts teacher matched Itzel with novels and nonfiction texts that mirrored and tapped into her experiences, including some by young adult authors such as Julia Alvarez, Thanhha Lai, and Sonia Nazario. Although these books were technically above Itzel's ascribed reading level, her enhanced interest, ability to tap into prior knowledge, and linguistic scaffolds provided by the teacher allowed her to access and enjoy these texts and interact in meaningful ways during the unit on immigration.

Stage 3 for Understanding and Language Development

Grounded in what research indicates to be common characteristics of sound instruction, Stage 3 of UbD prompts educators to design learning plans that immerse students in hands-on experiences with real-world application and personalization based on their particular backgrounds, abilities, and needs (Wiggins & McTighe, 2005). Within this constructivist context of learning, the teacher's primary role is to facilitate student learning, which includes modeling, coaching, prompting reflection, and providing feedback (Wiggins & McTighe, 2012). By purposefully designing the Stage 3 learning plan, our ultimate aim is to engage and effectively facilitate student learning.

With a language lens on Stage 3, we plan instruction that provides equitable access to authentic disciplinary learning experiences that support language development. Consistent with the equity lens highlighted throughout this book, our goal in Stage 3 is to maintain rigorous instruction while responding to students' varied backgrounds, abilities, and needs. Traditional approaches to instructional design for CLD students, particularly those labeled as ELs, emphasize the *coverage* of linguistic skills, such as grammar and spelling, drawing from a deficit-based perspective on learners' inability to engage with grade-level content. Conversely, embracing cultural and linguistic assets as resources for learning, we provide a framework to plan rigorous and authentic disciplinary instruction using research-based characteristics of engaging and effective instruction for CLD students (see, for example, Beeman & Urow, 2013; Bunch et al., 2012; Celic & Seltzer, 2011; Heritage et al., 2015; Herrera, 2016; Walqui & van Lier, 2010; Zwiers, 2014). In this way, teachers design instruction that enables Itzel to interact with peers in literature circles using culturally relevant texts that tap into her background knowledge and experiences, and allows Jin to collaborate with peers while using his L1 abilities and strengths to develop L2 with appropriate instructional supports.

In this chapter, we explore how to design unit-level learning trajectories with an explicit lens on language development. We first describe the five pedagogical factors guiding Stage 3 instructional design, followed by key characteristics and considerations to dynamically support students' language development and integrate their rich cultural backgrounds into teaching and learning.

Planning Instruction to Support Language Development

In sharing our framework for culturally and linguistically responsive instructional design, we have consistently emphasized the need to tap into students' background knowledge and explicitly attend to language development in authentic disciplinary learning (Gay, 2010; Herrera, 2016; Lucas et al., 2008; Walqui & van Lier, 2010; Wiggins & McTighe, 2005). In Chapter 4, we began the instructional design process in Stage 1 by uncovering educators' linguistic blind spots to highlight the importance of defining learning goals that include explicit lenses on language. We analyzed the functions and demands of disciplinary language, considering students' language development embedded in cognitive understandings and academic disciplines. Think back to our exploration of how language varies depending on sociocultural contexts of classrooms, including different topics, tasks, texts, register, and students (WIDA, 2012). In this chapter, we consider these five factors in terms of how to support students' disciplinary learning and language development in Stage 3 instructional design. Specifically, we examine *background knowledge,* which relates to topics; *collaborative cognitive tasks,* which relates to tasks; *complex and relevant texts,* which relates to texts; *transfer to real-world contexts,* which relates to register; and *differentiated scaffolds and supports,* which relates to students (see Figure 6.1).

Figure 6.1 | **Sociocultural Context of Disciplinary Learning and Language Development**

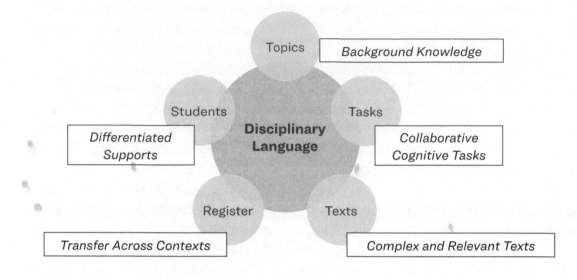

Source: Based on information from WIDA. (2012). *Amplification of the English Language Development Standards: Kindergarten–Grade 12.* Madison, WI: Author. Retrieved from https://www.wida.us/get.aspx?id=540.

Background Knowledge

How we support students' learning and language development in Stage 3 instruction varies based on unit *topics* and corresponding sets of background knowledge that students bring to classrooms. As noted earlier, background knowledge refers to previously compiled knowledge, skills, and experiences that shape learning, understanding, and participation in various settings and situations. When adding a language lens to UbD, we consider the rich and diverse resources that students bring to disciplinary units of study, including funds of knowledge from home, prior knowledge from the community, and academic knowledge from previous schooling. Due to its central role in culturally and linguistically responsive instruction, background knowledge has been discussed at length in previous stages of UbD, first in terms of discerning students' background knowledge during preplanning and then in using that lens to analyze and set goals in Stage 1 and to design authentic and appropriate assessments in Stage 2. Now, as we shift to designing the learning plan in Stage 3, we consider how students' unique and diverse sets of background knowledge connect to learning goals and provide opportunities to explicitly use cultural and linguistic resources to begin, continue, and extend learning. Integral to instructional design with a language lens, "background knowledge becomes the catalyst for accelerating the academic success of students from culturally and linguistically diverse backgrounds" (Herrera, 2016, p. 82).

Integrating background knowledge into the Stage 3 learning plan first requires teachers to discern students' resources and experiences that tie to focal learning in disciplinary units. We have to return to an important cautionary note regarding possible biases that may influence instructional design. School-based educators tend to prioritize academic knowledge, including connecting back to what a student learned or experienced in previous school years within the same discipline. When other sources of background knowledge are acknowledged, those sources often reflect mainstream American households and communities, such as taking family vacations or reading bedtime stories (Heath, 1983; Moll & Gonzalez, 1997). Nonetheless, at the heart of all students' learning and development, home- and community-derived resources are powerful tools to incorporate into instructional design (Herrera, 2016). Consider how teachers might incorporate the rich sources of background knowledge of the students profiled throughout this book. Absame, immersed in the Somali tradition of oral storytelling, has rich experiences and skills that connect to reading and writing units of study. Zaia brings firsthand knowledge and experience to various social studies topics, including social interaction, community structures, and economic exchanges. Lorenzo's roofing work with his father constitutes background knowledge and experience with aspects of mathematics such as measurement, estimation, and financial calculation. We encourage curriculum designers to be open-minded and creative, to think outside the box about how students' knowledge and experiences might connect in unique ways with unit topics.

Whereas previously collected preplanning data provide general profiles of students' backgrounds and abilities, strategically designed pre-assessments allow educators to capture more nuanced background knowledge related to particular disciplinary topics. For example, to begin a unit of study, students might be asked to brainstorm a particular topic or solve a problem using all cultural and linguistic resources available to them. By accessing background knowledge related to the unit, students tap into existing schema and resources for learning while teachers glean valuable data, such as students' direct and indirect knowledge of disciplinary topics that shape the overall learning plan and individual accommodations. Teachers then connect and affirm background knowledge throughout the unit by explicitly connecting background knowledge with learning goals, tapping into the expertise of particular students and making decisions regarding grouping configurations for various learning experiences (Herrera, 2016). Through purposeful instructional design, teachers continuously link learners' backgrounds with disciplinary topics to foster learning and language development, as well as maintain students' interest, engagement, and motivation.

In addition to background knowledge conceived broadly, language must be considered specifically. Because students store background knowledge using the language through which it was learned or experienced, we want to strategically incorporate students' L1 to access background knowledge, deepen understandings, and develop disciplinary language (Beeman & Urow, 2013; Celic & Seltzer, 2011). Two pedagogical concepts are helpful in shaping the integration of students' linguistic backgrounds into Stage 3 planning: translanguaging and bridging. Introduced in earlier chapters, *translanguaging* involves the authentic and dynamic use of multiple languages and linguistic repertoires, as when students brainstorm and discuss what they know about a disciplinary topic using any linguistic medium (Celic & Seltzer, 2011; Garcia, 2009a). Building from these L1 discussions, *bridging* makes the "explicit and consistent connection and transfer of knowledge and skills between languages" (Beeman & Urow, 2013, p. 51), exemplified by the ability to demonstrate similarities and differences between disciplinary terms and structures in different languages—for example, cognates in English and Spanish. Beyond providing equitable access to disciplinary topics by tapping into L1, bridging builds translanguaging abilities and metalinguistic awareness over time, as learners see that multiple languages have space in the classroom (Beeman & Urow, 2013; Celic & Seltzer, 2011; Herrera, 2016). Note that the L1 can and should be integrated into instruction across settings—bilingual, ESL, or general education—regardless of the teacher's language proficiency.

Collaborative Cognitive Tasks

In any unit of study, various *tasks* influence students' language usage and development, including ways that learners actively engage and collaborate to make meaning. When adding a language lens on UbD to design Stage 3 learning plans, we aim to foster autonomy by designing authentic, collaborative spaces for disciplinary learning and language development.

Sociocultural theory conceptualizes knowledge as coconstructed via social interaction with peers and expert others (Rogoff, 1995, 2003; Vygotsky, 1978; Wertsch, 2000). Further, language and cognition develop concurrently, as individuals rely on language to collaboratively and independently make meaning of ideas and understandings (Collier & Thomas, 2007; Walqui & van Lier, 2010). Thus learning plans must incorporate opportunities for students to interact around disciplinary topics with both teachers (as in modeling or guided practice) and peers (as in small-group settings or with partners). Whether teacher- or learner-centered, collaborative contexts should use strategic and flexible grouping to foster multiple interactions that scaffold learning and language development. Contexts and groups should change frequently across units of study as a way to engage learners and enhance learning (Echevarría, Vogt, & Short, 2013).

Learner-centered collaboration and critical thinking are particularly important when planning UbD instruction with a language lens. We want students to develop as autonomous learners while they deepen understandings, grapple with essential questions, and hone knowledge and skills through exploration and discovery (Wiggins & McTighe, 2005, 2011). Explicitly focused on language, authentic tasks prompt students to listen, speak, read, and write while wrestling with disciplinary ideas and problems (Beeman & Urow, 2013). An inductive learning experience—for example, historical investigation, scientific experimentation, problem-based learning, and creative expression (Heritage et al., 2015; Wiggins & McTighe, 2005)—provides an ideal learning medium within which to merge disciplinary learning and language development, with appropriate balance between focus (as related to content) and flexibility (as related to process). Disciplinary *focus* ensures productive dialogue centered on tasks that prompt higher-level thinking skills—for example, comparing ideas, generating and testing hypotheses, summarizing, reviewing and revising work—that are aligned to unit goals. *Flexibility* prioritizes the design of learning experiences that allow for multiple ways of knowing, encouraging students to tap into various resources and repertoires to make meaning and solve problems in diverse ways (Herrera, 2016; Rogoff, 2003). This balance can often be struck through use of discipline-specific collaborative contexts that simulate real-world practice (see Figure 6.2). Examples include book clubs in language arts, inquiry groups in mathematics, field teams in science, working groups in social studies, and sports teams in special areas. In such contexts, students participate in interactive disciplinary discussion and innovative meaning making to progress toward unit goals.

Figure 6.2 | Collaborative Contexts for Authentic Learning

Artistic collaborative	Interactive gamers	Study group
Advisory council	Laboratory partners	Workout partners
Book club	Learning community	Technology team
Colloquia	Literature circle	Theater cast and crew
Discussion group	Music group	Tutoring partners
Drama cast	Problem-solving team	Working group
Field team	Sports team	Writing collaborative
Inquiry group		

The use of multiple languages enhances the authenticity of collaborative contexts, reflecting the diverse communities and globalized world in which we live, with multilingual individuals interacting in varied linguistic mediums. Based on their work on translanguaging in classroom instruction, Celic and Seltzer

(2011) encourage teachers to think flexibly and strategically about the roles and functions of students' L1 and L2 during cooperative work. Flexibility implies the need for open-minded and creative thinking about the possible role of multiple languages and linguistic repertoires in mediating student learning, engagement, and achievement in classrooms. Further, effective curriculum designers strategically and explicitly define linguistic expectations that align with unit goals for transfer, meaning, and acquisition. In other words, teachers plan instruction to use students' multilingualism as a means to reaching Stage 1 goals for learning and language development. Examples include instructional decisions and experiences that prompt learners to (1) discuss, reflect, and negotiate in any language and share out in English, (2) brainstorm in any language and write in English, (3) preview in L1 and then collaborate in any language, and (4) listen in English and then discuss in any language (Celic & Seltzer, 2011). Pairing unit goals with linguistic strengths and preferences identified in preplanning data, teachers can craft the learning trajectory by organizing interactive groups and incorporating L1 to engage CLD students in learning, as well as to develop both the L1 and L2, support higher-order thinking, and deepen disciplinary understandings, knowledge, and skills (Celic & Seltzer, 2011; Garcia, 2009a).

While engaged in collaborative activity with teachers and peers, students use language to cognitively process and make meaning, ultimately supporting their individual development as autonomous learners, thinkers, and communicators (Collier & Thomas, 2007; Rogoff, 2003; Vygotsky, 1978; Walqui & van Lier, 2010). *Learning strategies* have been defined as "conscious mental and behavioral procedures that people engage in to gain control over the learning process" (Ortega, 2009, p. 208). Scholars have identified particular strategies (see Figure 6.3) that autonomous learners use to process and communicate ideas with others (Chamot & O'Malley, 1994; Herrera, 2016; Oxford, 1990). Strategies are organized into categories, including *cognitive* (thinking and processing), *metacognitive* (thinking about thinking), *memory* (mentally linking ideas), *linguistic* (comprehending and conveying ideas), *social* (collaborating with others), and *affective* (channeling emotions). After becoming aware of these varied learning strategies, we want to explicitly design instruction that embeds opportunities for students to use them in disciplinary learning and language development. Doing so includes teachers introducing and modeling strategies in daily instruction (aligned to unit goals and responding to learners), as well as supporting students in developing and using these strategies over time (Echevarría et al., 2013; Herrera, 2016). In this way, the design and implementation of collaborative cognitive tasks supports the progress of autonomous and resourceful individuals who can approach problems and discussion from multiple directions using varied tools and strategies.

Figure 6.3 | **Types and Examples of Learning Strategies**

Strategy Type	Strategy Examples
Cognitive	• Recognize and use formulas, patterns, and repetition. • Group, classify, and organize ideas (e.g., in graphic organizers). • Use reference materials (e.g., dictionaries, textbook, websites). • Write down key concepts in verbal, graphic, or numerical form. • Use visualization or auditory representation to learn information.
Metacognitive	• Center learning by previewing and linking to background knowledge. • Arrange and plan for learning (e.g., set goals, plan approach). • Monitor comprehension while listening and reading. • Monitor production while speaking and writing. • Evaluate learning through self-assessment and reflection.
Memory	• Create mental linkages to group, associate, or elaborate ideas. • Apply images, sounds, or keywords to remember ideas. • Employ action, such as using physical response or sensation.
Linguistic	• Translate into native language or use dynamic translanguaging. • Analyze words, phrases, and expressions contrastively across languages. • Recognize and use linguistic patterns in speech and written texts. • Adjust message using synonyms or other words (i.e., circumlocution). • Scaffold your message using mimes, gestures, and visuals.
Social	• Ask questions for explanation, clarification, or verification. • Cooperate with others (e.g., peers, proficient language users). • Empathize with others to develop awareness and cultural understanding.
Affective	• Lower anxiety using relaxation, music, or laughter. • Provide encouragement with positive statements and rewards. • Take emotional temperature about language learning.

Sources: Based on *The CALLA Handbook: Implementing the Cognitive Academic Language Learning Approach*, by A. U. Chamot and J. M. O'Malley, 1994, Boston: Addison-Wesley, and *Biography-Driven Culturally Responsive Teaching* (2nd ed.), by S. G. Herrera, 2016, New York: Teachers College Press, and *Language Learning Strategies: What Every Teacher Should Know*, by R. L. Oxford, 1990, Boston: Heinle, Cengage Learning.

Complex and Relevant Texts

In addition to topics and tasks, different *texts* mediate students' disciplinary learning and language development in Stage 3 instruction. *Complex texts* have emerged as the primary focus in contemporary classrooms, due to the emphasis in the Common Core State Standards on independent listening and reading with grade-level texts. Zwiers (2014) describes a complex text as "any written, visual, audio, or multimedia message that conveys information or ideas for learning purposes" (p. 63). This definition encompasses textbooks, articles, poetry, novels, online resources, oral histories, word problems, maps, photographs, and more. The complexity of any text is determined based on qualitative features, such as structure and language conventionality, and quantitative indicators, such as length of words and sentences. Most important for teachers and curriculum designers, text complexity also varies based on the reader (Fillmore & Fillmore, 2012; Zwiers, 2014). Specifically, readers with background knowledge aligned to the text demonstrate increased motivation, engagement, and comprehension, thus allowing them to access texts that are more complex per qualitative and quantitative measures (Ebe, 2011; Jiménez, García, & Pearson, 1996; Medina & Martínez-Roldán, 2011; Pierce, 1999; Smith, 2006). When designing Stage 3 learning plans, we want to select and incorporate complex texts that tap into students' background knowledge and strategically mediate students' learning while supporting disciplinary language development.

Culturally relevant texts align with students' rich experiences and varied interests, enabling students to read more complex texts than might be indicated by formal measures of reading proficiency. The UbD framework already pushes curriculum designers to move beyond the textbook and canned curriculum guides (Wiggins & McTighe, 2005). Adding the lens on culturally and linguistically responsive practice, we want to select and use high-quality texts that tap into students' backgrounds and experiences while aligning with unit goals. The emphasis in the term *culturally relevant texts* is on *culture*, which is much more than an ethnic ascription such Latino or African American. Conceptualized as complex and dynamic, culture involves multiple facets that shape identity, including family, language, community, religion, age, gender, and sexual orientation. When selecting books based on students' backgrounds, teachers should consider the multifaceted and complex nature of individual and collective students in their classrooms. Aligned to the unit goals, culturally relevant texts might serve as *mirrors* for some students to see themselves in texts, or *windows* to look into and connect with the lives of others (Sims-Bishop, 1990). Both mediate students' understanding—texts as mirrors that enhance interpretation and promote self-assessment and texts as windows that prompt learners to empathize and take perspective (Sims-Bishop, 1990; Wiggins & McTighe, 2005). By purposefully selecting texts, teachers tap into background knowledge as a means to deepen understandings and promote achievement of Stage 1 goals.

Teachers across grade levels and disciplines can plan Stage 3 instruction to integrate culturally relevant texts as a means to promote students' learning and language development. Language arts and social studies teachers can use culturally relevant fiction and nonfiction texts, either as primary texts to mediate learning (e.g., Laura Resau's *Red Glass*) or as supplemental texts linked to the focal text of the unit (e.g., J. D. Salinger's *The Catcher in the Rye*). Other teachers across disciplines can select or craft culturally relevant materials and resources that relate to unit goals, such as using culturally diverse myths in an earth science unit or culturally specific word problems in algebra. Regardless of the classroom context, remember that not all texts portraying CLD characters and themes are created equal. Depending on the portrayal of characters, settings, plots, and themes, so-called *multicultural* texts might do more harm than good in classrooms. Whether through the narrative or the illustrations, texts can either explicitly or implicitly epitomize the target culture and perpetuate stereotypes or maintain a surface-level focus on heroes and holidays (Cai, 2003; Morgan, 2009). Thus teachers should seek out texts that present accurate and nuanced portrayals of daily life, including language use, attitudes, values, gender roles, relationships between people, religion, and family structures (Barrera & Quiroa, 2003; Medina, 2006). To select relevant and authentic texts that align to unit topics and goals, teachers can begin by exploring texts, authors, and illustrators through various book awards, publishers, and social media (see Figure 6.4). Fortunately for educators seeking to craft effective Stage 3 learning plans, culturally relevant literature has grown in recent years, with more attention from publishers and practitioners alike.

Figure 6.4 | Resources for Culturally Relevant and Multilingual Texts

Book Awards	Publishers	Twitter
Américas Award	Arte Público Press	@ColorinColorado
Asian-Pacific American Literature Award	Children's Book Press	@diversebooks
Coretta Scott King Award	Cinco Puntos Press	@diversityinya
John Steptoe Award	Lee & Low Publishers	@KLUBooks
Pura Belpré Award	Piñata Books	@LatinosInKidLit
	Tu Books	

Just as culturally relevant texts connect with background knowledge, multilingual texts and materials tap into students' L1 abilities. This lens is particularly important when designing instruction for ELs in early stages of language proficiency, also referred to as *emergent bilinguals*. Because English proficiency is not a prerequisite to disciplinary learning and conceptual understanding, all students can engage in classroom instruction while developing the L2. Celic and Seltzer (2011) explain:

> By reading texts about a content-area topic in the home language, emergent bilinguals have more background knowledge to draw upon than when reading other texts about that same topic in English. As emergent

bilinguals gain more background knowledge, they can read and comprehend increasingly complex texts about the topic in English. This scaffolds their English language development and also develops home language literacy. (p. 51)

Whether in general education, ESL, or bilingual classrooms, teachers can integrate multilingual texts into the Stage 3 learning plan to mediate student learning and promote language development in both the L1 and L2. Instruction can include texts and materials in multiple languages for all students (either by selecting multilingual versions or creating translations) or supplemental L1 readings based on disciplinary topics and themes for individual students (Celic & Seltzer, 2011).

Beyond the cultural and linguistic relevance to the reader, complex texts offer qualitative features including meaning, structure, language conventions, clarity, and knowledge demands (Zwiers, 2014). Without influencing complexity, teachers can increase the accessibility of the text to enhance students' learning and language development (Clay & Cazden, 1990). Increasing access means *amplifying* texts with attention to these qualitative features (Walqui & van Lier, 2010), referred to in Chapter 4 as the language features at word, sentence, and discourse levels (WIDA, 2012). Thus, teachers select and use complex texts with needed modifications for features such as font type, font size, and font color as well as additions that may include margin notes, sticky notes, translations, and cognates, enabling learners to maneuver demanding language (Fillmore & Fillmore, 2012; Walqui & van Lier, 2010). Additionally, teachers design instruction to include various means to scaffold access to complex texts; examples include using different learning contexts, such as read-aloud and shared, guided, and interactive reading; implementing appropriate scaffolds before, during, and after reading, such as modeling strategies, using graphic organizers, and clarifying with L1; and considering the amount of reading and adjusting through use of a jigsaw of larger text or multiple reads (Herrera, 2016; Zwiers, 2014). Remember that amplifications are *not* simplifications (Walqui & van Lier, 2010). Rather than removing technical vocabulary or simplifying complex sentences, amplification maintains text complexity while fostering students' autonomy and increasing access to content. Thus teachers add marginal notes or use particular fonts to call attention to demanding language, such as text features, grammatical patterns, and technical terms.

Transfer to Real-World Contexts

The topics, tasks, and texts in units of study directly influence the language that we use to engage in learning, prompting our consideration of register when designing Stage 3 instruction. *Register* is a linguistic term that emphasizes the variance in language use across different contexts (such as home versus school), with varying purposes (such as a science experiment versus a soccer game) and particular audiences (such as L2 teachers versus L1 peers). Curricular design should seek to respond to the particular register of classroom instruction and to extend beyond it to consider how to develop learners' linguistic repertoires more broadly across settings so they can transfer disciplinary language to real-world contexts. To accomplish this, we want to facilitate students' learning about how language is both purposeful and patterned—planning instruction that probes the regularity and predictability of speech and text and contrasts linguistic elements across registers, languages, and language varieties (Heritage et al., 2015). The resulting metalinguistic awareness allows learners to tap into their own linguistic resources and repertoires across classrooms and disciplines, as well as between home, community, and school (Bialystok, 1993; Nagy & Anderson, 1995). This, in turn, supports student autonomy. Heritage and colleagues (2015) explain, "Recognizing patterns leads students to feel more in charge of their own learning—to be able to use language across contexts and to develop their agency as learners" (p. 41). By making the inner workings of language visible to students, we provide them with tools to reflect on language usage and development to transfer across both disciplines and languages.

As described earlier, instructional design targeting discipline-specific language development must include authentic learning experiences that integrate listening, speaking, reading, and writing both collaboratively and independently (Beeman & Urow, 2013). It is within these language-rich disciplinary tasks, mediated by complex and relevant texts, that we help students see and make connections across disciplinary units and courses of study. Consider how we use language not only within but across disciplines, including cross-cutting language functions (e.g., arguing, predicting) and language features (e.g., multiple-meaning words). Rather than operating within individual disciplines to develop language, teachers can support learners in making explicit connections between registers. They can do this in various ways, such as planning or coplanning interdisciplinary units (e.g., merging social studies and literacy), bringing in readings from different disciplines, and referencing relevant information and language across content areas (Celic & Seltzer, 2011). Whatever the approach, disciplinary integration supports students in deepening disciplinary understandings, increasing language development for academic purposes, and improving reading comprehension and writing abilities (Celic & Seltzer, 2011; Gibbons, 2002; Goldenberg, 2008; Samway, 2006). Interdisciplinary connections can also foster continued language development beyond the school day, as learners transfer and use disciplinary language in real-world contexts to deepen and solidify their linguistic understandings, knowledge, and skills.

In addition to fostering transfer across disciplines and classrooms, instruction should prompt students to transfer learning between languages and in so doing develop metalinguistic awareness. As described in Chapter 3, all languages have similarities and differences: languages can share features, such as cognates between English and Spanish; or diverge with separate features, such as the distinct sentence constructions in English and Spanish, or the different alphabets and text directionality in English and Arabic (Beeman & Urow, 2013; Cummins, 2000; Opitz, Rubin, & Erekson, 2011; Razfar & Rumenapp, 2014). After accessing linguistic background knowledge, as described earlier, teachers plan instruction that prompts students to analyze and evaluate the relationship between languages. Whether tracked formally through personal glossaries or noted informally in class discussions, linguistic analyses should probe similarities and differences in sounds (phonology), word parts (morphology), vocabulary (lexicon), grammar (syntax), and cultural norms (pragmatics) across students' languages (see Figure 6.5). The learning plan should align with Stage 1 goals and the previously analyzed language functions and features needed to access disciplinary learning. In other words, rather than comparing and contrasting every word, phrase, sentence, and text, prioritize the important language that students need to use and develop to reach the larger unit goals. Given consistent opportunities to examine, compare, and contrast their L1 and L2, students develop metalinguistic awareness, which then supports disciplinary learning, reading comprehension, writing abilities, and biliteracy development (Beeman & Urow, 2013; Bialystok, 1993; Celic & Seltzer, 2011; Jiménez et al., 1996; Nagy & Anderson, 1995).

Transfer to real-world contexts is challenging at first for many educators. The challenge connects to the very nature of formal schooling. Unfortunately, our current educational system consistently isolates both disciplines and languages in schools (Celic & Seltzer, 2011; Dressler, Carlo, Snow, August, & White, 2011). In elementary settings, the daily schedule dictates that students learn language arts, mathematics, science, social studies, and special areas within separate blocks of time across the day. Secondary students experience the barriers between disciplines even more, as they move to departmentalized classrooms with each ring of the school bell. The division between languages occurs across settings, such as ESL and general education classrooms facilitated in English only or bilingual classrooms that maintain rigid blocks for teaching and learning in Spanish only or English only. Even without explicit rules or guidelines for language usage, students recognize the implicit expectations: *I speak English at school, and I speak my L1 at home.* It is important to recognize and reflect upon the institutional context to consider how to design instruction that confronts these silos of discipline and language. After uncovering linguistic blind spots to recognize discipline-specific language functions and demands in Stage 1, Stage 3 provides educators with the opportunity to transparently develop and extend students' linguistic repertoires beyond the walls of the classroom.

Figure 6.5 | **Comparative Analyses of Languages**

Level of Analysis	Examples
Sounds	• Sound-spelling correspondences that vary by language, as in pronunciation of /j/ as /h/ in Spanish and /j/ in English • Silent letters, which vary across languages • Consonant digraphs and blends, such as the digraph /th/ that exists in English but not in Spanish • Vowels, as in no short vowel used in Arabic writing • *R*-controlled vowels, which are unique to English
Word Parts	• Similar prefixes and suffixes, such as English and Spanish words **imm**ediate/**inm**ediato; demo**cracy**/demo**cracia;** narra**tor**/narra**dor** • Omission of plural marker –s, when nouns do not change form in languages (e.g., Hmong, Tagalog) • Different uses of –ing, as infinitives and gerunds do not exist in certain languages (e.g., Khmer, Korean)
Words & Phrases	• Cognates across languages, such as *animal* (English), *el animal* (Spanish), *o animal* (Portuguese), *l'animal* (French), and *l'animale* (Italian)
Sentence Structure & Grammar	• Varying uses of articles, including frequent use (e.g., Arabic, Spanish) or underuse (e.g., Korean, Russian) • Word order, such as adjectives coming after nouns in Spanish, Hmong, Khmer, and Haitian Creole • Different use of verb tenses, including verbs that do not change form to express tense such as past or future (e.g., Cantonese, Vietnamese)
Discourse & Cultural Norms	• Varying cultural norms and social meanings of eye contact and certain head movements (e.g., nodding) • Appropriate amount of personal space and direct contact during various types of communication

Sources: Based on *Teaching for Biliteracy: Strengthening Bridges Between Languages,* by K. Beeman and C. Urow, 2013, Philadelphia, PA: Caslon, and *Reading Diagnosis and Improvement: Assessment and Instruction* (6th ed.), by M. Optiz, D. Rubin, and J. Erekson, 2011, Boston: Pearson.

Differentiated Scaffolds and Supports

The final Stage 3 instructional factor considers how disciplinary teaching and learning in support of language development shifts based on the unique learners in the classroom. Because of our emphasis on culturally and linguistically responsive practice, we have prioritized students' abilities, strengths, and needs throughout the planning process, including considerations for language demands in Stage 1 and assessments in Stage 2. Now in Stage 3, we design instruction with appropriate scaffolds and supports for students to reach Stage 1 goals and perform on Stage 2 assessments. Ultimately, our goal with this factor is to foster active and autonomous learning and language use by amplifying the accessibility of rigorous disciplinary topics, tasks, and texts.

Scaffolding is a word that is frequently thrown around in educational circles with regard to both planning and implementing instruction. It is important to flesh out what we mean by scaffolding, specifically with regard to supporting the disciplinary learning and language development of CLD students. In their book focused exclusively on scaffolding for ELs, Walqui and van Lier (2010) describe the metaphor of the scaffold:

> The builders put a scaffold around a building that needs to be renovated, but the scaffold itself is only useful to the extent that it facilitates the work that is to be done. The scaffold is constantly changed, dismantled, extended, and adapted in accordance with the needs of the workers. In itself, it has no value. (p. 24)

Effectively and soundly constructing the edifice is the ultimate goal, just like reaching the Stage 1 goals for transfer, meaning, and acquisition. Planned before construction, scaffolds provide a means to reach the end goal, which dynamically change over time as the work (or learning) evolves. Thus teachers scaffold through both intentional planning and on-the-spot decisions in daily practice (see Figure 6.6). But even when scaffolding occurs on the spot, effective instructional design that is both flexible and adaptable allows students to engage in authentic and innovative learning that deepens understandings and develops language (Herrera, 2016; Walqui & van Lier, 2010). Always designed with students in mind, Stage 3 integrates scaffolds into instructional structures and processes (Clay & Cazden, 1990; Heritage et al., 2015; Walqui & van Lier, 2010).

Figure 6.6 | **Examples of Scaffolding in Instructional Units**

Intentional Scaffolding in Unit Design	On-the-Spot Scaffolding in Flexible Units
• Modeling	• Contextualizing key vocabulary
• Think-alouds	• Paraphrasing using disciplinary language
• Demonstration	• Prompting elaboration of ideas
• Small-group discussion	• Providing appropriate wait and work time
• Independent application	• Reteaching content when necessary
• Graphic and sensory supports	• Using flexible grouping approaches
• Interactive learning supports	• Using various questioning strategies

(handwritten margin note: scaffolding techniques)

When considering unit-level instructional design, *structure-focused scaffolding* emphasizes the design and organization of learning experiences that support student learning in multiple contexts as a way to develop autonomy over time. As previously described, sociocultural theory supports our understanding that learning is coconstructed and mediated over time through various social interactions among teachers and learners. Using the theoretical construct of the zone of proximal development, we know that students learn and develop by engaging with teachers, other adults, more capable peers, equal peers, and less capable peers (Vygotsky, 1978; Walqui & van Lier, 2010). In addition, learning occurs through authentic experiences over time, prompting instruction that includes multiple interconnected opportunities for learners to think, reflect, and rehearse what they are learning (Herrera, 2016; Rogoff, 2003). In this way, based on students' backgrounds, abilities, and needs, teachers design instruction to scaffold the ongoing construction of understandings, knowledge, and skills. Doing so includes purposeful use of teachers modeling, thinking aloud, and demonstrating, as well as ongoing opportunities for learners to authentically discuss, negotiate, practice, and apply with peers (Echevarría et al., 2013). In addition to the intentional design of structural scaffolds, maintaining flexibility within curricular design allows for on-the-spot scaffolds to advance students' learning and language development as they grapple with disciplinary ideas and essential questions. Examples include teachers' use of various questioning techniques or revoicing to prompt, clarify, or elaborate upon particular ideas emergent from inquiry-based learning (Herrera, 2016).

Used within these varied structures, *process-focused scaffolding* further enhances learning experiences by providing individualized supports for students to access and actively engage with tasks and texts. Process-based scaffolds in instructional design are defined as "supports specifically designed to induce students' participation in meaningful and worthwhile activity while developing and increasing their autonomy" (Heritage et al., 2015, p. 46). The goal is to foster student independence by selecting the kinds of supports that are just right and within students' zone of proximal development (Heritage et al., 2015; Vygotsky, 1978; Wood, Bruner, & Ross, 1976). In other words, based on students' backgrounds, abilities, and needs, we strategically select and integrate instructional supports to promote equitable access and active engagement in disciplinary learning and language development. As noted in previous chapters, WIDA (2007) organizes supports into three categories: sensory, graphic, and interactive (see Figure 6.7). Embedded in scaffolded structures, instructional supports allow learners to more deeply and independently engage, understand, and apply. Consider how a teacher demonstration or peer discussion might enhance learning and language development by providing examples via illustrations and diagrams (sensory), documenting learning in graphic organizers (graphic), and negotiating understandings in students' L1 (interactive). Note that these are not strategies for strategy's sake, but rather purposefully selected and integrated supports to scaffold the learning and development of students with unique backgrounds and individualized needs.

Culturally and linguistically responsive instruction centers on students' unique and diverse backgrounds, abilities, strengths, and needs (Gay, 2010; Lucas et al., 2008). The factors described here support educators as they consider how the curriculum can dynamically support students' disciplinary learning and language development in Stage 3 of instructional design. Grounded in Stage 1 goals and Stage 2 assessments, teachers design instruction specifically for their classrooms by first considering the distinctive topics, tasks, texts, register, and students (WIDA, 2012). A rigorous and effective unit trajectory provides CLD students with equitable access to disciplinary learning by integrating background knowledge, collaborative cognitive tasks, complex and relevant texts, transfer to real-world contexts, and differentiated scaffolds and supports. In the next section, we consider these factors when designing instruction at the unit level, while the upcoming chapter will apply them to lesson-level planning.

Figure 6.7 | **Linguistic Supports to Scaffold Instruction**

Sensory Supports	Graphic Supports	Interactive Supports
Realia and manipulatives	Charts	Pairs or partners
Pictures and photographs	Graphic organizers	Triads or small groups
Illustrations and diagrams	Tables	Cooperative group structures
Magazines and newspapers	Graphs	Use of related technology
Gestures and movement	Time lines	Use of native language
Videos, films, and broadcasts	Number lines	Mentors
Models and figures	Concept maps	

Source: Based on WIDA ELP Standards © 2007, 2012 Board of Regents of the University of Wisconsin System. WIDA is a trademark of the Board of Regents of the University of Wisconsin System. For more information on using the WIDA ELD Standards, please visit the WIDA website at *www.wida.us*. Used with permission.

Considering WHERETO Elements with a Language Lens

Now that we have explored the five factors influencing students' disciplinary learning and language development, we shift to explore the specific steps involved in planning rigorous, authentic, and scaffolded learning plans in Stage 3 instructional design. Wiggins and McTighe (2005) use the acronym WHERETO to weave these key characteristics of good instructional design into the learning plan (see Figure 6.8). Incorporating the seven WHERETO elements, practitioners round out the design of units of study that support students in achieving the Stage 1 learning goals and demonstrating transfer and understandings on Stage 2 assessments. Thus, teachers' instructional planning includes (1) working out goals and expectations, (2) hooking and holding interest, (3) equipping for learning, (4) rethinking and revising, (5) evaluating and reflecting, (6) tailoring learning experiences, and (7) organizing and sequencing learning. In this section, we add a language lens to the WHERETO elements to foster students' disciplinary learning and language development, using Mr. Hassan's middle school science unit as an exemplar.

Figure 6.8 | **WHERETO Elements**

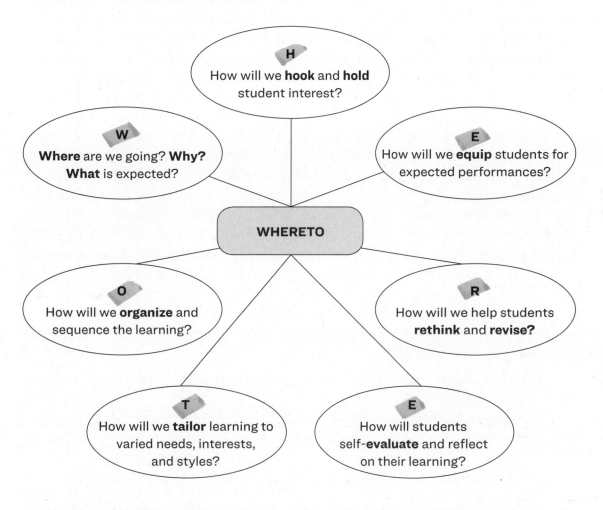

Source: From *Understanding by Design Professional Development Workbook* (p. 214), by Jay McTighe and Grant Wiggins, 2004, Alexandria, VA: ASCD. Copyright 2004 by ASCD. Adapted with permission.

Working Out Goals and Expectations

As we have noted, the UbD framework centers on the need to begin with the end in mind, with teachers first defining the goals for learning and development in Stage 1 of instructional design. But in authentic instruction, we want to develop learners' autonomy, which begins with students knowing the larger unit goals and setting a purpose for their own individual learning. McTighe and Wiggins (2004) explain, "Students are more likely to focus and put forth effort when they have clarity on the goals and expectations and see a purpose and value for the intended learning" (p. 215). With this in mind, the first WHERETO element emphasizes the need to start with clear goals and expectations, as well as pre-assess students' background knowledge, interests, and misconceptions. Considering the unique perspectives of students in the classroom, teachers first ask: *Where are we going? Why? What is expected?* Practitioners then craft the learning plan to explicitly define the goals and expectations of the units, including assessments and assignments, and clearly explain the purpose and benefits of achieving them. Additionally, this element prompts the inclusion of opportunities for teachers to determine learners' background knowledge, interests, and misconceptions.

When adding a lens on language to this first WHERETO element, we prioritize language development and respond to students' background knowledge when defining unit goals. Based on teachers' previous analyses of how students use language to actively engage with disciplinary learning, this element provides the opportunity to make language development explicit for learners—to call attention to linguistically focused goals and expectations within units of study. In addition to being aware of the desired results for their learning and language development, students should understand the overall importance and purpose, with a clear vision of how learning connects and transfers to real-world practice in homes, communities, and schools (Herrera, 2016; Wiggins & McTighe, 2011). Within this first WHERETO element focused on working out goals and expectations, consider the following:

- Do students know the unit goals, including goals for language development?
- How will students use language in assignments and assessments?
- How will this disciplinary language transfer to school and real-world topics?
- What related resources do students bring from home, community, and school?

To this point, we as curriculum designers have taken an explicit lens on disciplinary language development throughout the instructional planning process, including attention to Stage 1 goals and Stage 2 expectations for demonstrating learning. Here in Stage 3, our intention is to transparently share and substantiate language-focused goals and expectations with learners, prompting their awareness and ownership of language development.

Now let's consider what this element looks like in practice, using the middle school science unit on weather and climate (McTighe & Wiggins, 2004). In this section on WHERETO elements, we flesh out Mr. Hassan's language lens as he designs his Stage 3 plan for primarily bilingual learners and ELs from Mexico, Central America, and South America. Transfer goals center on students explaining weather patterns using models, with meaning and acquisition goals targeting causes and repercussions of weather (see Figure 6.9). To begin the unit, he wants to discuss goals and expectations and discern related sources of background knowledge from home, community, and school. Aligned to Stage 1 goals, Mr. Hassan first aims to glean his students' academic knowledge about weather from previous grades at the K–8 school, including terminology and concepts for observable weather patterns (e.g., wind, rain). With preplanning data indicating that students have either lived or visited family in other countries, he recognizes the value of linking their prior knowledge to new disciplinary learning. He forecasts that the end-of-unit performance task will focus on both the United States and Latin America. With these points in mind, Mr. Hassan designs a pre-assessment of background knowledge to both collect anecdotal data and frame the focus of the unit. He then integrates the opportunity to explicitly define and discuss unit goals, expectations, and relevance, including how students' background knowledge will support disciplinary learning and language development in the unit. By discerning background knowledge, defining goals and expectations, and previewing the culminating performance task, Mr. Hassan begins to craft a learning plan that provides equitable access for all learners.

Hooking and Holding Interest

Whereas sharing the unit outcomes and tasks with students is necessary, clear goals and explicit expectations alone are not always sufficient to make children and adolescents enthusiastic about new learning. Thus, we must consider ways to hook and hold learners' interest in the discipline-specific content of the unit to increase student engagement and motivation in learning (Echevarría et al., 2013). With this second WHERETO element, McTighe and Wiggins (2004) assert the importance of "*hooking* students at the beginning of a new learning experience and *holding* their interest throughout" (p. 217). Based on what teachers know about the learners in their classroom, they consider ways to engage students with the overall unit topic and begin to pique interest, inquiry, discussion, and learning related to the big ideas, essential questions, and performance tasks. In contrast to the explicit definition and explanation of the unit goals and expectations, the preliminary hook often involves creative inquiry, a discrepant event, and even surprise in the form of a challenge, a mystery, a problem, an experiment, a role-play, or a provocative entry question. Depending on the learners, teachers may opt to design hooks that specifically tap into related personal experiences, emotional connections, or humor (Wiggins & McTighe, 2011). Following inclusion of the initial hook, teachers design engaging learning to hold student interest throughout the rest of the unit.

Figure 6.9 | **Middle School Science Unit, Weather**

Stage 1—Desired Results

Established Goals

NGSS MS ESS2, S2-5 & S2-6

- Collect data to provide evidence for how the motions and complex interactions of air masses result in changes in weather conditions.
- Develop and use a model to describe how unequal heating and rotation of the Earth cause patterns of atmospheric and oceanic circulation that determine regional climates.

Transfer

Students will be able to independently use their learning to...

- Explain weather patterns by drawing from multiple disciplines, including earth, space, and physical science, as well as geography.
- Produce and use models to make meaning of scientific phenomena.

Meaning

Understandings

Students will understand that...

- Unequal heating between the equator and poles, Earth's rotation, and the distribution of land and ocean generate the global wind patterns that determine climate.
- Most of what goes on in the universe involves some form of energy being transformed into another.
- Transformations of energy usually produce energy in the form of heat, which spreads around by radiation and conduction into cooler places.

Essential Questions

Students will keep considering...

- What causes weather and wind patterns?
- What factors influence climate?
- How do events in one geographical area affect another?
- How does climate influence agriculture?
- How can I determine climate in a given location on Earth?

Acquisition

Students will know...

- Causes of wind and weather patterns.
- Factors influencing climate.
- Causes of Coriolis effect.
- How climate affects agriculture.
- Earth science text features (e.g., maps, tables, diagrams, figures).
- Sentence structures for cause/effect and other scientific relationships.
- Multiple meaning words (e.g., front, cycle).
- Related morphological constructions (e.g., morpho, meso, strato, thermo, exo).

Students will be skilled at...

- Describing how events in one geographical area influence another.
- Interpreting data illustrating the relationship between air pressure and temperature.
- Applying the concepts of Newton's First Law, the spherical geometry of Earth, and centripetal acceleration to the Coriolis effect.
- Communicating findings regarding climate and agriculture in writing.

Stage 2—Evidence

Evaluative Criteria	Assessment Evidence
• Evidence-based • Well-researched • Scientifically sound • Cross-disciplinary • Scientific language	**Performance Task(s)** Working in teams, students take on roles as consultants for farming companies in the United States and Latin America. Teams conduct research on the climates of three regions, including where they live, one U.S. region at the same latitude, and one Latin American region at the same longitude. Students compare and contrast climates using multiple sources of data, maps, and climate–determining factors. Teams produce and present reports to companies to support decisions regarding farms in each region.
• Accurate • Thorough • Scientific language	**Supplementary Evidence** • Open-book exam with selected- and constructed-response items on weather and climate • Ongoing quizzes on readings with problems requiring interpretation of charts and data

Stage 3—Learning Plan

Pre-assessment

• Access background knowledge about climate in regions where students have previously lived or visited, using provided graphic organizer and online resources.

• Share and compare regions, including L1 terminology to connect with L2 disciplinary language.

Learning Events

• Hypothesize the best place on campus and in the community to fly a kite. Test hypotheses with kites.

• Connect the above events as tied to unit goals, expectations, and relevance. Start a personal glossary.

• Model scientific text usage via annotation activity to access various features (e.g., diagram, maps).

• Guide students in evaluating circulation cell diagrams and explaining in terms of differential heating.

• Inquiry groups: Read articles, perform labs that illustrate Newton's First Law and centripetal acceleration, and relate information to the Coriolis effect.

• Interactive map study: Use isobars to label wind directions. Explain analyses and labeling.

• Hands-on lab: Solar rays and differential heating on different areas of Earth, using an energy budget diagram showing the energy flow between the sun, Earth's surface, and atmosphere.

• Independently describe airflow around high- and low-pressure centers using diagram analyses.

• Interpret case studies of how weather in one region influences weather in another, specifically tied to students' background knowledge (e.g., wildfires in California, earthquake in Chile).

• Complete the performance task, including reports, presentations, and self-evaluation.

• Take open-book exam based on unit understandings (with appropriate accommodations).

Formative Assessment

• Observations of annotated textbook activity

• Personal glossary of disciplinary language of unit, including technical vocabulary, multiple-meaning words, and morphological constructions

• Science journal entries to explain various approaches to interpretation and application

• Self-evaluations of learning throughout unit

Source: From Understanding by Design Professional Development Workbook (pp. 42–43), by Jay McTighe and Grant Wiggins, 2004, Alexandria, VA: ASCD. Copyright 2004 by ASCD. Adapted with permission.

When adding a language lens to this WHERETO element, we consider how to access students' unique sources of background knowledge, as well as integrate and account for students' L1 and L2. Remember that our overarching goal is equitable access to disciplinary learning. After defining Stage 1 goals and designing Stage 2 assessments, the goal is now to actively engage all learners in authentic experiences to reach those goals and expectations. As most any teacher will attest, it takes work to motivate and engage students in disciplinary learning, prompting thoughtful planning based on the unique and diverse learners in the classroom. Thus, preplanning data is the ideal place to start when designing instruction to consider students' cultural backgrounds and experiences, as well L1 and L2 preferences and abilities. Within this second WHERETO element focused on hooking and holding interest, consider the following:

- How can students' backgrounds be used to hook interest with personal experiences, pastimes, passions, or emotional connections?
- Are students' backgrounds integrated into instruction to continue to hold interest?
- Can students' L1 be used as the linguistic medium to hook (and hold) student interest?
- Is the language of instruction comprehensible in order to hold students' interest?

For learners to reach Stage 1 goals and demonstrate learning on Stage 2 assessments, the Stage 3 learning plan should engage learners in meaningful and authentic learning by tapping into their interests and background knowledge. Additionally, effective practitioners consider how students' language influences their motivation and engagement and design instruction that strategically incorporates L1 and L2 to maximize disciplinary learning.

Consider the middle school science unit focused on weather and climate. As described previously, Mr. Hassan began by designing a pre-assessment to access students' related background knowledge and frame unit goals and expectations. By prompting learners to brainstorm what they remember about weather and climates in places they previously lived in or visited, he recognizes, values, and uses students' lived experiences and backgrounds as mechanisms to hook interest in the focal topic of the unit. In a classroom with primarily bilingual students, Mr. Hassan purposefully encourages students to use their L1 during this activity, which he sees as a way to maximize brainstorming while both inciting and maintaining students' motivation and engagement in the unit topic. In addition to designing instruction to access prior knowledge, Mr. Hassan wants to incorporate an engaging, hands-on, problem-solving activity to further hook students' interest in connection to understandings, essential questions, knowledge, and skills. To accomplish this, he designs an inquiry-based experience in which learners make and test hypotheses about the best places to fly kites on campus and in the community. After students get out of the classroom to fly kites in their pre-determined areas, Mr. Hassan facilitates a discussion using emergent findings and ideas to serve as an engaging springboard into disciplinary learning about weather and climate.

Equipping for Learning

Beyond hooking and holding interest throughout units of study, we want to ensure that students have the needed knowledge and skills to actively engage in learning, develop understandings, and prepare for upcoming performance tasks. Based on Stage 1 goals and Stage 2 performances, this third WHERETO element focuses on ways to equip students for learning. In other words, curriculum designers first consider what students need to understand, know, and do, and then design learning experiences to prepare for the successful performances. McTighe and Wiggins (2004) describe how practitioners incorporate this element into the Stage 3 learning plan by designing "ways they will help students to *explore* the big ideas and essential questions and how they will *equip* students for their final performances" (p. 218). To prompt exploration of disciplinary concepts and ideas, practitioners design collaborative cognitive tasks for students to construct meaning across the six facets of understanding. Additionally, teachers use direct instruction and out-of-class activities to equip students with pertinent knowledge and skills for final performances. Depending on students' needs in relation to learning goals, teachers can craft appropriate trajectories to include opportunities for both student-centered exploration and teacher-guided instruction. The aim is to integrate experiences that equip students for disciplinary learning, as well as language development.

The language lens on this element emphasizes building from students' background knowledge and equipping learners with the language needed to develop understandings and grapple with essential questions. We have consistently underscored the importance of background knowledge and L1, but these resources need explicit connection and integration into the curriculum. Additionally, unit plans must strategically target and support language development using appropriate instructional contexts, which might include contextualizing disciplinary language via inductive learning experiences or building linguistic knowledge and skills via direct instruction or out-of-class experiences. Within this third WHERETO element of equipping for learning, consider the following:

- How is students' background knowledge explicitly connected with unit learning?
- How can students' L1 connect to language needed to engage with learning goals?
- Do any linguistic knowledge or skills need to be taught through direct instruction?

- How can disciplinary language be contextualized to support exploration of big ideas?
- What out-of-class experiences will further develop and extend disciplinary language?

Preplanning data, particularly the linguistic dimension, and Stage 1 linguistic analyses inform instructional design to equip students with pertinent discipline-specific language. Remember a key point emphasized in Chapter 4: our analysis of language demands in disciplinary topics, complex texts, and collaborative tasks is *not* done to remove demanding language in an attempt to shelter some students. Instead, after considering students' abilities and uncovering linguistic blind spots, educators design learning experiences to target language development and provide equitable access to learning goals.

In the science unit, we have discussed how Mr. Hassan strategically accesses students' background knowledge by brainstorming details about the weather and climate in regions they have lived in or visited around the world. He then has students share and compare regions, purposely bridging students' L1 to pertinent L2 terms in the unit. In addition to the strategic use of students' L1 and background knowledge to equip them for learning, personal glossaries further develop disciplinary language, using bilingualism as a resource. Later in the unit, Mr. Hassan returns to these sources of background knowledge to equip learners in exploring pertinent understandings, ideas, and concepts related to weather and climate, as well as to prepare for the culturally relevant and language-rich performance task. By having students interpret case studies that are specifically tied to their background knowledge and experiences, such as wildfires in California or earthquakes in Chile, he recognizes that students can dive deeper into the exploration of weather- and climate-related phenomena. Beyond integrating cultural background knowledge to challenge and support students, Mr. Hassan attends to previously brainstormed language demands to ensure that he appropriately equips learners and provides equitable access to content. For example, recognizing the discourse-level features of the scientific textbook structures and features, he incorporates a learning event to model text usage using an annotation activity. He also designs all other events and experiences to contextualize disciplinary language throughout the unit.

Rethinking and Revising

In addition to equipping students with knowledge, skills, tools, and experiences to prepare for learning, we must consider how learners can continue to discuss, negotiate, and deepen understandings. Pertinent here is instruction that emphasizes depth over breadth. Learners need time and extensive opportunities to engage in learning that allows for continuous grappling with essential questions and promotes transfer to real-world contexts. McTighe and Wiggins (2004) assert, "Understanding develops and deepens as a result of *rethinking* and *reflection*" (p. 221). Students need to come at problems and concepts in various ways to explain, interpret, apply, take perspective, empathize, and self-assess learning and understandings across units of study (McTighe & Wiggins, 2004). Thus, when designing instruction to promote understanding, teachers "provide students with numerous opportunities to rethink big ideas, reflect on progress, and revise their work" (Wiggins & McTighe, 2012, p. 38). Aiming to bolster learners' achievement of Stage 1 goals and performance on Stage 2 assessments, curriculum designers plan instruction that allows students to rethink important ideas, practice skills, improve products and performances, and reflect upon learning, thinking, and understanding. Additionally, they incorporate opportunities for learners to use and reflect upon learning strategies that transfer to other instructional contexts.

The language lens on this element emphasizes the importance of language-in-use: students developing language through use in meaningful ways in classrooms (Walqui & van Lier, 2010). Once equipped with knowledge, skills, tools, or strategies to access disciplinary learning activities, students learn and develop language while engaged in authentic, real-world practice. Learners should have ample time and meaningful opportunity to revisit and rehearse disciplinary language while deepening their understandings and grappling with essential questions. Further, purposeful rethinking and revising with a language lens also prompts instruction that fosters students' metalinguistic awareness. When teachers plan opportunities for learners to reflect upon language use and development, connections between L1, L2, and language varieties emerge—resulting in metalinguistic awareness that advances learning and language development (Bialystok, 1993; Nagy & Anderson, 1995). Within this fourth WHERETO element of rethinking and revising, consider the following:

- How do students revisit big ideas and reiterate vital disciplinary language?
- What linguistic skills require rehearsal embedded in disciplinary learning?
- Do students have opportunities to reflect on learning across sociocultural, cognitive, linguistic, and academic dimensions?
- How does instruction explicitly build students' metalinguistic awareness?

The key point here is that language develops through authentic disciplinary learning—not through separate lessons focused on grammar, spelling, or vocabulary. When crafting the Stage 3 learning plan, teachers design multiple learning experiences that prompt students to use language in meaningful, collaborative contexts. In this way, instruction supports learners in achieving Stage 1 goals for disciplinary learning and language development while priming for the language-rich performance tasks designed in Stage 2.

Let's return to Mr. Hassan's middle school science unit. In the Stage 3 learning plan, he designs multiple learning experiences that directly align to the Stage 1 goals and prepare students for the Stage 2 performance task. His overarching goal is to provide learners with a variety of collaborative, cognitively demanding tasks to deepen understandings, grapple with essential questions, and develop knowledge and skills. With this in mind, he crafts the learning plan to incorporate numerous experiences that prompt learners to rethink and revise understandings over time, including (1) inquiry groups to interpret complex texts and apply the Coriolis effect via laboratory work, (2) interactive map study groups to explain weather and wind with maps and isobars, and (3) hands-on laboratories to test hypotheses on heating patterns and energy transformations. These experiences prepare learners to rehearse and perform the task with roles as consultants who will first research and compare regional climates using texts, maps, and data, and then produce and present reports to farming companies. Designing responsive instruction for his students, Mr. Hassan incorporates bilingual word walls, sentence frames, and graphic organizers to ensure disciplinary language development during learner-centered tasks. Further, his consistent use of science journals and personal glossaries promotes metacognitive and metalinguistic awareness, respectively. After students have engaged in open-ended inquiry learning experiences with varied ways to solve problems, their science journals encourage reflection and explanation of solutions, and their personal glossaries call attention to bilingual translations, word parts, and cognates. Throughout the learning plan, Mr. Hassan provides time and space for learners to rethink and revise understandings, along with structures to develop disciplinary language and metalinguistic awareness.

Evaluating and Reflecting

Along with having instructional opportunities to rethink and revise understandings, students benefit from opportunities to self-evaluate and reflect upon their learning and performance. Accordingly, Wiggins and McTighe (2012) assert that effective teachers deliberately "build in opportunities for students to evaluate progress, self-assess, and self-adjust, based on formative assessment" (p. 38). Notice that this WHERETO element links to the self-knowledge facet of understanding explored in Chapter 4. These opportunities to self-evaluate and reflect also directly align to Stage 1, resulting in a clear and transparent system of learners setting and reflecting upon goals and teachers providing individualized feedback to push forward disciplinary learning and development.

When we add a language lens to this WHERETO element of evaluation and reflection, we consider opportunities for students to self-assess across multiple dimensions of learning and development (Herrera, 2016). Learners should consistently self-reflect on their individual growth and progress with regard to sociocultural, cognitive, linguistic, and academic learning, as well as receive feedback to scaffold learning and foster development over the course of the unit. Building from students' dynamic self-understandings, particularly those focused on disciplinary understandings and related language usage, teachers then design experiences for learners to extend their learning and language development. This effort includes providing opportunities (both inside and outside school) for learners to independently work toward personal goals for the unit, whether in students' L1 or L2. Within this fifth WHERETO element of evaluating and reflecting, consider the following:

- When do students have opportunities to self-assess learning across dimensions? What information can be gleaned via these self-assessments of student learning?
- How can students knowingly extend disciplinary language beyond the unit?
- How can students explicitly connect and extend learning in their L1?

Think back to the holistic student profiles described in Chapter 3, which prompt teachers to merge formal and anecdotal data across dimensions to set individualized goals that guide the design of culturally and linguistically responsive instruction (Gay, 2010; Herrera, 2016; Lucas et al., 2008). Learners can dynamically contribute to their profile by self-evaluating and reflecting during units. Teachers then use these data to monitor progress, provide targeted feedback, and design additional experiences for disciplinary learning and language development.

Thus far in the middle school science unit, we have explored how Mr. Hassan initially shares unit goals and expectations, accesses and builds background knowledge and hooks interest, and then purposefully engages and equips students for learning and provides locales to develop understandings and disciplinary language. He now wants to ensure that learners self-evaluate throughout the unit—reflecting upon their learning, development, performances, and progress—and extend their disciplinary learning and language development beyond classroom-based experiences. He incorporates opportunities for self-assessment that connect with the unit goals and expected performances, and that span dimensions of student learning and development (Herrera, 2016). Students self-evaluate throughout the unit by reflecting on their sources of background knowledge (the sociocultural dimension), elucidating their problem-solving processes in science journals (the cognitive dimension), and synthesizing their unit learning and language development following the performance task (the linguistic and academic dimensions). Mr. Hassan gathers additional self-evaluation data via checks for understanding in his daily lesson plans. To extend language development outside formal, school-based scientific learning and continue students' progress toward goals, Mr. Hassan incorporates learning events that integrate real-world practices and experiences, such as prior experiences in home countries and case studies of weather and climate. He also encourages use of languages other than English (LOTEs) and translanguaging throughout the unit, with the intent to extend disciplinary language development in students' L1, including Spanish, Chicano English, and indigenous languages.

Tailoring Learning Experiences

After defining goals and expectations, hooking and holding interest, and equipping students for learning, as well as designing experiences for all students to rethink, revise, evaluate and reflect, we consider how to differentiate instruction for individual learners. McTighe and Wiggins (2004) explain how the learning plan incorporates "ways of tailoring the [unit] design to address student differences in background knowledge and experiences, skill levels, interests, talents, and learning styles" (p. 224). This overarching WHERETO element focuses on personalizing instruction while maintaining the learning goals for the unit of study. In other words, based on the abilities and needs of individual students in classrooms, teachers should consider how to tailor learning to address the varied needs, interests, and styles of the students they serve. Teachers then differentiate the content, process, and products of learning experiences across the unit, including particular ways to make disciplinary topics accessible, accommodating learners in various ways, and providing options to demonstrate understanding (Tomlinson, 2007–2008; Wiggins & McTighe, 2005, 2011).

When adding a language lens to this WHERETO element, we consider how to tailor instruction for students with unique and diverse backgrounds, abilities, strengths, and needs. Using preplanning data, curriculum designers differentiate instruction based on the sociocultural, cognitive, linguistic, and academic dimensions of student learning and development (Collier & Thomas, 2007; Herrera, 2016). Teachers should differentiate with cultural and linguistic lenses throughout the learning plan, selecting texts for cultural relevance and scaffolding tasks with linguistic supports. Within this overarching WHERETO element of tailoring learning experiences, consider the following:

- How are tasks and texts that tap into students' background knowledge integrated?
- Do tasks and texts provide for unique ways of knowing, thinking, and responding?
- Are experiences language-rich, with scaffolds for oral language, reading, and writing?
- How do differentiated graphic, sensory, and interactive supports allow individual students equitable access to products and performances?

consider how we tailor lessons to those w/ needs

Keeping in mind our overarching intent of equitable access, we want to plan instruction so that all students—regardless of language proficiency, formal schooling experiences, or any other factors—achieve Stage 1 learning goals, demonstrate learning on Stage 2 assessments, and actively engage in Stage 3 instruction. Thus, tailoring learning experiences is integral. Although we have already woven this factor throughout UbD stages, this WHERETO element prompts us to holistically review the unit to further scaffold learning events for individual students.

Throughout the middle school science unit on weather and climate, Mr. Hassan has designed instruction in response to the unique learners in his classroom. Students attending his urban school are primarily Latino, including first- and second-generation immigrants from Mexico, Central America, and South America. Students' L1 backgrounds include Spanish, Chicano English, and various indigenous languages (including Kaqchikel, spoken by Itzel). Aiming to tailor learning experiences, he has integrated students' background knowledge throughout the unit—for example, by including strategically selected case study texts and focusing the performance task on regions in the United States and Latin America. He returns to the array of collaborative cognitive tasks—using inquiry groups, interactive map study groups, and hands-on lab teams—and specifically incorporates scaffolds to prompt authentic, language-rich experiences in which learners solve problems in various ways using oral language, reading, and writing. Based on his knowledge of his students, who include ELs and SLIFE students like Itzel, these interactive and hands-on disciplinary tasks incorporate targeted instructional supports, including realia, manipulatives, diagrams, models, figures, charts, graphic organizers, tables, graphs, and related technology (WIDA, 2007). By designing the learning plan in response to his learners' backgrounds, as well as incorporating differentiated scaffolds and supports to foster learning and language development, he makes students' equitable access to achieving unit goals the priority. Additional ideas for to differentiating daily lesson plans will be presented in the next chapter.

Organizing and Sequencing Learning

With differentiated learning experiences based on individual learners' abilities and needs, practitioners round out Stage 3 instructional design by organizing and sequencing the overall learning plan across the unit of study. The UbD framework challenges educators to push beyond linear progressions, such as simply following the pages of a textbook or teaching facts and skills according to the sequence listed in a standards document (Wiggins & McTighe, 2005). Such an approach suggests that the goal is simply content coverage, in which instruction aims to superficially *cover* particular standards or textbook topics. As described previously, instructional design must instead *uncover*, so that students learn, develop, and grapple with important big ideas and essential questions via authentic and inductive learning experiences. To accomplish this, designers arrange and structure learning as collaborative inquiry into an unfolding story or problem, with strategically designed and ongoing cycles of teaching, learning, and feedback (Wiggins & McTighe, 2005). Thus the final WHERETO element prompts teachers to first consider how to organize instruction to yield authentic, engaging, and effective learning. Teachers then finalize the Stage 3 design by strategically sequencing learning experiences to apprentice students into disciplinary content and mediate progress toward the desired results of the unit (Rogoff, 1995).

When adding a language lens to this element, we organize and sequence learning to maximize language development, engaging students in meaningful interaction with others and apprenticing learners into discipline-specific language use over time. Collaboration is integral to learning and language development, prompting use of flexible and strategic grouping to ensure that learners interact with diverse voices and perspectives in different collaborative contexts, such as partners and small groups. But collaboration does not always need to be among peers, as teachers' disciplinary expertise should also be used to mediate students' learning and language development. In this way, educators should consider how to organize and sequence learning to apprentice students into disciplinary learning and language development, using modeling, demonstration, practice, and application to foster autonomous learning. Within this WHERETO element of organizing and sequencing learning, consider the following:

- Are students consistently engaged in collaborative learning experiences?
- Do students learn and use disciplinary language in various contexts, such as whole-group, small-group, partnered, and individual experiences?
- Does the trajectory effectively apprentice students into disciplinary language use?
- How does the trajectory set learners up for success through modeling and practice?

As we know, the ultimate goal in backward design is that students achieve Stage 1 learning goals for transfer, meaning, and acquisition, which they demonstrate on Stage 2 assessments. After designing aligned learning experiences, curriculum designers organize and sequence those experiences in a progression that authentically fosters disciplinary learning and language development through meaningful collaboration in multiple contexts.

To finalize the UbD unit for his middle school science class, Mr. Hassan organizes and sequences the various experiences in the learning plan. Having designed authentic and language-rich experiences aligned to Stage 1 goals and Stage 2 performances, he reviews and revises the overall structure of the unit plan. With multiple interactive experiences already designed, he adds structural details regarding the collaborative contexts and grouping strategies: modeling and facilitating discussions with the whole group, guiding practice in smaller inquiry groups, prompting peer-guided learning in hands-on lab teams and case study groups, strategically matching partners for the interactive map study, and preparing learners for independent work. Because of the large number of SLIFE students and newcomers in his classroom, he recognizes the need to apprentice learners into the disciplinary understandings and applications in the science classroom. Thus, Mr. Hassan crafts the learning plan to showcase teacher-guided experiences early in the unit of study with increasingly more peer-guided and autonomous experiences later in the unit. He also strategically designs groups in the collaborative setting to tap into students' L1 abilities, which helps both emergent and established bilingual learners to access content and develop discipline-specific bilingualism and biliteracy. With a deliberate balance and arrangement of modeling, demonstration, discussion, and application across the Stage 3 trajectory, students engage in authentic learning experiences that purposefully support their disciplinary learning and language development over time.

Taken together, the WHERETO elements with a language lens provide practitioners with a set of guidelines for designing units in Stage 3 of UbD, further fostering students' disciplinary learning and language development. Figure 6.10 summarizes the WHERETO elements with a language lens.

Classroom Application: Tasks to Support Language Development

Having discussed the various considerations and elements of Stage 3 curricular design with explicit attention to language development, we now merge those ideas into actionable next steps to inform unit planning with the UbD framework. In this section, we outline how to support students' learning and language development throughout the learning plan in Stage 3 of the UbD planning template.

Revisit Student Data and Overarching Learning Goals

Embracing the principles of UbD's backward-planning framework requires a frequent return to the end goals for learning, as well as the dynamic data compiled on students' multidimensional development. Using holistic student profiles, maintained with up-to-date information following each unit of study, consider learners' abilities and needs at the start of instruction—Point A. Review your end goals for transfer, meaning, and acquisition, as well as the assessments through which students will demonstrate progress toward these goals—Point B. Think of your Stage 3 learning plan as the vehicle to support and challenge students in moving from Point A to Point B.

Figure 6.10 | **WHERETO Elements with a Language Lens**

Elements*	Language Lens
W	• Do students know the unit goals, including goals for language development? • How will students use language in assignments and assessments? • How will this disciplinary language transfer to school and real-world topics? • What related resources do students bring from home, community, and school?
H	• How can students' backgrounds be used to hook interest with personal experiences, pastimes, passions, and emotional connections? • Are students' backgrounds integrated into instruction to continue to hold interest? • Can students' L1 be used as the linguistic medium to hook and hold student interest? • Is the language of instruction comprehensible in order to hold students' interest?
E	• How is students' background knowledge explicitly connected with unit learning? • How can students' L1 connect to language needed to engage with learning goals? • Do any linguistic knowledge or skills need to be taught through direct instruction? • How can disciplinary language be contextualized to support exploration of big ideas? • What out-of-class experiences further develop and extend disciplinary language?
R	• How do students revisit big ideas and reiterate vital disciplinary language? • What linguistic skills require rehearsal embedded in disciplinary learning? • Do students have opportunities to reflect on learning across sociocultural, cognitive, linguistic, and academic dimensions? • How does instruction explicitly build students' metalinguistic awareness?
E	• When do students have opportunities to self-assess learning across dimensions? • What information can be gleaned via these self-assessments of student learning? • How can students knowingly extend disciplinary language beyond the unit? • How can students explicitly connect and extend learning in their L1?
T	• How are tasks and texts that tap into students' background knowledge integrated? • Do tasks and texts provide for unique ways of knowing, thinking, and responding? • Are experiences language-rich, with scaffolds for oral language, reading, and writing? • How do differentiated graphic, sensory, and interactive supports allow individual CLD students equitable access to products and performances?
O	• Are students consistently engaged in collaborative learning experiences? • Do students learn and use disciplinary language in various contexts, such as whole-group, small-group, partnered, and individual experiences? • Does the trajectory effectively apprentice students into disciplinary language use? • How does the trajectory set learners up for success through modeling and practice?

*See Appendix for explanation of WHERETO.

Draft a Learning Plan with Language-Rich Events

Plan the learning plan for students to reach Stage 1 goals and prepare them for Stage 2 assessments. Because those goals and assessments have been designed with a language lens, the unit plan should incorporate aligned disciplinary language by design. Keep in mind the goal to design disciplinary learning that simultaneously fosters language development, which is typically done through inductive, interactive, and authentic learning experiences. These meaningful learning contexts should integrate listening, speaking, reading, and writing with opportunities for learners to use both L1 and L2. In addition, consider how to support students' language development with appropriate instructional scaffolds.

Design Experiences That Tap into Students' Dimensions

In addition to applying a linguistic lens throughout the academic unit—including incorporating language-rich events and differentiated linguistic scaffolds—consider students' learning and development across the sociocultural and cognitive dimensions (Herrera, 2016). Students bring ample cultural resources to the classroom, such as background knowledge and cognitive learning strategies, which should be integrated into Stage 3 instruction in purposeful ways. Ensure that your learning plan consistently taps into students' resources, including connection with unique sources of background knowledge, flexibility for multiple modes of participating and making meaning, and integration of culturally relevant texts and materials.

Revise the Learning Plan with WHERETO Elements

With a thorough draft of your learning trajectory aligned to previous stages of unit-level instructional design, use the WHERETO elements to refine the plan: defining goals and expectations, tapping into background knowledge, hooking and holding interest, equipping students for learning, encouraging reflection and self-evaluation, and tailoring and sequencing learning events for engaging and effective teaching and learning (Wiggins & McTighe, 2005). Use the guiding questions in Figure 6.10 to consider how your learning plan fosters language development and integrates students' backgrounds. Make revisions accordingly to ensure rigorous instruction with equitable access that promotes students' disciplinary learning and language development.

Ensure Alignment Across Stages of Instructional Design

Once you have completed all three stages of instructional design, return to review your unit of study across all Stage 1 goals, Stage 2 assessments, and Stage 3 learning plans. Critically consider the alignment across design stages, particularly probing if instruction allows students to deepen understandings, grapple with essential questions, and transfer learning to new contexts and situations. Return to your preplanning data (which you have updated over time) to ensure that you have kept your students' complex and dynamic backgrounds, abilities, strengths, and needs at the center of your instructional planning with language-rich learning experiences and appropriate supports and scaffolds throughout the unit of study.

ex in social studies class →

Classroom Snapshot: Planning for Learning

Ms. Lindsay Niekra is a 1st grade teacher at Peter Reinberg Elementary School in the Portage Park community on the northwest side of Chicago. Once a predominantly Polish neighborhood, Portage Park is now home to many Latino families who have moved from other parts of the city over the past two decades. Reflecting the community's shifting demographics, 70 percent of Reinberg's 850 current students identify as Latino, with 55 percent speaking Spanish at home. Nonetheless, the historical roots of the region endure, with over 10 percent of students identifying as Polish-dominant, many of them attending a nearby Polish Saturday School to develop and maintain their L1 proficiency. In addition to Spanish, Polish, and English, other languages represented at Reinberg include Arabic, Tagalog, Ukrainian, Albanian, Romanian, Turkish, Assyrian, Bulgarian, Cantonese, Greek, Russian, Serbian, Telugu, and Vietnamese. Approximately 80 percent of students speak a LOTE at home, with 35 percent formally labeled as ELs based on standardized language proficiency scores. Fifty PreK–8 teachers support the learning of students at Reinberg Elementary, including those with proficiency in Spanish, Polish, and Arabic. To meet the diverse linguistic needs, each primary grade level has one Spanish bilingual classroom for Spanish-speaking ELs, one ESL classroom for ELs from diverse linguistic backgrounds, and one general education classroom for English-proficient students.

In her self-contained primary classroom, Ms. Niekra describes her role as a coach, mentor, and facilitator with the goal of fostering the learning, autonomy, and creativity of her young learners across the core disciplines of language arts, mathematics, science, and social studies. Multilingual in English, Polish, and Spanish and certified as an ESL and bilingual elementary teacher, Ms. Niekra teaches students with various L1 backgrounds, including Polish, Spanish, Arabic, Russian, Ukrainian, and Albanian. Of her 25 students, about half are formally labeled as ELs—spanning all levels of language proficiency from emergent to advanced—with the other half identifying as bilingual students speaking a LOTE at home. In addition to formal labels and ACCESS scores providing snapshots of language proficiency across domains, Ms. Niekra uses portfolios to compile scrapbooks detailing her students' holistic abilities and backgrounds. As most learners speak at least one of her three languages, she uses her multilingualism to connect with parents early in the school year to gather information on the rich sources of background knowledge that she can use in her classroom instruction. Ms. Niekra then designs UbD instruction to prepare students for real-world practices, making intentional decisions to provide rigorous and authentic disciplinary learning experiences that simultaneously support the language development of all students.

Early in the school year, Ms. Niekra implements an integrated literacy and social studies unit centered on community citizenship and social identities (see

Figure 6.11). Aligned to the Illinois Social Studies Standards and Common Core State Standards for English Language Arts, the unit intends to foster young learners' active and civic participation in home and school communities, as shaped by historic understandings of rules and expectations across social contexts and individual reflections on personal and familial identities. These social studies goals directly connect to desired literacy targets, as learners locate and evaluate information from a variety of sources, such as nonfiction texts, family interviews, and poetry, to support both historic understandings and identity constructions. Knowledge and skills include development of disciplinary language, including related vocabulary (c.g., routines), figurative language (e.g., personification), sentence structures (e.g., compare/contrast), and informational text structures (e.g., table of contents). Uniquely situated in the context of Reinberg School, the performance task prompts students to collaboratively create orientation videos with skits that explain, compare, and contrast rules and expectations at home and at school. Ms. Niekra designs a learning plan that includes students conducting family interviews, doing research projects, writing autobiographical poetry, and engaging in other learning activities. These, along with her own daily observations, provide ample opportunities to collect and analyze data to evaluate students' progress toward learning goals. To support her students in achieving Stage 1 goals and demonstrating learning on Stage 2 assessments, Ms. Niekra uses her in-depth understandings of language development to design a Stage 3 learning plan that taps into background knowledge, fosters collaboration and critical thinking, incorporates relevant and complex texts, extends language beyond classrooms, and differentiates for individual students.

Ms. Niekra begins the unit by tapping into her students' background knowledge and affinity for role-playing as a way to hook interest and introduce the unit goals. In pairs, students role-play different interactions at home, school, and other places in the community, such as playing with siblings at home, attending a birthday party in the community, or conducting a fire drill at school. Working in a whole-group setting, Ms. Niekra challenges learners by changing the context of or participants in their simulations, such as interacting with church with acquaintances as they do at home with siblings, prompting initial considerations of how rules and expectations vary across different settings. With her specific class in mind, she suspects that students will find humor and enjoyment in this activity to then carry over into the remainder of the unit. In addition, students' simulations and discussions provide keen insight into their background knowledge and experiences related to the unit goals on rules and expectations spanning social contexts. This is integral to shaping the implementation of the unit, as the learning plan incorporates various collaborative tasks that tap into students' background knowledge, including researching culturally diverse schooling experiences, inquiring into cultural and familial backgrounds, conducting family interviews

Figure 6.11 | **Ms. Niekra's 1st Grade Social Studies Unit**

Stage 1—Desired Results

Established Goals	Transfer
SS.CV.2.1: Identify and explain how rules function in various settings, inside and outside school. **SS.IS.4.K-2:** Evaluate a source by distinguishing between fact and opinion. **CCSS.ELA.W1.8:** With guidance and support from adults, recall information from experiences or gather information from provided sources to answer a question.	*Students will be able to independently use their learning to...* • Participate as an active and civil citizen by analyzing home and school rules. • Use historical knowledge to understand events in the present and future. • Locate and evaluate information from a variety of sources to support ideas.

	Meaning
	Understandings *Students will understand that...* • Each person's identity is multifaceted and unique. • People have similarities and differences that identify who they are as individuals. • Different social contexts include various relationships that influence behavioral expectations (teacher/student, parent/child).	**Essential Questions** *Students will keep considering...* • Who am I? • How do my culture and family influence my identity? • Why do we have different rules in different contexts, like at home or in school?

	Acquisition
	Students will know... • Different behavioral expectations in school and home/community settings. • Difference between fact and opinion. • Vocabulary (e.g., traditions, routines, holidays, beliefs, rules, expectations, individual, relationship). • Figurative language (e.g., metaphor, simile, personification, hyperbole). • Compare/contrast (e.g., is similar to, is different than, is unique because). • Informational text structures (e.g., headings, captions, glossaries).	*Students will be skilled at...* • Distinguishing fact from opinion. • Comparing and contrasting family members with themselves. • Comparing and contrasting individuals' accounts with informational texts. • Locating information in nonfiction texts on kids around the world. • Interviewing a family member and a person from a different background than their own. • Applying the rules of different social settings by role playing.

Stage 2—Evidence

Evaluative Criteria	Assessment Evidence
• Thorough • Evidence-based • Collaborative • Engaging	**Performance Task(s)** Your task is to create an orientation video for students new to Reinberg School who do not know the school rules. You need to communicate the expectations for behavior at our school and contrast them to rules in your home and community. You need to develop skits with your group to demonstrate and explain why we have different rules for home versus school. Your group will write the script and act in the video. Your video must compare and contrast home and school rules and explain *why* we need rules in these settings.
• Interactive • Interpretive • Precise language • Figurative language	**Supplementary Evidence** • Relate-to-a-relative interview: Students write interview questions to guide the interview, then document and code responses as fact or opinion. • Research diverse school experiences: Students identify different behavioral expectations of children in different parts of the world and make inferences to explain why that might be. • Autobiographical poetry: Students write poetry describing their personal characteristics using figurative language as compared to families.

Stage 3—Learning Plan

Pre-assessment

• First individually and then collaboratively brainstorm rules that students recognize as guiding their behavior in different settings (i.e., home, school, place of worship).

• Anticipatory set: Teacher provides list of facts and opinions related to home/school/community rules; students must mark which is fact and which is opinion.

Formative Assessment

• Observations of annotated textbook activity

• Personal glossary of disciplinary language of unit, including technical vocabulary, multiple-meaning words, and morphological constructions

• Science journal entries to explain various approaches to interpretation and application

• Self-evaluations of learning throughout unit

Learning Events

• Hook: Role-play behavior/interactions that might occur in various settings, including home, school, and other places, such as places of business, play, and worship. Then try them again with behavioral norms switched up, such as interacting with your teacher like you would with your mother.

• Post and discuss essential questions and knowledge/skill goals. Have students set their own personal goals as related to the unit. Refer and self-reflect on these goals throughout the unit.

• Read aloud *School Days Around the World*, by Margriet Ruurs, a nonfiction book made up of interviews.

• Grouped by L1, students collaboratively research culturally diverse school experiences.

• Self-inquiry into students' own cultural backgrounds. Create family trees, maps that show where families have lived, and family rules/norms. Use these to foster student discussion with their families and peers about their heritage, languages, values, hobbies, and interests.

• Using a Venn diagram, students compare and contrast to learn more about their identities and those of others.

• Invite guest speakers into the classroom from various backgrounds to be interviewed by students. Generate questions and document responses, following a style similar to *School Days Around the World*.

• Demonstration and application of drafting questions for relate-to-a-relative interviews, which are done at home with a relative chosen by the student (teacher gives directions and suggested criteria to select relative with differences from the student, such as age or country of origin).

• Students select an artifact from their home or the community to present to the class and describe the connection to the student's identity, culture, language, and family.

• Read aloud *The Best Part of Me*, by Wendy Ewald, a collection of poems and photographs by children reflecting on self-image. After modeling the text as seed idea, students write autobiographical poetry.

• Performance task planning, practice, and presentation: Students create and perform the new student school rules orientation video in pairs.

Source: Used with permission from Lindsay Niekra, Peter Reinberg Elementary School, Chicago.

about prior schooling experiences in unique settings, exploring identity through home and community artifacts, and writing autobiographical poetry.

To center her social studies unit, Ms. Niekra selects complex and relevant texts to mediate students' learning and language development aligned with Stage 1 learning goals. A nonfiction text that explores nuanced school and educational experiences around the world, *School Days Around the World* (Ruurs, 2015) serves as the anchor text throughout the unit. In addition to reading the text aloud, the class frequently returns to the text's various vignettes as seed ideas to guide their ongoing research into culturally diverse schooling and family interviews on nuanced educational experiences. Ms. Niekra strategically uses the text to build linguistic knowledge and skills related to such things as informational text structures (e.g., table of contents) and locating information in nonfiction texts. Later in the unit, 1st graders collaboratively read and explore *The Best Part of Me* (Ewald, 2002), a collection of poetry and photographs of children reflecting on identity and self-image. Now that her students have explored their roles in various social settings, she wants them to consider their own identities as shaped by their cultures, families, and experiences. After exploring poetry written by other children, students begin to write their own autobiographical poetry as a means of self-exploration and self-reflection. Spanning genres of poetry and nonfiction, the mediating texts provide both mirrors and windows for students in Ms. Neikra's vibrant 1st grade classroom.

In addition to integrating collaborative tasks and complex texts that tap into background knowledge, Ms. Niekra designs the learning plan to extend, scaffold, and support language development. Throughout the unit, she explicitly prompts students to consider their L1 when exploring and discussing family norms and individual identities. Using her own multilingualism and metalinguistic awareness, this language lens provides consistent opportunities for her to call attention to similarities and differences between languages. Students' L1 is also frequently used to support individuals' learning and language development, as exemplified by noting cognates in related vocabulary (e.g., expectation/expectativa, tradition/tradición in English/Spanish), translating texts for emergent bilinguals (e.g., an autobiographical poem in Polish), and forming strategic small groups and partners based on the L1. Beyond the scaffolded design of the Stage 3 learning plan, including learning events that span from teacher modeling to student inquiry, Ms. Niekra scaffolds and supports CLD students' learning and language development in daily practice. As a 1st grade teacher, particularly at this early point in the school year, she recognizes the need to differentiate for individual student learning within every lesson of the larger unit. Lesson-level planning with a language lens is described in depth in the next chapter.

Chapter Summary

Focused on Stage 3 of UbD, this chapter has centered on educators designing learning plans that support diverse students' disciplinary learning and language development. We have considered how to scaffold for language development throughout units of study, including accessing background knowledge, fostering meaningful collaboration, using complex and relevant texts, promoting transfer across contexts, and implementing differentiated supports. Similar to the previous stages' overarching focus on equity, Stage 3 aims for educators to design language-rich instruction that engages and supports students in reaching rigorous transfer and meaning goals, as well as acquisition goals for disciplinary learning and language development. After drafting Stage 3 UbD, educators return to the learning plan to integrate effective and appropriate scaffolds, supports, and materials to support language development and engage CLD students. Based on this larger unit-level learning trajectory, teachers then design individual lesson plans to guide daily instruction. We explore lesson-level planning within the UbD framework in the next chapter.

PART III

Learning and
Language
Development
in Classrooms
and Schools

7

Differentiating Daily Learning: Lesson Planning for Language Development

CHAPTER GOALS

- **Transfer**: Educators will be able to independently use their learning to…

  – Design effective and engaging lessons that simultaneously foster students' language development and rigorous disciplinary learning.

- **Understandings**: Educators will understand that…

  – Backward design at the lesson level includes defining objectives and sequencing learning connected to unit-level learning goals.
  – Effective lessons sequence learning events to engage students by tapping into interests, challenging with complex texts and tasks, integrating meaningful interaction, and reflecting upon learning and language development.

- **Essential questions**: Educators will keep considering…

  – How do lesson plans connect to the broader unit of study?
  – What role do learning objectives play in learning and language development?
  – How can lessons integrate language from beginning to end?

- **Knowledge**: Educators will know…

  – Contextual and situational factors influencing language development.
  – Three components of language-focused learning objectives.
  – Learning events that activate background knowledge.
  – Learning events that innovate disciplinary learning.
  – Learning events that extend language development.
  – Learning events that check for understanding.

- **Skills**: Educators will be skilled at…

  – Writing learning objectives that target disciplinary learning and scaffold language development.
  – Sequencing lessons with appropriate learning events, strategies, and supports for all students.
  – Integrating formative assessments to check students' understanding and progress toward unit goals.

In this chapter, we consider how to support students' language development in daily instruction by adding a language lens to backward design at the lesson level. Similar to the equity focus emphasized across design stages at the unit level, we want to plan lessons that build knowledge and skills while also targeting and supporting language development.

Language Development in Daily Classroom Instruction

Once again we introduce two students whose linguistic and cultural backgrounds illustrate the diversity of today's classrooms. Their stories provide a context for our discussion of UbD at the lesson level.

Jesus, 4th Grader

Born and raised in the United States, Jesus lives with his grandmother in a predominantly Latino community in a large city. He was labeled as an EL upon entering kindergarten, although his dominant and preferred language is English. With enrollment documents indicating that his grandmother and parents occasionally spoke Spanish at home, the school administered the standardized language proficiency test; he scored high in oral language but low in literacy. In 1st grade, his teacher initiated the intervention process for special education services, which labeled him as having a learning disability that influenced his reading fluency and comprehension. In addition to having needs related to language and literacy development, Jesus often misbehaved in class, something that his 3rd grade teacher attributed to the fact that both of his parents were frequently in and out of jail. Now in 4th grade, Jesus has a teacher who has specifically worked to foster a positive classroom environment to support his social and emotional needs as a learner, as well as cognitive, linguistic, and academic dimensions. As a part of the intervention and monitoring process, the classroom teacher, the special education teacher, and the bilingual resource teacher have consistently collaborated to support his learning and development in daily classroom instruction. Jesus thrives by having clear goals and steps to guide daily learning, as well as ample interaction and instructional scaffolds to engage with his teachers, his peers, and the disciplinary content. By regularly checking his understanding as related to daily learning objectives, his teachers have been able to better monitor and support his learning.

Astryd, 11th Grader

Following the natural disaster in Haiti in 2010, Astryd and her younger sister were adopted by a U.S. family and moved into their home in a rural community. Enrolled in the local public school with primarily white and Latino students, Astryd was the only Haitian Creole speaker in her class. Outgoing and confident, she established a circle of friends with whom she interacted regularly. Astryd tested out of EL services in middle school, no longer having a formal label ascribed to her language proficiency and abilities. When she moved on to high school, her outgoing personality often masked her linguistic needs, specifically related to language development in disciplinary instruction. As Astryd moved across class periods, her various teachers perceived her English to be strong, based on daily conversations on topics such as her participation on the varsity volleyball team and student council. With Astryd now in 11th grade, her parents have noticed a pattern: her grades overall are average, but her achievement varies within specific content areas depending on the teacher. After her parents discuss their observations with Astryd, she self-reflects and realizes that she struggles with teachers who lecture and give traditional tests and quizzes but excels with those who scaffold and support her learning in collaborative, inquiry-based settings. After Astryd shares this realization at school, her guidance counselor works with teachers to recognize and find ways to support her language development within disciplinary classes, including chemistry, physics, trigonometry, psychology, and history.

Lesson Planning for Understanding and Language Development

As shown in Figure 7.1, the UbD design principles can be applied across layers of instructional design, all centered on the notion of beginning with the end in mind (Wiggins & McTighe, 2005, 2007, 2012). When using the UbD framework at the macro level, such as within states, districts, and schools, educators set long-term goals for learners, design cornerstone performance tasks, and draft curriculum maps to guide instruction across K–12 learning trajectories. When using the framework in classrooms, teachers first draft larger course-level goals, assessments, and trajectories, and then design units of study aimed at fostering deep and authentic learning around disciplinary concepts and ideas. Applied at the lesson level, the UbD framework prompts educators to begin with clear goals for learning, incorporate aligned formative assessment, and sequence learning events for optimal engagement and effectiveness with the aim of having students progress toward the larger goals of the unit (Wiggins & McTighe, 2012). All these layers of instructional design must be aligned and interconnected to support students' overall learning, development, and achievement: lessons support students' progress toward unit goals, units foster learning related to annual course goals, and courses bolster development toward long-term subject and curricular goals across the K–12 trajectory. In this way, lessons play an important role in students' overall learning, development, and achievement.

Teachers can respond to students' backgrounds, strengths, and needs through their daily instructional decisions, such as providing Jesus with the clear learning goals and instructional scaffolds that he needs to thrive, or Astryd with consistent opportunities to engage in collaborative and interactive learning. By merging the principles of UbD and culturally and linguistically responsive practice, our aim is to design lessons that foster language development in the dynamic moment-to-moment events in classrooms and directly connect to broader course and unit goals (Heritage et al., 2015; Herrera, 2016). This effort includes defining lesson objectives with emphases on both disciplinary learning and language development; determining ways to formatively assess students' progress toward learning and language goals; and designing learning events that activate background knowledge, use language in new ways in disciplinary learning, and extend language development beyond the classroom. Before considering specific components of lesson-level backward design, let's consider the contextual and situational features of daily instruction more broadly.

Figure 7.1 | **Layers of Instructional Design**

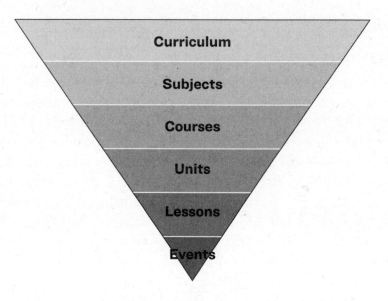

Source: Based on Wiggins, G., & McTighe, J. (2011). *The Understanding by Design Guide to Creating High-Quality Units.* Alexandria, VA: ASCD.

Supporting Language Development in Daily Practice

Think back to the principles of culturally and linguistically responsive practice that we described in Chapter 3 and have integrated at the unit level throughout this book. Those same principles remain at the lesson level. Specifically, we support students' disciplinary learning and language development by first responding to students' backgrounds, abilities, and needs and then explicitly attending to and scaffolding language. Using data from the updated profiles of students' learning and development across dimensions (sociocultural, cognitive, linguistic, academic), we purposefully design instructional contexts and situations (see Figure 7.2). *Contextual features* are implicit instructional components that are embedded in the day-to-day physical setting of the classroom. *Situational features* of instruction are explicit events that constitute and guide classroom instruction, including both strategic instructional planning and those in-the-moment decisions that teachers make to dynamically monitor and mediate student learning (Herrera, 2016). In this section, we explore how to foster and support students' language development in daily practice, including the use of contextual features in classroom environments and situational features in lesson-level instruction.

Figure 7.2 | **Contextual and Situational Features of Instruction**

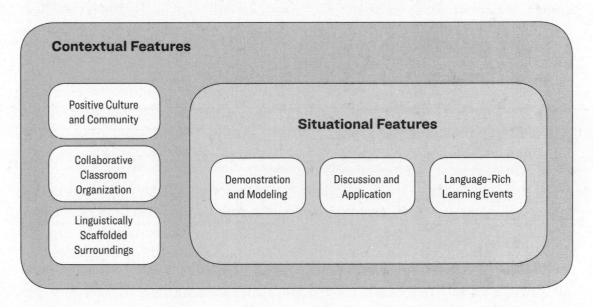

Classroom Environment

The *classroom environment* can be conceptualized as all that learners see, hear, and feel in educational settings, including physical setup, wall displays, and general climate. Designed for both students' needs and instructional goals, classrooms should be appealing, comfortable, organized, and functional to foster inclusivity and cooperation (Bucholz & Sheffler, 2009). Research has indicated that well-designed classroom environments positively influence students' learning (Fraser, 2012). In addition to the benefits for all students, high-quality classroom environments have been pinpointed as particularly efficacious in supporting the social, emotional, cultural, linguistic, and academic development of CLD students (Coleman & Goldenberg, 2010; Herrera, 2016; Wrigley, 2000). Adding a lens on language, we consider how to design classroom environments that integrate such various contextual features of daily practice as (1) classroom culture and community, (2) collaborative classroom organization, and (3) linguistically scaffolded surroundings.

Classroom culture and community

Classroom culture and community refers to safe and welcoming environments where students feel secure and comfortable to take risks with language while engaged in disciplinary learning. Stephen Krashen's *affective filter hypothesis* (Krashen, 1981, 1982, 2003) reminds us of the importance of affect in learning, as stress and fear negatively affect students' willingness to participate in classroom practice. When students' affective filter is high, or they feel insecure, stressed, or scared, they tend not to participate or take risks with language. When the affective filter is low, learners feel safe, supported, and comfortable with participating and taking risks without worrying about possible errors (Horwitz, 2001; Young, 1991). An overall positive classroom culture and community lowers students' affective filters to foster language usage and development. In addition to the connection between affect and language development, students become and remain motivated and engaged in learning when teachers and peers value and incorporate their unique cultural and linguistic backgrounds and identities (Harklau, 2000; McInerney, 2008; McKay & Wong, 1996).

Relationships drive the various contextual factors that foster language development in classrooms. Whether in a kindergarten or a high school classroom, students and teachers must come together as a holistic community to support one another in learning and mutually respect each other's unique backgrounds, strengths, and needs. Building rapport begins on the first day of school, when teachers foster safe spaces and guide opportunities for learners to introduce and share details about themselves. Teachers may prompt learners to collaboratively draft classroom visions, shared expectations, and consistent procedures to maintain positive cultures of classrooms, such as a daily community circle to close each school day, with students sharing personal feelings, thoughts, questions, and ideas. With strong relationships, rapport, and respect established in classrooms, students embrace safe spaces and ample time to learn and develop dynamically. Rather than being stigmatized for taking risks and making errors, these behaviors are considered to be central components of authentic learning. In addition to

English, all languages are welcomed, esteemed, displayed, and encouraged both inside and outside classrooms. In this way, teachers promote the shared value and celebration of students' varied and unique backgrounds and identities.

Positive classroom cultures reflect the students, incorporating their backgrounds and identities in a way that fosters community across diverse individuals. Creating such cultures includes getting to know students as individuals at the beginning of and throughout the school year to build rapport and community. Let's think back to the vignette of Jesus, whose 4th grade teacher has worked to build a welcoming and safe classroom context based on his background and needs as a learner. With two parents frequently incarcerated, Jesus thrives with consistent attention and a strong sense of belonging in the classroom, specifically taking on the role of teacher's assistant, with responsibilities that tap into his strengths and resources. His teacher regularly posts student work, and Jesus picks out his proudest accomplishments to be displayed and celebrated by his peers. With community-building a central facet of the classroom since the beginning of the school year, the rapport with both teachers and students encourages Jesus to share ideas and take risks. Astryd's language development at the high school level draws support from similar contextual factors, such as warm and welcoming classroom settings where students and teachers respect one another, rapport among participants provides the needed time and safe space to think and share, and opportunities are available to celebrate and value multilingual and multicultural backgrounds and identities.

Collaborative classroom organization

Collaborative classroom organization refers to interactive contexts that consistently engage students in learning through meaningful, language-rich tasks that simulate real-world practice with texts, ideas, and content. Learning occurs when individuals interact with one another, as knowledge is socially and culturally constructed (Vygotsky, 1978). *Communities of learners* actively engage students in learning from one another—learners from teachers, teachers from learners, and learners from learners (Rogoff, 1997). Peers work together on meaningful and real-world tasks, maintaining joint responsibility for learning and sharing of resources. In this way, learners produce authentic language across domains as they engage in learning that is grounded in particular academic disciplines. Collaborative classrooms are necessary to support students' learning and language development. Although some might view this as an instructional element, such as the incorporation of interactive strategies in a lesson or unit, collaboration should be woven into the fabric of the classroom environment.

Classrooms should be collaborative spaces that foster active learning in multiple languages through classroom setup, grouping techniques, and interactive structures. Because students develop language by using it, desks and other

know what your students strengths are

classroom furniture should be organized to maximize opportunities for students to collaborate. When forming pairs and small groups for collaborative learning, teachers can use flexible or strategic grouping, depending on the learning goals. Flexible grouping strategies prompt students to interact with learners representing various perspectives, backgrounds, and abilities. Teachers can purposefully bring together particular students through strategic grouping, such as matching learners of the same L1 to encourage translanguaging, biliteracy, and mutually beneficial learning supports. Simply organizing furniture and students into groups does not necessarily yield productive communication and interaction, however, as students need to build cooperative learning skills to engage in constructive dialogue with peers. In addition, teachers can purposefully structure collaborative work to authentically integrate listening, speaking, reading, and writing into disciplinary learning by using particular constructs (e.g., literature circles, inquiry groups, and laboratory partners) and roles (e.g., facilitator, recorder, and reporter).

Effective practitioners design and foster collaborative learning in the classroom environment, drawing from students' unique backgrounds and abilities to advance the learning of the class as a whole. For Jesus, meaningful collaboration occurs in the inclusive classroom context where he interacts with 4th grade peers throughout the school day. Mediated by the coteaching approach of the ESL, special education, and classroom teachers, who strategically scaffold and support learning in the least restrictive environment, Jesus actively participates in disciplinary learning via both flexible and strategic grouping. The coteachers have discovered that Jesus best engages in small-group work when he takes on an important and active role; Jesus particularly prefers to be the timekeeper, which allows him to contribute to interactive learning on his terms while simultaneously maintaining the group's productivity. Astryd thrives as a learner in high school classrooms that similarly stimulate collaboration. Teachers promote her learning and language development by organizing desks into small groups rather than rows, and by integrating consistent procedures and frequent opportunities to interact with peers around disciplinary concepts.

Linguistically scaffolded surroundings

Language-rich classrooms purposefully scaffold and support students' learning through the targeted use of languages and literacies around the classroom. We know that students are resourceful, tapping into various available scaffolds and supports when engaged in meaningful and authentic learning experiences (Zhao, 2012). This resourcefulness is more evident with nonnative English speakers in English-dominant learning contexts, as they seek to make meaning and find support in various facets of classroom instruction and surroundings (Genishi, 2002; Stein, 1999). The classroom environment should provide students with consistent and targeted language and literacy supports for learning. Research has consistently demonstrated the value and efficacy of students' home languages as resources for learning both content and language (see, for example, Bialystok, 2016; Cummins, 1981, 2005; Krashen, 1985, 1990; Rossell & Baker, 1996; Willig, 1985). As students use their existing linguistic repertoires to make meaning of classroom language use, research calls for building on and extending those repertoires by using, developing, displaying, and engaging in multiple languages (de Jong, 2011).

Envision classrooms that use all available space and time to support students' language development—using wall space for meaningful displays, filling shelf space with helpful resources, and designing daily routines to incorporate language and literacy. Wall displays can make language development a priority by featuring such things as sentence stems focused on particular grammar patterns and word walls that target bilingual cognates or disciplinary vocabulary. Text- and technology-based resources such as bilingual dictionaries and translation software available in all represented languages can scaffold learning based on students' linguistic backgrounds and needs. Using these resources, students' metalinguistic awareness and dynamic multilingual abilities can be further fostered with specific procedures, such as using personal glossaries that encourage the documentation of learning in multiple languages. Considering classroom practice more broadly across daily routines, teachers can creatively and deliberately use related procedural discourse to develop oral language and literacy when they welcome learners, give directions, and distribute materials.

Print-based literacy materials in and around a classroom should not be available simply for print's sake; instead, print should serve a specific purpose in supporting language development. In linguistically responsive classrooms, print-rich environments respond to students' linguistic backgrounds and needs as related to disciplinary learning. Because of his 4th grade teacher's repetitive disciplinary discourse tied to daily learning routines, Jesus frequently uses targeted words, phrases, and sentence structures. His ESL and special education teachers have designed individualized procedures that target his language abilities and needs, prompting Jesus to use particular graphic organizers to take notes, document vocabulary, and reflect upon learning. In addition to the ample print-rich labels and cues that he uses as resources for learning, Jesus thrives in the classroom library, which the teacher has stocked with culturally relevant texts, such as fiction and nonfiction books related to his favorite topic, *lucha libre,* a form of professional wrestling. In the high school context, disciplinary word walls, sentence stems, and technological tools support all students' language development embedded in content area classrooms. Teachers specifically encourage Astryd to use her Haitian Creole as a resource for learning through consistent use of a bilingual dictionary and creation of personal glossaries for units of study.

Classroom Instruction

In addition to key principles for instruction at the unit level—including background knowledge, collaborative cognitive tasks, complex and relevant texts, transfer to real-world concepts, and differentiated scaffolds and supports—other principles must be considered to integrate language development at the lesson level. Other frameworks have been put forth to support ELs and language development at the lesson level, such as the well-known and widely used Sheltered Instruction Observational Protocol, or SIOP (Echevarría et al., 2013). Unlike other approaches to lesson-level planning for language development, the UbD approach allows for pedagogical flexibility while maintaining the principles of backward design, including learning goals (Stage 1), assessment (Stage 2), and corresponding learning events (Stage 3). In addition to the contextual factors described previously, *situational factors* influence CLD student learning, and they must be considered for both instructional planning and on-the-spot support (Herrera, 2016). In the next sections, we explore three overarching situational factors of instruction: (1) demonstration and modeling, (2) discussion and application, and (3) language-rich learning events. Please note that there is no need to follow a linear trajectory in instructional design, such as a gradual release of responsibility from teacher to student, but various contexts are needed to support students in achieving the transfer, meaning, and acquisition goals.

Demonstration and modeling

Demonstration and modeling refers to how teachers introduce ideas and model practice in daily classroom instruction in ways that learners can understand. This concept is theoretically grounded in the notion of *comprehensible input*, which centers on teachers' authentic communication and language use that includes linguistic features and functions that are "just beyond" students' language proficiency levels (Krashen, 1981, 2003). In other words, we want students to understand what they listen to and read by ensuring that our speech and selected texts challenge and support their learning and language development, rather than frustrate, overwhelm, or submerse them. Because of the emphasis on teachers' use of language, considerations regarding comprehensible input are situated toward the teacher-directed side of the continuum of classroom learning contexts (see Figure 7.3). Teachers can promote comprehensible input by demonstrating and modeling disciplinary concepts, ideas, and directions using language that students understand, with the goal of both supporting and challenging their thinking, learning, and understanding. These situational factors are incorporated into classroom instruction in two ways: (1) deliberate opportunities for demonstration and modeling integrated into formal lesson plans and (2) on-the-spot decisions using formative data to amplify language usage to ensure student understanding (Herrera, 2016).

Figure 7.3 | **Continuum of Classroom Learning Contexts**

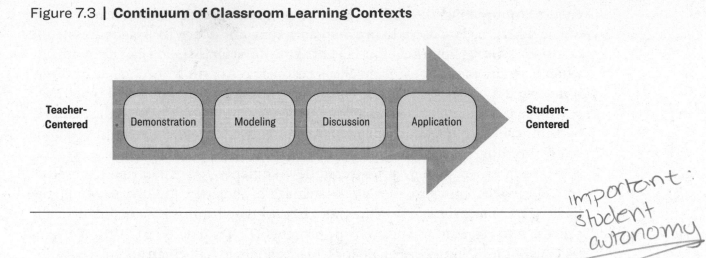

handwritten note: important: student autonomy

When planning for daily instruction, teachers include explicit opportunities and learning events that allow them to demonstrate and model disciplinary concepts and language, as well as procedural directions and expectations. Even in student-centered classrooms where lessons aim to promote inquiry and collaboration among learners, demonstration and modeling play an integral role in setting students up for success in reaching the learning objectives. Put yourselves in the shoes of many CLD students: you're in a classroom with your peers, learning and exploring disciplinary concepts and ideas in your nonnative language, such as Khmer, Urdu, or Spanish. Standing in front of the room, the teacher has just briefly stated information and directions to guide your work in small groups, but you remain unclear on the goals or expectations for learning. Whether you're an emergent EL who is just beginning to learn the language or you've had ample experience with the language outside a formal classroom environment, the teacher simply telling you what to do does not necessarily result in understanding. Demonstration and modeling provide opportunities for teachers to scaffold understanding and therefore set students up for success in student-centered learning. By explicitly including the demonstration of disciplinary concepts or modeling of procedural expectations for group work into lesson-level instruction, teachers scaffold oral language with visual and kinesthetic prompts and ensure comprehensibility for all students. Please note that demonstration and modeling do not always have to come from the teacher. Instructional design can prompt peers to both demonstrate and model, with approaches that include mediation of learning through the use of L1 and translanguaging.

Educators can also *read the room* to provide on-the-spot instruction to challenge and support learners in classrooms. Formative data collected during instruction by means such as observations and checks for understanding allow teachers to monitor students' understanding and modify speech and texts to make them comprehensible. With flexibility built into lesson design, teachers can ensure comprehensible input by modifying the *pace* of the lesson, such as recognizing when to slow down to provide more time and space for teacher modeling or student discussion (Echevarría et al., 2013). Formative data can also indicate when learners may benefit from clarification or reiteration of concepts or directions, such as *paraphrasing* ideas in other words or providing oral or written narrative in students' *native language*. Teachers should be aware of the comprehensibility of the questions and prompts they use to mediate student learning, understanding, and discussion. Strategically *scaffolded questions* (e.g., yes/no, short phrases, extended responses) allow students to respond and therefore actively participate across levels of language proficiency. Finally, allowing adequate *wait time* gives learners the time they need to cognitively and linguistically process and respond to questions or prompts (Echevarría et al., 2013). Perhaps one of simplest things we can do for CLD students in daily instruction, wait time often falls by the wayside in efforts to maintain active dialogue or get through a packed lesson agenda. Nonetheless, it is imperative to give students—particularly those who speak a language other than English—the time they need to make meaning, grapple with questions, and respond in various learning contexts.

Discussion and application

Discussion and application refers to opportunities to produce language in classrooms, specifically language that is embedded in authentic disciplinary learning tasks. In the previous section we focused on comprehensible input, which emphasizes the need for teachers' language to be clear, coherent, and understandable to learners (Krashen, 1981, 2003). But to holistically develop language, students must do more than passively receive language from teachers via listening and reading. The term *meaningful output* refers to how learners (1) produce language in daily instruction by speaking and writing and (2) learn and develop through interaction with one another (Fillmore, 1991). To foster learning and language development, students must frequently and consistently use language during daily instruction. These situational factors of discussion and application may seem obvious to many educators, particularly after the ample exploration in this book on the dynamic and interactive nature of language learning. Classrooms should not be consistently quiet, nor should they be dominated by teacher talk. Whereas educators should indeed model, demonstrate, and scaffold through comprehensible input, learners require ample time to discuss ideas, grapple with essential questions, and apply learning through authentic tasks and texts in daily instruction.

Collaboration is the central tenet behind both how and why to integrate discussion into daily instruction. Through collaboration, we make discussion a priority as an integral factor guiding teaching and learning—specifically, how students' interactions with peers and expert others mediate disciplinary learning and language development (Vygostky, 1978). We have explored collaboration as a central facet of authentic learning in other chapters, particularly thinking through collaborative and tailored learning experiences in Stage 3 with the WHERETO elements of the unit-level curricular trajectory. At the lesson level, we add specific details to the instructional plan to ensure that productive dialogue is embedded in disciplinary learning and differentiated based on students' abilities and needs. Because of its centrality to culturally and linguistically responsive practice, differentiation—including the use of preplanning data to select and tailor instructional supports for students to enable equitable access to unit-level assessment and instruction—has been discussed throughout this book. Nonetheless, differentiation becomes more pronounced at the lesson level, as we aim to both plan instruction and provide on-the-spot scaffolding with sensory, graphic, and interactive supports for learning (WIDA, 2007, 2012). Grouping in particular becomes integral when planning daily instruction. Teachers can strategically or flexibly cluster students—for example, based on L1 background or using heterogeneous language proficiency levels—to foster learning and development related to overall goals.

Although collaboration is a highly effective method to promote learning, the ultimate goal of instruction is student autonomy. Grounded in the sociocultural perspective, educators apprentice students over time through multiple learning contexts and with the support of expert others (Rogoff, 2003; Vygotsky, 1978). We want students to independently demonstrate knowledge and skills so they can be successful in classroom instruction but also (and more important) so they can transfer learning and understandings as autonomous individuals working and interacting in authentic settings both inside and outside school (Wiggins & McTighe, 2005, 2007, 2012). With this in mind, teachers provide students with appropriate instructional scaffolds, such as graphic organizers or visual illustrations, to facilitate independent practice and application of learning (Echevarría et al., 2013; WIDA, 2007). After independently considering, applying, and reflecting upon their individual learning, students share these understandings with teachers and peers. Whether students share learning through informal or formal means, teachers then have the opportunity to check for understanding and examine language development. Please note the connection back to the interrelated contextual factors of classroom environment described previously, as learners must feel safe, comfortable, and valued to take risks and communicate with peers across small- and whole-group classroom learning contexts.

Language-rich learning events

Students learn and develop language by actively communicating and using language to engage with authentic disciplinary tasks and texts. By merging the principles of comprehensible input and meaningful output (Fillmore, 1991;

Krashen, 1981, 2003) teachers can incorporate authentic opportunities for learners to listen, speak, read, and write from the beginning to the end of every lesson. Students should use language in meaningful ways in classroom instruction as they grapple with essential questions and build disciplinary understandings, knowledge, and skills. This situational factor of daily instruction could be perceived as an inevitable result of UbD instructional design, with its emphasis on authentic learning and communicative experiences invoking the language domains and functions tied to the six facets of understandings (Wiggins & McTighe, 2005). Nonetheless, historical approaches and traditional tendencies in the field of language education tend toward the behaviorist teaching of discrete language skills, through such means as rote grammar drills, spelling tests, and vocabulary lists. In today's classrooms, students should develop linguistic knowledge and skills spanning domains (reading, writing, listening, speaking) that are embedded in disciplinary learning. While learners are prompted to use all language domains across the span of daily instruction, teachers can specifically target and scaffold particular areas in need of development, as described in Chapter 3.

Language-rich learning events also strategically integrate the teaching and learning of vocabulary into authentic disciplinary tasks. Traditional approaches to vocabulary instruction have centered on preteaching academic terminology, thus separating academic language from disciplinary learning. For ELs in particular, we often see content-based learning in sheltered classrooms reduced to having students learn and define from memory a list of related vocabulary terms, rather than having them engage in rigorous cognitive tasks with complex texts. Instead, in lesson-level UbD design with a lens on language, we encourage the purposeful merging of language and content learning (Lucas et al., 2008; van Lier & Walqui, 2012). In this way, teachers support language development by contextualizing vocabulary, or providing learners with instructional scaffolds to recognize and use key terms within the context of disciplinary texts and tasks (Walqui & van Lier, 2010). Educators should indeed pinpoint the language needed for CLD students to equitably engage in daily classroom learning—including the word-, sentence-, and discourse-level language features described in Chapter 4—at the unit level (WIDA, 2012). After uncovering the linguistic blind spot at the lesson level, teachers can then contextualize vocabulary (word-level demands) and support students' overall language development (sentence- and discourse-level demands) through both planned learning events and on-the-spot scaffolds in classrooms.

English is not the only language that contributes to language-rich learning events in daily practice. Classroom instruction should embrace students' holistic linguistic abilities to foster their participation and communication in multiple languages and language varieties. As described in Chapter 3, L1 is the basis for developing both language and conceptual understandings, prompting daily instruction that emphasizes and integrates students' L1 as a primary resource for learning (Herrera, 2016). Consider our discussion of vocabulary. When contextualizing terms to foster word-level language development, teachers can build students' awareness of *cognates*—words that look and sound the same between languages, such as English and Spanish (see Figure 7.4). In addition, students should be encouraged to *translanguage*, or draw from their holistic linguistic repertoires to incorporate and build bilingualism and biliteracy (Celic & Seltzer, 2011). In addition to connecting to students' linguistic backgrounds, translanguaging further simulates authentic settings, as people use multiple languages and language varieties when interacting in a diverse and globalized world. This situational factor applies to all classrooms across disciplines, including language arts, mathematics, science, social studies, fine arts, physical education, health, foreign language, and beyond. Regardless of the language background of the teacher, daily instruction should purposefully integrate students' L1 to value students' linguistic resources, simulate authentic learning experiences, and foster disciplinary learning and language development.

Figure 7.4 | **Cognate Examples in English and Spanish**

Language Arts	Mathematics	Science	Social Studies
biography/*biografía*	congruent/*congruente*	atmosphere/*atmósfera*	candidate/*candidato*
describe/*describir*	divide/*dividir*	atomic/*atómica*	congress/*congreso*
discuss/*discutir*	multiply/*multiplicar*	cells/*células*	democracy/*democracia*
exclaim/*exclamar*	numerator/*numerador*	classify/*clasificar*	document/*documento*
finally/*finalmente*	parallel/*paralelo*	concept/*concepto*	history/*historia*
list/*lista*	product/*producto*	diagram/*diagrama*	pioneer/*pionero*
novel/*novela*	quadrant/*cuadrante*	electricity/*electricidad*	population/*población*
object/*objeto*	rhombus/*rombo*	elements/*elementos*	president/*presidente*
poem/*poema*	symmetry/*simetría*	geology/*geología*	society/*sociedad*
problem/*problema*	vertex/*vértice*	laboratory/*laboratorio*	space/*espacio*
verb/*verbo*	volume/*volumen*	limitations/*limitaciones*	state/*estado*

In summary, teachers can cultivate students' disciplinary learning and language development in daily instruction by designing and implementing various contextual and situational factors into classroom practice (Herrera, 2016). Contextual features in daily practice consist of fostering positive cultures and communities, organizing collaborative contexts, and designing language-rich classroom environments. Situational features of daily practice include mediating student learning through demonstration and modeling, discussion and application, and language-rich learning events in classroom instruction. Grounded in these broad contextual and situational features of daily instruction, we now share specific considerations to guide lesson planning.

Designing Lessons for Disciplinary Learning and Language Development

Backward design for language development at the lesson level features five elements: learning objectives, activation, innovation, extension, and checks for understanding. *Learning objectives* define the goals for the lesson, specifically corresponding to unit goals and targeting language as embedded in students' abilities and needs. *Activation* refers to learning events or strategies that tap into students' background knowledge, capture interest and motivation, build needed background, and set a purpose for learning. *Innovation* centers on the facilitation of students' meaningful and authentic use of disciplinary language. *Extension* focuses on widening the scope of the lesson to the unit, the course, and the real world. Assessment in the form of *checks for understanding* ensures that students reach lesson-level objectives and make progress toward unit-level goals for transfer, meaning, and acquisition. Activation, innovation, extension, and checks for understanding do not need to follow a sequential trajectory. For example, you may start with inquiry into a problem (innovation) and then use that to present and discuss learning goals (activation). Or you may formatively assess students' progress toward objectives (check for understanding) and then extend beyond to real-world practices (extension). The lesson trajectory will correspond to the unit goals and student strengths and needs. In other words, how can you best facilitate learning so that students reach lesson objectives?

Throughout this section, we use the previously introduced high school English unit as an example of how to design UbD instruction with a lens on language development at the lesson level (Brown, 2014; McTighe & Wiggins, 2004). Centered on J. D. Salinger's quintessential American novel, *The Catcher in the Rye*, the unit prompts students to evaluate how novels connect with human experience by critically considering if and how the protagonist represents adolescence. Astryd's English teacher, Mr. Kolodziej, seeks to plan instruction for primarily white and Latino junior-year students from rural farming communities, first recognizing that the text uses ample colloquial language unique to upper-class white adolescents in 1950s New York City. Although the author's language is likely to be demanding for his students, it is integral to achieving the larger transfer and meaning goals of the unit. Thus the teacher aims to explicitly call attention to the language used in the text by connecting with contemporary portrayals of adolescents. Within the overarching goals and trajectory of the larger unit, Mr. Kolodziej designs a lesson in which students can grapple with essential questions about the focal text by exploring other portrayals of adolescents in popular movies throughout recent history. With an explicit lens on language development, he drafts a lesson plan for a 1.5-hour block class session that includes learning objectives, a check for understanding, and learning events to activate, innovate, and extend language in disciplinary instruction (see Figure 7.5). We will explore these learning events and decisions more deeply throughout this section.

Defining Learning Objectives

Learning objectives define the desired outcomes for student learning at the culmination of lesson-level instruction. Central to UbD instructional design, lesson objectives connect explicitly to unit-level goals, including both the disciplinary goals and related linguistic knowledge and skills defined in Stage 1. In traditional approaches to planning instruction for ELs, specifically the SIOP model, content and language objectives are written separately, with content objectives derived from state standards and language objectives specifying the "academic language they [students] need to understand the content and perform the activities in the lesson" (Echevarría et al., 2013, p. 32). This approach ensures that teachers add an explicit lens on language, but it often results in either separating linguistic knowledge and skills from disciplinary learning or unnecessarily repeating the content objective in different words. When adding a lens on language to UbD instructional design, we instead merge content and language objectives, specifically drawing from the WIDA consortium's framework for drafting *model performance indicators* as a way to set goals for teaching language in meaningful disciplinary contexts (WIDA, 2012). In addition to maintaining rigor via simultaneous lenses on disciplinary learning and language development, we find this approach to be more reasonable for teachers in both planning and implementation.

When written with an explicit lens on language, learning objectives have three components: (1) language function, (2) content stem, and (3) instructional support (WIDA, 2012). Every learning objective begins with a verb that describes an observable behavior, specifically indicating the desired way that students use language to engage in social interaction, cognitive processing, and authentic learning. This observable verb connects to the *language domain* (listening, speaking, reading, writing) and *language function*. Discussed in Chapter 4, language functions align to cognitive processes, such as classifying, describing, analyzing, predicting, arguing, and evaluating (AACCW, 2010). The second component, *the content stem*, stipulates the disciplinary context for instruction, specifically aligned to the larger unit-level goals—established standards, transfer goals, understandings. Finally, learning objectives pinpoint *instructional supports* to guide teachers in selecting resources to support and differentiate for learners. As described in Chapters 5 and 6, sensory supports, such as realia and physical activities; graphic supports, such as charts and time lines; and interactive supports,

Figure 7.5 | **High School English Lesson, *The Catcher in the Rye***

Established Goals	Corresponding Unit Goals
CCSS ELA-Literacy (RL.11-12.2) Determine two or more themes or central ideas of a text and analyze their development over the course of the text.	• Transfer Goal: Consider and evaluate how fictional texts contribute to our broader understanding of real-life experiences. • Understanding: Holden Caulfield reflects common adolescent experiences but masks deep-seated personal problems related to growing up and relating to others. • Essential Questions: Does Holden represent adolescence? Is he abnormal, or are all adolescents abnormal?

	Learning Objectives
	Students will be able to… • Identify common features used to portray adolescents by using videos in small groups. • Compare and contrast representations of adolescents by using a graphic organizer.

Check for Understanding	Other Evidence
Tweet: In 140 characters or less, connect Holden Caulfield to other adolescents. You can compare and contrast with a particular adolescent character or yourself, or span out to connect to all teenagers.	• Save the Last Word and Gallery Walk graphic organizers and posters • Observational notes during paired, small-group, and whole-group work

Learning Plan

• Before lesson: Read from *Catcher* and prepare for "Save the Last Word" by writing notable quotes related to adolescence in your journal, as well as your response to each quote as connected to essential questions.

• Show brief clip from the movie *Superbad* to capture students' interest and preview video-clip activity.

• Connect to lesson goals, expectations, and trajectory, as tied to unit goals and previous instruction.

• "Save the Last Word": In pairs, take turns sharing quotes and responses, allowing a partner to respond to your quote before giving your own response. In whole group, share key ideas related to essential questions.

• After teacher modeling, small groups watch movie clips portraying adolescents: *Grease, The Breakfast Club, Igby Goes Down, Mean Girls,* and *Juno.* Discuss clip and chart observations and ideas about both behavior and language: What does it mean to be an adolescent? What are the clichés? What do they get wrong?

• Hang posters for Gallery Walk. Jot down notes on graphic organizer about adolescent portrayals. How have portrayals of adolescents changed over time? How do the portrayals compare to Holden Caulfield?

• *Tweet:* In 140 characters or less, connect Holden Caulfield to other adolescents. You can compare and contrast with a particular adolescent character or yourself, or span out to connect to all teenagers.

• Homework: Plan and conduct interviews of family members about what it means to be an adolescent.

such as L1 partners and mentors, can be purposefully integrated to scaffold language development that is embedded in disciplinary learning (WIDA, 2007). By merging these three components into clear and concise statements, teachers draft learning objectives that explicitly define the end goals for lesson-level instruction.

Teachers can differentiate learning objectives based on students' language proficiency. Remember that our ultimate goal when adding a lens on language to UbD instructional design is maintaining disciplinary rigor while ensuring equitable access and appropriate scaffolding for language development. Using these three components of learning objectives, teachers can differentiate expected outcomes for ELs as they progress in L2 proficiency by (1) increasing the complexity of language functions, (2) maintaining content stems, and (3) decreasing instructional supports (WIDA, 2012). As described in Chapter 4, language functions vary in complexity. Emergent ELs might demonstrate learning by sequencing or labeling, whereas advanced or proficient students may synthesize or generalize (AACCW, 2010). Thus, teachers modify the verb, allowing ELs to demonstrate learning by using language in varying ways. Whereas language functions increase in complexity as students progress with language, instructional supports should decrease in intensity and number to foster autonomy. With this in mind, differentiated learning objectives pinpoint multiple supports for emergent ELs, including sensory, graphic, and interactive resources, whereas advanced or proficient students are expected to perform with little to no scaffolds. The unchanged content stem ensures the maintained focus on disciplinary learning tied to unit-level goals. For teachers with ELs, we recommend further exploration of the WIDA framework to better understand how to draft differentiated learning objectives based on students' levels of language proficiency, specifically referred to as *model performance indicators* (WIDA, 2012).

When planning the lesson for the English unit focused on *The Catcher in the Rye*, Mr. Kolodziej first drafts learning objectives to guide instruction in support of students' learning and language development. The overall focus of the lesson comes from his Stage 3 learning plan, which aligns to Stage 1 learning goals and Stage 2 assessments. Nonetheless, to ensure that all daily instruction supports students in achieving larger transfer and meaning goals, he begins lesson-level design by targeting select Stage 1 goals in the unit of study. For this lesson, learners specifically work toward transfer goals ("Consider and evaluate how fictional texts contribute to our broader understanding of real-life experiences"), build understandings ("Holden Caulfield reflects common adolescent experiences but masks deep-seated personal problems related to growing up and relating to others"), and grapple with essential questions ("Does Holden represent adolescence? Is he abnormal, or are all adolescents abnormal?"). Mr. Kolodziej also revisits the related language demands that may challenge students in reaching unit goals, particularly how Holden's use of vernacular language supports his overall portrayal of adolescence. Grounded in these unit-level goals and using the three components described earlier (see Figure 7.6), he drafts the following learning objectives: *Students will be able to (1) identify common features used to portray adolescents by using videos in small groups,* and *(2) compare and contrast representations of adolescents by using a graphic organizer.* He chooses not to differentiate these objectives for ELs, considering that his junior-year students have previously demonstrated English proficiency. Nonetheless, knowing that some students bring L1 abilities in Spanish and Haitian Creole, he plans to integrate opportunities for translanguaging into the lesson plan.

Figure 7.6 | **Examples of Lesson-Level Learning Objectives**

Language Function	Content Stem	Instructional Support
Identify	Common features used to portray adolescents	Using videos in small groups
Compare and Contrast	Representations of adolescents	Using a graphic organizer

Activating Background Knowledge

A topic that has been woven throughout this book because of its centrality to instructional design for CLD students, *background knowledge* refers to resources that learners bring from homes, communities, and schools (Herrera, 2016). As described in Chapter 6 at the unit level, sound instruction requires educators to tap into students' background knowledge and then connect it directly to classroom learning. The same principles operate in daily instruction, as each lesson should incorporate learning events that build needed background for learning by accessing students' prior experiences and unique resources. Students should know that they bring valuable sources of expertise to classroom learning, which serve as springboards to reaching lesson-level objectives (McTighe & Wiggins, 2004; Wiggins & McTighe, 2005). By explicitly connecting students' backgrounds to defined learning goals, teachers hook student interest to foster motivation, investment, and engagement in the goals and trajectory of the lesson. Various learning events can be incorporated into daily lessons to activate students' background knowledge with the intention of preparing them for disciplinary learning and language development (see Figure 7.7).

Let's consider the activation of background knowledge in Mr. Kolodziej's lesson plan. When the unit began, he used culturally relevant short stories, such as

Figure 7.7 | **Learning Events to Activate Language**

Activating Background Knowledge

Instructional Event	Directions and Language Considerations
Artifact-Based Prompts	Teachers can tap into learners' senses using artifacts and visuals to activate prior knowledge. Using strategically selected _illustrations_, _photos_, or _realia_, students collaboratively discuss or write emergent connections, ideas, and predictions. These are then used to connect directly to discipline-specific concepts and language.
Brainstorming	Brainstorming events provide structures to access background knowledge using oral and written disciplinary language. Events range from open brainstorming of anything that comes to mind on a _word splash_; listing what students know, wonder, and learned on the _KWL chart_; providing specific prompts on separate pages passed around to peers in _carousel brainstorming_; and completing an acrostic with a particular disciplinary word in _the first word_.
Creative Response	Creative responses allow learners to activate and share prior knowledge by producing and explaining drawings. In instructional events such as _talking drawings_ and _sketch-to-stretch_, students draw their responses to a topic-based prompt and then use those as scaffolds to orally share their related background knowledge.
Idea-Based Prompts	Idea-based prompts center on students' responses to various statements or questions related to the lesson or unit. For instructional events like _graffiti_ and _chalk talk_, teachers place sheets of newsprint or poster paper around the room—each with a thought-provoking statement or question. Students move around to posters and respond to each prompt, writing while engaging in conversation with peers.
Interactive Surveys	Anticipatory sets have long been used to access prior knowledge using statements related to lesson learning. To foster language development, teachers can integrate interaction through events including _walk around survey_ and _find-someone-who_, as well as interactive, survey-based technology (e.g., Poll Everywhere, Kahoot).
Previewing	Previewing events are ideal for accessing and building from academic knowledge, such as students' understandings from previous units and lessons. Teachers can use _word walls_ to review topics and terms, _textbook activities_ to prepare for complex text usage, and _picture walks_ to preview and discuss other books.
Prompted Pairings	Because all students bring varied background knowledge on any given topic, teachers can simply prompt collaborative thinking and sharing. Prompted pairings merge students into pairs or small groups to share ideas based on a given topic, via activities such as _think-pair-share_, _read-write-pair-share_, _two-minute talk_, or _three-step interview_.
Reader Responses	Reader responses prompt learners to collaboratively connect with previously read texts. Because students often read mediating texts (e.g., novels, trade books, textbooks) before lessons, reader responses support meaningful reflection and discussion to activate knowledge gleaned from reading. Examples include _time lines_, _story maps_, _webbing_, _written conversations_, and _cloning the author_ (Short, Harste, & Burke, 1996).
Student Interests	Teachers can activate background knowledge by tapping into students' interests and opinions related to instruction. Designed around key topics using disciplinary language, teachers design _interest surveys_, _questionnaires_, _opinionnaires_, and _interviews_ for students to read, write, and orally discuss with peers.
Word-Based Prompts	Word-based prompts center on activating students' prior knowledge with discipline-specific words and phrases. Teachers draft questions and prompts that integrate vocabulary terms that are pertinent to the upcoming lesson. Students can respond to focal words in drawing, writing, or oral language with peers.

"Baseball in April" by Gary Soto, and poems, such as "Cool Salsa" by Lori Carlson, as coming-of-age portrayals connected to the unit's transfer goal (*Consider and evaluate how fictional texts contribute to understanding of real-life experiences*). The close readings and reflections on culturally relevant texts prepared students for the close reading of *The Catcher in the Rye*, specifically prompting them to look for poignant and notable passages that allow for further grappling with the essential questions. Throughout the unit, learners have maintained double-entry journals while reading: first copying meaningful quotes and then responding based on personal experiences in adolescence. To begin the lesson, Mr. Kolodziej uses this consistent reader-response procedure to tap into students' independent reading and personal interactions with the text. He uses the "Save the Last Word for Me" strategy (Short et al., 1996), in which one student reads a selected passage from the first column of the double-entry journal, allowing the partner to respond based on previous experiences. After the partner provides insight, the original student reads the personal response from the second column to prompt dialogue about the passage. This process continues, alternating between partners, to foster collaborative and balanced dialogue that purposefully integrates disciplinary language from the focal text. Mr. Kolodziej facilitates a whole-group discussion after the paired activity to connect emergent ideas to lesson objectives, including clarifying and contextualizing vocabulary from the selected passages.

Although the reader response connects to previous independent reading and personal experiences, the teacher is not convinced that this will get students excited about the lesson. Thus he strategically incorporates a hook for the lesson to tap into students' affinity for popular culture, particularly their shared passion for watching movies they can connect with because the films portray kids similar in age. *Superbad* is a well-known comedic film produced in 2007, featuring two high school seniors and best friends who embark upon a mission to throw an epic graduation party to gain acceptance into the in crowd. Mr. Kolodziej shows a brief clip of the movie and has students share preliminary thoughts in response to the essential question: *Are all adolescents abnormal?* With interest hooked, he then explicitly connects to the lesson goals, expectations, and learning trajectory situated in the larger unit of study. The white board in the front of the classroom displays the unit-level essential questions, pertinent disciplinary language—vocabulary, sentence stems—and the lesson-level objectives and agenda. Because much of the lesson is interactive and student-centered, students gain a clear vision of where they're headed, what they will be doing, and how the learning events will help them reach their goals.

Innovating Disciplinary Learning

Innovating disciplinary learning for language development centers on meaningful collaboration as learners grapple with essential questions, build understandings, and develop knowledge and skills. In Chapter 6 we explored the integration of collaborative cognitive tasks for all students, as well as specific scaffolds to support language development for individual learners. Whereas educators can integrate collaborative tasks and complex texts into the unit's trajectory in Stage 3, daily lessons are the primary locale for considering how to organize instructional contexts, design learning events, and individualize experiences for CLD learners. In other words, guided by learning objectives, lesson plans can foster critical thinking, cognitive strategies, and collaborative dialogue by strategically grouping learners—by L1, for example, to intermix language proficiency levels—to provide various collaborative contexts, such as pairs and small groups. Practitioners can use varied learning events to innovate language embedded in disciplinary learning and simultaneously support students' conceptual processing and language development (see Figure 7.8). Within these events, individualized supports for language development—sensory, graphic, and interactive—are used to actively engage and challenge CLD students in disciplinary learning with the goal of providing equitable access to lesson-level goals.

Within the larger unit focused on *The Catcher in the Rye,* Mr. Kolodziej innovates instruction by integrating various contexts to foster critical thinking and dialogue via flexible and strategic grouping. As previously described, collaboration in the lesson begins with reader responses using partners, with students strategically paired to allow them to use their L1. After modeling how to make behavioral and linguistic observations about adolescents from *Superbad,* Mr. Kolodziej uses video groups to provide learners with visual portrayals of adolescents and prompt the hands-on creation of posters to share with the class. Students move into small groups to engage in collaborative critical thinking using clips from movies portraying adolescents in a time range spanning from the 1950s, when *Catcher* was published, to the more recent past (*Grease, The Breakfast Club, Igby Goes Down, Mean Girls, Juno*). Aligned to unit goals and lesson objectives, the small-group context is organized for students to grapple with the essential question related to Holden's representation of adolescents by identifying, comparing, and contrasting common features of adolescent depictions. Mr. Kolodziej assigns heterogeneous groups based on students' classroom performance and participation, aiming to balance groups so that students can support the disciplinary learning and language development of one another. Learners self-select roles to mediate collaborative work toward lesson objectives: the *leader* facilitates the group, the *scribe* documents observations and ideas, the *cinematographer* stops and starts the video, the *behaviorist* records specific behavior observed in the clips, the *linguist* highlights language use, and the *character coach* makes connections to Holden.

Through this time and space for active engagement in meaningful interaction in small groups, learners build understandings, grapple with essential questions, and develop disciplinary language. The teacher uses the smaller video

Figure 7.8 | **Learning Events to Innovate Language**

Handwritten margin note: Innovatng knowledge – help students learn from each other

Instructional Event	Directions and Language Considerations
Graphic Organizers	Graphic organizers scaffold language production and organization of conceptual understandings. Graphic organizers are selected based on conceptual processes (e.g., cycle, decision tree, flow diagram, matrix), language functions (e.g., describing main ideas and details, sequencing events, describing objects, retelling stories), or language demands (e.g., cause-effect, problem-solution, compare-contrast).
Hands-on Application	Emergent from one of the six facets of understanding, hands-on application fosters authentic learning and disciplinary language development during instruction. Teachers can support student learning and scaffold for language development via body movements (e.g., total physical response), hands-on materials (e.g., realia, manipulatives), and collaborative contexts (e.g., centers, labs).
Information Gap	Information-gap events require students to communicate with one another to fill in gaps in knowledge or understandings in the lesson. In *expert groups*, students first build expertise in one particular facet of an issue and then work together in groups to share expertise and solve problems. *Gallery walks* prompt learners to explore and display one facet of instruction for others to read, discuss, and learn.
Inquiry Groups	Student-centered approaches foster collaborative learning across disciplines, thus allowing learners to develop understandings and grapple with essential questions. Approaches including *inquiry groups* and *literature circles* foster investigation and discussion related to learning goals. *Problem-solving groups* can be facilitated with teacher-derived *academic prompts,* or students can *send a problem* between groups.
Jigsaw	These events divide tasks and texts across individuals or small groups. In *jigsaw,* teachers might divide a text into smaller chunks, each of which is read and described by a student to then relay to the group. In *four corners,* students explore one related subtopic to then share with the whole group. In this way, students holistically explore concepts with more precision and less reading.
Roles	Roles, such as facilitator, recorder, or friendly critic, provide structure to guide students engaged in various approaches to collaborative learning (e.g., book clubs, discussion groups). Certain instructional events also divide responsibility and assign students to roles, such as *reader-writer-speaker* and *numbered heads*.
Role-Playing	*Role-playing* embedded in instructional topics and goals prompts learners to take perspectives and empathize with others. With approaches ranging from *puppetry* to *debates*, as well as events like *hot seat, take-a-stand* and *question the author*, students must take on specific personae to discuss, argue, and interact.
Semantic Mapping	Students create *semantic maps* or *semantic webs* to graphically explore and document conceptual understandings with related disciplinary language as they learn and grapple with essential questions. Learners begin with a core question or concepts in the center and then extend strands to explain, clarify, and support ideas.
Simulation	Simulations prompt rehearsal and participation in authentic events that connect to learning goals. Students can attend a *dinner party* where they espouse roles to converse with one another. They can create *tableaus* to enact moments in a story or event. *Fishbowls* simulate small-group discussions while others observe.
Workshops	The workshop model is a collaborative approach to teaching literacy and supporting learners' language development; examples include *reader's workshop* and *writer's workshop*. Students engage in authentic reading and writing practices while teachers provide differentiated scaffolds and supports based on learners' strengths and needs.

groups to transition into a whole-class gallery walk, an information-gap learning event in which students rely on the work of others to reach the lesson objectives. In other words, rather than having students watch all the videos as a whole group to identify, compare, and contrast representations of adolescents, this approach fosters students' deep explorations of individual movies to then merge, share, and make meaning across movies with peers. Around the classroom, groups hang posters that display the collaborative documentation of their observations and ideas. To encourage flexible grouping and interaction with multiple peers, Mr. Kolodziej has students move around freely to explore and discuss posters with others nearby. Students use a graphic organizer, designed specifically to guide learning and language development related to the goals for the lesson. He also moves around the room to provide individual scaffolds for learners, such as asking Astryd questions peppered with specific disciplinary language.

Extending Language Development

Central to UbD instruction is the transfer of learning to real-world contexts, as expressed in the transfer goals set in Stage 1 and the authentic performance tasks designed in Stage 2. As described in Chapter 6, Stage 3 instructional design with a language lens specifically aims to build students' linguistic registers and repertoires, as well as to extend their language development beyond the classroom. At the unit level, we explored how to design learning plans that foster connections across units and disciplines. At the lesson level, we consider how to extend language development following daily instruction, including specific ways to (1) widen the scope of the lesson to connect with unit and course goals, (2) connect beyond the classroom to authentic and real-world practice, (3) preview upcoming learning in relation to the lesson, and (4) design additional learning experiences inside and outside school. Homework emerges as a consideration within this aspect of lesson-level design. Rather than the traditional practice of assigning homework consisting of random exercises or drills, teachers can continue students' engagement in meaningful and authentic learning and language use around disciplinary concepts and ideas. For example, rather than assigning rote worksheets or textbook assignments, teachers can encourage related independent reading or the writing of blogs. When planning lessons, teachers integrate both learning events and consistent procedures that purposefully extend students' disciplinary language development beyond the scope of the lesson (see Figure 7.9).

In Mr. Kolodziej's English class, students have recently completed the gallery walk to explore various portrayals of male and female adolescents, specifically connected to the protagonist in *The Catcher in the Rye*. Following small-group discussions in the gallery walk, Mr. Kolodziej brings students together to debrief and widen the scope to connect with unit-level goals, including transfer goals,

Figure 7.9 | **Learning Events to Extend Language**

Instructional Event	Directions and Language Considerations
Blogs or Vlogs	*Blogs* are regularly updated websites where individuals or small groups use writing to produce new material. *Vlogs* are blogs in video form that prompt oral language use, paired with supporting text and images. Students can maintain blogs or vlogs to document and share disciplinary learning with peers or parents.
Independent Reading	When students read independently, they build autonomy as learners and continue to develop language knowledge (e.g., vocabulary, text structures) and skills (e.g., reading, interpreting). Teachers can strategically stock classrooms and display texts related to disciplinary learning, including *bilingual texts* in students' L1, as well as find ways to encourage independent reading in and out of classrooms.
Interdisciplinary Projects	*Interdisciplinary projects* prompt students to make conceptual and linguistic connections across disciplines, thus extending language beyond lessons and units. Through authentic projects, learners holistically develop linguistic knowledge and skills, including language features, functions, and domains.
Goal Setting and Reflecting	Teachers can design procedures that purposefully integrate language into the regular practice of *goal setting* and *reflecting on learning*. Students can write personal learning goals on sticky notes, which are posted near the class goals for the unit. As students self-reflect on learning in each lesson, they draft new sticky notes.
Language Detectives	Teachers design procedures prompting students to be *language detectives*, who aim to find and use disciplinary language inside and outside school. Students keep a notepad to document where and when they heard or observed disciplinary words or phrases outside the classroom.
Journals	*Journals* prompt students to reflect and share learning. In addition to traditional journals of thoughts and wonderings, teachers can target disciplinary learning and language (e.g., math journals, science journals). *Dialogue journals* can further extend language, with teachers and students writing back and forth, thus prompting students to write and to read teachers' targeted and scaffolded feedback.
Personal Dictionaries	Students maintain *personal dictionaries* or *personal glossaries* to document language development, such as academic vocabulary, multiple-meaning words, idioms, and collocations. Teachers design procedures to support learners, such as the use of the *Frayer template,* with separate boxes to note facets of each word or phrase, including the definition, L1 translation, synonyms, sketch, or applied use in context. These are tools for daily use.
Social Media	Social media, specifically Twitter, provide opportunities for learners to follow and interact online with authors, scientists, mathematicians, historians, researchers, artists, and athletes. Students can use disciplinary language to read posts, pose questions, and share ideas with individuals connected to units of study.
Wikis	Wikis are websites designed for collaborative writing and revising of various content topics. Through *Wikispaces Classroom* or *Wikispaces Campus*, educators can host and provide their own wikis, where students across disciplines and grades draft, revise, and maintain pages based on ongoing classroom learning.
Word Walls	Classrooms spanning K–12 can benefit from word walls, which teachers build across units or courses to document pertinent words and phrases (e.g., content word walls, bilingual word walls, cognate word walls). Students then use word walls as resources to prompt discipline-specific oral and written language production.

[handwritten margin note: ways to expand language w/ students]

understandings, and essential questions. He then previews upcoming learning in relation to the lesson so that students can situate their learning in the larger unit trajectory—specifically, how they will continue to grapple with essential questions and understandings to prepare for the forthcoming performance task. For homework, he aims to extend students' learning and language development beyond the classroom by having learners interview various family members— parents and grandparents, for example—about what it means or meant to be an adolescent, based on their unique sociohistorical and sociocultural experiences. Students draft, read, and orally discuss questions and ideas about adolescence using disciplinary language related to the lesson, unit, and mediating text. For those who speak Spanish at home with family members, he supports students in bridging languages to draft interview questions in Spanish. In addition to extending language in an authentic manner, this homework task supports students' overall preparation for the unit performance task: creating podcast scripts to make arguments about Holden Caulfield's portrayal of adolescence.

Whereas *The Catcher in the Rye* is the focal text of the unit and required reading for juniors in the district curriculum, the teacher recognizes that other texts better connect to students' experiences as adolescents. Mr. Kolodziej begins the unit with snippets from culturally relevant texts, aiming to first activate learners' personal experiences to build background related to the text. With the goal now to extend students' language development, he encourages students to use time both inside and outside school to read independently. A bookshelf in the front of his classroom showcases texts that relate to unit learning on adolescence and coming of age, while targeting and appealing to students as windows and mirrors (Sims-Bishop, 1990). Students can find and read novels with relatable main characters and stories, including *Mexican White Boy* (de la Peña, 2008), *Ball Don't Lie* (de la Peña, 2005), *Gabi: A Girl in Pieces* (Quintero, 2014), and *The Tequila Worm* (Canales, 2005). Despite limited options, the teacher seeks out texts with Haitian protagonists, such as *In Darkness* (Lake, 2012) and *Touching Snow* (Felin, 2007). Living in a rural community, students particularly connect to unique settings behind the adolescent protagonists in *Dark Dude* (Hijuelos, 2008) and *The Absolutely True Diary of a Part-Time Indian* (Alexie, 2007). Mr. Kolodziej also provides an array of genres, including poetry and graphic novels, with selections such as *Under the Mesquite* (McCall, 2011) and *American Born Chinese* (Yang, 2006). By recommending and making texts available for independent reading, he extends students' language development related to learning goals.

Checking for Understanding

Introduced as one component of formative assessment in Chapter 5, *checks for understanding* are actions that prompt students to reveal their current level of learning and self-evaluate their progress toward lesson objectives and unit goals. Purposefully planned and typically situated at the close of individual lessons, checks for understanding provide teachers with data points that are imperative for evaluating the efficacy of daily instruction in fostering student learning, thereby informing ongoing teaching within the unit of study. When considering how to incorporate checks for understandings into lesson-level instructional design, we need to ensure an explicit but simultaneous lens on language in addition to disciplinary learning. The goal is to prompt learners to first cognitively reflect upon learning and then share understandings using related disciplinary language—words, phrases, sentences—as aligned to the language functions (e.g., compare/contrast) and domains (e.g., speaking, writing) specified in the lesson-level learning objectives. When applying the UbD framework with a language lens at the lesson level, teachers strategically select learning events to check for understanding in lesson plans, based on available time and resources and aligned to lesson- and unit-level goals for both disciplinary learning and language development (see Figure 7.10).

Let's return one last time to the high school English lesson, part of the larger unit of study mediated by *The Catcher in the Rye*. Guided by language-infused learning objectives, the lesson has included learning events that activate background knowledge, innovate language-rich disciplinary learning, and extend language development beyond the classroom. Mr. Kolodziej has collected anecdotal data throughout the lesson, using a checklist and observational notes regarding how students engage in disciplinary learning and language use as they move between paired, small-group, and whole-group settings. Graphic organizers, posters, and other artifacts provide other evidence of students' understandings and misunderstandings as they grapple with essential questions and work toward the unit-level transfer, meaning, and acquisition goals.

In addition to observations and artifacts, Mr. Kolodziej wants to directly check for understanding before students leave the classroom. He uses social networking in the form of Twitter as a quick and engaging way for students to self-assess and synthesize learning: *In 140 characters or less, connect Holden Caulfield to other adolescents. You can compare and contrast with a particular adolescent character or yourself, or span out to connect to all teenagers.* The prompt explicitly ties to lesson-level objectives and unit-level essential questions and yields critical thinking about the most important ideas and how to portray those ideas creatively and succinctly. Using social networking sites and organizing each class section into a different user list, Mr. Kolodziej collects valuable data to inform progress toward learning goals and directions for future lessons.

Whether activating background knowledge, innovating disciplinary learning, extending language development, or checking for understanding, lesson plans incorporate learning events to support students in reaching the defined learning objectives. We have provided various summaries of learning events to give ideas

Figure 7.10 | **Learning Events to Check for Understanding**

Instructional Event	Directions and Language Considerations
Concept Connections	These events prompt students to make and explain connections between concepts. Focusing on word-level linguistic knowledge, students read and write to create *concept maps*, *concept ladders*, or *concept categories* (Allen, 2007) to spatially organize disciplinary concepts and terminology.
Creative Representations	Creative representations engage students in interpreting and applying understandings in artistic contexts. Students reflect and creatively express disciplinary understandings using figurative language in oral or written form. Examples include *poems*, *similes*, and *analogies*. Despite the obvious literary focus, these events can be used across disciplines.
Hand Signals	Hand signals prompt students to self-evaluate learning. Teachers provide a statement, such as the objective, to which students respond with a gesture (e.g., thumbs-up or thumbs-down, fist-to-five) to rate understanding. Signals provide teachers with quick data on students' understandings and possible need for reteaching.
Question and Answer	Students show understanding by posing and answering questions. Teachers can use a *question box* or *question board* to collect questions for peers or an individual (e.g., character, scientist). For quick responses, *take-and-pass* prompts students to ask and answer one another's questions via collaborative writing.
Rapid Response	Rapid-response events assess acquisition goals that students can recall and produce quickly, such as facts and discrete skills. To align with the domain of the learning objective, teachers might use oral (e.g., timed pair-share) or written responses (e.g., one-minute essay, quick write, exit slip).
Reflective Probes	Probes give students structure to reflect and share understandings. *Triangle-square-circle* asks learners to write important points, what squared with their thinking, and what is circling around their heads. The *3-2-1* activity similarly prompts sharing of 3 things learned, 2 things found interesting, and 1 lingering question, with flexibility in drafting prompts based on learning objectives.
Social Media	Aligned with students' technological abilities, social media such as Twitter and Facebook can provide engaging ways to check understanding. For example, students can use smartphones or computers to tweet reflections or responses to a prompt, including a hashtag related to the unit of study.
Summarization	These checks for understanding prompt students to write summaries of learning. Events can be straightforward written products, such as *index card summaries*. Teachers can prompt creativity and transfer when students summarize learning by *writing a headline*, *creating a bumper sticker*, or *designing an advertisement*.
Technological Responses	When available, various technologies allow teachers to check students' understanding and document data to inform future instruction. Examples include student use of *clicker-based audience response systems* to self-evaluate learning or *mind maps* to web ideas using various software or online platforms.
Visual Representations	Visual representations prompt students to *think-and-draw*, synthesizing and sharing understandings through drawing or spatial organization of ideas. Whether sketching on paper or a whiteboard, students share learning with options for teachers to differentiate based on language proficiency.

for lesson-level planning. The events draw from other books dedicated to strategies for ELs and disciplinary language and literacy (Allen, 2007; Fisher, Brozo, Frey, & Ivey, 2011; Herrell & Jordan, 2016; Reiss, 2008; Short et al., 1996; Vogt & Echevarría, 2008). These full texts can further inform educators in fleshing out lesson-level instruction to support language and content learning; however, these events should be incorporated strategically to support students' disciplinary learning and language development as tied to Stage 1 goals. To align with principles of UbD and culturally and linguistically responsive practice, learning events connect to unit-level goals, assessment, and instruction, as well as students' backgrounds, abilities, strengths, and needs.

Classroom Application:
Lesson Plans for Language Development

In the previous sections, we shared considerations and strategies to prioritize language in daily disciplinary learning. In this section, we outline how to design lessons to support students' learning and language development, specifically connecting lesson plans to transfer, meaning, and acquisition goals at the unit level.

Begin with the Unit of Study
and Students' Holistic Profiles

Lessons must directly connect to unit-level instruction to support students' progress toward transfer, meaning, and acquisition goals and related assessments. Using your Stage 3 learning plan, determine the right grain size to break up the unit trajectory into individual lessons. Then return to your students' holistic profiles, which you recently updated after your last unit of study to maintain dynamic data based on students' learning and development across dimensions. Use this information to respond to students' individual backgrounds, abilities, and needs in lesson-level instructional planning.

Consider Contextual Features
to Support Student Learning

Whereas the crux of lesson planning focuses on the instruction itself, consider how contextual factors of daily instruction within your classroom environment might support your students' disciplinary learning and language development. Incorporate ways to continue to build your classroom community, allowing students to feel valued, safe, and comfortable in taking risks with language. Integrate collaborative spaces and flexible grouping that give learners frequent opportunities to actively engage in disciplinary learning that includes various students' perspectives. Incorporate related disciplinary print materials in and around the classroom to provide consistent supports for language development.

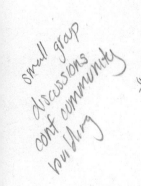

Cont to see students holistically take into consideration their backgrounds + culture

small group discussions cont community building

Write Learning Objectives with Lenses on Content and Language

Following the principles of backward design, begin with the end in mind by setting goals for each lesson. The specific lesson objectives should connect to the broader unit goals for both disciplinary learning and language development. Use the three components of language-infused learning objectives: language function, content stem, and instructional supports (WIDA, 2012). Begin each learning objective with the verb that pinpoints the targeted language function and domain—for example, *describe, compare, evaluate*. To simultaneously maintain disciplinary learning and language development, incorporate the content stem that connects the larger goals of the unit. Finally, indicate the instructional supports (graphic, sensory, interactive) that will scaffold students' learning and language development.

[handwritten margin note: backwards learning - know end goal - state obj.]

Plan Lesson Trajectory to Activate, Innovate, and Extend Language

Design a learning trajectory that supports students in reaching the lesson-level objectives. Integrate the appropriate learning events that will activate students' background knowledge; innovate discipline-specific language use with collaboration, complex texts, and critical thinking; and extend language development beyond the scope of the lesson. Consider the best way to sequence learning events within a lesson to meet objectives and actively engage students with disciplinary concepts, ideas, and related language. Rather than producing a detailed script for a lesson plan, maintain some flexibility within the trajectory to allow for the natural progression of learning as students negotiate understandings and grapple with essential questions.

[handwritten margin note: plan activities that req background knowledge · allow flexibility don't go by the book if alls good.]

Determine How to Monitor Students' Progress Toward Objectives

Based on the learning objectives, determine how you will formatively assess students' learning during and after the focal lesson. Consider procedures to observe and monitor students' progress throughout the lesson, allowing you to dynamically support students' learning and language development in the moment. Incorporate ways to check for understanding before closing the lesson, encouraging students to self-assess their progress toward learning objectives. Use these assessment data to inform subsequent lessons within the unit of study—for example, identifying concepts and ideas that need revisiting for students to continue to progress toward unit-level learning goals.

[handwritten margin note: assessments throughout - formative assessments]

Classroom Snapshot: Planning Daily Practice

Ms. Bridget Heneghan teaches 6th grade mathematics and science on the northwest side of Chicago at William G. Hibbard Elementary School, where approximately 1,200 students attend preschool through 6th grade before heading to middle school across the street at Albany Park Multicultural Academy. Although the majority of Hibbard students speak a LOTE at home, approximately 45 percent of students are formally labeled as ELs as measured by the ACCESS language proficiency test. With the school's population being 75 percent Latino, Spanish is the majority language spoken by children and families, including language varieties from regions in Mexico, Central America, Ecuador, and Colombia. Arabic is the next most prevalent L1, and other languages include French, Urdu, Tagalog, Bosnian, Hindi, Bengali, Farsi, Yoruba, Serbian, Romanian, Malay, Gujarati, Korean, Mongolian, and Burmese. One of 65 teachers at this neighborhood elementary school, Ms. Heneghan teaches approximately 54 6th graders, organized into equal class sections. Whereas 50 of her students use a LOTE at home, approximately 10 are labeled as ELs, with half of those being dual-labeled as having special needs.

The first science unit of the school year focuses on space systems (see Figure 7.11). After compiling holistic student profiles for her new 6th graders, Ms. Heneghan analyzes the disciplinary language needed to reach Stage 1 goals, including vocabulary (e.g., gravitational pull), nominalization (e.g., illuminate/ illumination), idioms (e.g., everything under the sun), sentence structures (e.g., compare/contrast), and informational text features (e.g., diagrams). She then fleshes out the Stage 2 assessments, including the Mars Rover Team performance task and supplementary evidence of students' learning and language development. Her Stage 3 plan targets disciplinary language and integrates students' cultural backgrounds throughout the unit, not just at one point in time. Ms. Heneghan taps into background knowledge from home, community, and school to begin the unit, and she builds from students' previous experiences and L1 knowledge. Aligned with her inquiry-based approach to science teaching, collaborative cognitive tasks pervade the unit with rich opportunities for students to use disciplinary language to investigate space systems and related models and images. The unit extends disciplinary language related to space systems by incorporating complex and culturally relevant texts, such as *Boy, Were We Wrong About the Solar System!* (Kudlinski, 2008), *The Librarian Who Measured the Earth* (Lasky, 1994), *How Night Came from the Sea: A Story from Brazil* (Gerson, 1994), *Child of the Sun: A Cuban Legend* (Arnold, 1995), and *Myths from Around the World* (Keenan, 2016). Designed with CLD students in mind, the learning plan outlines Ms. Heneghan's overall instructional trajectory for students to successfully achieve unit goals.

Using the unit-level goals, assessments, and learning plan, Ms. Heneghan fleshes out detailed lesson plans to foster student learning, development, and achievement. She maintains a consistent framework to guide her interactive,

Figure 7.11 | **Ms. Heneghan's 6th Grade Science Unit**

Stage 1—Desired Results

Established Goals

NGSS-MS-ESS1-1: Develop and use a model of the Earth-sun-moon system to describe cyclic patterns of lunar phases, eclipses of the sun and moon, and seasons.

NGSS-MS-ESS1-2: Develop and use a model to describe the role of gravity in the motions within galaxies and the solar system.

NGSS-MS-ESS1-3: Analyze and interpret data to determine scale and properties of objects in the solar system.

CCSS-RST.6–8.7: Integrate quantitative or technical information expressed in words in a text with a version of that information expressed visually (e.g., diagram, table).

CCSS-WHST.6–8.2.D: Use precise language and domain-specific vocabulary to inform about or explain the topic.

Transfer

Students will be able to independently use their learning to...

• Collect data as evidence to make logical inferences about natural phenomena.

• Use modeling and mathematics as strategies for understanding systems and relationships in the natural world.

• Apply knowledge of science engineering to engage in public discuss ons on relevant issues in a changing world.

Meaning

Understandings

Students will understand that...

• Science assumes objects and events in natural systems occur in consistent patterns understandable through measurement and observation.

• Engineering advances have led to important scientific discoveries that further build related industries.

• We use patterns to identify cause-and-effect relationships.

• We study time, space, and energy phenomena using scale models of systems large and small.

• We use models to represent systems and their interactions.

• We use models to observe, describe, predict, and explain motion patterns of the sun, moon, and stars. (NGSS Lead States, 2013)

Essential Questions

Students will keep considering...

• How do we learn about space from Earth?

• What could we learn from a space mission that we cannot learn here on Earth?

• How does light from space influence our world?

• How does light from space influence our daily lives?

• What makes our solar system?

• What happens in our solar system?

Acquisition

Students will know...

• Solar system components and terminology (e.g., sun, planets, moons, asteroids; orbit, gravitational pull).

• Other disciplinary concepts and terminology (e.g., galaxies, Milky Way galaxy, universe).

• Formation of the solar system from dust, gas, and gravity.

• Sun and moon eclipses.

• Seasons and connection to Earth's tilt.

• Informational text features (e.g., tables, graphs, models, diagrams, illustrations).

• Compare/contrast sentence frames.

• Related idioms (e.g., over the moon, everything under the sun).

• Nominalization (e.g., infer/inference, observe/observation, predict/prediction).

Students will be skilled at...

• Describing the formation and components of solar system.

• Reading and evaluating two- and three-dimensional models.

• Reading and following sequential, multistep procedures.

• Writing explanations of scientific phenomena using domain-specific vocabulary.

• Explaining scientific phenomena integrating information from models, observations, and numerical data.

• Comparing and contrasting objects to describe changes using sentence frames.

(continued)

Figure 7.11 | **Ms. Heneghan's 6th Grade Science Unit—**(*continued*)

Stage 2—Evidence

Evaluative Criteria	Assessment Evidence
• Thorough analyses • Accurate assertions • Innovative design • Detailed model • Precise language	**Performance Task(s)** **MARS Rover Team** Your task is to design and send a rover safely to Mars to collect additional data about the red planet. You are a member of a team of NASA scientists exploring Mars. You will present your findings to your colleagues at NASA. The challenge involves analyzing and interpreting data to determine when to send the solar-powered rover to Mars, designing a way to keep equipment safe as it lands on Mars, and using a scale-relief map to send directions to the rover on where it should travel after landing. You will produce an interactive presentation on the computer that includes data tables demonstrating the best time to land the rover, design for a rover casing that could survive the landing, and a scale map to identify the travel distance for the rover.
• Thorough narrative • Detailed displays • Cross-disciplinary language (e.g., science, math, engineering)	**Supplementary Evidence** • Space mission notebook (maintained individually by students; includes journal prompts and personal glossary) • Various student artifacts (e.g., models, displays, graphic organizers)

Stage 3—Learning Plan

Pre-assessment

• Prompted pairings to glean background knowledge from math (e.g., data collection, measurement, ratios, proportions) and social studies (e.g., ancient architecture, history of telescopes and space travel).

Learning Events

• Starting our space mission: Review class goals and set personal learning goals. Students design and share mission patches that represent their goals for the school year and unit of study.

• Hook: Read aloud *The Librarian Who Measured the Earth* (Lasky, 1994) and simulate Eratosthenes' experiment (whole group and small groups) with toothpicks in cardstock paper and flashlight.

• Start space mission notebooks (and continue regular use with each lesson), including observe-infer-predict tables, disciplinary language (e.g., vocabulary and sentence stems with illustrations and L1 translations), and responses to formative assessment prompts.

Formative Assessments

• Formative assessment probes (used to begin each daily lesson; Keeley, Eberle, & Dorsey, 2008)

Learning Events—(continued)	Formative Assessments —(continued)
• Earth model comparison: Spherical versus flat using light source (realia and video examples). • Small-group exploration of light's effects on transparent, translucent, and opaque objects in stations. • Earth-and-sun model simulation: Light source, shadows, and illumination (realia and video examples). • Seasons exploration: Students compare seasons in Chicago and places they have lived (e.g., Mexico, Ecuador, Iraq, India) doing *Walk and Talk Dots* with *Reason for the Seasons* agree/disagree statements. • Seasons exploration: Use realia (e.g., globe, rubber band, flashlight) and city-specific temperature and daylight tables to observe patterns in different regions (e.g., Chicago, Mexico City, Melbourne). • Earth-sun-moon models in small groups: Use realia (sphere on a stick, flashlight) and Galileo's drawings of the moon to investigate moon patterns (e.g., shadow, illumination) and eclipses. • Solar system photograph observations (L1 groups): Students discuss, sort, and categorize cards by characteristics (graphic organizer, sentence stems for compare/contrast). Use observations to build understandings and reinforce vocabulary (e.g., planets, asteroids, comets, moons, atmosphere). • Solar system exploration: Model how to collect and arrange data in tables; have groups make claims about temperature, size of planets, compositions, length of year, number of moons, atmospheres, etc. • Modeling of gravity, followed by gravity exploration in expert groups: jigsaw different gravitational scenarios in expert groups, then move to mixed groups to explain the solutions to others. • Scale exploration using various historical models of the solar system (see Library of Congress), as well as student scale drawings using distances between planets (compare/critique among students). • Performance task: Prepare and put students into teams for Mars rover task; time to plan and carry out. • Extension: Ongoing compilation of multilingual word wall with related terminology for the unit and classroom moon journal (i.e., what the moon looks like each day and the time it "rises" with pictures). • Extension: Providing book bins in classroom for students to independently read and explore, including (a) star stories (fiction), (b) space myths, legends, and folktales, and (c) related informational texts.	• Checks for understanding (following each learning event) • Observations with WIDA rubrics and anecdotal note-taking, particularly during small-group activities

Source: Used with permission from Bridget Henghan, William G. Hibbard Elementary School, Chicago.

inquiry-based approach to daily instruction. Based on Stage 1 unit goals, she defines learning objectives with lenses on scientific learning and related disciplinary language development. Ms. Heneghan collects similar assessment data in each lesson to determine if students achieve learning objectives, using formative assessment probes to begin instruction (Keeley et al., 2008), space-mission notebooks during instruction, and mini-performance tasks to close instruction. Drawing from her thorough preparation as an elementary and middle grades science teacher, she plans lessons using an inquiry-based learning trajectory that prompts and challenges learners to engage, explore, explain, and elaborate (Bybee, 2015). Aligned to the principles of authentic learning in the UbD framework, these facets prompt her to integrate learning events that *engage,* by hooking student interest and motivation; *explore,* through teacher demonstration and student discussion; *explain,* via teacher modeling and student application; and *elaborate,* by extending learning and language development. To maintain the contextual and situational factors across daily instruction, Ms. Heneghan consistently extends language for all learners with tools such as a multilingual word wall and the classroom moon journal, and she provides individualized supports to particular students through graphic organizers, bilingual dictionaries, and mission buddies.

As part of the larger 6th grade science unit on space systems, Ms. Heneghan designs a lesson focused on light and shadows (see Figure 7.12). To define her learning objectives, she begins by connecting back to the unit-level goals, including transfer goal (*Use modeling and mathematics as strategies for understanding systems and relationships in the natural world*), understanding (*We use models to represent systems and their interactions*), and essential question (*How does light from space influence our daily lives?*). As an early lesson in the unit, she drafts objectives that emphasize (1) prerequisite disciplinary learning on light and shadows and (2) less complex language functions and features (*Describe the key characteristics of light using realia and a graphic organizer; Explain light-based phenomena…using images and models*). Whereas these objectives target disciplinary language functions (describing, explaining) with related academic terminology (transparent, translucent, opaque, light source, illumination, shadow, viewpoint), lesson objectives across the unit increase in cognitive and linguistic rigor over time. The final component of the learning objectives, the instructional supports (realia, graphic organizer, images, models) prompt the design of the learning trajectory, with the realia-based stations corresponding to the first objective and the exploration of various models and images related to the second objective. With student-centered inquiry driving the lesson, Ms. Heneghan cultivates learning and language development by strategically grouping students in various collaborative structures, while simultaneously differentiating for individual students' abilities and needs.

Figure 7.12 | **Ms. Heneghan's 6th Grade Science Lesson**

Established Goals	Corresponding Unit Goals
NGSS-MS-ESS1-1: Develop and use a model of the Earth-sun-moon system to describe the cyclic patterns of lunar phases, eclipses of the sun and moon, and seasons. **CCSS-WHST.6-8.2.D:** Use precise language and domain-specific vocabulary to inform about or explain the topic.	• Transfer goal: Use modeling and mathematics as strategies for understanding systems and relationships in the natural world. • Understanding: We use models to represent systems and their interactions. • Essential question: How does light from space influence our daily lives?

	Learning Objectives
	Students will be able to… • Describe the key characteristics of light using realia and a graphic organizer. • Explain light-based phenomena (i.e., light source, illumination, shadow, and viewpoint) using images and models.

Check for Understanding	Other Evidence
Ancient Astronomical Architecture As a class, take a virtual tour of ancient structures that have specific effects on certain days of the year (e.g., Abu Simbel, Chichen Itza). Using a shoebox and a flashlight (as the sun), students work in small groups to design a room that would have a specific effect on the day that the sun hit a certain location. Students label the light source, viewpoint, illumination, and shadow.	• Formative assessment probe ("Me and My Shadow," Keeley et al., 2008) • Space mission notebooks and other student artifacts • Observations of student learning and interaction in small groups (stations, small-group application)

Learning Plan

• Introduce the lesson in the broader context of the unit and provide space mission challenge: What information can we get from observing light and shadows?
• Formative assessment probe: Read "Me and My Shadow" (Keeley et al., 2008) and quick-write: Where do you see light and shadow? (Prompt connections to home, community, and school.)
• Hook via heterogeneous small-group light stations: Let's look at what affects light.
  - Station 1: After viewing three websites, students observe that light travels in straight lines.
  - Station 2: Using a flashlight with objects in three bins, students observe the differences between transparent, translucent, and opaque objects.
  - Station 3: Students experiment with making shadows with different-shaped objects, such as making them bigger or smaller based on the angle of the light source.
• Whole-group simulation: Share station findings. Make a shadow in center of room with students standing in different places. Sketch how views of the shadow change based on where they stand. Provide *if-then* sentence frame (e.g., If Marisol stands in the corner, then the shadow …).
• Modeling and application: Draw a model of the shadow including vocabulary (e.g., light source, illumination, shadow, viewpoint). In small groups, make sketches and identify the light source, illumination, shadow, and viewpoint. Exchange drawings with another group to analyze.
• Demonstration and discussion: Look at pictures/videos of Earth from space to develop a model of the sun and Earth. Discuss in small groups: What is our light source on Earth? When would we be illuminated? When would we be in shadow? Return to formative probe, "Me and My Shadow."
• Small-group application: Whole-group exploration of ancient structures, small-group (organized by L1 to provide interactive supports) room design using flashlight and box (above).
• Extensions: Add to multilingual word wall for unit (e.g., light source, illumination, shadow, viewpoint) and make recommendations for independent reading (e.g., related nonfiction texts, picture books).

Source: Used with permission fom Bridget Heneghan, William G. Hibbard Elementary School, Chicago.

Chapter Summary

Whereas the crux of this book has focused on unit-level instructional design, this chapter has honed in on planning at the lesson level, with a lens on language. Many of the concepts may be familiar to you, as lesson-level and strategy-based instruction has been the traditional locale for differentiating learning for CLD students. Unlike other approaches, we use principles of backward design at the lesson level to define objectives, assess mastery, and design learning events. In this way, rather than adding a one-size-fits-all strategy or filling in a box with differentiated supports at the end of the lesson plan, we integrate a language lens throughout the lesson to foster active participation, meaningful interaction, and authentic learning. In addition, we emphasize the need to situate daily lesson plans in broader units of study, ensuring that lessons come together to support all students in achieving the unit- and course-level goals for disciplinary learning and language development. In summary, by setting long-term goals for all students' learning and development, designing rigorous disciplinary units of study with a language lens, and planning corresponding lessons to reach course- and unit-level goals, educators can develop students' language and provide equitable access to high-quality curriculum and instruction. In the next chapter, we conclude and extend learning by considering how to collaboratively use this framework to build capacity in schools to support students' learning and development over time.

8

Maintaining a Language Lens: Building Capacity at Schools

CHAPTER GOALS

- **Transfer**: Educators will be able to independently use their learning to...
  - Sustain support for language development across classrooms and schools.

- **Understandings**: Educators will understand that...
  - Supporting the holistic development of all students requires an *all-hands-on-deck* approach in which multiple stakeholders collaborate around instruction.

- **Essential questions**: Educators will keep considering...
  - How can curriculum design extend beyond individual classrooms to ensure greater coherence and vertical alignment?
  - How can various stakeholders prioritize language development in schools and districts?

- **Knowledge**: Educators will know...
  - The key tenets of designing curriculum and instruction for CLD students.
  - UbD design standards with considerations for language development.
  - Foundations and structures to support CLD students across schools.

- **Skills**: Educators will be skilled at...
  - Reviewing UbD units of study with a lens on language development.
  - Analyzing how multiple stakeholders across classrooms and schools support and prioritize students' language development.

Throughout this book, we have introduced you to students in K–12 schools. These 10 student vignettes only begin to scratch the surface of the rich cultural and linguistic diversity in classrooms, as well as the complexity and heterogeneity within the homogenous labels that teachers typically use to guide instructional design and implementation. Students enter schools with a plethora of social, cultural, linguistic, and academic resources for learning, although those may diverge from the resources of native-English-speaking children who grew up in what we might perceive as mainstream homes and monolingual communities. Recognizing that language is the medium for all learning and communication in schools, we have integrated this pertinent language lens into the UbD framework so that classroom teachers can support all students' holistic learning and development, embedded in authentic learning experiences.

Moving beyond the four walls of classrooms, we assert that the prioritization of language development cannot remain as the compartmentalized work of individual teachers. Research consistently demonstrates that learning a second language—particularly English, with its many irregularities and idiosyncrasies—is a lengthy and complex process spanning 4 to 10 years (Collier, 1989; Hakuta et al., 2000). Add to that the challenges of learning mathematics, science, social studies, and other disciplines simultaneously, typically in schools that mandate academic performance in the second language that is still developing (de Jong, 2011; de Jong & Harper, 2005). In the context of U.S. schools, it is estimated that CLD students must make 15-month gains in a 10-month school year, in contrast to 10-month gains in a 10-month school year of English-proficient peers, in order to catch up academically in six years (Cummins, 2009). With this in mind, we assert that multiple stakeholders spanning classrooms, schools, districts, and communities must embrace the responsibility and commit to systemically supporting students' language development.

Consider the students introduced throughout the text. Like Jin, Absame, Zaia, and Jesus, elementary students learn from a variety of educators across the school day and year, including ESL teachers, special education teachers, special-area teachers, social workers, school psychologists, after-school tutors, teacher candidates, and paraprofessionals. Middle school students like Emma, Fatima, and Itzel move throughout the school building to engage in daily learning in ELA, math, science, social studies, foreign language, and special areas, and then extend their learning through after-school extracurricular activities and community-based interest groups including sports and fine arts. Vinh, Astryd, Lorenzo, and other high school students move around to different classroom contexts with increasing amounts of specialization within disciplines, including offerings in Advanced Placement (AP) and International Baccalaureate (IB) programs, and at community colleges, technical colleges, and universities as they prepare for postsecondary school and work. In addition to consistent movement across classrooms within one school, students progress longitudinally across grade levels, moving from elementary to middle to high school settings within districts, neighborhoods, and communities.

Recognizing both the central importance of developing language embedded in authentic learning experiences and the extensive time needed to do so, we close this book by considering how readers can extend this work beyond their individual roles and settings. We propose ways to prioritize language diversity and development, design programmatic and curricular structures, build internal and external capacity, and collaborate with other educators across classrooms, schools, and communities (Heineke et al., 2012; Wiggins & McTighe, 2007). We begin by summarizing the key elements of UbD with a language lens explored throughout this book. We then build upon these understandings of classroom-based instructional design for authentic and language-rich learning by putting forth a collaborative framework for school stakeholders to use to improve educational policies, programs, and practices.

Language Development and Understanding by Design

UbD as a curricular planning framework embraces the challenge and opportunity to design instruction that provides students with rigorous, thought-provoking, and authentic learning in classrooms. Organized into three stages and beginning with the end in mind, UbD emphasizes the backward nature of instructional design to support students' in-depth understandings within disciplinary units of study.

In this book, we add a lens on language to the widely used UbD framework. Language is the medium of learning and communication both inside and outside schools, with ample complexity when considering various linguistic components, such as phonology and syntax; domains, such as listening and writing; and functions, such as inferring and evaluating (AACCW, 2010; Halliday, 1998). In addition, language is directly tied to cognition, as we use language to make meaning, solve problems, and share ideas with others. By adding a lens on language to the UbD framework, we specifically recognize these linguistic complexities and plan instruction that both develops language and ensures equitable access to academic learning. Recognizing the unique and diverse needs of today's students, many of whom speak languages other than standard English at home, UbD for language development embraces the centrality and complexity of language to design authentic and meaningful instruction for deep learning across monolingual, bilingual, and multilingual contexts.

The complexity of language means there is no one-size-fits-all approach to instructional design—no lists of vocabulary terms or silver-bullet strategies that will work for every student. Despite the homogenous labels ascribed to CLD students in schools, they are heterogeneous in terms of native languages, language varieties, countries of origin, cultural backgrounds, circumstances of immigration, citizenship status, prior schooling, parental employment, family structures, religious traditions, literacy abilities, and more (Herrera, 2016; Suárez-Orozco & Suárez-Orozco, 2006). Recognizing that students bring rich resources for learning to the classroom, teachers should get to know students' backgrounds, strengths, and needs to begin planning relevant, responsive, appropriate, and effective instruction (Gay, 2010; Lucas et al., 2008). Conceptualizing the holistic nature and multiple dimensions of learning and development, teachers use formal and anecdotal assessment data to discern students' sociocultural background knowledge from homes and communities, dynamic linguistic abilities in L1 and L2, culturally shaped cognitive processing, and academic competencies across school-based disciplines (Herrera, 2016). In this way, they embrace students' social, cultural, and linguistic backgrounds as the starting place for UbD instructional design with a lens on language.

Digging into the unique backgrounds, strengths, and needs of students is integral for culturally and linguistically responsive practice, but rigorous goals for learning are maintained across the board. In Stage 1 of UbD, we define desired results for deep understanding and authentic learning for all students; when adding a language lens, we ensure that CLD students have equitable access to achieve these results. To this end, we identify long-term transfer goals, understandings, and essential questions while concurrently analyzing language demands inherent in units of study to allow equitable access to learning and simultaneously develop language (Walqui & van Lier, 2010; Zwiers, 2014). Deconstructing the *linguistic blind spot*, teachers uncover the language students need to engage with goals for understanding and learning. These language demands are then pinpointed in acquisition goals. Knowledge indicators include discipline-specific language features, including words, phrases, sentences, texts, and classroom discourse, that students need to achieve transfer and meaning goals (WIDA, 2012). Skill indicators focus on the specific language functions related to the unit goals (e.g., explain, predict, infer, evaluate), and highlight language development in particular domains—that is, listening, speaking, reading, and writing (AACCW, 2010; O'Malley & Pierce, 1996). When considering knowledge and skills together, linguistically focused acquisition goals aim to develop students' language authentically and holistically, through means that include multilingual mediums and translanguaging between English and other languages (de Jong, 2011; Garcia, 2009a).

After Stage 1's focus on maintaining transfer and meaning goals, analyzing language demands, and drafting language-based acquisition goals, Stage 2 of UbD seeks to collect evidence of students' understanding, learning, and language development. Performance tasks serve as the preferred source of evidence in UbD, engaging students in complex challenges that are embedded in genuine, real-world situations, issues, and problems (Wiggins & McTighe, 2005). Because of the focus on real-world complexity, performance tasks are ideal assessments for CLD students, inciting meaningful applications and extensions of learning while prompting authentic language use across domains (O'Malley & Pierce, 1996). Whether in oral, written, or displayed tasks, students use language to explain, represent, apply, take perspective, empathize, and self-assess. Because the UbD framework typically requires students to demonstrate understanding in novel contexts, assessment tasks should allow for equitable achievement, tapping into students' cultural and linguistic background knowledge and scaffolding performance indicators based on language proficiency. In this way, performance tasks provide all students with authentic opportunities to demonstrate understanding without privileging students from mainstream, English-speaking homes.

In addition to performance tasks, effective teachers incorporate opportunities to collect supplementary evidence of learning. Recognizing learners in classrooms as holistic individuals, teachers should put together well-rounded repertoires of assessment tools to capture students' multiple dimensions of learning and development (Herrera, 2016; Moll & González, 1997). When using formal assessment tools, such as tests, quizzes, and academic prompts, the primary challenge lies in reducing cultural and linguistic biases to ensure accurate evaluation of students' content knowledge and skills, rather than language proficiency (Gottlieb, 2006; Luykx & Lee, 2007; Martiniello, 2009). When seeking out anecdotal data via observations, dialogues, and checks for understanding, consider how to collect and analyze data that simultaneously capture progress toward goals for disciplinary learning and language development (O'Malley & Pierce, 1996; Spinelli, 2008). Because all students are unique across sociocultural, linguistic, cognitive, and academic dimensions, teachers should document and track these data on individual students and then purposefully use the information to guide and plan future goals, assessments, and instruction (Herrera, 2016).

Stage 3 of UbD follows the WHERETO principles to design instruction that mediates students' learning and achievement of Stage 1 goals (Wiggins & McTighe, 2005). Recognizing the many resources for learning that students bring to classrooms from homes, communities, and prior schooling, instruction begins by accessing background knowledge to hook interest and explicitly connect to cultural schema, native languages, and previous learning (Herrera, 2016). Throughout units of study, teachers design instruction to maintain students' access to transfer and meaning goals while scaffolding and differentiating learning experiences to support language development. Unlike traditional approaches, UbD instruction does *not* separate the learning trajectories of ELs through use of simplified texts, decontextualized vocabulary lists, or grammar drills. Instead, all students engage in authentic and interactive learning experiences as their teachers select texts and tasks and provide scaffolds and supports based on cultural and linguistic backgrounds, strengths, and needs. Units also include experiences that extend students' learning and language development beyond the scope of study, connecting understandings, knowledge, and skills (including those focused on language) to prior and subsequent units of study, across academic disciplines, and beyond the classroom to real-world practice. Formative assessments are integrated into the learning plan to capture authentic language-in-use data that inform students' progress toward unit goals and teachers' subsequent instruction.

Although the crux of this book focuses on instructional design for language development at the unit level, lesson-level considerations remain important to support teaching and learning in daily practice. Lesson planning has been the traditional focus of approaches to EL teaching and learning, with teachers writing language objectives and including particular strategies for ELs (see, for example, Echevarría et al., 2013). We argue that lesson planning is most meaningful and supportive of students' holistic learning and development when it is situated in long-term goals at both the unit and course levels. In this way, following the planning of Stage 3 at the unit level, teachers organize the learning trajectory into lesson plans (Wiggins & McTighe, 2012). Similar tenets of UbD for language at the unit level can be applied to the lesson level, including setting goals, collecting formative data, designing tasks, and selecting texts with an explicit lens on language development. Working toward the larger goals of the unit, lesson plans begin with learning objectives that capture both content and language. To support students in achieving objectives, teachers then plan appropriate events that tap into background knowledge and check for understanding, as well as appropriate scaffolds and materials to foster disciplinary learning and language development simultaneously.

By now, you have started to wrap your head around big ideas related to UbD for language development. In addition to your reading, we hope that you have applied your learning to instructional planning and discussed it with colleagues. We know that effective professional learning and development should be both collaborative and applicable to daily practice (Gulamhussein, 2013). Once you have completed a draft of your first UbD unit with a lens on language, you should continue to improve and refine instructional plans by reviewing your work and tapping into the expertise of your peers. As Wiggins and McTighe (2012) remind us, unit design is "an extended and cyclical process of continuous improvement, involving drafting and refinement based on feedback from reviews, implementation, and results" (p. 118).

Introduced in Chapter 1, UbD design standards serve as the starting point to review and revise units of study (Wiggins & McTighe, 2012), providing criteria for designers, colleagues, and outside experts to approach draft units. When designers feel prepared, they should also use the additional language considerations that supplement these design standards (see Figure 8.1), which include the analyses of language demands to ensure the linguistic accessibility to unit goals and target specific goals for language development, as well as assessment and instruction that taps into background knowledge and provides appropriate scaffolds, supports, and materials to support unique and diverse students' language development.

In addition to individual and collaborative review using UbD design standards *before* the implementation of units of study, educators resume the process of

Figure 8.1 | **UbD Design Standards with a Language Lens**

To what extent does the unit plan...		
	UbD Design Standards	**Language Lens**
Stage 1	1. Identify important, transferable ideas worth exploring and understanding?	
	2. Identify understandings stated as full-sentence generalizations: *Students will understand that...*?	Analyze disciplinary understandings for language demands?
	3. Specify the desired long-term transfer goals that involve genuine accomplishment?	
	4. Frame open-ended, thought-provoking, and focusing essential questions?	Word questions to be linguistically accessible for all students?
	5. Identify relevant standards, mission, or program goals to be addressed in all three stages?	
	6. Identify knowledge and skills needed to achieve understanding and address the established goals?	Target knowledge and skills to further language development?
	7. Align all the elements so that Stage 1 is focused and coherent?	
Stage 2	8. Specify valid assessment evidence of all desired results (i.e., Stage 2 aligns with Stage 1?)	Reduce potential bias for students from diverse backgrounds?
	9. Include authentic performance tasks based on one or more facets of understanding?	Use tasks that tap into students' background knowledge?
	10. Provide sufficient opportunities for students to reveal their achievement?	Provide language-rich opportunities to demonstrate language development?
	11. Include evaluative criteria to align each task to desired results and to provide suitable feedback on performance?	Differentiate assessments based on linguistic abilities?
Stage 3	12. Include learning events and instruction needed to help learners— 　Acquire targeted knowledge and skills? 　Make meaning of important ideas? 　Transfer their learning to new situations?	Provide appropriate scaffolds, supports, and materials to support language development?
	13. Effectively incorporate the WHERETO elements so that the unit is likely to be engaging and effective for all learners?	Differentiate based on the backgrounds, abilities, and needs of students from diverse backgrounds?
Overall	14. Align all three stages as a coherent whole?	

Source: From *The Understanding by Design Guide to Creating High-Quality Units* (p. 27), by G. Wiggins and J. McTighe, 2011, Alexandria, VA: ASCD. Copyright 2011 by G. Wiggins and J. McTighe. Adapted with permission.

continuous improvement both *during* and *after* instruction (Wiggins & McTighe, 2012). Teachers know that instruction on paper does not always end up looking the same in practice, due to the myriad variables of day-to-day life in classrooms. All classrooms are complex and dynamic locales, situating diverse students' learning and development across multiple dimensions (Herrera, 2016; Wrigley, 2000). In today's classrooms, particularly considering the diversity among students, we know that a unit of study may need to be tweaked and changed at any point to meet students' backgrounds, strengths, and needs. Often working intuitively, educators should formalize processes to collect, organize, synthesize, and reflect upon multiple sources of data. Teachers also should welcome peer observations and feedback from colleagues, administrators, and external partners. To maintain a lens on language development, consider inviting EL teachers, coaches, or instructors to your classroom. This ongoing review should be done *during* unit implementation to allow for real-time revisions to the learning plan, as well as *after* completion to note enhancements and considerations for subsequent iterations.

As illustrated in Figure 8.2, educators can individually tackle iterations of UbD, including Stages 1, 2, and 3 of instructional design and what has been termed Stages 4, 5, and 6 of the follow-up and continuous feedback loop before, during, and after instruction (Wiggins & McTighe, 2012). However, as suggested in the cycles of review and revision just described, collaboration can greatly enhance curriculum and instruction by tapping into the expertise and support of colleagues. Ample research supports the notion of collaborative professional development, with educators coming together to study a problem of practice, discuss common readings, analyze student work, debrief peer observations, and more (see, for example, Cochran-Smith & Lytle, 1998; Florio-Ruane, 2001; Grossman, Wineburg, & Woolworth, 2001; Lewis & Ketter, 2004; Rogers & Mosely, 2008; Smith & Hudelson, 2001). We encourage you to collaborate with your colleagues within and across grades and disciplines as you work to understand language development, collect and analyze data on student learning, and integrate the language lens into units of study.

To better facilitate collaborative professional learning structures for educators, leaders can prioritize UbD for language development in schools and districts by engaging in backward design—or what Wiggins and McTighe (2007) have called *Schooling by Design*. In the next section, we broaden our perspective to share a framework for how stakeholders can define macro-level goals and plan to maximize the long-term supports for students' learning.

Figure 8.2 | **Unit Design and Feedback Loop**

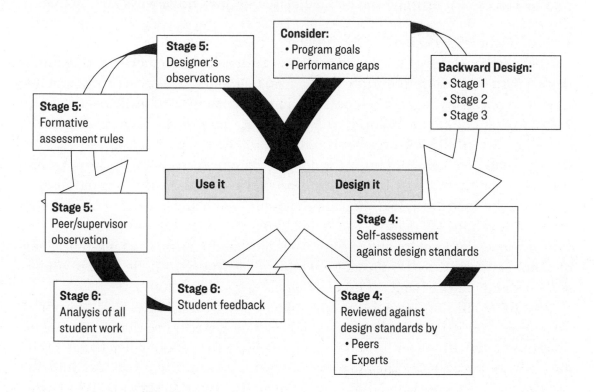

Understanding by Design for Language Across Schools

The classroom teacher is the number one in-school factor influencing student achievement, confirming the integral role of daily instruction in students' learning and language development (Cochran-Smith & Lytle, 2008; Gándara & Maxwell-Jolly, 2006; Sanders & Rivers, 1996). Nonetheless, we know that various educators influence learning throughout the school day, week, year, and experience, as students move between classes, specialty areas, resource rooms, grade levels, and schools. For CLD students, learning a second language at the same time they are learning academic content can take up to 10 years, necessitating an all-hands-on-deck approach in schools (Collier, 1989; Cummins, 2009; Hakuta et al., 2000). With this in mind, we assert the need to extend UbD with a lens on language across schools and districts by starting with the end goals for learning (Wiggins & McTighe, 2007). Stakeholders first define a mission for student learning, which then guides the design and implementation of programs, curriculum, and instruction for CLD students, and capacity-building efforts develop educators' expertise in culturally and linguistically responsive practice.

Defining the School's Mission

Extending the explicit foci on CLD students and language development begins with a mission that unites school stakeholders and drives daily practice (Heineke et al., 2012). A school's mission has the potential to bring together individuals throughout the building with common, unifying goals that become the shared responsibility of the school community (Schmoker, 2011; Wrigley, 2000). Rather than teachers serving as independent contractors in their individual classrooms, a shared mission statement becomes a collaborative commitment to fostering the long-term learning, development, and achievement of all students across the school (Wiggins & McTighe, 2007). Student-focused in nature, this statement serves to drive and maintain a relentless focus on the long-term goals of schools, which centers around enabling all learners to demonstrate understanding and mature habits of mind (Wiggins & McTighe, 2007).

By first defining aspirations for students' education and then specifying long-term goals to get there, backward design becomes more than a process for designing curriculum units; it serves as a vehicle for schoolwide change (Wiggins & McTighe, 2007). The *mission* defines our commitment for the education of students. We recommend that school and district mission statements be cast in terms of long-term transfer goals, or what we want students to be able to do with the learning once they complete their educational careers in K–12 schools. For example, in addition to developing academic skills, a school's mission statement might declare a commitment to developing critical and creative thinkers, collaborative workers, responsible risk takers, and civically engaged members of the community. To formulate or update an educational mission statement, key stakeholders must come together to discuss, deconstruct, and define a portrait of the graduate—a long-term picture of what students will be able to do. Once identified, the mission then serves as the north star to help prioritize and plan curriculum, assessments, and instruction backward with long-term ends in mind.

Throughout this book, the message has been consistent: we do not plan separate instruction for CLD students, but rather maintain rigorous goals and expectations in inclusive classrooms with a lens on language development. That message does not change when we shift our focus to changing practice across schools. Thus, school stakeholders should not define a separate mission for CLD students but rather consider the existing mission statement with a lens on language. For example, when considering our long-term goals for students, how does language come into play? Perhaps we envision and set goals for our learners to be versatile communicators who are bilingual, biliterate, culturally competent, and globally minded. Grounded in theory and research, these language-focused goals specifically target the linguistic strengths and rich backgrounds of CLD students but also broadly benefit the learning and development of all students (de Jong, 2011; de Jong & Harper, 2008; Herrera, 2016). By adding the language lens to the mission that drives practice in schools, stakeholders explicitly include CLD students as part of the school community and prioritize language diversity and development as being integral to daily work across the building (see Figure 8.3).

Figure 8.3 | **Features of Linguistically Responsive Schools and Classrooms**

School Features

• Multiple languages are portrayed around the school through bulletin boards and displays.

• Multiple languages are represented in oral school communications, such as the morning announcements and discourse around the school building.

• Multiple languages are represented in written school communications, such as newsletters, report cards, and parent notifications.

• Culture is a consideration when welcoming students and families into the school and preparing them for success in U.S. schools.

• Mirroring the linguistic diversity of students, school personnel are bilingual.

• All students have access to special areas, the library, and extracurricular activities.

• The school library has a wide variety of bilingual and L1 books and materials.

• The school library has a wide variety of books and audiovisual materials that are culturally relevant and portray diverse individuals and families.

• Faculty members have access to multilingual resources to support instruction.

• Faculty members recognize the importance and value of language diversity.

Classroom Features

• Classrooms are welcoming environments where students feel comfortable taking risks.

• Classrooms provide consistent procedures and routines to focus students on learning.

• Teachers consistently work to foster community and collaboration within the classroom.

• Teachers celebrate students' assets and make them a central part of the curriculum.

• Teachers recognize and use students' native languages as resources.

• Teachers understand the appropriate ways to accommodate student language, such as by using wait time and appropriately responding to linguistic errors.

• Classrooms are print-rich environments with multilingual supports.

• Classrooms provide collaborative opportunities for students to creatively make meaning.

• Teachers set short-term and long-term goals for academic and language achievement.

• Teachers collect data on students' backgrounds and abilities to guide decision making.

• Teachers incorporate background knowledge from homes, communities, and schools.

• Teachers value and involve parents and families in meaningful ways.

Supporting Curriculum and Instruction

With clarity about the school's long-term mission, stakeholders can put structures in place for schoolwide design and implementation of curriculum and instruction to support student learning, development, and achievement. In *Schooling by Design*, Wiggins and McTighe (2007) describe the need for schools to develop a curricular framework that honors and works toward the student-centered mission of deep understanding and authentic learning, ensuring that content coverage is not the tacit approach to instruction across classrooms. Indeed, consistency in the approach to teaching and learning throughout the school is important as stakeholders collaboratively work toward shared goals. Consider a 2nd grade classroom that engages students in inquiry-based learning designed around understandings and essential questions, only to be followed by a 3rd grade classroom typified by thematic activities, spelling tests, and rote worksheets. To reach the long-term goals of schooling for students, stakeholders collaboratively design and implement curriculum and instruction spanning the school across grade levels, content areas, and special areas. In addition, school leaders prioritize the school mission, structures, and commitments when making decisions related to policies, job descriptions, and use of resources (Wiggins & McTighe, 2007).

To support students' long-term language development, stakeholders must also explicitly define how language is used and supported in programs, curriculum, and instruction across the school, as illustrated in Figure 8.4 (Hilliard & Hamayan, 2012). This is particularly important for students labeled as ELs, as both federal and state language policies require formal program models that are research-based, appropriately funded, and effective in demonstrating students' language development and academic achievement (Gándara & Hopkins, 2010). At the *programmatic level*, stakeholders strategically determine the appropriate EL or bilingual program model and specifically designate language allocations across the entirety of the program. Examples of these programs include two-way immersion, transitional bilingual education, or sheltered instruction that ties specific percentages to language use as students progress through school. Directly embedded in the broader program model, the *curricular level* refers to stakeholders' determination of which subjects to teach in each language at each grade level. The *instructional level*, the focus of this text, encompasses the day-to-day decisions regarding linguistic use in classroom instruction by students and teachers, such as separating, merging, or bridging students' first and second languages.

In this way, program models emerge as the schoolwide structure that situates and aligns classroom curriculum and instruction across grade-level and content-area classes. In other words, classroom-by-classroom instructional scaffolds are no substitute for sound schoolwide supports for students' longitudinal language development (Santos, Darling-Hammond, & Cheuk, 2012). Responding to the backgrounds and needs of students, as well as the mission defined by stakeholders, schools design and implement programs that guide decisions related to curriculum and instruction. For example, with balanced numbers of native Spanish and English speakers, as well as a faculty committed to bilingualism and biliteracy, a school designs and implements a two-way immersion program with equal allocations of languages across grade levels (a 50-50 model). The literacy curriculum is provided in both languages, with math and science in Spanish, and social studies and special areas in English. To reach the school's goals for bilingualism and biliteracy, linguistic bridging strategies become integral in daily instruction to connect content concepts and develop disciplinary language in both Spanish and English. With a clearly defined program model that informs curriculum and instruction, as well as the appropriate human and material resources to implement the model effectively, school stakeholders work toward shared goals for students' language development and academic achievement.

Figure 8.4 | **Schoolwide Programs for CLD Students**

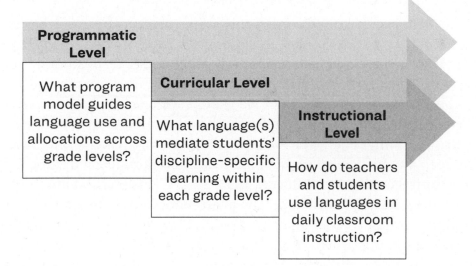

Source: Based on "How Do We Plan for Language Development?" by J. Hilliard and E. Hamayan, in E. Hamayan and R. Field (Eds.), *English Language Learners at School: A Guide for Practitioners* (2nd ed., pp. 121–123), 2012, Philadelphia: Caslon.

Building Professional Capacity in Schools

With a clear mission and associated programs in place to support CLD students, schools then focus on building professional capacity so that teachers and other stakeholders are able to successfully work toward goals and enact programs in practice. Research has demonstrated that macro-level foundations and policies, such as school mission statements or bilingual program models, often differ from what actually occurs in classroom practice (see, for example, Coburn & Stein, 2006; Colón & Heineke, 2015; Datnow, Lasky, Stringfield, & Teddlie, 2006; Heineke & Cameron, 2011, 2013; Honig, 2006). In other words, in their daily practice with students, educators actively make decisions that might include enacting, modifying, or ignoring the existing school structures. To influence daily practice aligned to the larger mission of the school, stakeholders first set goals for faculty related to UbD and language development and then design experiences to build their professional capacity. Recognizing the complexity of building teacher expertise to incite meaningful school change, we embrace a sociocultural framework to consider individual, interpersonal, and institutional facets of professional learning (Rogoff, 1995). To build professional capacity in schools, educators should engage in *individual* learning around a set of principles to support classroom decision making, *interpersonal* learning about effective pedagogy in collaboration with school colleagues, and *institutional* learning related to the unique educational and policy context.

Teaching and learning as principled practice

All teachers are decision makers; they make myriad choices every day that influence teaching and learning (de Jong, 2011; Ricento & Hornberger, 1996). Whether setting expectations for learning, posing questions to students, or organizing groups in classrooms, teachers often make choices unknowingly as they engage in complex daily work. What we want is for teachers to be *informed* and *principled* decision makers. In our sociocultural approach to capacity building in schools, this individual layer focuses on developing teacher expertise starting with deep and principled understandings of learners, learning, and language learning (Heritage et al., 2015; Rogoff, 1995, 2003). This method might require a shift for many educators because of the overreliance on immediately applicable learning and overemphasis of one-size-fits-all strategies in professional development, particularly in the field of EL teaching and learning. By taking the time to build understandings, educators gain much more than a handful of teaching strategies; they construct a pertinent and principled lens with which to view, enact, and influence every facet of student learning.

Thus, we recommend that educators seeking to incite broader school change use a shared set of learning principles to support all classroom- and school-based decisions about pedagogy and planning. In Chapters 1 and 2, we shared the seven overarching tenets of learning that guide the UbD framework, and the three that relate specifically to adding a language lens. These principles have guided the ideas presented throughout this book. In seeking to construct deeper understandings to guide decision making as connected to the UbD approach for language development, it is useful to revisit the 10 principles for using UbD in culturally and linguistically diverse classrooms. These can serve as a place to begin to build buy-in and develop professional capacity with educators focused on supporting authentic and rigorous learning with CLD students:

1. Learning is enhanced when teachers think purposefully about curricular planning. The UbD framework supports thoughtful curriculum design without offering a rigid process or prescriptive program.

2. The UbD framework helps focus curriculum and teaching on the development and deepening of student understanding and transfer of learning—that is, the ability to effectively use content knowledge and skill.

3. Understanding is revealed when students can make sense of, and transfer, their learning through authentic performance. Six facets of understanding—the capacity to explain, interpret, apply, shift perspective, empathize, and self-assess—can serve as indicators of understanding.

4. Effective curriculum is planned *backward* from long-term outcomes through a three-stage design process. This process helps avoid three common educational problems: (a) treating the textbook as the curriculum rather than a resource, (b) activity-oriented teaching in which no clear priorities and purposes are apparent, and (c) test prep in which students practice the format of standardized tests (usually selected-response items) while concentrating only on tested content.

5. Teachers are coaches of understanding, not mere purveyors of content knowledge, skill, or activity. They focus on ensuring that transfer of learning happens; they do not just assume that what was taught was learned.

6. Regular reviews of curriculum against UbD Design Standards enhance curricular quality, leading to deeper learning, while concomitant reviews of student work in professional learning communities (PLCs) inform needed adjustments in curriculum and instruction to maximize student learning.

7. Teachers, schools, and districts can *work smarter* and more effectively by sharing their curriculum and assessment designs with others in various ways, including through web-based tools such as the Eduplanet21 Unit Planner and shared database (https://www.eduplanet21.com/).

8. All teachers have the responsibility to support students' learning and language development. Language develops in the context of disciplinary learning, such as mathematics, social studies, sciences, and fine arts. Thus, language cannot be separated and maintained as the sole obligation of particular classrooms (e.g., ESL) or courses (e.g., English language arts).

9. All students are capable of achieving rigorous, grade-level goals for learning and understanding, regardless of ascribed labels or particular variables that have often unintentionally prompted lower expectations in

classrooms and schools (e.g., students who speak languages or language varieties other than Standard English, recent immigrants, and refugees from other countries).

10. All students bring rich resources for learning to the classroom, including those with knowledge, experiences, and language repertoires that differ from those of white, middle-class, English-dominant students. Teachers should embrace and integrate students' backgrounds and multifaceted language abilities into instructional design to support learning and language development.

Collaborating to support student learning

In addition to building the capacity of principled decision makers in classrooms, educators coconstruct knowledge to support students' authentic learning and language development. By strategically designing professional learning experiences and opportunities, school stakeholders can expand principled work from the classroom level to the school level. We know that learning is social and interactive in nature, which makes collaboration among educators pertinent (Rogoff, 2003; Vygotsky, 1978). Whether collaborating horizontally in grade-level or departmental teams or vertically in cross-grade teams or professional learning communities, teachers support one another in purposeful planning and implementation to reach determined goals for both student learning and development and their own professional learning and development. Collaborative professional learning should be consistent and ongoing, as well as structured through formal procedures, protocols, and practices related to such things as professional learning communities and peer observations. We argue that supporting CLD students' learning and language development should be incorporated into existing collaborative learning structures in schools, explicitly adding the language lens to extant areas of professional learning and development. In line with the 10 principles of CLD student learning (de Jong, 2011; Wiggins & McTighe, 2007), this stance reinforces the pertinent message that supporting students' language development is not an add-on or a "this too shall pass" initiative, but rather a pertinent lens taken on all we do in schools.

Teachers have been the focal audience of this book because of our concentration on curricular and instructional design. Nonetheless, schools employ many adults who have distinctive roles in fostering the learning and development of CLD students, whether physical, social, emotional, behavioral, cultural, linguistic, cognitive, or academic (Herrera, 2016; Wrigley, 2000). Thus principled decision making and collaborative professional learning opportunities extend beyond classroom teachers, embracing, as suggested earlier, an all-hands-on-deck approach to involve all stakeholders in supporting the holistic CLD learner in schools (Heineke et al., 2012). As schools work toward their mission for student learning, development, and achievement, stakeholders should recognize and embrace the reality that every employee plays a unique and important role in the education of students. Tapping into the rich and varied human resources in the school building, collaborative learning experiences should consider the valuable expertise that each stakeholder brings to the school community of practice (see Figure 8.5). Whether a teacher, a librarian, a social worker, or a psychologist, faculty members must commit to and participate in professional learning to realize the shared vision for CLD student learning and development.

Looking beyond classroom and school walls

The all-hands-on-deck approach to improve schools cannot stop at the property lines of the school building (Heineke et al., 2012). Schools exist within larger communities, which should be viewed as resources when considering ways to reach the school's mission, to design programs and curriculum, and to build capacity for supporting students' holistic learning and development. Parents and families are the primary partners of school-based educators, as they can contribute unique insight into the cultures, backgrounds, experiences, and identities of the learner and explicate rich funds of knowledge, including home language, literacy, and numeracy skills (Moll & González, 1997). In addition to families, other external actors have distinctive human and material resources that can contribute to the school's mission, programs, and capacity-building work for student learning and language development, including those working at local universities, community organizations, and cultural institutions (see Figure 8.5). School-based educators should become aware of external resources and then partner with stakeholders in strategic ways to support students, parents, and families.

In addition to being situated in communities, schools typically operate within larger districts or institutional hierarchies. To build capacity for supporting students' learning and language development, districts can provide professional learning opportunities that span stakeholders across schools and communities. Recognizing the unique needs of students in particular educational contexts, such as early childhood or science education, district leaders can bring together educators from across schools to engage in deeper, context-specific learning related to UbD for language development. In addition to these horizontal opportunities for collaboration within disciplines, cross-school professional learning should also bring together educators vertically across grade levels, such as elementary, middle, and high school teachers who serve students in the same community. To accomplish these types of collaboration focused on language at the district level, leaders must recognize the importance of language development and prioritize CLD students' learning within the larger policies, programs, and practices in the district. We contend that this should not be approached as another initiative, but rather become a central tenet of the district's approach to teaching and learning.

Figure 8.5 | **Stakeholder Contributions to CLD Student Learning**

Role	Examples of Contributions
Teacher	Knowledge of individual students' backgrounds, abilities, and needs, as well as content knowledge within and across disciplines
Bilingual Teacher	Skills in building, maintaining, and bridging students' native languages in support of second language and literacy development
ESL Teacher	Knowledge of linguistics, including the components, functions, domains, and developmental stages of English language proficiency
Administrator	Knowledge of longitudinal student progress and cross-school practices that support long-term learning and language development
Librarian	Knowledge of culturally relevant texts and materials to mediate learning, including those in students' native languages
Social Worker	Skills in understanding and supporting social and emotional learning, as connected to cultural experiences and expectations
School Psychologist	Skills in administering culturally and linguistically valid assessments to accurately determine students' abilities and needs
Counselor	Skills in supporting students through academic transitions, such as when moving across program models or schools
Case Manager	Knowledge of students' parents, families, homes, communities, and other external support systems for learning and development
School Nurse	Knowledge of students' physical development, including culturally specific health and wellness patterns and trends
Parent/Family Member	Knowledge of interests, experiences, and abilities of the learner, including social, emotional, cultural, linguistic, and academic
Community Member	Knowledge of the social and historical context of the community, as well as available cultural and linguistic resources
University Partner	Knowledge of federal and state language policies, effective bilingual and EL programs, and research-based practices for CLD students
Teacher Candidate	Knowledge of up-to-date research and related practice to support CLD students' learning and language development
Cultural Institution	Skills in designing out-of-school learning experiences to support students' disciplinary learning and language development
Community Organization	Skills in seeking out social, economic, cultural, and linguistic resources and supports for students, parents, and families

By no means an exhaustive outline of next steps, our suggestions provide a preliminary set of ideas to encourage readers to think of ways to extend the lens on language development beyond individual classroom practice. For more all-encompassing exploration, we recommend reading *Schooling by Design: Mission, Action, and Achievement* (Wiggins & McTighe, 2007) for an overarching conceptual and practical approach to school-level change that is connected to the principles and practices of backward design. To add specific lenses on CLD students' learning and development, you can supplement with articles (e.g., Heineke, Coleman, Ferrell, & Kersemeier, 2012), chapters (e.g., Lucas et al., 2008), policy reports (e.g., Tung et al., 2011), or texts (e.g., Miramontes, Nadeau, & Commins, 2011; Soltero, 2011) focused at the school level. This book can serve as a starting place for you and your colleagues to grapple with the challenges and opportunities of using the UbD framework with CLD students. You can also read and discuss to collectively build understandings, knowledge, and skills to implement supports for language development within and beyond school buildings. To illustrate what this might look like in your context, we close by pulling together the individual teachers featured throughout this book to share the ongoing, collaborative work within and across schools on Chicago's Northwest Side.

Maintaining a Language Lens Across Schools

Earlier chapters introduced teachers who are doing the important work of designing UbD instruction with a language lens to support students' learning, development, and achievement. Chapter 3 profiled Mrs. Tellez at Newton Bateman Elementary School in her design of English language arts instruction that responds to the diverse backgrounds and unique needs of her middle schoolers. Chapter 4 explored how Ms. Hartmann supports the disciplinary language demands and functions in her earth science class at Theodore Roosevelt High School. Chapter 5 probed how Mr. Carman uses multiple forms of authentic and culturally responsive assessment in the middle school mathematics classroom at Albany Park Multicultural Academy. Chapter 6 described the 1st grade classroom of Ms. Niekra at Peter Reinberg Elementary School, specifically the language-rich learning trajectory of the integrated social studies and literacy unit. Chapter 7 connected to lesson-level backward design, exemplified by Ms. Heneghan and her scientific inquirers at William G. Hibbard Elementary School. These teachers and schools are situated in the diverse and vibrant communities of Albany Park and Portage Park on the Northwest Side of Chicago. They are supported by a team of instructional leaders at Network One, a regional subdistrict of the Chicago Public Schools with over 80 languages spoken by learners and their families, including 10,000 students labeled as ELs.

Although they do not require a particular approach to curricular design at the K–12 schools in their region, Network One leaders had long preferred the UbD approach, reaching back to their days as classroom teachers and school leaders. With many schools seeking to improve their instructional effectiveness and rigor for CLD students, the team decided to focus network-level capacity-building efforts on the UbD framework with an explicit lens on language development. Aware of the limitations in directly reaching the thousands of teachers across the region, network coaches prioritized schools with both interest and need, enlisting teams from each site that purposefully included both school leaders and teacher leaders. Guided by the school- and district-level backward design principles of *Schooling by Design* (Wiggins & McTighe, 2007), the network team planned professional development with the ultimate goal that educators would collaboratively value and use UbD with a language lens to plan instruction for CLD students in classrooms and schools (see Figure 8.6). Keeping in mind the specific contexts of the focal schools, the plan centered on deepening understandings and grappling with students' unique backgrounds and dynamic needs as a means to design responsive instruction that authentically fosters learning and language development. Further, school leadership teams needed to understand and negotiate how to carry out UbD for language development in practice to build capacity and understanding of other colleagues. To yield these larger transfer and meaning goals, the acquisition goals centered on the foundations, components, and applications of UbD for CLD students, spanning preplanning using multidimensional data, Stage 1 goals, Stage 2 assessments, and Stage 3 learning plans. Evidence of this learning would emerge in the resultant curriculum that educators backward-designed for their students, including curriculum maps, unit plans, assessments, and instructional practices.

To achieve these goals in classrooms and schools across the network, the action plan spanned two calendar years and incorporated both independent and collaborative strands for teachers and leaders. Recognizing the complexity of both dimensions of this work—UbD and language development—the team opted to sequentially develop related understandings, knowledge, and skills. First focused on UbD, teams traveled to Connecticut for three days of intensive learning, followed by a semester-long workshop series allowing time and space for educators to explore, grapple, and apply UbD principles in practice. Responding to those areas where teachers indicated a need for additional support, the network team designed five sessions to deepen learning and understanding of transfer goals, meaning goals, performance tasks, rubric creation, and cross-stage alignment. Professional development then added the lens of language development with a semester-long workshop series that prompted teams to analyze data to determine multidimensional abilities and needs (preplanning), set rigorous goals for disciplinary learning and language development (Stage 1), design culturally and responsive assessments (Stage 2), and plan authentic, language-rich instruction to support and challenge students (Stage 3). After building the awareness and expertise of individuals on each school team, the action plan prompted, supported, and provided various tools for teachers and leaders to design capacity-building efforts for on-site implementation of UbD for language development.

School teams developed professional development plans based on educators' expertise and overall professional capacity within their unique contexts. This flexibility was integral in meeting the particular needs of schools and communities, recognizing that curricular design and capacity-building efforts would vary based on factors such as educator experience, school structures, student population, and EL/bilingual programming. Some schools, like Hibbard Elementary and Albany Park Multicultural Academy, had history and experience with UbD as a general framework for curricular design and therefore focused capacity-building efforts on adding the language lens across units of study. Situated across the street from one another and serving the same students and families, these schools strategically selected leadership teams (spanning elementary grade levels and middle school disciplines) who then facilitated the learning and application of their colleagues focused on one stage each quarter (e.g., Stage 1 in Quarter 1). For other schools, like Reinberg Elementary and Roosevelt High, these network-level efforts provided initial exposure to UbD, prompting capacity building focused on the foundations of both curricular design and language development. Thus school and teacher leaders began by collaboratively defining the school mission and and curricular approach of UbD for their diverse student population, followed by designing long-term efforts to purposefully build capacity for colleagues to design instructional units with CLD students at the center. By designing professional development to expand educators' understandings, knowledge, and skills for using UbD in diverse classrooms, the network empowered leadership teams to apply learning in ways that responded to their unique school contexts.

The shared commitment to this important work by teachers and leaders across the network has had a marked impact in schools. Educators in diverse classrooms and schools have described integral shifts in their overall perceptions of CLD students and corresponding instructional practices (Heineke et al., 2017). Teachers plan instruction that scaffolds for language demands, emphasizes language-rich collaboration around disciplinary ideas, and integrates culturally relevant resources. School leaders design schoolwide missions and programs that prioritize language development, as well as implement collaborative strategies to support teachers spanning grade levels and content areas. Network leaders report collaborative planning across schools, mediated by the online portal EduPlanet21 Unit Planner (www.eduplanet21.com). Because of this work, teachers observe enhanced engagement and learning in classrooms, while school and network leaders describe increases in CLD students' achievement as measured by standardized tests of disciplinary content and language proficiency. Building from short-term successes, the long-term benefits of these intensive regional efforts are promising. The benefits of constructing a coherent and vertically aligned curriculum become evident in the lives of students in the vibrant Albany Park community who begin at Hibbard for elementary school, move across the

Figure 8.6 | **Network One Capacity-Building Plan**

	Stage 1—Desired Results	

Transfer

Educators will be able to independently use their learning to…
- Teachers and leaders see the value of a backward design approach to instructional planning.
- School teams build capacity around the UbD framework, language development, and leading adult learning.
- Teachers share practice both within schools and across networks.
- Teachers engage in reflective practices to ensure planning meets the needs of diverse populations of students.
- School teams engage in vertical and horizontal curriculum mapping.

Meaning

Educators will keep considering…
- Who are the students in our highly diverse classrooms and schools?
- How can we design instruction to support students' learning and language development?
- To what extent does UbD with a language lens shift classroom practice?
- How do adults learn and make changes in their daily practice?

Educators will understand that…
- We construct coherent and aligned instructional pathways for CLD students when we plan with the end in mind and determine evidence to be collected along the way.
- Teachers learn best when they see relevance and therefore *buy in*, have support for learning along the way, and work collaboratively with peers.
- Teacher leadership teams need an opportunity to reflect upon the systems and structures of their building and how to best move this work forward to meet the needs of their communities.

Acquisition

Educators will be skilled at…
- Setting rigorous Stage 1 goals, using standards to design transfer goals, essential questions, understandings, knowledge, and skills.
- Analyzing language demands to construct language-specific and integrated learning goals.
- Incorporating authentic and varied Stage 2 assessments to capture student progress toward all goals with aligned evaluative criteria.
- Designing language-rich GRASPS tasks with appropriate analytical rubrics.
- Planning Stage 3 instruction shaped by CLD students' background and proficiency levels.
- Developing content and language objectives.
- Constructing units and analyze curriculum maps for alignment and gaps in instruction.

Established Goals

Professional Standards for Educational Leaders (2015)
- S1: Mission, Vision, & Values
- S4: Curriculum, Instruction, & Assessment
- S7: Professional Community for Teachers and Staff
- S10: School Improvement

Educators will know…
- Components of Stage 1, including transfer goals, enduring understandings, essential questions, knowledge, skills, and related language demands.
- Components of Stage 2, including varied assessments (i.e., formative, summative; informal, formal), evaluative criteria, performance tasks and GRASPS, and student-friendly rubrics/checklists to assess learning and language development.
- Components of Stage 3, including progression of learning events with language lens, including differentiating by background and proficiency and writing language targets using WIDA tools.
- EduPlanet21 Unit Planner platform, a tool for vertical and horizontal alignment across schools.

Stage 2—Evidence	
Direct Evidence	**Indirect Evidence**
• School-level curriculum maps	• Professional development survey feedback
• Schooling by Design plans by school team	• Collaborative teacher practice observations
• Teacher-developed UbD units with language lens	• Agendas from UbD team meetings, professional development, and grade-level teams
• Classroom assessments and rubrics for meaning making, transfer, and language development	• Instructional practices designed for meaning making and transfer
• ACCESS assessment data plots and corresponding analyses of disciplinary language demands	• Differentiated instruction based on students' language development
• Language and content objectives	

Stage 3—Action Plan

• UbD Conference with School Teams (*Summer 2015*)
- Meet with principals to gauge interest and build UbD teams of teacher leaders
- Participate in 3 days of learning on UbD and plan implementation across schools

• Principal Development with School Leaders (*Fall 2015 – Spring 2016*)
- Monthly principal collaboration via UbD-focused professional learning community
- Semester 1: Focus on building understandings of UbD (McTighe & Wiggins, 2004)
- Semester 2: Focus on building schoolwide structures (Wiggins & McTighe, 2007)

• Network UbD Workshops with School Teams (*Fall 2015*)
- Session 1: Transfer Goals
- Session 2: Essential Questions & Enduring Understandings
- Session 3: Balanced Assessment with Focus on Performance Tasks
- Session 4: Rubric Creation
- Session 5: Alignment Across All Stages

• Language Matters Workshops with School Teams (*Spring 2016*)
- Session 1: UbD for Language Development
- Session 2: Stage 1 with Language Lens
- Session 3: Stage 2 with Language Lens
- Session 4: Stage 3 with Language Lens
- Session 5: Capacity Building and Roll-Out at Schools

• EduPlanet21 Unit Planner with School Teams (*Summer 2016*)
- Language integration into online Unit Planner template
- Preliminary workshop on Unit Planner template with school leaders
- Workshop on Unit Planner template with language integration to school teams
- School team collaborative planning: Roll-out efforts at school sites using template

Source: Used with permission from Kate Ramos and Camille Unger, Chicago Public Schools.

street to Albany Park Multicultural Academy for middle school, and round out high school at Roosevelt. From day one of these students' academic careers, their teachers have prioritized and provided equitable access to rigorous, authentic, and high-quality disciplinary learning that taps into rich cultural and linguistic resources as a means to support language development. Multilingual with content and language expertise spanning disciplines, these students will complete their K–12 experiences ready to take on the world.

Closing Thoughts

Today's classrooms continue to grow in cultural and linguistic diversity, with rapidly changing student populations in all corners of the United States and in immigrant destinations around the world (Gándara & Hopkins, 2010; Wrigley, 2000). While students bring in rich linguistic resources needed for multilingualism in a global world, they face challenges in simultaneously learning another language and the content of academic disciplines. Nevertheless, educational institutions have not kept up with the growing diversity to either assuage challenges or tap into opportunities. Teachers often enter classrooms underprepared for CLD students, a situation that results in deficit-based mindsets, low expectations, and simplified approaches to teaching and learning (de Cohen & Clewell, 2007). Schools and districts often use program models that rush students to English proficiency and struggle to appropriately label CLD students for gifted and special education services (de Jong, 2011). Macro-level curricular policies emphasize and measure achievement primarily in English, with states like Arizona going so far as to require students to demonstrate proficiency in English before being able to access disciplinary learning (Heineke, 2016). Overall, the failures of the educational system to meet the needs of CLD students have resulted in low student achievement and soaring high school dropout rates (Fry, 2008).

It is within this realistic context of today's educational system that we write this book, which holds promise for preparing educators to meet the needs of this large, growing, and richly diverse population of students. Situated at the center of the educational institution, local educators have the capacity to transform teaching and learning in diverse classrooms and schools (Heineke, 2016; Ricento & Hornberger, 1996; Sutton & Levinson, 2001). Consider the work being done by the knowledgeable, skilled, and committed teachers and leaders in Chicago Public Schools. Working in schools with students speaking more than 140 languages, Chicago educators balance the challenges and opportunities of the rich diversity from Rogers Park to Albany Park to Portage Park. Teachers like Bridget, Luke, Jillian, Lindsay, and Karen work every day to improve their professional practice so they can better foster the learning and language development of students like Absame, Itzel, Lorenzo, and Fatima. Whether analyzing unit goals for language demands, crafting language-rich performance tasks, designing learning trajectories to support language development, or implementing instruction that taps into and builds upon students' rich cultural and linguistic backgrounds, *teachers* positively influence students' learning, development, and achievement.

By using of the UbD framework, educators provide high-quality, meaningful curriculum and instruction that maintain rigorous goals that are situated in authentic teaching and learning (Wiggins & McTighe, 2005, 2012). These goals remain consistent for all students and maintain high expectations for CLD students, including those who may still be developing proficiency in English. The premise of adding a lens on language to UbD is that students develop language at the same time that they engage in authentic learning across school-based disciplines (Walqui & Heritage, 2012; Walqui & van Lier, 2010). Thus, the purpose of UbD for language development is to ensure that CLD students have equitable access to achieve learning goals, with teachers who recognize the language progressions, demands, scaffolds, and supports needed to reach learning goals (Santos et al., 2012). In addition, this approach centers on instruction that values, incorporates, and maintains students' cultural identities and native language abilities (Herrera, 2016).

In sum, we hope that this book helps you to craft your understandings, knowledge, skills, and habits of mind about UbD for language development so that you can continue to support the increasingly diverse students who come into your teaching context ready and eager to inquire, grapple, discover, and explore.

References

Alexie, S. (2007). *The absolutely true diary of a part-time Indian*. New York: Little, Brown.

Allen, J. (2007). *Inside words: Tools for teaching academic vocabulary, grades 4–12*. Portland, ME: Stenhouse.

American Community Survey. (2015). *Detailed languages spoken at home and ability to speak English for the population 5 years and over for United States: 2009 to 2013*. Washington, DC: U.S. Census Bureau. Retrieved on November 22, 2017, from https://www.census.gov/newsroom/press-releases/2015/cb15-185.html

Ankiel, J. M. (2016). Pictures tell the story: Improving comprehension with *Persepolis*. International Literacy Association. Retrieved from http://www.readwritethink.org/classroom-resources/lesson-plans/pictures-tell-story-improving-1102.html

Arnold, S. (1995). *Child of the sun: A Cuban legend*. Mahwah, NJ: Troll Associates.

Assessment and Accountability Comprehensive Center at WestEd (AACCW). (2010). Language for achievement: A framework for academic English language [Handout]. San Francisco: WestEd.

August, D., & Shanahan, T. (2008). *Developing reading and writing in second-language learners: Lessons from the report of the National Literacy Panel on language-minority children and youth*. Abingdon, UK: Taylor & Francis.

Barrera, R., & Quiroa, R. (2003). The use of Spanish in Latino children's literature in English: What makes for cultural authenticity? In D. L. Fox & K. G. Short (Eds.), *Stories matter: The complexity of cultural authenticity in children's literature* (pp. 247–265). Urbana, IL: National Council of Teachers of English.

Beeman, K., & Urow, C. (2013). *Teaching for biliteracy: Strengthening bridges between languages*. Philadelphia, PA: Caslon.

Bialystok, E. (1993). Metalinguistic awareness: The development of children's representations of language. In C. Pratt & A. Garton (Eds.), *Systems of representation in children: Development and use* (pp. 211–233). London: Wiley.

Bialystok, E. (2016). Bilingual education for young children: review of the effects and consequences. *International Journal of Bilingual Education and Bilingualism*. Retrieved from http://www.tandfonline.com/doi/abs/10.1080/13670050.2016.1203859

Bloom, B. S. (Ed.). (1956). *Taxonomy of educational objectives, handbook 1: Cognitive domain*. New York: Longman.

Bloom, P. (2007). More than words: A reply to Malt and Sloman. *Cognition, 105*(3), 649–655.

Bowerman, M., & Levinson, S. C. (Eds.). (2001). *Language acquisition and conceptual development*. Cambridge, UK: Cambridge University Press.

Bransford, J. D., Brown, A. L., & Cocking, R. R. (Eds.). (2000). *How people learn: Brain, mind, experience, and school*. Washington, DC: National Academy Press.

Brown, A. C. (2014, October 23). Text to text: 'The Catcher and the Rye' and 'The Case for Delayed Adulthood.' *New York Times*. Retrieved from https://learning.blogs.nytimes.com/2014/10/23/text-to-text-catcher-in-the-rye-and-the-case-for-delayed-adulthood/?_r=1

Brown, H. D., & Abeywickrama, P. (2010). Principles of language assessment. In *Language assessment: Principles and classroom practices* (2nd ed., pp. 25–51). Boston: Pearson.

Bucholz, J. L., & Sheffler, J. L. (2009). Creating a warm and inclusive classroom environment: Planning for all children to feel welcome. *Electronic Journal for Inclusive Education, 2*(4). Retrieved from http://corescholar.libraries.wright.edu/cgi/viewcontent.cgi?article=1102&context=ejie

Bunch, G. C., Kibler, A., & Pimentel, S. (2012, January). Realizing opportunities for English learners in the Common Core English language arts and disciplinary literacy standards. Paper presented at the Understanding Language Conference, Stanford, CA. Available: http://ell.stanford.edu/sites/default/files/pdf/academic-papers/01_Bunch_Kibler_Pimentel_RealizingOpp%20in%20ELA_FINAL_0.pdf

Bybee, R. (2015). Scientific literacy. In R. Gunstone (Ed.), *Encyclopedia of science education* (Vol. 2, pp. 944–947). New York: Springer.

Cai, M. (2003). Can we fly across cultural gaps on the wings of imagination? Ethnicity, experience, and cultural authenticity. In D. L. Fox & K. G. Short (Eds.), *Stories matter: The complexity of cultural authenticity in children's literature* (pp. 167–181). Urbana, IL: National Council of Teachers of English.

Calloway-Thomas, C. (2010). *Empathy in the global world: An intercultural perspective.* Thousand Oaks, CA: Sage.

Canales, V. (2005). *The tequila worm.* New York: Random House.

Celic, C., & Seltzer, K. (2011). *Translanguaging: A CUNY-NYSIEB guide for educators.* New York: CUNY-NYSIEB.

Chamot, A. U., & O'Malley, J. M. (1994). *The CALLA handbook: Implementing the cognitive academic language learning approach.* Boston: Addison-Wesley.

Clark, E. V. (2004). How language acquisition builds on cognitive development. *Trends in Cognitive Sciences, 8*(10), 472–478.

Clay, M., & Cazden, C. (1990). A Vygotskian interpretation of Reading Recovery and applications of sociohistorical psychology. In L. C. Moll (Ed.), *Vygotsky and education: Instructional implications* (pp. 206–222). Cambridge, UK: Cambridge University Press.

Cloud, N., Genessee, F., & Hamayan, E. (2009). *Literacy instruction for English language learners: A teacher's guide to research-based practices.* Portsmouth, NH: Heinemann.

Coburn, C. E., & Stein, M. K. (2006). Communities of practice theory and the role of teacher professional community in policy implementation. In M. I. Honig (Ed.), *New directions in education policy implementation: Confronting complexity* (pp. 25–46). Albany, NY: SUNY Press.

Cochran-Smith, M., & Lytle, S. L. (1998). Teacher research: The question that persists. *International Journal of Leadership in Education Theory and Practice, 1*(1), 19–36.

Cohen, J., & Daniel, M. C. (2013). What is a teacher to do with a newcomer? *Illinois Reading Council Journal, 41*(4), 25–34.

Coleman, R., & Goldenberg, C. (2010). What does research say about effective practices for English learners? Part IV: Models for schools and districts. *Kappa Delta Pi Record, 46*(4), 156–163.

Collier, V. P. (1989). How long? A synthesis of research on academic achievement in a second language. *TESOL Quarterly, 23*(3), 509–531.

Collier, V. P., & Thomas, W. P. (2007). Predicting second language academic success in English using the prism model. In J. Cummins & C. Davison (Eds.), *International handbook of English language teaching, Part 1* (pp. 333–348). New York: Springer.

Colón, I., & Heineke, A. J. (2015). Bilingual education in English-only: A qualitative case study of language policy in practice at Lincoln Elementary School. *Mid-Western Educational Researcher, 27*(4), 271–295.

Constantinou, P., & Wuest, D. A. (2015). Using academic language to level the playing field for English-language learners in physical education. *Strategies, 28*(5), 28–33.

Costello, D. P. (2000). The language of *The Catcher in the Rye*. In H. Bloom (Ed.), *Bloom's modern critical interpretations: J. D. Salinger's* The Catcher in the Rye (pp. 11–20). Philadelphia: Chelsea House.

Council of Chief State School Officers, National Governors Association. (n.d.). *Common core state standards initiative*. Washington, DC: Author. Retrieved from http://www.corestandards. org/]

Covey, S. R. (1989). *The 7 habits of highly effective people*. New York: Free Press.

Cruz, B. C., & Thornton, S. J. (2013). *Teaching social studies to English language learners* (2nd ed.). New York: Routledge.

Cummins, J. (1981). The role of primary language development in promoting educational success for language minority students. In California State Department of Education (Eds.), *Schooling and language minority students: A theoretical framework* (pp. 3–50), Los Angeles: California State University.

Cummins, J. (2000). *Language, power, and pedagogy: Bilingual children in the crossfire*. Bristol, UK: Multilingual Matters.

Cummins, J. (2005). A proposal for action: Strategies for recognizing heritage language competence as a learning resource within the mainstream classroom. *Modern Language Journal, 89*, 585–592.

Cummins, J. (2009). Fundamental psycholinguistic and sociological principles underlying educational success for linguistic minority students. In T. Skutnabb-Kangas, R. Phillipson, A. K. Mohanty, & M. Panda (Eds.), *Social justice through multilingual education* (pp. 19–35). Bristol, UK: Multilingual Matters.

Datnow, A., Lasky, S., Stringfield, S., & Teddlie, C. (2006). *Integrating educational systems for successful reform in diverse contexts*. Cambridge, UK: Cambridge University Press.

De Cohen, C. C., & Clewell, B. C. (2007, May). Putting English language learners on the educational map: The *No Child Left Behind* act implemented. *Education in focus: Urban institute policy brief*. Retrieved from https://www.urban.org/sites/default/files/publication/46276/311468-Putting-English-Language-Learners-on-the-Educational-Map.PDF

De Jong, E. J. (2011). *Foundations for multilingualism in education: From principles to practice*. Philadelphia: Caslon.

De Jong, E. J., & Harper, C. A. (2005). Preparing mainstream teachers for English language learners: Is being a good teacher good enough? *Teacher Education Quarterly, 32*(2), 101–124.

De la Peña, M. (2005). *Ball don't lie*. New York: Random House.

De la Peña, M. (2008). *Mexican whiteboy*. New York: Random House.

Delpit, L. D. (2006). *Other people's children: Cultural conflict in the classroom*. New York: New Press.

Dressler, C., Carlo, M. S., Snow, C. E., August, D., & White, C. E. (2011). Spanish-speaking students' use of cognate knowledge to infer the meaning of English words. *Bilingualism: Language and Cognition, 14*(2), 243–255.

Dromi, E. (1993). *Language and cognition: A developmental perspective*. New York: Ablex.

Ebe, A. E. (2011). Culturally relevant books: Bridges to reading engagement for English language learners. *Insights on Learning Disabilities: From Prevailing Theories to Validated Practices, 8*(2), 31–45.

Echevarría, J. J., Vogt, M. J., & Short, D. J. (2013). *Making content comprehensible for elementary English learners: The SIOP model* (2nd ed.). Boston: Pearson.

Ewald, W. (2002). *The best part of me: Children talk about their bodies in pictures and words*. Boston: Little, Brown.

Fairclough, N. (2003). *Analyzing discourse: Textual analysis for social research.* Abingdon, UK: Routledge.

Felin, M. S. (2007). *Touching snow.* New York: Atheneum.

Fillmore, L. W. (1991). When learning a second language means losing the first. *Early Childhood Research Quarterly, 6*(3), 323–346.

Fillmore, L. W., & Fillmore, C. J. (2012, January). What does text complexity mean for English learners and language minority students? Paper presented at the Understanding Language Conference, Stanford, CA. Retrieved from http://ell.stanford.edu/sites/default/files/pdf/academic-papers/06-LWF%20CJF%20Text%20Complexity%20FINAL_0.pdf

Fisher, D., Brozo, W. G., Frey, N., & Ivey, G. (2011). *50 instructional routines to develop content literacy* (3rd ed.). Boston: Pearson.

Flaitz, J. (2006). *Understanding your refugee and immigrant student: An educational, cultural, and linguistic guide.* Ann Arbor, MI: University of Michigan Press.

Florio-Ruane, S. (2001). *Teacher education and the cultural imagination: Autobiography, conversation, and narrative.* New York: Routledge.

Fraser, B. J. (2012). *Classroom environment.* Abingdon, UK: Routledge.

Fry, R. (2008, June 26). The role of schools in the English language learner achievement gap. Pew Research Center: Hispanic Trends. Retrieved from http://www.pewhispanic.org/2008/06/26/the-role-of-schools-in-the-english-language-learner-achievement-gap/

Gándara, P., & Hopkins, M. (Eds.). (2010). *Forbidden language: English learners and restrictive language policies.* New York: Teachers College Press.

Gándara, P., & Maxwell-Jolly, J. (2006). Critical issues in developing the teacher corps for English learners. In K. Téllez & H. C. Waxman (Eds.), *Preparing quality educators for English language learners: Research, policies, and practices* (pp. 99–120). Mahwah, NJ: Lawrence Erlbaum Associates.

Garcia, O. (2009a). Education, multilingualism and translanguaging in the 21st century. In T. Skutnabb-Kangas, R. Phillipson, A. K. Mohanty, & M. Panda (Eds.), *Social justice through multilingual education* (pp. 140–158). Bristol, UK: Multilingual Matters.

Garcia, O. (2009b). Emergent bilinguals and TESOL: What's in a name? *TESOL Quarterly, 43*(2), 322–326.

García-Sánchez, I. M., Orellana, M. F., & Hopkins, M. (2011). Facilitating intercultural communication in parent-teacher conferences: Lessons from child translators. *Multicultural Perspectives, 13*(3), 148–154.

Gay, G. (2010). *Culturally responsive teaching: Theory, research, and practice* (2nd ed.). New York: Teachers College Press.

Genishi, C. (2002). Young English language learners: Resourceful in the classroom. Research in review. *Young Children, 57*(4), 66–72.

Gerson, M.-J. (1994). *How night came from the sea: A story from Brazil.* New York: Little, Brown.

Gibbons, P. (2002). *Scaffolding language, scaffolding learning: Teaching second language learners in the mainstream classroom.* Portsmouth, NH: Heinemann.

Goldenberg, C. (2008). Teaching English language learners: What the research does—and does not—say. *American Educator 32*(2), 8–23, 42–44.

Goodman, P. (1973). Freedom and learning: The need for choice. *National Elementary Principal, 52*(6), 38–42.

Gottlieb, M. (2006). *Assessing English language learners: Bridges from language proficiency to academic achievement.* Thousand Oaks, CA: Corwin Press.

Grosjean, F. (1989). Neurolinguists, beware! The bilingual is not two monolinguals in one person. *Brain and Language, 36*(1), 3–15.

Grossman, P., Wineburg, S., & Woolworth, S. (2001). Toward a theory of teacher community. *Teachers College Record, 103*(6), 942–1012.

Gulamhussein, A. (2013). *Teaching the teachers: Effective professional development in an era of high stakes accountability.* Alexandria, VA: Center for Public Education. Retrieved from http://www.centerforpubliceducation.org/Main-Menu/Staffingstudents/Teaching-the-Teachers-Effective-Professional-Development-in-an-Era-of-High-Stakes-Accountability/Teaching-the-Teachers-Full-Report.pdf

Hakuta, K., Butler, Y. G., & Witt, D. (2000). *How long does it take English learners to attain proficiency?* Policy Report 2000-1. Berkeley, CA: University of California Linguistic Minority Research Institute.

Halliday, M. A. K. (1975). *Learning how to mean: Explorations in the development of language.* London: Edward Arnold.

Halliday, M. A. K. (1998). Things and relations: Regrammatising experience as technical knowledge. In J. R. Martin & R. Veel (Eds.), *Reading science: Critical and functional perspectives on discourses of science* (pp. 185–235). London: Routledge.

Harklau, L. (2000). From the "good kids" to the "worst": Representations of English language learners across educational settings. *TESOL Quarterly, 34*(1), 35–67.

Heath, S. B. (1983). *Ways with words: Language, life and work in communities and classrooms.* Cambridge, UK: Cambridge University Press.

Heineke, A. J. (2016). *Restrictive language policy in practice: English learners in Arizona.* Bristol, UK: Multilingual Matters.

Heineke, A. J., & Cameron, Q. (2011). Closing the classroom door and the achievement gap: Teach for America alumni teachers' appropriation of Arizona language policy. *Education and Urban Society, 45*(4), 483–505.

Heineke, A. J., & Cameron, Q. (2013). Teacher preparation and language policy appropriation: A qualitative investigation of Teach for America teachers in Arizona. *Education Policy Analysis Archives, 21*(33), 1–25.

Heineke, A. J., Coleman, E., Ferrell, E., & Kersemeier, C. (2012). Opening doors for bilingual students: Recommendations for building linguistically responsive schools. *Improving Schools, 15*(2), 130–147.

Heineke, A. J., Ellis, A., Davin, K., Cohen, S., Roudebush, A., Wright, B., & Fendt, C. (in press). Language matters: Developing urban educators' expertise for English learners in linguistically diverse communities. *Language, Culture, and Curriculum.*

Heineke, A. J., & Neugebauer, S. (in press). The complexity of language and learning: Deconstructing teachers' conceptions of academic language. *Issues in Teacher Education, 27*(2), 1–17.

Heritage, M., Walqui, A., & Linquanti, R. (2015). *English language learners and the new standards: Developing language, content knowledge, and analytical practices in the classroom.* Cambridge, MA: Harvard Education Press.

Herrell, A. L., & Jordan, M. (2016). *50 strategies for teaching English language learners* (5th ed.). Boston: Pearson.

Herrera, S. G. (2016). *Biography-driven culturally responsive teaching* (2nd ed.). New York: Teachers College Press.

Hijuelos, O. (2008). *Dark dude.* New York: Atheneum.

Hilliard, J., & Hamayan, E. (2012). How do we plan for language development? In E. Hamayan & R. F. Field (Eds.), *English language learners at school: A guide for administrators* (2nd ed., pp. 121–123). Philadelphia: Caslon.

Honig, M. I. (2006). *New directions in education policy implementation.* Albany, NY: SUNY Press.

Horwitz, E. (2001). Language anxiety and achievement. *Annual Review of Applied Linguistics, 21,* 112–126.

Jiménez, R. T., García, G. E., & Pearson, P. D. (1996). The reading strategies of bilingual Latina/o students who are successful English readers: Opportunities and obstacles. *Reading Research Quarterly, 31*(1), 90–112.

Keeley, P., Eberle, F., & Dorsey, C. (2008). *Uncovering student ideas in science: Another 25 formative assessment probes* (vol. 3). Arlington, VA: NSTA Press.

Keenan, S. (2016). *Myths from around the world.* New York: Scholastic. Retrieved on November 22, 2017, from https://www.scholastic.com/teachers/activities/teaching-content/myths-around -world-writing-writers-activity/)

Kenner, C., & Ruby, M. (2013). Connecting children's worlds: Creating a multilingual syncretic curriculum through partnership between complementary and mainstream schools. *Journal of Early Childhood Literacy, 13*(3), 395–417.

Kersaint, G., Thompson, D. R., & Petkova, M. (2013). *Teaching mathematics to English language learners* (2nd ed.). New York: Routledge.

Krashen, S. D. (1981). Bilingual education and second language acquisition theory. In *Schooling and language minority students: A theoretical framework* (pp. 51–79). Los Angeles: Evaluation, Dissemination, and Assessment Center, California State University.

Krashen, S. D. (1982). *Principles and practice in second language acquisition.* Oxford: Pergamon Press.

Krashen, S. D. (1985). *The input hypothesis: Issues and implications.* New York: Longman.

Krashen, S. D. (1990). How reading and writing make you smarter, or, how smart people read and write. In J. E. Alatis (Ed.), *Georgetown University round table on languages and linguistics* (pp. 364–376). Washington, DC: Georgetown University Press.

Krashen, S. D. (2003). *Explorations in language acquisition and use: The Taipei lectures.* Portsmouth, NH: Heinemann.

Kudlinski, K. V. (2008). *Boy, were we wrong about the solar system!* New York: Dutton.

Kurpaska, M. (2010). *Chinese language(s): A look through the prism of* The Great Dictionary of Modern Chinese Dialects. Berlin: Walter de Gruyter.

Lake, N. (2012). *In darkness.* New York: Bloomsbury.

Lasky, K. (1994). *The librarian who measured the earth.* New York: Little, Brown.

Latta, M. M., & Chan, E. (2010). *Teaching the arts to engage English language learners.* New York: Routledge.

LeMoine, N. (1999). *English for your success: A language development program for African American children.* New York: Peoples Publishing Group.

Lewis, C., & Ketter, J. (2004). Learning as social interaction: Interdiscursivity in a teacher and researcher study group. In R. Rogers (Ed.), *An introduction to critical discourse analysis in education* (2nd ed., pp. 128–153). New York: Routledge.

Lindholm-Leary, K., & Borsato, G. (2006). Academic achievement. In F. Genesee, K. Lindholm-Leary, W. Saunders, & D. Christian (Eds.), *Educating English language learners: A synthesis of research evidence* (pp. 176–222). Cambridge, UK: Cambridge University Press.

Linquanti, R., & Cook, H. G. (2013, February 1). *Toward a "common definition of English learner": A brief defining policy and technical issues and opportunities for state assessment consortia.* Washington, DC: Council of Chief State School Officers.

Lippi-Green, R. (1997). *English with an accent: Language, ideology, and discrimination in the United States.* Abingdon, UK: Routledge.

Lipski, J. M. (2008). *Varieties of Spanish in the United States*. Washington, DC: Georgetown University Press.

Lucas, T., & Villegas, A. M. (2010). The missing piece in teacher education: The preparation of linguistically responsive teachers. *National Society for the Study of Education, 109*(2), 297–318.

Lucas, T., Villegas, A. M., & Freedson-Gonzalez, M. (2008). Linguistically responsive teacher education: Preparing classroom teachers to teach English language learners. *Journal of Teacher Education, 59*(4), 361–373.

Luykx, A., & Lee, O. (2007, March). Measuring instructional congruence in elementary science classrooms: Pedagogical and methodological components of a theoretical framework. *Journal of Research in Science Teaching, 44*(3), 424–447.

Martiniello, M. (2009). Linguistic complexity, schematic representations, and differential item functioning for English language learners in math tests. *Educational Assessment, 14*(3–4), 160–179.

McCall, G. G. (2011). *Under the mesquite*. New York: Lee & Low.

McFarland, J. (2016, February 18). Diversity in home languages: Examining English learners in US public schools [blog post]. Retrieved from *National Center for Education Statistics Blog* at https://nces.ed.gov/blogs/nces/post/diversity-in-home-languages-examining-english-learners-in-u-s-public-schools

McInerney, D. M. (2008). Personal investment, culture and learning: Insights into school achievement across Anglo, Aboriginal, Asian and Lebanese students in Australia. *International Journal of Psychology, 43*(5), 870–879.

McKay, S. L., & Wong, S. L. C. (1996). Multiple discourses, multiple identities: Investment and agency in second-language learning among Chinese adolescent immigrant students. *Harvard Educational Review, 66*(3), 577–609.

McMillan, J. H. (2010). The practical implications of educational aims and contexts for formative assessment. In H. L. Andrade & G. J. Cizek (Eds.), *Handbook of formative assessment* (pp. 41–58). New York: Routledge.

McTighe, J. & Wiggins, G. (2004). *Understanding by design professional development workbook*. Alexandria, VA: ASCD.

Medina, C. L. (2006). Interpreting Latino/a literature as critical fictions. *The ALAN Review, 33*(2), 71–77.

Medina, C. L., & Martínez-Roldán, C. (2011). Culturally relevant literature pedagogies: Latino students reading in the borderlands. In J. C. Naidoo (Ed.), *Celebrating* cuentos: *Promoting Latino children's literature and literacy in classrooms and libraries* (pp. 259–272). Santa Barbara, CA: ABC-CLIO.

Menken, K., & Kleyn, T. (2009, April). The difficult road for long-term English learners. *Educational Leadership, 66*(7). Retrieved from http://www.ascd.org/publications/educational_leadership/apr09/vol66/num07/The_Difficult_Road_for_Long-Term_English_Learners.aspx

Miramontes, O. B., Nadeau, A., & Commins, N. L. (2011). *Restructuring schools for linguistic diversity: Linking decision making to effective programs* (2nd ed.). New York: Teachers College Press.

Moll, L. C., Amanti, C., Neff, D., & Gonzalez N. (1992). Funds of knowledge for teaching: Using a qualitative approach to connect homes and classrooms. *Theory into Practice, 31*(1), 132–141.

Moll, L. C., & González, N. (1997). Teachers as social scientists: Learning about culture from household research. In P. Hall (Ed.), *Race, ethnicity, and multiculturalism* (vol. 1, pp. 89–114). New York: Garland.

Morales, A., & Hanson, W. E. (2005). Language brokering: An integrative review of the literature. *Hispanic Journal of Behavioral Sciences, 27*(4), 471–503.

Morgan, H. (2009). Gender, racial, and ethnic misrepresentation in children's books: A comparative look. *Childhood Education, 85*(3), 187–190.

Moschkovich, J. (2013). Principles and guidelines for equitable mathematics teaching practices and materials for English language learners. *Journal of Urban Mathematics Education, 6*(1), 45–57.

Nagy, W. E., & Anderson, R. C. (1995). *Metalinguistic awareness and literacy acquisition in different languages.* Champaign, IL: University of Illinois.

Nagy, W., & Townsend, D. (2012). Words as tools: Learning academic vocabulary as language acquisition. *Reading Research Quarterly, 47*, 91–108.

National Center for Education Statistics. (2015). EDFacts file 141, Data Group 678; Common Core of Data, "State Nonfiscal Survey of Public Elementary and Secondary Education." Table 204.27.

National Center for Education Statistics. (2017). *English language learners in public schools.* Retrieved on November 22, 2017 from https://nces.ed.gov/programs/coe/indicator_cgf.asp

National Council for the Social Studies. (2016). *About National Council for the Social Studies.* Retrieved on December 12, 2016, from http://www.socialstudies.org/about

National Council for the Social Studies. (2017). *College, career, and civic life framework for social studies state standards.* Retrieved on February 18, 2017, from http://www.socialstudies.org/c3

National Research Council. (2013). *Next generation science standards: For states, by states.* Washington, DC: National Academies Press.

National Science Teachers Association (NSTA). (2000). NSTA position statement: The nature of science. Retrieved from http://www.nsta.org/about/positions/natureofscience.aspx

NGSS Lead States. (2013). *Next Generation Science Standards: For states, by states.* Washington, DC: The National Academies Press.

Nutta, J., Bautista, N. U., & Butler, M. B. (2011). *Teaching science to English language learners.* New York: Routledge.

Olsen, L. (2014). *Meeting the unique needs of long term English language learners: A guide for educators.* Washington, DC: National Education Association.

O'Malley, J. M., & Pierce, L. V. (1996). *Authentic assessment for English language learners: Practical approaches for teachers.* New York: Longman.

Opitz, M., Rubin, D., & Erekson, J. (2011). *Reading diagnosis and improvement: Assessment and instruction* (6th ed.). Boston: Pearson.

Orellana, M. F. (2001). The work kids do: Mexican and Central American immigrant children's contributions to households and schools in California. *Harvard Educational Review, 71*(3), 366–390.

Ortega. (2009). U*nderstanding second language acquisition.* London: Hodder Education.

Oxford, R. L. (1990). *Language learning strategies: What every teacher should know.* Boston: Heinle, Cengage Learning.

Paulson, E. J., & Freeman, A. E. (2003). *Insight from the eyes: The science of effective reading instruction.* Portsmouth, NH: Heinemann.

Perry, T., & Delpit, L. D. (1998). *The real Ebonics debate: Power, language, and the education of African-American children.* Boston: Beacon Press.

Pierce, K. M. (1999). I am a Level 3 reader: Children's perceptions of themselves as readers. *New Advocate, 12*(4), 359–375.

Quintero, I. (2014). *Gabi: A girl in pieces.* El Paso, TX: Cinco Puntos Press.

Ranney, S., Dillard-Paltrineri, B., Maguire, C., & Schornack, M. (2014). Academic language demands: Texts, tasks, and levels of language. *Minnetesol Journal.* Retrieved from http://

minnetesoljournal.org/spring-2014/academic-language-demands-texts-tasks-and-levels-of
-language

Razfar, A., & Rumenapp, J. C. (2014). *Applying linguistics in the classroom: A sociocultural approach*. New York: Routledge.

Reiss, J. (2008). *102 content strategies for English language learners: Teaching for academic success in grades 3–12*. Upper Saddle River, NJ: Merrill Prentice Hall.

Resau, L. (2009). *Red glass*. New York: Delacorte Press.

Ricento, T. K., & Hornberger, N. H. (1996). Unpeeling the onion: Language planning and policy and the ELT professional. *TESOL Quarterly, 30*(3), 401–427.

Rivera, C., Collum, E., Willner, L. S., & Sia, J. K., Jr. (2005). An analysis of state assessment policies regarding the accommodation of English language learners. In C. Rivera & Collum, E. (Eds.), *State assessment policy and practice for English language learners: A national perspective* (pp. 1–174). Mahwah, NJ: Lawrence Erlbaum.

Roe, B. D., & Ross, E. P. (2005). *Integrating language arts through literature and thematic units*. Boston: Pearson Allyn Bacon.

Rogers, R., & Mosley, M. (2008). A critical discourse analysis of racial literacy in teacher education. *Linguistics and Education, 19*(2), 107–131.

Rogoff, B. (1995). Observing sociocultural activity on three planes: Participatory appropriation, guided participation, and apprenticeship. In J. V. Wertsch, P. del Río, & A. Alvarez (Eds.), *Sociocultural studies of mind* (pp. 139–164). Cambridge, UK: Cambridge University Press.

Rogoff, B. (1997). Evaluating development in the process of participation: Theory, methods, and practice building on each other. In E. Amsel & K. A. Renninger (Eds.), *Change and development: Issues of theory, method, and application* (pp. 265–285). Mahwah, NJ: Lawrence Erlbaum Associates.

Rogoff, B. (2003). *The cultural nature of human development*. Oxford, UK: Oxford University Press.

Rosenblatt, L. M. (2004). The transactional theory of reading and writing. In R. B Ruddell & N. J. Unrau (Eds.), *Theoretical models and processes of reading, 5th edition* (pp. 1363–1398). International Reading Association.

Rossell, C. H., & Baker, K. (1996). The educational effectiveness of bilingual education. *Research in the Teaching of English, 30*(1), 7–74.

Ruurs, M. (2015). *School days around the world*. Toronto: Kids Can Press.

Salinger, J. D. (1951). *The catcher in the rye*. New York: Little, Brown.

Samway, K. D. (2006). *When English language learners write: Connecting research to practice, K–8*. Portsmouth, NH: Heinemann.

Sanders, W. L., & Rivers, J. C. (1996). *Cumulative and residual effects of teachers on future student academic achievement*. Knoxville, TN: University of Tennessee Value-Added Research and Assessment Center.

Santos, M., Darling-Hammond, L., & Cheuk, T. (2012). Teacher development to support English language learners in the context of the Common Core State Standards. Paper presented at the Understanding Language Conference, Stanford, CA: Stanford University. Retrieved from http://ell.stanford.edu/sites/default/files/pdf/academic-papers/10-Santos%20LDH%20Teacher%20Development%20FINAL.pdf

Schmoker, M. (2011). *Focus: Elevating the essentials to radically improve student learning*. Alexandria, VA: ASCD.

Siegel, J. (2006). Language ideologies and the education of speakers of marginalized langauge varieties: Adopting a critical awareness approach. *Linguistics & Education, 17*(2), 157–174.

Short, D. J., Vogt, M. E., & Echevarría, J. (2011). *The SIOP model for teaching history-social studies to English learners*. Boston: Pearson.

Short, K. G., Harste, J. C., & Burke, C. (1996). *Creating classrooms for authors and inquirers* (2nd ed.). Portsmouth, NH: Heinemann.

Sims-Bishop, R. S. (1990). Walk tall in the world: African American literature for today's children. *Journal of Negro Education, 59*(4), 556–565.

Sin-wai, C. (Ed.). (2016). *The Routledge encyclopedia of the Chinese language.* Abingdon, UK: Routledge.

Smith, F. (2006). *Reading without nonsense* (4th ed.). New York: Teachers College Press.

Smith, K., & Hudelson, S. (2001). The NCTE reading initiative: Politics, pedagogy, and possibilities. *Language Arts, 79*(1), 29–37.

Soltero, S. W. (2011). *Schoolwide approaches to educating ELLs: Creating linguistically and culturally responsive K–12 schools.* Portsmouth, NH: Heinemann.

Spady, W. G. (1994) *Outcome-based education: Critical issues and answers.* Alexandria, VA: American Association of School Administrators.

Spinelli, C. G. (2008). Addressing the issue of cultural and linguistic diversity and assessment: Informal evaluation measures for English language learners. *Reading & Writing Quarterly, 24*(1), 101–118.

Stein, M. (1999, May). Developing oral proficiency in the immersion classroom. *ACIE Newsletter, 2*(3). Retrieved from http://carla.umn.edu/immersion/acie/vol2/May1999.pdf

Suárez-Orozco, M., & Suárez-Orozco, C.. (2006). Globalization, immigration, and education: Recent US trends. *Pontifical Academy of Sciences, 28.* Retrieved on November 22, 2017, from http://www.pas.va/content/dam/accademia/pdf/es28/es28-suarezorozco.pdf

Sutton, M., & Levinson, B. A. U. (Eds.). (2001). *Policy as practice: Toward a comparative sociocultural analysis of educational policy* (vol. 1). Westport, CT: Ablex.

Thomas, W. P., & Collier, V. (1997). School effectiveness for language minority students. *NCBE Resource Collection Series, No. 9.* Retrieved from http://www.ncela.us/files/rcd/BE020890/School_effectiveness_for_langu.pdf

Toliver, K. (1993). The Kay Toliver mathematics program. *Journal of Negro Education, 62*(1), 35–46.

Tomlinson, C. A. (2007, December–2008, January). Learning to love assessment. *Educational Leadership, 65*(4), 8–13.

Truax, E. (2015). *Dreamers: An immigrant generation's fight for their American dream.* Boston: Beacon Press.

Tung, R., Diez, V., Gagnon, L., Uriarte, M., Stazesky, P., de los Reyes, E., & Bolomey, A. (2011). *Learning from consistently high performing and improving schools for English language learners in Boston Public Schools.* Boston: Center for Collaborative Education.

Tyler, R. W. (1949). *Basic principles of curriculum and instruction.* Chicago: University of Chicago Press.

Uccelli, P., Galloway, E. P., Barr, C. D., Meneses, A., & Dobbs, C. L. (2015). Beyond vocabulary: Exploring cross-disciplinary academic-language proficiency and its association with reading comprehension. *Reading Research Quarterly, 50,* 337–356.

Van Lier, L., & Walqui, A. (2012). Language and the Common Core State Standards. In K. Hakuta & M. Santos (Eds.). *Understanding language: Language, literacy, and learning in the content areas.* Stanford, CA: Stanford University. Available: http://ell.stanford.edu/sites/default/files/pdf/academic-papers/04-Van%20Lier%20Walqui%20Language%20and%20CCSS%20FINAL.pdf

Versteegh, K. (2014). *The Arabic language* (2nd ed.). Edinburgh, UK: Edinburgh University Press.

Vogt, M., & Echevarría, J. (2008). *99 Ideas and activities for teaching English learners with the SIOP Model.* Boston: Pearson.

Vygotsky, L. S. (1962). *Language and thought.* Boston: Massachusetts Institute of Technology Press.

Vygotsky, L. S. (1978). *Mind in society: The development of higher psychological processes.* Cambridge, MA: Harvard University Press.

Walqui, A., & Heritage, M. (2012). Instruction for diverse groups of English language learners. Stanford, CA: Stanford University, Understanding Language Initiative. Available: http://ell .stanford.edu/sites/default/files/pdf/academic-papers/09-Walqui%20Heritage%20Instruction%20for%20Diverse%20Groups%20FINAL_0.pdf

Walqui, A., & van Lier, L. (2010). *Scaffolding the academic success of adolescent English language learners: A pedagogy of promise.* San Francisco: WestEd.

Wertsch, J. V. (2000). Is it possible to teach beliefs, as well as knowledge about history? In P. N. Stearns, P. Seixas, & S. Wineburg (Eds.), *Knowing, teaching, and learning history: National and international perspectives* (pp. 38–50). New York: New York University Press.

WIDA. (2007). *English language proficiency standards and resource guide.* Madison, WI: Author. Retrieved from https://www.wida.us/get.aspx?id=4

WIDA. (2012). *Amplification of the English language development standards: Kindergarten–grade 12.* Madison, WI: Author. Retrieved from https://www.wida.us/get.aspx?id=540

WIDA. (2016). *Can-do descriptors: Key uses edition, grades K–12.* Madison, WI: Author. Retrieved from https://www.wida.us/get.aspx?id=2043

Wiggins, G., & McTighe, J. (2005). *Understanding by design* (2nd ed.). Alexandria, VA: ASCD.

Wiggins, G., & McTighe, J. (2007). *Schooling by design: Mission, action, and achievement.* Alexandria, VA: ASCD.

Wiggins, G., & McTighe, J. (2011). *The Understanding by Design guide to creating high-quality units.* Alexandria, VA: ASCD.

Wiggins, G., & McTighe, J. (2012). *The Understanding by Design guide to advanced concepts in creating and reviewing units.* Alexandria, VA: ASCD.

Willig, A. C. (1985). A meta-analysis of selected studies on the effectiveness of bilingual education. *Review of Educational Research, 55*(3), 269–317.

Willis, J. (2006). *Research-based strategies to ignite student learning: Insights from a neurologist and classroom teacher.* Alexandria, VA: ASCD.

Wisconsin Center for Education Research. (2014). *SLIFE: Students with limited or interrupted formal education.* Madison, WI: Author.

Wood, D., Bruner, J. S., & Ross, G. (1976). The role of tutoring in problem solving. *Journal of Child Psychology and Psychiatry, 17*(2), 89–100.

Wrigley, T. (2000). *The power to learn: Stories of success in the education of Asian and other bilingual pupils.* London: Trentham Books.

Yang, G. L. (2006). *American born Chinese.* New York: First Second.

Young, D. J. (1991). Creating a low-anxiety classroom environment: What does language anxiety research suggest? *Modern Language Journal, 75*(4), 426–439.

Zentella, A. C. (Ed.). (2005). *Building on strength: Language and literacy in Latino families and communities.* New York: Teachers College Press.

Zhao, Y. (2012). *World class learners: Educating creative and entrepreneurial students.* Thousand Oaks, CA: Corwin.

Zwiers, J. (2014). *Building academic language: Meeting common core standards across disciplines, grades 5–12* (2nd ed.). Hoboken, NJ: Wiley.

Appendix:
Guide to Abbreviations and Acronyms

Abbreviation/ Acronym	**Explanation**
504	Section 504 Plan
AAVE	African American Vernacular English
ACCESS	Assessing Comprehension and Communication in English State-to-State
AP	Advanced Placement
CCSS	Common Core State Standards
CLD	Culturally and Linguistically Diverse
EB	Emergent Bilingual
EL	English Learner
ELA	English Language Arts
ELD	English Language Development
ELL	English Language Learner
ELP	English Language Proficiency
ESL	English as a Second Language
FEP	Fluent English Proficient
GRASPS	Goal; Role; Audience; Situation; Product, Performance, and Purpose; Success Criteria
HSP	Holistic Student Profile
IB	International Baccalaureate
IEP	Individualized Education Plan
L1	Dominant, Home, or Native Language
L2	Second Language
LEP	Limited English Proficient
LOTE	Language Other Than English

LTEL	Long-Term English Learner
NCELA	National Clearinghouse for English Language Acquisition
NCES	National Center for Education Statistics
NCSS	National Council for the Social Studies
NCTE	National Council of Teachers of English
NGSS	Next Generation Science Standards
NSTA	National Science Teachers Association
PARCC	Partnership for Assessment of Readiness for College and Careers
PLC	Professional Learning Community
RtI	Response to Intervention
SEL	Standard English Learner
SIFE	Student with Interrupted Formal Education
SIOP	Sheltered Instruction Observational Protocol
SLA	Second Language Acquisition
SLIFE	Student with Limited or Interrupted Formal Education
STEM	Science, Technology, Engineering, and Mathematics
UbD	Understanding by Design
WHERETO	**W**—How will I help students know what they should be learning? Why is this worth learning? What evidence will show their learning? **H**—How will I hook and engage the learners? In what ways will I help them connect desired learning to their experiences and interests? **E**—How will I equip students to master identified standards and succeed with the targeted performances? What learning experiences will help develop and deepen understanding of important ideas? **R**—How will I encourage the learners to rethink previous learning? How will I encourage ongoing revision and refinement? **E**—How will I promote students' self-evaluation and reflection? **T**—How will I tailor the learning activities and my teaching to address the different readiness levels, learning profiles, and interests of my students? **O**—How will the learning experiences be organized to maximize engaging and effective learning? What sequence will work best for my students and this content?

Index

Note: The letter *f* following a page number denotes a figure.

language functions
  academic, 74
  communicative, 74
  and features, 76–77*f*
  in learning objectives, 217
  use of, 23
language other than English (LOTE) speakers, 33–34, 38, 50
learners, communities of, 207
learning
  the academic dimension, 55
  affect in, 206
  applicable, 5
  authentic opportunities for, incorporating, 214
  background knowledge for, 55–59, 56*f*
  the brain and, 6
  cognitive dimension of, 54–55
  collaboration to support, 254–255
  collaborative, 207–208
  culture's role in, 53–55
  disciplinary, 216–217, 222–223, 224*f*, 225
  linguistic dimension of, 41–42
  as principled practice, 252–254
  role of language in, 21–22, 55
  a second language, time required for, 240
  sociocultural dimension of, 55–59, 56*f*
  stakeholder contributions to, 256*f*
  strategies for, 164, 165*f*
learning events, language-rich, 213–216
learning objectives, 216, 217, 219–220, 220*f*, 231
lesson planning
  activation in, 216
  background knowledge, activating, 220, 221*f*, 222
  checking for understanding, 227–228, 229*f*, 230
  collaboration benefits, 246
  for disciplinary learning and language development, 216–217
  English lesson example, 218*f*, 219–220, 223, 225, 228
  extending language development, 225, 226*f*, 227
  extension in, 216
  innovating disciplinary learning, 222–223, 224*f*, 225
  innovation in, 216
  instructional design, layers of, 204*f*
  learning objectives, 216, 217, 219–220, 220*f*
  revision in, 246

lesson planning—(*continued*)
  student vignettes, 202–203
  supporting language development in daily practice, 204–205
  UbD in, 244
  for understanding and language development, 203–204
lesson planning, classroom application
  begin with unit of study and students' holistic profiles, 230
  consider contextual features to support student learning, 230
  determine how to monitor students' progress toward objectives, 231
  plan lesson trajectory to activate, innovate, and extend language, 231
  science unit example, 232, 233–235*f*, 236, 237*f*
  write learning objectives with lenses on content and language, 231
limited English proficient (LEP), 39
linguistic bias in assessment, 139
linguistic dimension, assessment, 143
linguistic learning strategies, 164, 165*f*
listening, 46–48, 47*f*, 78–79
long-term English learners (LTEL), 39–40, 40*f*

mathematics, language demands in, 85–86, 86*f*, 87*f*, 88
meaning goals, 74–76, 78, 80, 82, 88, 93, 99–102, 104–105, 114–115, 132, 141
memory, 164, 165*f*
metacognition, 82
metacognitive strategies, 164, 165*f*
modeling and demonstration, 210–212, 211*f*
multilinguals, 38, 50, 52
music education, language demands in, 98–99

native language abilities, 42–45, 43*f*
newcomers, 39–40
novice knowledge, 5

objectives, monitoring progress toward, 231
observations, 140*f*, 141
Organizing and sequencing learning (WHERETO), 175*f*, 187–189, 190*f*
output, meaningful, 212

performance tasks
  on the continuum, 113*f*
  cultural lens on, 124–128

About the Authors

Amy J. Heineke

Amy Heineke is an associate professor of Bilingual and Bicultural Education in the School of Education at Loyola University Chicago, specializing in teacher preparation for English learners. She earned a master's and a doctorate in Curriculum and Instruction from Arizona State University, as well as an undergraduate degree from Northwestern University. Coming from a family of educators, Amy started her career as a kindergarten teacher in the Roosevelt School District in Phoenix, Arizona, where she began developing her advocacy and expertise for teaching English learners. In the last 15 years, she has facilitated students' learning in both elementary and secondary classroom settings and supported a wide array of practitioners working with linguistically diverse students in English-medium and bilingual settings around the United States and Latin America.

Amy's current work centers on preparing preservice and inservice teachers to promote students' disciplinary learning and language development across K–12 schools, with particular focus on English learners. She has published several journal articles on preparing teachers to support students' language development in academic publications, including the *Journal of Teacher Education, Action in Teacher Education, Teacher Education and Practice, Urban Education, Improving Schools, TESOL Journal,* and *Teacher Education Quarterly.* In 2016, she published a research-based monograph entitled *Restrictive Language Policy in Practice: English Learners in Arizona,* which explores the current approach to teaching English learners in Arizona. Overall, Amy's work converges around one primary goal: promoting educational equity for students from diverse cultural and linguistic backgrounds. She can be reached by e-mail at aheineke@luc.edu and on Twitter @DrAJHeineke.

Jay McTighe

 Jay McTighe brings a wealth of experience from a rich and varied career in education. He served as director of the Maryland Assessment Consortium, a collaboration of school districts working together to develop and share formative performance assessments. Previously he was involved with school improvement projects at the Maryland State Department of Education, where he helped lead standards-based reforms, including development of performance-based statewide assessments. He directed development of the Instructional Framework, a multimedia database on teaching. Well known for his work with thinking skills, Jay coordinated statewide efforts to develop instructional strategies, curriculum models, and assessment procedures for improving the quality of student thinking. In addition to his work at the state level, Jay has experience at the district level in Prince George's County, Maryland, as a classroom teacher, resource specialist, and program coordinator. He also directed a state residential enrichment program for gifted and talented students.

Jay is an accomplished author, having coauthored 14 books, including the award-winning and best-selling *Understanding by Design* series with Grant Wiggins. His books have been translated into six languages. Jay has also written more than 35 articles and book chapters, and has been published in leading journals, including *Educational Leadership* and *Education Week*.

With an extensive background in professional development, Jay is a regular speaker at national, state, and district conferences and workshops. He has made presentations in 47 states within the United States, in 7 Canadian provinces, and internationally to educators in 37 countries on six continents.

Jay received his undergraduate degree from the College of William and Mary, earned his master's degree from the University of Maryland, and completed postgraduate studies at the Johns Hopkins University. He was selected to participate in the Educational Policy Fellowship Program through the Institute for Educational Leadership in Washington, D.C., and served as a member of the National Assessment Forum, a coalition of education and civil rights organizations advocating reforms in national, state, and local assessment policies and practices. Jay may be reached at via e-mail at jay@mctighe-associates.com and on Twitter @ jaymctighe.

Related ASCD Resources

At the time of publication, the following resources were available (ASCD stock numbers in parentheses).

Print Products

Assessing Multilingual Learners: A Month-by-Month Guide (ASCD Arias), by Margo Gottlieb (#SF 117076)

Building Equity: Policies and Practices to Empower All Learners, by Dominique Smith, Nancy E. Frey, Ian Pumpian, and Douglas E. Fisher (#117031)

Creating the Opportunity to Learn: Moving from Research to Practice to Close the Achievement Gap, by A. Wade Boykin and Pedro Noguera (#107016)

Disrupting Poverty: Five Powerful Classroom Practices, by Kathleen M. Budge and William H. Parrett (#116012)

Essential Questions: Opening Doors to Student Understanding, by Jay McTighe and Grant Wiggins (#109004)

Even on Your Worst Day, You Can Be a Student's Best Hope, by Manny Scott (#117077)

Getting Started with English Language Learners: How Educators Can Meet the Challenge, by Judi Haynes, (#106048)

Keeping It Real and Relevant: Building Authentic Relationships in Your Diverse Classroom, by Ignacio Lopez (#117049)

Meeting Students Where They Live: Motivation in Urban Schools, by Richard L. Curwin (#109110)

Motivating Black Males to Achieve in School & in Life, by Baruti K. Kafele (#109013)

Raising Black Students' Achievement Through Culturally Responsive Teaching, by Johnnie McKinley (#110004)

Reaching Out to Latino Families of English Language Learners, by David Campos, Rocio Delgado, and Mary Esther Soto Huerta McNulty (#110005)

Schooling by Design: Mission, Action, and Achievement, by Grant Wiggins and Jay McTighe (#107018)

Solving 25 Problems in Unit Design: How do I refine my units to enhance student learning? (ASCD Arias), by Jay McTighe and Grant Wiggins (#SF115046)

The Teacher 50: Critical Questions for Inspiring Classroom Excellence, by Baruti K. Kafele (#117009)

Turning High-Poverty Schools into High-Performing Schools, by William H. Parrett and Kathleen M. Budge (#109003)

The Understanding by Design Guide to Advanced Concepts in Creating and Reviewing Units, by Grant Wiggins and Jay McTighe (#112026)

The Understanding by Design Guide to Creating High-Quality Units, by Grant Wiggins and Jay McTighe (#109107)

Understanding by Design, Expanded 2nd Edition, by Grant Wiggins and Jay McTighe (#103055)

For up-to-date information about ASCD resources, go to **www.ascd.org**. You can search the complete archives of *Educational Leadership* at **www.ascd.org/el**.

ASCD myTeachSource®

Download resources from a professional learning platform with hundreds of research-based best practices and tools for your classroom at http://myteachsource.ascd.org/

For more information, send an e-mail to member@ascd.org; call 1-800-933-2723 or 703-578-9600; send a fax to 703-575-5400; or write to Information Services, ASCD, 1703 N. Beauregard St., Alexandria, VA 22311-1714 USA.

WHOLE CHILD
TENETS

1 **HEALTHY**
Each student enters school healthy and learns about and practices a healthy lifestyle.

2 **SAFE**
Each student learns in an environment that is physically and emotionally safe for students and adults.

3 **ENGAGED**
Each student is actively engaged in learning and is connected to the school and broader community.

4 **SUPPORTED**
Each student has access to personalized learning and is supported by qualified, caring adults.

5 **CHALLENGED**
Each student is challenged academically and prepared for success in college or further study and for employment and participation in a global environment.

THE WHOLE CHILD

The ASCD Whole Child approach is an effort to transition from a focus on narrowly defined academic achievement to one that promotes the long-term development and success of all children. Through this approach, ASCD supports educators, families, community members, and policymakers as they move from a vision about educating the whole child to sustainable, collaborative actions.

Using Understanding by Design in the Culturally and Linguistically Diverse Classroom relates to the **safe**, **engaged**, and **challenged** tenets. *For more about the ASCD Whole Child approach, visit* **www.ascd.org/wholechild.**

Become an ASCD member today!
Go to www.ascd.org/joinascd
or call toll-free: 800-933-ASCD (2723)

LEARN. TEACH. LEAD.